Fodor's 95
Walt Disney
World® and
the Orlando
Area

Fodor's Travel Publications, Inc.
New York • Toronto • London • Sydney • Auckland

Copyright © 1994
by Fodor's Travel Publications, Inc.

Fodor's Walt Disney World® and the Orlando Area

Executive Editor: Karen Cure
Editor: Chelsea Mauldin
Contributors: Lysle Buchbinder, Marianne Camas, Catherine Fredman, Barbara Freitag, Echo Garrett, Andrew Holleran, Laura M. Kidder, Bevin McLaughlin, Mary Meehan, Dee Rivers, Ed Schmidt Jr., Lindy Shepherd, Mary Ellen Shultz, Nancy van Itallie
Creative Director: Fabrizio La Rocca
Cartographer: David Lindroth
Illustrator: Karl Tanner
Cover Photograph: Comstock, Inc.

Design: Vignelli Associates

Special Sales

Contents

4 Sea World, Universal Studios, and Beyond   *145*

5 Away from the Theme Parks   *203*

6 Shopping   *216*

7 Sports and the Outdoors   *228*

8 Dining   *242*

9 Lodging   *264*

10 After Dark   *301*

11 The Cocoa Beach Area   *315*

Index

Maps

Foreword

Many years ago, I wrote the *Official Guide to Walt Disney World.* After that, I was for many years the book's executive editor, and I followed the field of WDW books as it grew. And grew. And grew. But not until we at Fodor's produced the volume you now hold in your hands have I ever felt that there was a perfect guidebook to the most unusual of vacation kingdoms.

It's the best book for visiting with kids, for instance. If a ride routinely scares toddlers, we say so. I have two of my own, so I know how important that can be. But it's also a great guide for grownups on their own—that's how I traveled when I first visited Orlando. And it's also the book for peop[le who can't stand waiting in line; I hate queuing up as much as you do, so we made sure to tell you how to avoid the crowds. I love what Disney does, and I've seen it at very close range and from behind the scenes. Yet we're not in Disney's pocket: The information in this guide originated with the authors and revisors and has not been authorized or endorsed by The Walt Disney Company or any of its affiliates. That way we can always say what we really think. We can also cover all of Orlando's many attractions with equal care, to help you decide how you want to spend your time.

Because this is a Fodor's guide, you'll find great writing. Our descriptions of the various theme park rides don't merely recite historical facts or repeat what you read in a brochure. We also capture the magic of each attraction or ride, and we tell you enough about it so you can easily plan in advance what you want to see—and what you could miss.

Many of our writers are specialists in the fields they write about: Dining chapter author Barbara Freitag, for instance, has been eating out around Orlando for more than 20 years; she knows the good, the bad, and the ugly of the Orlando dining scene. And all our authors live in the Orlando area.

Best of all, the Fodor's format makes information easily accessible. Headings in the margin, a great index, and our signature computer-generated maps help you find what you want fast.

Although every care has been taken to ensure the accuracy of the information in this guide, the passage of time will always bring changes, and consequently the publisher cannot accept responsibility for errors that may occur. All prices and operating schedules quoted here are based on information supplied to us at press time. Operating hours, maps, resort policies, coming attractions, and admission fees and other costs may change, however, and it's always best to call ahead.

Walt Disney World is a registered trademark of The Walt Disney Company. Some of the attractions, products, and locations described in this guide are registered trademarks of The Walt Disney Company and other trademark owners. The use in this guide of trademarked names is strictly for editorial purposes, and neither commercial claim to their use nor suggestion of sponsorship or endorsement is made by the author or publisher.

We hope you'll have a great trip and we'd love to hear about your travel experiences, both pleasant and unpleasant. When a hotel or restaurant fails to live up to its billing, let us know and we will investigate the complaint and revise our entries when the facts warrant it.

Send your letters to me at Fodor's Travel Publications, 201 East 50th Street, New York, NY 10022.

Karen Cure

Editorial Director

Highlights '95 and Fodor's Choice

Highlights '95

Orlando seems to have adopted as its motto "If you build it, they will come." This marsh-of-dreams turned tourist mecca sees constant construction and renovation: Area theme parks, hotels, and other attractions fight for a share of your vacation dollars by presenting ever more spectacular rides or shows or amenities.

Theme Parks The big news at Walt Disney World (WDW) is the revamping of
Walt Disney the Magic Kingdom's Tomorrowland, which was so badly in need
World of updating that locals had taken to calling it "Yesterdayland." Disney's Imagineers have created a Fantasy Future City with a friendly atmosphere. Gone is the outdated Mission to Mars, replaced with **Alien Encounter,** a show with groundbreaking audio and visual effects that show what happens when a demonstration with a "teletransporter" (a device that beams folks from Earth to another planet and back) goes awry. Other new attractions include **Visionarium**—which may still be renamed the Transportarium—a CircleVision 360 presentation in which the audience travels back and forth in time, and **AstroOrbiter,** a ride that's a revamping of the 1950s-vintage Star Jets. Instead of looking like the space shuttle, the cars look like oversize Buck Rogers toys. They are surrounded by whirling planets that swing around the center of the new Tomorrowland.

Future World, in Epcot Center, is also expanding before the future passes it by. **Innoventions,** a major display area featuring the latest in gadgetry, electronics, and telecommunications products, is one of Disney's ongoing attempts to keep the park from falling behind the times.

The latest thrill ride at Disney-MGM Studios is the **Twilight Zone Tower of Terror,** a deserted hotel where you'd be better off taking the stairs: The building's 200-foot tower—the tallest structure of all the Disney parks—houses an elevator cage that plunges straight down. The attraction is on **Sunset Boulevard,** an avenue of Hollywoodesque shops and restaurants where much of the park's expansion will be concentrated.

Some exciting developments are still in the planning stages: **Blizzard Beach,** the third and biggest of Disney's water parks, centers on a seemingly impossible theme: a Florida Winter Sports resort. There will be numerous water slides and "icy" bobsled runs that stay comfortably warm and thrillingly fast. Built on the sides and around the base of a "snowcapped" mountain are thrill rides with winter-related themes such as a bobsled run where four-man tube sleds twist down a 1,200-foot water run. Special areas for teenagers and young children, as well as a 1-acre wave pool, are also planned. It is hoped this "beach" area will divert some of the crowds from the perennially popular Typhoon Lagoon. Opening day is set for mid to late 1995.

Universal
Studios

All of the major rides, including Jaws, are now up and running smoothly after several years of technical problems. Universal has also made a bow to the studio's latest blockbuster, *Jurassic Park,* with an exhibit of memorabilia from the movie; look for **Jurassic Park: The Ride** in the near future. A new Flintstones-themed ride, based on the John Goodman movie, may soon be opening as well. Universal recently announced plans to triple its park size by building a second theme park, five hotels, a night-time entertainment complex, more studios, and other attractions. This is a 10-year plan, so don't expect to find attractions immediately; construction is tentatively scheduled to begin in 1995.

Sea World

Sea World is now offering a glimpse behind its most famous attraction—Shamu the killer whale. The **Shamu Stadium Breeding and Research Pool** is the park's newest addition and offers underwater viewing of the whales and their latest offspring. There is currently an unprecedented pair of "Baby Shamus" at the park.

Splendid China

Central Florida has a new theme park to add to its collection. Splendid China won't terrify you with roller coasters, but its 76 magnificently landscaped acres of miniaturized Asian landmarks can be equally entertaining. Chinese investors spent $100 million to produce exactingly detailed scale replicas of the Great Wall and the Imperial Palace, among others. Besides the exhibits, Splendid China also offers demonstrations of martial arts, acrobatics, and various craft skills; excellent shops; and some of the best theme-park dining around. It's part recreational and part educational—a nice contrast to the frenzied pace of most area parks—and it's a lot closer to WDW than Cypress Gardens, its only competitor in mood.

Sports

One of Disney's most ambitious projects this decade is the **International Sports Center,** set to open prior to the '96 Olympics in Atlanta. The multimillion-dollar complex will cover nearly 100 acres on Disney property; facilities will include a 5,000-seat main-event stadium, a multipurpose field house, a tennis arena, multisports practice fields, running tracks, a fitness center, and training areas. All in all, there will be professional-caliber training and competition sites and vacation-fitness facilities for at least 25 individual and team sports.

Dining

After years of anticipation, Arnold, Sly, Bruce, and Demi have joined forces with Mickey. No word on how Mr. Schwarzenegger, Mr. Stallone, Mr. Willis, and Ms. Moore felt about working with a scene-stealer like Mr. Mouse, but **Planet Hollywood,** one of the stars' movie-memorabilia-filled restaurants, is now orbiting on Pleasure Island.

Lodging

On the hotel front, Disney continues to expand its moderately priced All-Star Resorts. The **All-Star Music Resort,** set to open in mid-1995, will revolve around Broadway, country, jazz, rock and roll, and calypso themes. Oversize appointments such as a three-story pair of cowboy boots, a guitar-shaped swimming pool, and a walk-through neon-lit jukebox will promote the music theme. Non-Disney projects include the 215-room **Holi-**

day Inn Castle, which will look like an Austrian fantasy castle; it's slated to open late in 1994 on International Drive. The 1,335-room **Omni/Rosen Hotel,** currently under construction adjacent to the Orange County Convention Center, is scheduled to open in late 1995.

After Dark   Orlando's nightlife continues to bloom. Pleasure Island, Disney's hot spot for after-hours entertainment, has new clubs: **8trax** revives the sounds of the '70s, while the **Pleasure Island Jazz Company** is making a real attempt to showcase contemporary talent. Downtown there's a bumper crop of new bars and nightclubs; they range from **Howl at the Moon,** a rowdy sing-along bar, to **Yab Yum,** a bohemian coffeehouse that hosts local alternative bands. If you're looking for family entertainment—complete with all the soda you can drink—check out one of Orlando's ever-popular dinner shows. Choose from new offerings with Asian, Chicago-mobster, or murder-mystery themes.

Fodor's Choice

No two people will agree on what makes a perfect vacation, but it's fun and helpful to know what others think. We hope you'll have a chance to experience some of Fodor's Choices yourself while visiting Walt Disney World and the Orlando area. For detailed information about each entry, refer to the appropriate chapters in this guidebook.

Lodging

Hilton at Walt Disney World Village ($$$$)

Chalet Suzanne ($$–$$$)

Park Plaza Hotel ($$–$$$)

Caribbean Beach Resort ($$)

Ramada Resort Maingate at the Parkway ($$)

Casa Rosa Inn ($)

Dining

Victoria and Albert's ($$$$)

Christini's ($$$)

Dux ($$$)

Bistro de Paris ($$–$$$)

Chatham's Place ($$–$$$)

Enzo's ($$–$$$)

Hemingway's ($$–$$$)

La Scala ($$–$$$)

Biergarten ($$)

Le Coq au Vin ($$)

Linda's La Cantina ($$)

Forbidden City ($)

Rolando's Cuban Restaurant ($)

Any meal with Disney characters

Walt Disney World

Magic Kingdom

Big Thunder Mountain Railroad

Haunted Mansion

Jungle Cruise

Pirates of the Caribbean

Space Mountain

Splash Mountain

Epcot Center Body Wars and "The Making of Me" in Wonders of Life (Future World)

Journey into Imagination's Image Works (Future World)

Spaceship Earth (Future World)

Impressions de France (World Showcase)

Wonders of China (World Showcase)

Disney-MGM Studios The Great Movie Ride

Indiana Jones Epic Stunt Spectacular

Magic of Disney Animation

Monster Sound Show

Star Tours

Twilight Zone Tower of Terror

Sea World, Universal Studios, and Beyond

Sea World Dolphin Community Pool, Caribbean Tide Pool, and Sting Ray Lagoon

Penguin Encounter

Terrors of the Deep

Tropical Reef

Universal Studios Florida Back to the Future . . . The Ride

Earthquake—the Big One

E. T. Adventure

Ghostbusters

Jaws

Kongfrontation

Production Tram Tour

Busch Gardens Congo River Rapids

Elephant Display

Kumba

Cypress Gardens Botanical Gardens

Water ski shows

Splendid China Great Wall

Imperial Palace

Away from the Theme Parks

Alexander Springs, Ocala National Forest

Bok Tower Gardens

Gatorland

Mount Dora

Wekiwa Springs State Park

Winter Park

Cocoa Beach Area

Canaveral National Seashore, especially Playalinda Beach

Sebastian Inlet State Recreation Area

Spaceport USA, especially shuttle launches

Sunrise on Cocoa Beach

After Dark

Adventurers Club (Pleasure Island at WDW)

Church Street Station (downtown Orlando)

Dekko's (downtown Orlando)

Drinks at the Top of the World (Contemporary Resort, WDW)

Hoop Dee Doo Revue (Fort Wilderness, WDW)

IllumiNations (Epcot Center, WDW)

The after-dark SpectroMagic parade (in the Magic Kingdom, in busy seasons only)

Shopping

Belz Factory Outlet World

Bountiful Harvest (China Pavilion, Epcot Center)

Flea World

Longwood

Mickey's Character Shop (Disney Village Marketplace)

Park Avenue (Winter Park)

Sanford

Sid Cahuenga's One-of-a-Kind (Disney-MGM Studios)

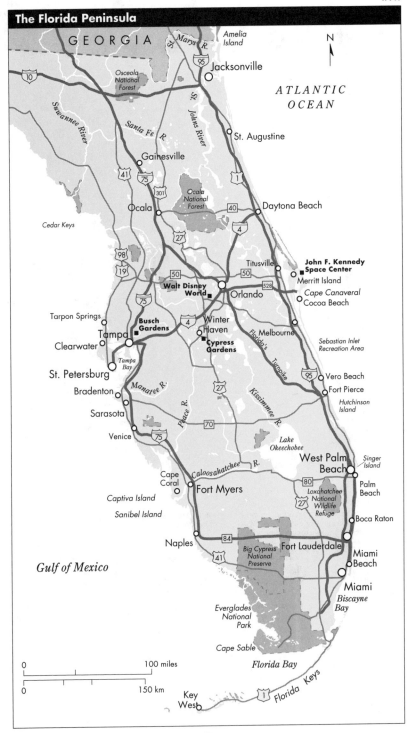

The Florida Peninsula

GEORGIA

St. Marys R.

Amelia Island

N

10

95

Jacksonville

ATLANTIC OCEAN

Osceola National Forest

Suwannee River

Santa Fe R.

St. Johns River

St. Augustine

41

75

Gainesville

301

1

Ocala

Ocala National Forest

40

Daytona Beach

Cedar Keys

27

4

98

19

50

Titusville

50

528

John F. Kennedy Space Center

Merritt Island

75

Walt Disney World

Orlando

Cape Canaveral

Cocoa Beach

Tarpon Springs

Busch Gardens

4

Winter Haven

Florida's Turnpike

Melbourne

Sebastian Inlet Recreation Area

Tampa

Clearwater

Cypress Gardens

Tampa Bay

St. Petersburg

Manatee R.

95

Vero Beach

Bradenton

27

Fort Pierce

Hutchinson Island

Sarasota

Peace R.

Kissimmee R.

Venice

75

70

Lake Okeechobee

West Palm Beach

Singer Island

Cape Coral

Caloosahatchee R.

80

Palm Beach

Fort Myers

27

Loxahatchee National Wildlife Refuge

Boca Raton

Captiva Island

Sanibel Island

Naples

84

Big Cypress National Preserve

Fort Lauderdale

41

Miami Beach

Gulf of Mexico

Miami

Biscayne Bay

Everglades National Park

Cape Sable

Florida Bay

0   100 miles

0   150 km

Florida Keys

1

Key West

World Time Zones

Numbers below vertical bands relate each zone to Greenwich Mean Time (0 hrs.).
Local times frequently differ from these general indications,
as indicated by light-face numbers on map.

Algiers, **29**

Anchorage, **3**

Athens, **41**

Auckland, **1**

Baghdad, **46**

Bangkok, **50**

Beijing, **54**

Berlin, **34**

Bogotá, **19**

Budapest, **37**

Buenos Aires, **24**

Caracas, **22**

Chicago, **9**

Copenhagen, **33**

Dallas, **10**

Delhi, **48**

Denver, **8**

Djakarta, **53**

Dublin, **26**

Edmonton, **7**

Hong Kong, **56**

Honolulu, **2**

Istanbul, **40**

Jerusalem, **42**

Johannesburg, **44**

Lima, **20**

Lisbon, **28**

London (Greenwich), **27**

Los Angeles, **6**

Madrid, **38**

Manila, **57**

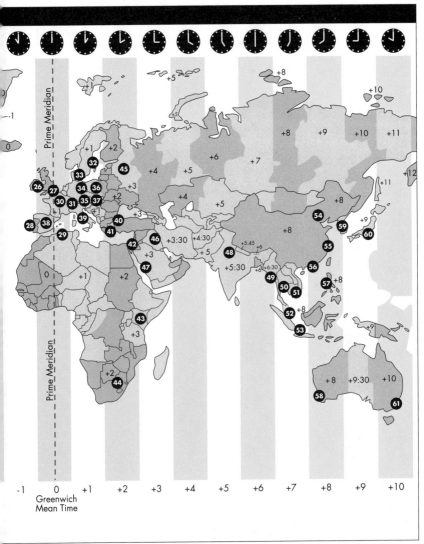

Mecca, **47**
Mexico City, **12**
Miami, **18**
Montréal, **15**
Moscow, **45**
Nairobi, **43**
New Orleans, **11**
New York City, **16**

Ottawa, **14**
Paris, **30**
Perth, **58**
Reykjavík, **25**
Rio de Janeiro, **23**
Rome, **39**
Saigon (Ho Chi Minh City), **51**

San Francisco, **5**
Santiago, **21**
Seoul, **59**
Shanghai, **55**
Singapore, **52**
Stockholm, **32**
Sydney, **61**
Tokyo, **60**

Toronto, **13**
Vancouver, **4**
Vienna, **35**
Warsaw, **36**
Washington, D.C., **17**
Yangon, **49**
Zürich, **31**

1 Essential Information

Before You Go

Tourist Information

*Updated by
Marianne
Camas*

For general information about Mickey's realm, contact **Walt Disney World Information** (Box 10040, Lake Buena Vista, FL 32830, tel. 407/824–4321; TDD 407/827–5141). Request the free *Walt Disney World Vacation Guide.* For reservations for accommodations and entertainment, phone the **Central Reservations Office** (CRO, tel. 407/W–DISNEY; TDD, 407/345–5984). To be a member of the audience at a show being taped at Disney-MGM Studios, call **Production Information** (tel. 407/560–4651).

For information about the Kissimmee area on U.S. 192, contact the **Kissimmee/St. Cloud Convention and Visitors Bureau** (1925 E. Irlo Bronson Memorial Hwy., Kissimmee, FL 34744, tel. 407/847–5000 or 800/327–9159).

For Greater Orlando area information, contact the **Orlando/Orange County Convention and Visitors Bureau** (8445 International Dr., Orlando, FL 32819, tel. 407/363–5871). Ask for the free *Discover Orlando* guidebook; it includes the Orlando Magicard, good for discounts on area attractions.

For information about the tony suburb of Winter Park, contact the **Winter Park Chamber of Commerce** (Box 280, Winter Park, FL 32790, tel. 407/644–8281).

For information on destinations outside the immediate Orlando-Kissimmee area, contact the **Florida Department of Commerce Division of Tourism** (126 W. Van Buren St., Tallahassee, FL 32399–2000, tel. 904/487–1462).

Tours and Packages

Should you buy your travel arrangements to the Orlando area packaged, or should you do it yourself? There are advantages either way. Buying packaged arrangements can save you money, particularly if you can find a program that includes exactly the features you want. You also get from the outset a pretty good idea of what your trip will cost. For most destinations, you have two options: fully escorted tours and independent packages. Here, most travelers opt for independent packages, which generally include airline travel and hotels, theme park admissions, sightseeing, car rental, and excursions. Often you can get a room in your choice of hotel through a package operator for the very dates that Walt Disney World's own Central Reservations Office informs you that there's no room.

Fully escorted tours are another option, though most that include Walt Disney World allow only a day or two as part of a weeklong tour of Florida and may not even include the other area theme parks; if you really want to see everything the area has to offer, look carefully at what's offered before you sign up. Escorted tours are most often via motor coach, with a tour director in charge. Your baggage is handled, your time rigorously scheduled, and most meals planned. It's usually hassle free and cost wise.

Travel agents are your best source of recommendations for both tours and packages. They will have the largest selection, and the cost to you is the same as buying direct. Whatever program you ultimately choose, however, be sure to find out exactly what is included: taxes, tips, transfers, meals, baggage handling, ground transportation, entertainment, excursions, sports or recreation, and rental equipment for any sports you plan to pursue. Ask about the level of hotel used, the size of the rooms, the kind of beds, and hotel amenities—such as pool, room service, or programs for children—if they're important to you. Find out the operator's cancellation penalties. Nearly all operators charge them, and the only way to avoid them is to buy trip cancellation insurance, available from travel agents and insurance agents. Also ask about the single supplement—a surcharge assessed to solo travelers. Some operators do not make you pay it if you agree to be matched up with a roommate of the same sex, even if one is not found by departure time. Remember that a program that has features you won't use, whether for rental sporting equipment or discounted museum admissions, may not be the most cost-wise choice for you. Pay attention to the location of the accommodations the tour or package includes; they may be miles and miles away from the theme parks if the price is rock-bottom—a fact you need to take into consideration when you plan your days. Make sure that any admission media that are included do not limit you to certain days of the week.

Fully Escorted Tours Escorted tours are usually sold in three categories: deluxe, first class, and tourist or budget class. The most important differences among them are the price and the level of accommodations. Some operators specialize in one category; others offer a range.

In the moderate price range, your options include **Certified Vacations** (Box 1525, Ft. Lauderdale, FL 33302, tel. 305/522–1414 or 800/233–7260), **Cosmos Tourama** (5301 S. Federal Cir., Littleton, CO 80123, tel. 303/797–2800 or 800/221–0090), **Domenico Tours** (751 Broadway, Bayonne, NJ, tel. 201/823–8687 or 800/554–8687), and **Travel Impressions/Cavalcade** (465 Smith St., Farmingdale, NY 11735, tel. 516/845–8000 or 800/284–0044). In the higher price range are **Gadabout Tours** (700 E. Tahquitz Canyon Way, Palm Springs, CA 92262, tel. 619/325–5556 or 800/952–5068), **Globus** (a sister company of **Cosmos Tourama,** *above*), and **Tauck Tours** (Box 5027, Westport, CT 06881, tel. 203/226–6911 or 800/468–2825).

Typically, escorted-tour itineraries are jam-packed with sightseeing, so you see a lot in a short period of time (usually one place per day). To judge just how fast paced the tour is, review the itinerary carefully. If you are in a different hotel each night, you will be getting up early each day to head out, travel to your next destination, do some sightseeing, have dinner, and go to bed; then you'll start all over again. If you want some free time, make sure it's mentioned in the tour brochure; if you want to be escorted to every meal, confirm that any tour you consider does that. Also, when comparing programs, be sure to find out if the motor coach is air-conditioned and has a rest room on board. Make your selection based on price and itinerary.

Independent Packages

Independent packages are offered by airlines, tour operators who may also do escorted programs, and any number of other companies, from large, established firms to small, new entrepreneurs. Just about all the airlines that fly to Florida have tour programs; look into **American Airlines Fly AAway Vacations** (tel. 800/321–2121), **Continental Airlines' Grand Destinations** (tel. 800/634–5555), and **Delta Dream Vacations** (tel. 800/872–7786 or 800/221–6666); you can also book packages through **United Airlines' Vacations Planning Center** (tel. 800/328–6877). **American Express Vacations** (300 Pinnacle Way, Norcross, GA 30093, tel. 800/241–1700) offers dozens of packages with an optional rental car. **Olson-Travelworld** (Box 10066, Manhattan Beach, CA 90226, tel. 800/421–5785; in CA, 800/421–2255) has similar packages.

These programs come in a wide range of prices based on levels of luxury and options—in addition to hotel and airfare, sightseeing, car rental, transfers, admission to local attractions, and other extras. Note that when you are pricing different packages, it sometimes pays to purchase the same arrangements separately, as when a rock-bottom promotional airfare is being offered, for example. Again, base your choice on what's available at your budget for the destinations you want to visit.

If you want to spend most of your vacation enjoying Walt Disney World theme parks and resort properties, you may want to consider the all-inclusive **Disney Vacation Packages** offered by Disney's own Central Reservations Office (tel. 407/W-DISNEY), a group of land-only packages that include not only your on-property hotel accommodations but also all admissions, many or all meals, transportation, fees for the use of the sports facilities, and even tips. These packages seem rather pricey, but if you have an active family and you plan to use many WDW facilities, they represent real value.

Cruises

Joint Walt Disney World–cruise packages have become increasingly popular since they debuted a few years ago. Two of the most popular include three- and four-day land packages to Walt Disney World plus cruises to the Bahamas on **Carnival Cruise Lines'** *Fantasy* (Box 526170, Miami, FL 33152-6170, tel. 305/599–2600 or 800/327–9501) or aboard the *Atlantic, Majestic,* and *Oceanic,* the three Big Red Boats of **Premier Cruise Lines** (400 Challenger Rd., Cape Canaveral, FL 32920, tel. 407/783–5061 or 800/473–3262).

Tips for British Travelers

Tourist Offices

Direct inquiries to **Walt Disney Co.** (20th Century House, 31–32 Soho Sq., London W1V 5DG, tel. 0171/734–8111); for travel outside Disney World, contact the **U. S. Travel and Tourism Administration** (Box 1EN, London W1A 1EN, tel. 0171/495–4466, fax 0171/409–0566) for a free USA pack).

Passports and Visas British citizens need a valid 10-year passport. A visa is not necessary unless you are planning to stay more than 90 days; your trip is for purposes other than vacation; you have at some time been refused a visa or refused admission to the United States, or have been required to leave by the U.S. Immigration and Naturalization Service; or you do not have a return or onward ticket. You will need to fill out the Visa Waiver form 1–94W, supplied by the airline.

To apply for a visa or for more information, call the **U.S. Embassy's Visa Information Line** (tel. 01891/200–290; calls cost 48p per minute or 36p per minute cheap rate).

Customs From countries outside the European Union you may import duty-free 200 cigarettes, 100 cigarillos, 50 cigars, or 250 grams of tobacco; 1 liter of spirits or 2 liters of fortified or sparkling wine; 2 liters of still table wine; 60 milliliters of perfume; 250 milliliters of toilet water; and £36 worth of other goods, including gifts and souvenirs.

For further information or a copy of "A Guide for Travellers," which details standard customs procedures as well as what you may bring into the United Kingdom from abroad, contact **HM Customs and Excise** (New King's Beam House, 22 Upper Ground, London SE1 9PJ, tel. 0171/620–1313).

Insurance Most tour operators, travel agents, and insurance agents sell specialized policies covering accidents, medical expenses, personal liability, trip cancellation, and loss or theft of personal property. Some policies include coverage for delayed departure and legal expenses, winter sports and motoring abroad. You can also purchase an annual travel insurance policy valid for every trip you make during the year in which it's purchased (usually only trips of fewer than 90 days). Before you leave, make sure you will be covered if you have a preexisting medical condition or are pregnant; your insurers may not pay for routine or continuing treatment, or they may require a note from your doctor certifying your fitness to travel. The **Association of British Insurers,** a trade association representing 450 insurance companies, advises extra medical coverage for visitors to the United States.

For advice by phone or a free booklet, "Holiday Insurance," that sets out what to expect from a holiday insurance policy and gives price guidelines, contact the **Association of British Insurers** (51 Gresham St., London EC2V 7HQ, tel. 0171/600–3333; 30 Gordon St., Glasgow G1 3PU, tel. 041/226–3905; Scottish Provincial Bldg., Donegall Sq. W, Belfast BT1 6JE, tel. 01232/249176; call for other locations).

Tour Operators Tour operators offering packages to Walt Disney World and the Orlando area are **British Airways Holidays** (Atlantic House, Hazelwick Ave., Three Bridges, Crawley, W. Sussex RH10 1NP, tel. 01293/518022), **Jetsave Travel Ltd.** (Sussex House, London Rd., E. Grinstead, W. Sussex RH19 1LD, tel. 01342/312033), **Key to America** (15 Feltham Rd., Ashford, Middlesex TW15 1DQ, tel. 01784/248777), **Kuoni Travel** (Kuoni House, Dorking, Surrey RH5

4AZ, tel. 01306/742222), and **Premier Holidays** (Westbrook, Milton Rd., Cambridge CB4 1YQ, tel. 01223/355977). Car rental is included in all Florida holidays.

Airfares Fares vary enormously. Fares from consolidators are usually the cheapest, followed by promotional fares such as APEX. A few phone calls should reveal the current picture. When comparing fares, don't forget to figure airport taxes and weekend supplements. Once you know which airline is going your way at the right time for the least money, book immediately, since seats at the lowest prices often sell out quickly. Travel agents will generally hold a reservation for up to five days, especially if you give a credit card number.

Some travel companies that offer cheap fares to Orlando and Miami include **Trailfinders** (42–50 Earl's Court Rd., London W8 6EJ, tel. 0171/937–5400), specialists in Round-the-World fares and independent travel; **Travel Cuts** (295a Regent St., London W1R 7YA, tel. 0171/637–3616), the Canadian students' travel service; and **Flightfile** (49 Tottenham Court Rd., London W1P 9RE, tel. 0171/700–2722), a flight-only agency.

Flying as an on-board courier to Orlando is not a possibility, but you can get to Miami. A courier is someone who accompanies a shipment between designated points so it can clear customs quickly as personal baggage. Because the courier company actually purchases a seat for the package, which uses the seat's checked-baggage allowance, it can allow you to occupy the paid seat at a vastly reduced rate. You must have a flexible schedule, however, as well as the ability to travel light, because you usually must make do with only carry-on baggage. Contact **Courier Travel Services** (346 Fulham Rd., London SW10 9UH, tel. 0171/351–0300) for details.

Car Rentals Make arrangements from home to avoid inconvenience, save money, and guarantee yourself a vehicle. Major firms include **Alamo** (tel. 0800/272–200), **Budget** (tel. 0800/181–181), **EuroDollar** (tel. 01895/233–300), **Europcar** (tel. 0181/950–5050), and **Hertz** (tel. 0181/679–1799).

In the United States, you must be 21 to rent a car; rates may be higher for those under 25. Extra costs cover child seats, compulsory for children under 5 (about $3 per day); additional drivers (around $1.50 per day); and the all-but-compulsory Collision Damage Waiver (*see* Car Rentals, *below*). To pick up your reserved car, you will need the reservation voucher, a passport, a U.K. driver's license, and a travel insurance policy covering each driver.

Travelers with Disabilities Your main sources are the **Royal Association for Disability and Rehabilitation** (RADAR, 25 Mortimer St., London W1N 8AB, tel. 0171/637–5400), which publishes travel information for the disabled in Britain, and **Mobility International** (228 Borough High St., London SE1 1JX, tel. 0171/403–5688), the headquarters of an international organization that serves as a clearinghouse of travel information for people with disabilities.

When to Go

Timing can spell the difference between a good vacation in the theme parks and a great one. During certain periods, the parks are oppressively crowded, with discouraging lines. At other times, you can step right in to the major rides and attractions. During busy periods, the parks have longer hours, run all rides at full capacity, and add entertainment and parades (like SpectroMagic in Disney's Magic Kingdom) that you can't see in quiet periods. If you have children, it's more fun to travel when you can count on there being plenty of other children around; if you prefer a more adult experience, you will be happier skipping school vacation periods.

Crowds The most crowded times of the year in all of the central Florida theme parks are when school is out. The single busiest week is from Christmas through New Year's Day. All of the area's attractions are also packed around Easter. Memorial Day weekend is not only crowded but also hot and humid. Other busy periods are from mid-June through mid-August, Thanksgiving week in November, the week of Presidents' Day in mid-February, and the weeks of college spring break in late March.

Are crowds inescapable, then? Not at all. Particularly from early September until just before Thanksgiving, visitation is very light. Mid-afternoons will still feel busy, but you're not packed in body-to-body as during the most crowded seasons. The least crowded time of all is from just after the Thanksgiving weekend until the beginning of the Christmas holidays. Another excellent time is January and the first week of February. If you must go in summer, late August is best.

Cypress Gardens is different. It attracts older travelers, so it is busier during the winter.

Climate The following are average daily maximum and minimum temperatures for Orlando.

Jan.	70F	21C	May	88F	31C	Sept.	88F	31C
	49	9		67	19		74	23
Feb.	72F	22C	June	90F	32C	Oct.	83F	28C
	54	12		74	23		67	19
Mar.	76F	24C	July	90F	32C	Nov.	76F	24C
	56	13		74	23		58	14
Apr.	81F	27C	Aug.	90F	32C	Dec.	70F	21C
	63	17		74	23		52	11

Information Sources For current weather conditions for cities in the United States and abroad, plus the local time and helpful travel tips, call the **Weather Channel Connection** (tel. 900/WEATHER, 95¢ per minute) from a touch-tone phone.

You may also want to call ahead for current Orlando weather (tel. 407/976–1611).

Attraction Maintenance Before you finalize your travel schedule, call the theme parks you plan to visit in order to find out about any planned maintenance that will close major attractions you want to see.

Opening and Closing Times

Most major attractions, restaurants, hotels, and shops are open for business seven days a week year-round.

Daily Hours Theme park hours vary from season to season; daily hours are extended mornings and evenings in busy periods. Walt Disney World's Magic Kingdom, for instance, closes at 7 PM in November but stays open until 2 AM on New Year's Eve. Cypress Gardens is open 9:30–5:30 daily year-round.

Holidays Some public and private establishments close on holidays—not only the traditional holidays of New Year's Day, Easter, Memorial Day, Fourth of July, Labor Day, Thanksgiving, and Christmas but also January 15 (Martin Luther King, Jr.'s, Birthday), February 12 (Lincoln's Birthday), the third Monday in February (Robert E. Lee's Birthday), April 26 (Confederate Memorial Day), June 3 (Jefferson Davis's Birthday), and the second Monday in October (Columbus Day).

Festivals and Seasonal Events

Top area events include the Florida Citrus Bowl on New Year's Day, the Walt Disney World Wine Festival in February, Light Up Orlando in November, and the Walt Disney World Halloween and Christmas celebrations.

January The **Florida Citrus Bowl Football Classic** (tel. 407/423–2476) takes place at the Orlando Citrus Bowl on January 1. At the end of the month, **Scottish Highland Games** are played at Orlando's Central Florida Fairgrounds (tel. 407/339–3335).

February Early in the month, the **Walt Disney World Village Wine Festival** (tel. 407/934–6743) showcases the vintages of 60 participating wineries from all over the country, and the **National Championship Rodeo Finals** at the Orlando Arena (tel. 407/849–2000) give cowboys from all over a chance to compete. It's followed at the end of the month by Kissimmee's **Silver Spurs Rodeo** (tel. 407/847–5000), one of the oldest and largest events of its kind in the South, drawing cowboys from all over the United States and Canada. At about the same time, or early in March, the **Annual Central Florida Fair** is held at Orlando's Central Florida Fairgrounds (tel. 407/295–3247), with shows, rides, exhibits, and entertainment.

March It's baseball spring-training time, with the **Houston Astros** at Osceola County Stadium in Kissimmee (tel. 407/933–5500) and the **Kansas City Royals** at Baseball City Stadium (tel. 813/424–2424). Cypress Gardens kicks off its **Spring Flower Festival** (tel. 813/324–2111), which runs through May and features extraordinary floral topiaries and a profusion of spring blossoms.

One weekend in early March, the **Kissimmee Bluegrass Festival** showcases bluegrass bands and gospel music at the Silver Springs Arena (tel. 407/856–0246). On March 17, the **St. Patrick's Day Street Party** encourages the "wearin' o' the green" at Church Street Station (tel. 407/422–2434). Mid-month, the **Nestle Invitational,** a regular PGA Tour event, stops at Orlando's Bay Hill Club (tel. 407/876–2888), and the **Winter Park Sidewalk Art Festival** (tel. 407/644–8281) draws thousands of art enthusiasts to trendy Park Avenue.

April and May   From early April through early May, the **Orlando Shakespeare Festival** pays tribute to the Bard at Orlando's Lake Eola Amphitheater (tel. 407/423–6905). Also early in April, the **Dr. Pepper Annual Surf Festival** (tel. 407/783–5813) draws professional and amateur surfers to Cocoa Beach. On Easter Sunday there are **Easter Sunrise Services** at Sea World's Atlantis Theater (tel. 407/351–3600) and an **Easter Parade** down Main Street at Walt Disney World. From the end of April until early May, the **Orlando International Fringe Festival** brings 200 artists and theater troupes to perform in downtown Orlando. Cypress Gardens' Spring Flower Festival also wraps up in early May. Leading into June, the annual **"Up, Up and Away" Airport Art Show** takes place at Orlando International Airport (tel. 407/826–2055).

June   Late in the month and early in July is the **Silver Spurs Rodeo** (tel. 407/847–5000); there's another in early February.

July   The **Fourth of July** is a big day in and around Orlando. Walt Disney World's fireworks are legendary; recent years have brought record crowds. There are also fireworks at Kissimmee as part of its old-fashioned celebration in Lakefront Park, which also features games, rides, entertainment, and food (tel. 407/932–7223), and in Cypress Gardens, which mounts special ski shows as well (tel. 813/324–2111).

September   **Oktoberfest at Church Street Station** (tel. 407/422–2434) means oompah bands and German folk dancers, food, and beer.

October   Early in the month, the **Universal Art Show** is held on Orlando's Central Florida Parkgrounds (tel. 407/422–8226). Midmonth is the season for the **Walt Disney World Oldsmobile Golf Classic,** played on three of Walt Disney World's 18-hole golf courses (tel. 407/824–2250); for Cypress Gardens' **Annual Mustang Roundup** (tel. 800/282–2123), which draws aficionados of that most famous Ford to exhibit and ogle models from 1965 to the present; and for the **Winter Park Autumn Art Festival** at Rollins College (tel. 407/644–8281). Later on is the **Pioneer Days Folk Festival,** with craftspeople and musicians on the grounds of the Folk Art Center on East Fairlane Avenue in suburban Pine Castle (tel. 407/855–7461). For **Halloween,** there's a street party at Church Street Station (tel. 407/422–2434).

November   Early in the month, the **American Indian Powwow** (tel. 407/295–3247) takes place at the Central Florida Fairgrounds. Midmonth is the **Festival of the Masters,** with 230 top artists exhibiting their creations at Disney Village Marketplace (tel. 407/934–6743). **Light Up Orlando** is a street party downtown with live entertainment (tel. 407/648–4010). Cypress Gardens hosts its monthlong **Chrysanthemum Festival.**

December Early in the month, Orlando's Loch Haven Park stages a **Pet Fair & Winterfest** (tel. 407/644–2739). For Christmastime, Cypress Gardens mounts its annual **Pointsettia Festival** (tel. 813/324–2111), featuring 48,000 multicolored blooms. Walt Disney World gears up by decorating Main Street in perfect Victorian style, complete with a magnificent Christmas tree in Town Square, strolling characters, special afternoon parades, and entertainment. A Nativity Pageant takes place at Disney Village Marketplace (tel. 407/824–4321). December 31 occasions the **Citrus Bowl Parade** in Orlando (tel. 407/629–4944), a street party at Church Street Station (tel. 407/422–2434), and a double fireworks display and extra-late hours in Walt Disney World's Magic Kingdom, which usually records some of the biggest crowds of the year for the occasion.

What to Pack

Airlines generally allow two pieces of check-in luggage and one carry-on piece per passenger.

Clothing Comfortable walking shoes or sneakers are essential. The entire area is extremely casual, day and night, so men will need a jacket and tie in only a handful of restaurants. For sightseeing and theme park visits, pack shorts, sundresses, cotton slacks or jeans, T-shirts, and a light sweater as protection against the sometimes glacial air-conditioning. Don't forget your sunglasses!

In winter, be prepared for a range of temperatures: Take clothing that you can layer, including a sweater and warm jacket. For summer, you'll want a sun hat, sunscreen lotion, and a poncho and folding umbrella in case of sudden thunderstorms.

Miscellaneous If you have a health problem that requires you to take a prescription drug, pack enough to last the duration of the trip. Bring an extra pair of eyeglasses or contact lenses. Put these vital items in your carry-on bag, so you won't be out of commission if your luggage goes astray. And don't forget to pack a list of the addresses of offices that supply refunds for lost or stolen traveler's checks. You may also want to bring film and blank VCR tape (more expensive here than at home). Experienced theme park visitors also suggest using a waist pouch rather than a tote bag or purse.

Luggage Certain toy guns, toy knives, and the like sold in Frontierland and Adventureland should be packed in checked luggage. Security may give you a hard time if you try to carry them on board.

Regulations Free baggage allowances on an airline depend on the airline, the route, and the class of your ticket. In general, on domestic flights you are entitled to check two bags—neither exceeding 62 inches (158 centimeters) (length + width + height), or weighing more than 70 pounds (32 kilograms). A third piece may be brought aboard as a carry-on; its total dimensions are generally limited to less than 45 inches (114 centimeters), so it will fit easily under the seat in front of you or in the overhead compartment. In the United States, the Federal Aviation Administration (FAA) gives airlines broad latitude to limit carry-on allowances and tailor them to different aircraft and operational conditions. Charges for excess, oversize, or overweight pieces vary.

Safeguarding Your Luggage Before leaving home, itemize your bags' contents and their worth; such a list will help you estimate the extent of your loss if your bags go astray. To minimize that risk, tag them inside and outside with your name, address, and phone number. (If you use your home address, cover it so that potential thieves can't see it.) Put a copy of your itinerary inside each bag, so that you can easily be tracked. At check-in, make sure that the tag attached by baggage handlers bears the correct three-letter code for your destination. If your bags do not arrive with you or if you detect damage, do not leave the airport until you've filed a written report with the airline.

Insurance In the event of loss, damage, or theft on domestic flights, airlines' liability is $1,250 per passenger, excluding the valuable items such as jewelry, cameras, and more that are listed in the fine print on your ticket. Excess-valuation insurance can be bought directly from the airline at check-in. Your homeowner's policy may fill the gap; or firms such as **The Travelers Companies** (1 Tower Sq., Hartford, CT 06183, tel. 203/277–0111 or 800/243–3174) and **Wallach and Company** (107 W. Federal St., Box 480, Middleburg, VA 22117, tel. 703/687–3166 or 800/237–6615) sell baggage insurance.

Traveler's Checks

Traveler's checks are preferable in metropolitan centers, although you'll need cash in rural areas and small towns. The most widely recognized are **American Express, Citicorp, Diners Club, Thomas Cook,** and **Visa,** which are sold by major commercial banks. Both American Express and Thomas Cook issue checks that can be countersigned and used by you and your traveling companion. Typically, the issuing company or the bank at which you make your purchase charges 1% to 3% of the checks' face value as a fee. Some foreign banks charge as much as 20% of the face value as the fee for cashing travelers' checks in a foreign currency. Buy a few checks in small denominations to cash toward the end of your trip, so you won't be left with excess foreign currency. Record the numbers of checks as you spend them, and keep this list separate from the checks.

Getting Money from Home

Cash Machines Many automated-teller machines (ATMs) are tied to international networks such as **Cirrus** and **Plus.** You can use your bank card at ATMs away from home to withdraw money from an account and get cash advances on a credit-card account if your card has been programmed with a personal identification number, or PIN. Check in advance on limits on withdrawals and cash advances within specified periods. On cash advances you are charged interest from the day you receive the money—whether you withdraw it using an ATM or with the help of a teller. Transaction fees for ATM withdrawals outside your home turf will probably be higher than for withdrawals at home.

For specific Cirrus locations in the United States and Canada, call 800/424–7787, and press the area code and first three digits of the number you're calling from (or the calling area where you want an ATM). For U.S. Plus locations, call 800/843–7587.

Wiring Money You don't have to be a cardholder to send or receive a **MoneyGram from American Express** for up to $10,000. Go to a MoneyGram agent in retail and convenience stores and American Express travel offices, pay up to $1,000 with a credit card and anything over that in cash. You are allowed a free long-distance call to give the transaction code to your intended recipient, who needs only to present identification and the transaction reference number to the nearest MoneyGram agent to pick up the cash. MoneyGram agents are in more than 70 countries (call 800/926–9400 for locations). Fees range from 3% to 10%, depending on the amount you send and how you pay.

You can also use **Western Union.** To wire money, take either cash or a cashier's check to the nearest office or call and use MasterCard or Visa. Money sent from the United States or Canada will be available for pick up at agent locations in Florida within minutes. Once the money is in the system it can be picked up at *any* one of hundreds of locations (call 800/325–6000 for the one nearest you).

Traveling with Cameras, Camcorders, and Laptops

Rental disk and 35mm cameras and even VCRs are widely available in all the central Florida theme parks. So are film and blank videotape—though certainly not at the discount prices you may be able to get at home.

Film and Cameras If your own camera is new or you haven't used it for a while, shoot and develop a few rolls of film before leaving home. Pack some lens tissue and an extra battery for your built-in light meter, and invest in an inexpensive skylight filter, to both protect your lens and provide some definition in hazy shots. Store film in a cool, dry place—never in a car's glove compartment or on the shelf under the rear window.

Airport security X-rays generally aren't harmful to film with ISO below 400. To protect your film, carry it with you in a plastic bag and ask for a hand inspection. Such requests are honored at American airports. Don't depend on a lead-lined bag to protect film in checked luggage—the airline may very well turn up the dosage of radiation to see what you've got in there. Airport metal detectors do not harm film, although you'll set off the alarm if you walk through one with a roll in your pocket. Call the Kodak Information Center (tel. 800/242–2424) for details.

Camcorders Before your trip, put camcorders through their paces, invest in a skylight filter to protect the lens, and check all the batteries.

Videotape Videotape is not damaged by X-rays, but it may be harmed by the magnetic field of a walk-through metal detector, so ask for a hand-check. Airport security personnel may ask you to turn on the camcorder to prove that it's what it appears to be, so make sure the battery is charged.

Laptops Security X-rays do not harm hard-disk or floppy-disk storage, but you may request a hand-check, at which point you may be asked to turn on the computer to prove that it's what it appears to be. (Check your battery before departure.) Most airlines allow you to use your laptop aloft except during takeoff and landing, when operation can interfere with navigation equipment.

Car Rentals

Though public transportation in Orlando is practically nonexistent and taxis are expensive because of the distances involved, it is by no means absolutely necessary to rent a car when you are in Orlando. If you are staying at a Disney hotel or purchase a multiday passport instead of buying daily admission tickets to the Disney parks, your transportation within Walt Disney World is free. Outside Walt Disney World, just about every lodging is linked by private shuttle to area attractions. However, should you want to visit the major theme parks outside Walt Disney World, venture off the beaten track, or eat where most tourists don't, then a rental car is essential. Fortunately, Orlando offers some of the lowest rental car rates in the United States.

Most major car-rental companies are represented in Orlando, including **Alamo** (tel. 800/327–9633); **Avis** (tel. 800/331–1212, 800/879–2847 in Canada); **Budget** (tel. 800/527–0700); **Dollar** (tel. 800/800–4000); **Hertz** (tel. 800/654–3131, 800/263–0600 in Canada); and **National** (tel. 800/227–7368). Unlimited-mileage rates range from $28 per day for an economy car to $38 for a large car; weekly unlimited-mileage rates range from $133 to $205. This does not include tax, which in Florida is 8% on car rentals.

Extra Charges Picking up the car in one city and leaving it in another may entail substantial drop-off charges or one-way service fees. The cost of a collision or loss-damage waiver (*see below*) can be high, also. Some rental agencies will charge you extra if you return the car *before* the time specified on your contract. Ask before making unscheduled drop-offs. Fill the tank before you turn in the vehicle to avoid being charged for refueling at what you'll swear is the most expensive pump in town.

Cutting Costs Major international companies have programs that discount their standard rates by 15%–30% if you make the reservation before departure (anywhere from 24 hours to 14 days), rent for a minimum number of days (typically three or four), and prepay the rental. More economical rentals may come as part of fly/drive or other packages, even bare-bones deals that only combine the rental and an airline ticket (*see* Tours and Packages, *above*).

Insurance and Collision Damage Waiver Before you rent a car, find out exactly what coverage, if any, is provided by your personal auto insurer and by the rental company. Don't assume that you are covered. If you do want insurance from the rental company, secondary coverage may be the only type offered. You may already have secondary coverage if you charge the rental to a credit card. Only Diner's Club (tel. 800/234–6377) provides primary coverage in the United States and worldwide.

In general, if you have an accident, you are responsible for the automobile. Car rental companies may offer a collision damage waiver (CDW), which costs from $4 to $14 a day. You should decline the CDW only if you're certain that you are covered through your personal insurer or credit card company. In many states, laws mandate that renters be told what the CDW costs, that it's optional, and that their own auto insurance may provide the same protection.

Traveling with Children

All the theme parks get high marks from young travelers. Hotel facilities for children range from okay to fabulous. The only problem is that the times when your kids are out of school are the times when every other child in the universe is out of school and every other parent is packing up the car to drive to Orlando as well. Preschoolers can find these crowds overwhelming. So if your children are of varying ages and those in school are good students, consider taking them out so that you can visit in the less congested off-season. Educational programs and the broadening experience of travel itself may persuade your children's teachers to excuse the absence. Teachers may also arrange special study assignments relating to the trip.

If your children cannot afford to miss school, try to take your vacation in late May or early June (as soon as the school year ends).

Publications *Newsletter* *Family Travel Times,* published 10 times a year by **Travel With Your Children** (TWYCH, 45 W. 18th St., 7th Floor Tower, New York, NY 10011, tel. 212/206–0688, annual subscription $55), covers destinations, types of vacations, and modes of travel.

Books *Great Vacations with Your Kids,* by Dorothy Jordan and Marjorie Cohen ($13; Penguin USA, 120 Woodbine St., Bergenfield, NJ 07621, tel. 800/253–6476), and *Traveling with Children—and Enjoying It,* by Arlene K. Butler ($11.95 plus $3 shipping per book; Globe Pequot Press, Box 833, 6 Business Park Rd., Old Saybrook, CT 06475, tel. 800/243–0495, or 800/962–0973 in CT) help plan your trip with children, from toddlers to teens. From the same publisher are *Recommended Family Resorts in the United States, Canada, and the Caribbean,* by Jane Wilford with Janet Tice ($12.95), and *Recommended Family Inns of America* ($12.95).

Tour Operator **Rascals in Paradise** (650 5th St., Suite 505, San Francisco, CA 94107, tel. 415/978–9800 or 800/872–7225) specializes adventurous, exotic and fun-filled vacations for families to carefully screened resorts and hotels around the world.

Getting
There
Airfares

On domestic flights, children under 2 not occupying a seat travel free, and older children currently travel on the "lowest-applicable" adult fare.

Baggage

In general, infants paying 10% of the adult fare are allowed one carry-on bag, not to exceed 70 pounds or 45 inches (length + width + height) and a collapsible stroller; check with the airline before departure, because you may be allowed less if the flight is full. The adult baggage allowance applies for children paying half or more of the adult fare. Check with the airline for particulars.

Safety Seats

The Federal Aviation Administration (FAA) recommends the use of safety seats aloft and details approved models in the free leaflet "**Child/Infant Safety Seats Recommended for Use in Aircraft**" (available from the Federal Aviation Administration, APA–200, 800 Independence Ave. SW, Washington, DC 20591, tel. 202/267–3479; Information Hot Line, tel. 800/322–7873). Airline policy varies. U.S. carriers allow FAA-approved models bearing a sticker declaring their FAA approval. Because these seats are strapped into regular passenger seats, airlines may require that a ticket be bought for an infant who would otherwise ride for free.

Facilities
Aloft

Airlines do provide other facilities and services for children, such as children's meals and freestanding bassinets (to those sitting in seats on the bulkhead, where there's enough legroom to accommodate them). Make your request when reserving. The annual February/March issue of *Family Travel Times* gives details of the children's services of dozens of airlines ($10) (*see above*). "Kids and Teens in Flight" (free from the U.S. Department of Transportation's Office of Consumer Affairs, R-25, Washington, D.C. 20590, tel. 202/366–2220) offers tips for children flying alone.

Lodging

In all but the smallest motels there is little or no charge for children under 18 who share a room with an adult.

Playgrounds,
Game
Rooms,
Theme Pools

All hotels on Disney property and many others in the area have playgrounds and arcades with video games and pinball machines. The one in Disney's **Contemporary Resort** is, hands down, the biggest game room in any hotel in the area. Parrot Cay, a little island in the **Caribbean Beach Resort**'s lagoon, is anchored by a winning little playground with soft white sand underfoot. Swimming pools—such as the one here (it has a pirate stronghold and a cannon that lets out periodic booms) the Stormalong Bay area between Disney's **Yacht and Beach Club,** and the lagoon at Disney's **Dixielandings Resort**—are long on Disney charm.

Child Care,
Baby-Sitting

Baby-sitting is widely available; ask at your hotel desk. **Fairy Godmothers** (tel. 407/277–3724) will care for infants and children in your hotel room or will take your youngsters to the theme parks. Walt Disney World's preschool and drop-off day-care facilities in the Lake Buena Vista area, **KinderCare,** will also send baby-sitters to your hotel room (tel. 407/827–5444). The Kinder-

Care center proper accepts children who are potty trained and walking (tel. 407/827–5437; available daily 6 AM–8 PM), and you don't have to stay at Disney to use the program. These programs (and the hotels below) charge between $5 and $10 an hour, depending on the ages and number of children and the type of service provided.

On-site, there are strong children's facilities and programs at the **Contemporary, Dolphin, Grand Floridian, Polynesian Village,** and **Swan;** the Polynesian Village's Neverland Club will enchant you and your offspring with its Peter Pan–theme clubhouse and youngsters-only dinner show. The **Hilton,** near Disney Village Marketplace, has a Youth Hotel where parents can leave their offspring until midnight for a night on the World; meals are served and there's even a dormitory. Off-site, many hotels have supervised children's programs. Standouts are the camplike programs at the **Stouffer Orlando Resort** opposite Sea World (it's called Shamu's Playhouse); at the **Hyatt Regency Grand Cypress** near Disney Village (which has a separate teens-only evening program); the **Sonesta Villa Resort Orlando;** and the **Holiday Inn at Lake Buena Vista** and the **Holiday Inn Maingate East.** These have trained counselors and planned activities as well as attractive facilities; some even have mascots. The age range varies from 4 or 5 to 15; some accept children as young as 2, however. The **Peabody Hotel** has an evening program that allows you to drop off your youngsters while you dine in the hotel's restaurants; call ahead. *See also* Chapter 9, Lodging.

Meals   Many restaurants in the Orlando area have a special children's menu. And providing that reassuring taste of home, franchised fast-food eateries abound. The **McDonald's** on International Drive has an elaborate multilevel playground that seems almost bigger than the restaurant.

Character   At these special breakfasts, brunches, and dinners offered by
Meals   many **Walt Disney World** restaurants, Mickey, Donald, Goofy, Chip 'n' Dale, and other favorite characters sign autographs and pose for snapshots. Reservations are not always necessary— just show up early if you don't like to wait. *See* Chapter 8, Dining. **Universal Studios** has its own character meal, right in the park before official park-opening hours; Woody Woodpecker, the Flintstones, and other favorites are on hand, and you will be strategically positioned to head the stampede to Back to the Future . . . The Ride. Plan your character meal for toward the end of your visit, when your little ones will be used to seeing these large and sometimes frightening figures; they're a good way to kill the morning on the day you check out. *See also* Chapter 4, Sea World, Universal Studios, and Beyond, and Chapter 8, Dining.

Stroller   Stroller rentals are available in theme parks, but you may want
Rentals   to bring your own, since fees run $5–$6 per day (plus a deposit) and you will probably need a stroller in places you can't rent one—to explore Orlando off the beaten track, to explore Orlando malls, even just to get around your hotel, if it's big. No one rents

double strollers, and singles available in Walt Disney World are sturdy but unyielding, not optimal for infants.

If you do rent a stroller, there is always the possibility that it will be taken. Experienced park visitors suggest either taping a large card with your name to the stroller or leaving some small personal item with it, such as a bandanna, a T-shirt, even a clear plastic bag with diapers inside; the theory is that people who wouldn't think twice about purloining theme park property that they will subsequently return hesitate to make off with something that belongs to a fellow parent. If your stroller does disappear, you can easily pick up a replacement; ask any park staffer for the nearest location.

Baby Swap Parents with small children under the height limit for major attractions have to take turns waiting in the long lines, right? Wrong. In what's unofficially known as the Baby Swap, both of you queue up, and when it's your turn to board, one stays with the youngsters until the other returns; the waiting partner then rides without waiting again. (Universal Studios calls it a Baby Exchange, and has Baby Exchange areas at all rides.)

Educational Programs Be sure to reserve ahead for any of these behind-the-scenes tours.

Walt Disney World Walt Disney World offers its six-hour Wonders Program courses year-round for those aged 10–15 (tel. 407/354–1855, $79 per course). Your youngsters can sign up for **Wildlife Adventure: Exploring the Environment,** which visits Discovery Island and WDW's 7,500-acre conservation preserve, where several rare species have found refuge from encroaching development; **Art Magic: Bringing Illusion to Life,** which introduces students to animation, costuming, landscaping and set design in movies, stage shows, and theme parks; or **Showbiz Magic: The Walt Disney World of Entertainment,** during which students get to meet the performers and technicians who create the Disney shows, and get an understanding of how music, lighting, costumes, and timing all combine to beguile an audience. In summer there is also a separate four-hour **Kidventure Program,** which focuses on Discovery Island plants and wildlife and is open to students aged 8–14 (tel. 407/824–3784; $30, including boat transportation).

Sea World Three year-round **Sea Safari** programs ($5.95 adults, $4.95 children 3–9) offer behind-the-scenes looks at park operations: **Backstage Explorations** and **Animal Lover's Adventure** are 90-minute guided tours of park facilities; **Animal Training Discoveries** consists of a 45-minute chat and demonstration with the park's trainers. For a wide selection of age-specific classes on wildlife and ecology, you'll have to wait for summer, when the calendar is chockablock with programs ranging from one day to one week in length (most $15–$60, tel. 407/363–2380). In addition, the bring-your-own-sleeping-bag Education Sleepovers, offered exclusively to school groups in winter, are open to individual visitors. (How about bedding down in the shark exhibit at **Terrors of the Sleep?** Or try **Cool Nights with Penguins** to see the nightlife of the tuxedoed masses.) There's even talk of conducting overseas trips that combine classes at the park with a few days in Belize or the Bahamas.

Busch　**Multiday Zoo Camps** (tel. 813/987–5555) keep children learning
Gardens　here from June through October. There's a different program
for each age group, from kindergartners through 10th graders,
and each program lasts several days ($80–$100 per session).
Youngsters can also sign up for classes that last just a few hours
($15–$20), from a hands-on introduction to wildlife for toddlers
to a night hike for preteens.

Hints for Older Travelers

Bear in mind that school vacation times can spell ordeal rather
than adventure if you have limited energy (or patience). What
you have will go farther if you arrive in the theme parks at opening time or even before. Do a little homework about your destination, and have a plan of action. Take in first those attractions
that you most want to see. Spend the morning taking in the attractions so that you can take it easy when the day warms up.
Then relax in the shade, have a nice long lunch, see some shows
in air-conditioned theaters, and maybe even go back to your
hotel to relax around the pool, read, or nap. Refreshed, you can
return to one of the theme parks, when they're open late, or
explore Pleasure Island, Church Street Station, or Orlando's
other after-dark options. Don't overdo it.

Most hotels and restaurants in the area have senior-citizen discounts. Pick up brochures as you visit places, read the newspapers (especially the *Orlando Sentinel*), and don't be shy about
asking for suggestions at your hotel.

Fairy Godmothers (tel. 407/277–3724) squires older travelers as
well as youngsters around the parks.

Organizations　The **American Association of Retired Persons** (AARP, 601 E St.
NW, Washington, DC 20049, tel. 202/434–2277) provides independent travelers who are members of AARP (open to those age
50 or older; $8 per person or couple annually) with the Purchase
Privilege Program, which offers discounts on lodging, car rentals, and sightseeing, and the AARP Motoring Plan, which furnishes domestic trip-routing information and emergency
road-service aid for an annual fee of $39.95 per person or couple
($59.95 for a premium version). AARP also arranges group
tours, cruises, and apartment living through AARP Travel Experience from American Express (400 Pinnacle Way, Suite 450,
Norcross, GA 30071, tel. 800/927–0111 or 800/745–4567).

Two other organizations offer discounts on lodgings, car rentals,
and other travel products, along with such nontravel perks as
magazines and newsletters: the **National Council of Senior Citizens** (1331 F St. NW, Washington, DC 20004, tel. 202/347–8800;
membership $12 annually) and **Mature Outlook** (6001 N. Clark
St., Chicago, IL 60660, tel. 800/336–6330; $9.95 annually).

Note: When using any senior-citizen identification card for reduced hotel rates, mention it when booking, not when checking out. At restaurants, show your card before you're seated; discounts may be limited to certain menus, days, or hours. If you are renting a car, ask about promotional rates that might improve even your senior-citizen discount.

Educational Travel   The nonprofit **Elderhostel** (75 Federal St., 3rd Floor, Boston, MA 02110, tel. 617/426–7788) has offered inexpensive study programs for people 60 and older since 1975. Held at more than 1,800 educational institutions, courses cover everything from marine science to Greek myths to cowboy poetry. Participants usually attend lectures in the morning and spend the afternoon sightseeing or on field trips; they live in dorms on the host campuses. Fees for programs in the United States and Canada, which usually last one week, run about $300, not including transportation.

Tour Operators   **Saga International Holidays** (222 Berkeley St., Boston, MA 02116, tel. 800/343–0273), which specializes in group travel for people older than 60, offers a selection of variously priced tours. **SeniorTours** (508 Irvington Rd., Drexel Hill, PA 19026, tel. 215/626–1977 or 800/227–1100) arranges motor-coach tours throughout the United States and Nova Scotia, as well as Caribbean cruises.

Publications   *The 50+ Traveler's Guidebook: Where to Go, Where to Stay, What to Do* by Anita Williams and Merrimac Dillon (St. Martin's Press, 175 5th Ave., New York, NY 10010; $12.95) is available in bookstores and offers many useful tips. "The Mature Traveler" (Box 50820, Reno, NV 89513, tel. 702/786–7419; $29.95), a monthly newsletter, contains many travel deals.

Hints for Travelers with Disabilities

Central Florida attractions are among the most accessible destinations in the world for people who have disabilities. The hospitality industry continues to spend millions on barrier-removing renovations. Though some challenges remain, most can be overcome with planning.

Local Information and Assistance   The **Disabled Traveler's Helpline of Central Florida** (tel. 407/352–5209 or 800/945–2045, fax 407/351–1901 or 800/677–5224) can answer questions about the accessibility of many area attractions, hotels, and restaurants. Both Walt Disney World (tel. 407/824–4321) and Universal Studios (tel. 407/363–8000) publish guidebooks for guests with disabilities; allow six weeks for delivery. If you need the information in a hurry, send a large, self-addressed envelope with at least $1 in postage to the **Disabled Travelers Friendship Network** (Box 690801, Orlando, FL 32869–0801), which operates under the wing of the Disabled Traveler's Helpline and is affiliated with **Friends of the Family** (Box 690801, Orlando, FL 32869–0801, tel. 407/856–7676 or 800/945–2045), which will develop a custom itinerary, supply tour guides that push wheelchairs, and meet you at the airport.

On-Site Information   The main park information centers (*see* Chapters 3 and 4) can answer specific questions and dispense general information for guests with disabilities.

Local Transpor- tation   Although there are some lift-equipped vans for rent and some shuttle service available, guests need to plan itineraries in advance. The exception is on Disney property: Every other Disney bus on each route is lift equipped, so there's never more than a 30-minute wait for hotel-to-theme-park trips. Consult transportation companies (*see below*) for more information.

Designated parking is available for guests with disabilities. It's near the turnstile area for most parks. The Magic Kingdom's special lot is near the Transportation and Ticket Center, where ferries depart for the Magic Kingdom and monorails travel there and to Epcot Center. Monorail entrances are level, but the ramp up is quite steep.

Medical Supplies   Undoubtedly the best in town, **Care Medical Equipment** (tel. 407/856–2273 or 800/741–2282) does everything from renting wheelchairs and scooters to supplying oxygen. They are particularly effective at coordinating with hometown medical personnel to ensure the appropriate equipment. Prices are reasonable, and reliability is superior.

Nursing Services   **Rescare** (1801 Lee Rd., Suite 175, Winter Park 32789, tel. 407/740–5650, fax 407/740–7178) reliably provides LPNs, home health aides, therapists, and RNs on call around the clock. Prices are reasonable, although professional services are never cheap. **CareTeam** (1085 W. Morse Blvd., Suite A, Winter Park 32789, tel. 407/628–8845) has a similar setup, with similar prices and reliability.

Wheelchairs   Probably the most comfortable course is to bring your wheelchair from home. However, except in theater-style shows, access may be difficult if it's wider than 24½ inches and longer than 32 inches (44 inches for scooters); consult hosts and hostesses at the attraction. Thefts of personal wheelchairs while guests are inside attractions are rare but have been known to occur; take the precautions you would in any public place.

Wheelchair **rentals** are available from area medical supply companies that will deliver to your hotel and let you keep the chair for the duration of your vacation. You can also rent by the day in major theme parks ($5 a day for wheelchairs, $25 daily for the limited number of scooters, plus a deposit; *see* Chapters 3 and 4 for specifics).

In Disney parks, since rental locations are relatively close to parking, it may be a good idea to send someone ahead to get the wheelchair and bring it back to the car; at day's end, a Disney host or hostess may escort you to your car and then return the wheelchair for you. Here and at the other major area theme parks, rented wheelchairs that disappear while you're in a ride can be replaced throughout the parks—ask any staffer for the nearest location. Attaching some small personal item to the wheelchair may prevent other guests from taking yours by mistake.

Theme Parks At press time, guests with disabilities could take advantage of a
Discounts wide variety of discounts: 50% at **Busch Gardens** for wheelchair users and the visually or hearing impaired; at least 50% at **Cypress Gardens** and **Sea World** for guests with visual or hearing impairments; and 20% at **Universal Studios** for those with a disability that limits enjoyment of the park.

Guests Using Accessibility in the area is constantly improving for people who
Wheelchairs use wheelchairs. At **Walt Disney World,** a new standard of access was set with the opening of the Disney-MGM Studios. All of its restaurants, shops, and attractions, except one thrill ride, can be enjoyed right from a wheelchair. Epcot Center comes in a close second; some of the rides have a tailgate that drops down to provide a level entrance to the ride vehicle. Though the Magic Kingdom, now in its third decade, was designed before architects gave consideration to access issues, renovation plans are under way. Even so, the 18 accessible attractions combine with the live entertainment around the park to provide a most memorable experience. For specific accessibility information, *see* the Access for Travelers with Disabilities section for each park.

Universal Studios and **Sea World** are both substantially barrier-free. Universal has retrofitted its major attractions, with the exception of Back to the Future, for wheelchair accessibility. At Sea World, most shows are in stadiums or theaters and have always been barrier-free. Now guests can even take their wheelchairs on the Behind the Scenes tours. **Cypress Gardens** and **Splendid China** are accessible by guests with disabilities.

In some attractions, guests who use scooters may be required to transfer to a wheelchair. In others, guests must be able to leave their own wheelchair to board the ride vehicle (and must have a traveling companion assist them, as park staff cannot do so). Attractions with emergency evacuation routes that have narrow walkways or steps require additional mobility. Turbulence on other attractions poses a problem for some guests.

Rest rooms at all of these parks have standard accessible stalls. Yet more spacious facilities are available in First Aid stations.

Guests with **WDW** and **Universal Studios** have produced descriptive cassette
Visual tapes that can be borrowed, along with portable tape recorders
Impairments (deposit required); **Sea World** has no cassette program but does offer a braille guidebook and a free tour. The other parks have no services for the visually impaired. Service animals, while welcome, must be leashed or in a harness; they may board many rides, but not all—usually not those with loud noises, pyrotechnics, and other intense effects.

Guests with **Walt Disney World** publishes a special guidebook describing the
Hearing theme and story of various attractions in the three parks. At
Impairments Epcot Center, you can rent personal translator units that amplify the sound tracks of seven shows ($4 plus $40 deposit).

There and in the Magic Kingdom (but not Disney-MGM Studios), four-hour guided tours in sign language are available by advance reservation ($5 for adults, $3.50 for children 3–9; tel. 407/560–6233; TTY 407/827–5141).

Both **Universal Studios** (tel. 407/354–6356; TTY, 407/363–8265) and **Sea World** (tel. 407/351–3600; TTY, 407/363–2395) can with advance notice provide guides fluent in sign; Universal also has scripts available for all its shows. **Busch Gardens, Cypress Gardens,** and **Splendid China** do not offer assistance in sign.

Lodging Hotels and motels here are continually being renovated in order to comply with the Americans with Disabilities Act. Call the **Disabled Traveler's Helpline of Central Florida** (*see above*) for up-to-the-minute information. For questions about or reservations at Disney-owned properties only, call **WDW Special Request Reservations** (tel. 407/354–1853).

Guests Using Staying at Disney-owned resort hotels is particularly conven-
Wheelchairs ient, since the Disney transportation system has dozens of lift-equipped vehicles. Most resorts here in every price range have rooms with roll-in showers or transfer benches in the bathrooms. The **Yacht and Beach Club** ($$$$; Walt Disney World Central Reservations, tel. 407/934–7639; TTY, 407/939–7670), within walking distance of the International Gateway entrance to Epcot Center, has four rooms with roll-in showers in addition to 16 with bathtubs and grab bars. Another accessible Disney-owned resort is **Dixie Landings** ($$; tel. 407/W–DISNEY; TTY, 407/939–7670), containing 22 accessible rooms with roll-in showers with bench seats. For guests with oversize wheelchairs, the most accessible rooms are at the **Embassy Suites Resorts.** The one at Lake Buena Vista ($$$$; tel. 407/239–1144 or 800/857–8483) provides free transportation to the Disney parks; the one on International Drive South ($$$; tel. or TTY 407/352–1400 or 800/433–7275) was recently renovated to accommodate guests with disabilities, and it costs less because of its somewhat greater distance from WDW. *See also* Chapter 9 for details.

The **Hilton Gateway** on U.S. 192 in Kissimmee ($$–$$$; tel. 407/396–4400 or 800/327–9170) has recently added a tower that contains 13 accessible rooms with roll-in showers; unfortunately, its shuttle bus to Disney attractions is not accessible. The **Hampton Inn** ($–$$; tel. 407/351–6716 or 800/231–8395), opposite Universal Studios Florida, has accessible rooms but only with king-size beds; you can reserve transportation to the theme parks on lift-equipped vehicles, and the shuttle to Universal Studios is free. Finally, you'll find clean, comfortable, no-frills quarters with excellent bathroom facilities at the **Motel Six** locations, both on U.S. 192 and both in the inexpensive category (5731 W. Irlo Bronson Memorial Hwy., Kissimmee 34746, tel. 407/396–6333; and 7455 W. Irlo Bronson Memorial Hwy., Kissimmee 34747, tel. 407/396–6422).

Guests with You will be comfortable at any number of on-property Disney
Some resorts. Especially worthwhile and convenient is the **Grand**
Mobility **Floridian,** a luxurious monorail resort ($$$$), and **Port Orleans**

has all the advantages of Dixie Landings but a much more intimate feel ($$); contact Walt Disney World Central Reservations (*see above*).

One of the most accommodating off-site resorts is the **Marriott Orlando World Center** ($$$–$$$$; tel. 407/239–4200 or 800/621–0638; TTY, 407/238–0833); its level of commitment is especially apparent on Sunday mornings, when the Garden Terrace Restaurant hosts one of the most delicious and hospitable Sunday brunches in central Florida. **Howard Johnson Park Square Inn and Suites** in Lake Buena Vista offers superior amenities and accessibility ($$; tel. 407/239–6900 or 800/635–8684).

Guests with Visual Impairments In most properties, only elevators are braille equipped, but some have programs to help employees understand how best to assist guests with visual impairments. Particularly outstanding is the **Buena Vista Palace** on Hotel Plaza Boulevard in Walt Disney World Village (Expensive–Very Expensive; tel. 407/827–2727 or 800/327–2990); its Australian-themed Outback Restaurant has a tableside storyteller who truly paints pictures with words. The **Embassy Suites Resorts** at Lake Buena Vista and International Drive (tel. 800/362–2779; TTY, 800/451–4833) offer services such as talking alarm clocks and braille or recorded menus.

Guests with Hearing Impairments Most area properties have purchased the equipment necessary to accommodate guests with hearing impairments. Telecommunications devices for the deaf, flashing or vibrating phones and alarms, and close captioning are common; an industry-wide effort to teach some employees sign language is under way. The **Grosvenor Resort** (tel. 407/828–4444 or 800/624–4109), on Hotel Plaza Boulevard, has excellent facilities but no teletype reservations line.

Organizations Several organizations provide travel information for people with disabilities, usually for a membership fee, and some public newsletters and bulletins. Among them are the **Information Center for Individuals with Disabilities** (Fort Point Pl., 27–43 Wormwood St., Boston, MA 02210, tel. 617/727–5540 or 800/462–5015; TTY, 617/345–9743); **Mobility International USA** (Box 10767, Eugene, OR 97440; tel. or TTY, 503/343–1284 fax 503/343–6812), the U.S. branch of an international organization based in Britain and present in 30 countries; **MossRehab Hospital Travel Information Service** (tel. 215/456–9603; TTY, 215/456–9602), a referral line; the **Travel Industry and Disabled Exchange** (TIDE, 5435 Donna Ave., Tarzana, CA 91356, tel. 818/344–3640, fax 818/344–0078); and **Travelin' Talk** (Box 3534, Clarksville, TN 37043, tel. 615/552–6670, fax 615/552–1182).

In the United Kingdom Important information sources include the **Royal Association for Disability and Rehabilitation** (RADAR, 25 Mortimer St., London W1N 8AB, tel. 0171/637–5400), which publishes travel information for people with disabilities in Britain, and **Mobility International** (228 Borough High St., London SE1 1JX, tel. 0171/403–5688), an international clearinghouse of travel information for people with disabilities.

Travel Agencies and Tour Operators **Flying Wheels Travel** (143 W. Bridge St., Box 382, Owatonna, MN 55060, tel. 507/451–5005 or 800/535–6790) is a travel agency that specializes in domestic and worldwide cruises, tours, and independent travel itineraries for people with mobility problems. Adventurers should contact **Wilderness Inquiry** (1313 Fifth St. S.E., Minneapolis, MN 55414, tel. and TTY 612/379–3838), which orchestrates action-packed trips with activities such as white-water rafting, sea kayaking, and dogsledding for people with disabilities. Tours are designed to bring people who have disabilities together with those who don't.

Publications Several free publications are available from the **Consumer Information Center** (Pueblo, CO 81009, tel. 719/948–3334): "New Horizons for the Air Traveler with a Disability," a U.S. Department of Transportation booklet costing $.50 that describes changes resulting from the 1986 Air Carrier Access Act and the 1990 Americans with Disabilities Act (include Department 355A, Attn. R. Woods, in the address); and the Airport Operators Council's *Access Travel: Airports* (Dept. 575A), which describes facilities and services for people with disabilities at more than 500 airports worldwide.

Travelin' Talk Directory (*see* Organizations, *above*) was published in 1993. This 500-page book ($35) is packed with information for travelers with disabilities. **Twin Peaks Press** (Box 129, Vancouver, WA 98666, tel. 206/694–2462 for information, or 800/637–2256 for orders) publishes the *Directory of Travel Agencies for the Disabled* ($19.95), listing more than 370 agencies worldwide, and *Wheelchair Vagabond* ($14.95), a collection of personal travel tips. Add $2 per book for shipping. Fodor's publishes *Great American Vacations for Travelers with Disabilities,* which details services and accessible attractions, restaurants, and hotels in Florida and other U.S. destinations (available in bookstores, or call 800/533–6478).

Hints for Gay and Lesbian Travelers

Organizations The **International Gay Travel Association** (Box 4974, Key West, FL 33041, tel. 305/292–0217, 800/999–7925, or 800/448–8550), which has 700 members, will provide you with names of travel agents and tour operators who specialize in gay travel. The **Gay & Lesbian Visitors Center of New York Inc.** (135 W. 20th St., 3rd Floor, New York, NY 10011, tel. 212/463–9030 or 800/395–2315; $100 annually) mails a monthly newsletter, valuable coupons, and more to its members.

Tour Operators and Travel Agencies The dominant travel agency in the market is **Above and Beyond** (3568 Sacramento St., San Francisco, CA 94118, tel. 415/922–2683 or 800/397–2681). Tour operator **Olympus Vacations** (8424 Santa Monica Blvd. #721, West Hollywood, CA 90069; tel. 310/657–2220 or 800/965–9678) offers all-gay-and-lesbian resort holidays. **Skylink Women's Travel** (746 Ashland Ave., Santa Monica, CA 90405, tel. 310/452–0506 or 800/225–5759) handles individual travel for lesbians all over the world and conducts two international and five domestic group trips annually.

Publications The premiere international travel magazine for gays and lesbians is **Our World** (1104 N. Nova Road, Suite 251, Daytona Beach, FL 32117, tel. 904/441–5367; $35 for 10 issues). **Out & About** (tel. 203/789–8518 or 800/929–2268; $49 for 10 issues, full refund if you aren't satisfied) is a 16-page monthly newsletter with extensive information on resorts, hotels, and airlines that are gay-friendly.

Planning Your Visit

Careful planning is your key to the most hassle-free visit to the Orlando area. Figure out everything you want to see and do in the area. Will you be staying put in the Orlando area, or do you want to spend some time at the beach? Once you've settled on your sightseeing priorities, you can figure out how long you want to stay, make reservations, and buy tickets.

How Long to Stay There are a couple of ways to approach this question. If your objective is to enjoy the complete Walt Disney World resort experience, five days is a comfortable period to allow; this gives you time to see all of its major and minor parks, to sample the restaurants and entertainment, and to spend some time around the pool. Six days would be better. Figure on an additional day for every other area theme park you want to visit, and then add your travel time to and from home.

If you're coming to the area mostly to go on the rides and see the theme parks, allow one day per theme park (this supposes that you're willing to start out early every day, move quickly, breeze through shops, and hurry through meals). Then add your travel time to and from home.

In either case, add time for visiting the minor theme parks, for exploring Orlando off the beaten track, and for shopping in Orlando's flea markets and discount malls. Add an extra day or two if you're traveling with small children, who may have limited patience for marathon touring; if you want to linger during your stays; if you're staying off Disney property or using local shuttle transportation rather than your own or a rental car (to accommodate the extra time you will spend just getting to and from your destinations); or if you're visiting during a busy period, when long lines will make it nearly impossible to see all the most popular attractions (unless you have a lot of stamina for long days on your feet and are willing to be on the go from early in the morning until park closing). You could easily spend two weeks in the area and still not have seen it all.

Creating an Itinerary Once you know what you want to see and do, the first step is to lay out a day-by-day touring plan, using the Strategies for Your Visit sections of our theme parks sections in Chapters 3 and 4 and the italicized Crowds and Strategy information following each review. Don't try to plot your route from hour to hour; instead break the day up into morning, afternoon, and evening sections. Finally, make a schedule for calling for any reservations you will need. Put each day's plan on a separate index card, and carry the card with you as you explore.

What to See First find out the busy days of the week in the parks you want
When to visit (*see* When to Go in the Strategies for Your Visit section
preceding every theme park tour in Chapters 3 and 4). Then,
beginning with the dates on which you plan to visit, decide which
parks you will see on each day.

Think creatively. If you're staying on Walt Disney World property in a not-too-busy period and have at least five days, consider
spending afternoons at one of the water parks, at your hotel
swimming pool, or at a spa or sports facility. If you buy a multiday pass, which is good for unlimited visits to WDW's major
parks, you can also visit two or more theme parks in a single
day—say, combine a visit to the Magic Kingdom in the morning,
when the park isn't crowded, with an afternoon in Epcot Center's Future World, that area's least busy time.

Making Make a list of all the things you want to do that require reser-
Reservations vations. Note on the list how far in advance you can book for
each. (In this book, this information is usually in the italicized
information following each review.) Then, based on your travel
schedule, designate the date on which you should call for the
reservations you want. Some reservations can be made as soon
as you book your hotel; others will have to wait until you're in
the area.

Buying Your If you aren't signing up for an escorted tour or travel package,
Tickets buy your WDW admission tickets from **Walt Disney World Ticket
Mail Order** (Box 10030, Lake Buena Vista 32830-0030, tel.
407/824–4321) as soon as your travel dates have firmed up.
Prices typically go up two or three times a year, so you may just
beat a price hike and save some money. Many local offices of the
American Automobile Association (AAA) also sell tickets to
WDW; you don't have to be a AAA member to buy these tickets.

Before you get your tickets for other Orlando-area attractions,check into various money-saving offers. The **Orlando
Magicard,** available free from the Orlando/Orange County Convention and Visitor's Bureau, entitles you to discounts at restaurants, dinner shows, and sometimes even theme parks (though
never WDW). AAA members can often qualify for 10%–20% discounts on non-Disney theme park tickets; call your branch office
for more information. If applicable, also *see* Hints for Travelers
with Disabilities and Hints for Older Travelers, *above,* for further discount information.

Further Reading

Still the most perceptive book on Disney is *The Disney Version,*
by Richard Schickel (Simon & Schuster, 1985). Disney's art is
featured in *Disneyland: Inside Story,* by Randy Bright (Harry
N. Abrams). For a good read about Disney and other animators,
look for *Of Mice and Magic* (NAL Dutton, 1987), by Leonard
Maltin. *Walt Disney: An American Original* (Pocket Books,
1980), by Bob Thomas, is full of anecdotes about the development of WDW, and Marc Elliot's *Walt Disney: Hollywood's Dark
Prince* (Birch Lane Press, 1993) is a controversial look at the life

of WDW's creator. Much of the action in Tom Wolfe's *The Right Stuff* (Bantam, 1984) takes place at Cape Canaveral, on the Atlantic coast east of Orlando.

Arriving and Departing

By Plane

Flights are either nonstop, direct, or connecting. A **nonstop** flight requires no change of plane and makes no stops. A **direct** flight stops at least once and can involve a change of plane, although the flight number remains the same; if the first leg is late, the second waits. This is not the case with a **connecting** flight, which involves a different plane and a different flight number.

Airport and Airlines More than 20 scheduled airlines and more than 30 charter firms operate flights in and out of **Orlando International Airport,** providing direct service to more than 100 cities in the United States and many more in Europe, South America, Canada, and even Asia.

At last count, **Delta** (tel. 800/221–2121), the official airline of Walt Disney World, had more than 65 flights daily to and from Orlando International. The airport is also a major hub for **United Airlines** (tel. 800/241–6522), which has 20 daily flights to and from Orlando. **Continental** (tel. 800/525–0280) has 15 nonstops daily from its hubs in Houston, Denver, New York/Newark, and Cleveland. Other major airlines that serve Orlando include **America West,** (tel. 800/247–5692), **American** (tel. 800/433–7300), **Bahamasair** (tel. 800/562–7661), **British Airways** (tel. 800/247–9297), **Icelandair** (tel. 800/223–5500), **KLM** (tel. 800/374–7747), **Mexicana** (tel. 800/531–7921), **Northwest** (tel. 800/225–2525), **TransBrasil** (tel. 800/872–3153), **TWA** (tel. 800/221–2000), **USAir** (tel. 800/428–4322), and **Virgin Atlantic** (tel. 800/862–8621).

The Orlando airport has Universal Studios and Walt Disney World gift shops, where tickets, maps, and information are available. Buying tickets here while waiting for your bags to be unloaded will save time later.

Cutting Costs The Sunday travel section of most newspapers is a good source for deals. When booking, particularly through an unfamiliar company, call the Better Business Bureau or your local or state consumer protection bureau to find out whether any complaints have been registered against the company, pay with a credit card if you can, and consider trip cancellation and default insurance.

Promotional Airfares Less expensive fares, called promotional or discount fares, are round-trip and involve restrictions, which vary according to the route and the season. You must usually buy the ticket—commonly called an APEX (advance purchase excursion) when it's for international travel—in advance (seven, 14, or 21 days are usual), although some of the major airlines have added no-frills, cheap flights to compete with new bargain airlines on certain routes. These new low-cost carriers include: **Kiwi** (tel. 800/538–

5494), based in Newark, NJ, and serving Chicago, Atlanta, Tampa, Orlando, West Palm Beach, and San Juan; and **ValuJet** (tel. 800/825–8538 or 404/994–8258), based in Atlanta and flying to Jacksonville, Orlando, Memphis, Louisville, Tampa, New Orleans, and Ft. Lauderdale.

With the major airlines, the cheaper fares generally require minimum and maximum stays (for instance, over a Saturday night or at least seven and no more than 30 days). Airlines generally allow some return-date changes for a $25 to $50 fee, but most low-fare tickets are nonrefundable. Only a death in the family would prompt the airline to return any of your money if you canceled a nonrefundable ticket. You can, however, apply an unused nonrefundable ticket toward a new ticket, again with a small fee. The lowest fare is subject to availability, and only a small percentage of the plane's total seats will be sold at that price. Contact the U.S. Department of Transportation's Office of Consumer Affairs (I–25, Washington, DC 20590, tel. 202/366–2220) for a copy of "Fly-Rights: A Guide to Air Travel in the U.S." *The Official Frequent Flyer Guidebook* by Randy Petersen (4715-C Town Center Dr., Colorado Springs, CO 80916, tel. 719/597–8899 or 800/487–8893; $14.99, plus $3 shipping and handling) yields valuable hints on how to get the most for your air-travel dollars.

Consolidators Consolidators or bulk-fare operators buy blocks of seats on scheduled flights that airlines anticipate they won't be able to sell. They pay wholesale prices, add a markup, and resell the seats to travel agents or directly to the public at prices that still undercut the airline's promotional or discount fares. You pay more than on a charter but ordinarily less than for an APEX ticket. Moreover, some consolidators sometimes give you your money back. Carefully read the fine print detailing penalties for changes and cancellations. If you doubt the reliability of a company, call the airline once you've made your booking and confirm that you do, indeed, have a reservation on the flight.

Discount Travel Clubs Travel clubs offer members unsold space on airplanes, cruise ships, and package tours at as much as 50% below regular prices. Membership may include a regular bulletin or access to a toll-free hot line that provides details of available trips departing from three or four days to several months in the future. Most also offer 50% discounts off hotel rack rates, but double check with the hotel to make sure it isn't offering a better promotional rate independent of the club. Clubs include **Discount Travel International** (114 Forrest Ave., Suite 203, Narberth, PA 19072, tel. 215/668–7184; $45 annually, single or family), **Entertainment Travel Editions** (Box 1014 Trumbull, CT 06611, tel. 800/445–4137; price ranges $28–$48), **Great American Traveler** (Box 27965, Salt Lake City, UT 84127, tel. 800/548–2812; $29.95 annually), **Moment's Notice Discount Travel Club** (425 Madison Ave., New York, NY 10017, tel. 212/486–0503; $45 annually, single or family), **Privilege Card** (3391 Peachtree Rd. NE, Suite 110, Atlanta GA 30326, tel. 404/262–0222 or 800/236–9732; domestic annual membership $49.95, international, $74.95), **Travelers**

Advantage (CUC Travel Service, 49 Music Sq. W, Nashville, TN 37203, tel. 800/548–1116; $49 annually, single or family), and **Worldwide Discount Travel Club** (1674 Meridian Ave., Miami Beach, FL 33139, tel. 305/534–2082; $50 annually for family, $40 single).

Publications The newsletter "Travel Smart" (40 Beechdale Rd., Dobbs Ferry, NY 10522, tel. 800/327–3633; $44 a year) has a wealth of travel deals in each monthly issue.

Smoking Since February 1990, smoking has been banned on all domestic flights of less than six hours' duration; the ban also applies to domestic segments of international flights aboard U.S. and foreign carriers.

Between the Airport and the Hotels Several shuttle and limousine services offer both regularly scheduled and charter service. Departures are every half hour to Disney properties, every hour to other destinations. Ticket counters are in the baggage claim area. Find out in advance whether your hotel offers free airport shuttles; if not, ask for a recommendation.

By Bus Public buses operate between the airport and the main terminal of the **Tri-County Transit Authority** (1200 W. South St., Orlando, tel. 407/841–8240), downtown. Though the cost is 75¢, other options are preferable because center-city Orlando is far from most of the hotels used by theme park vacationers.

By Limousine **Mears Transportation Group** (tel. 407/423–5566) has meet-and-greet service—they'll meet you at the gate, help you with your luggage, and whisk you away, in either an 11-passenger van, a town car, or a limo. Vans run to Walt Disney World and along U.S. 192 every 30 minutes; prices range from $12.50 one-way for adults ($8.50 for children 4–11) to $22 round-trip for adults ($16 children 4–11). Limo rates run around $50–$60 for a town car that will accommodate three or four and $90 for a stretch limo that will seat six. **Town & Country Limo** (tel. 407/828–3035) charges $30–$40 one-way for up to seven, depending on the hotel, and **First Class Transportation** (tel. 407/578–0022) charges $45 one-way for up to four people.

By Taxi Taxis take only a half hour to get from the airport to most hotels used by WDW visitors; they charge about $25 plus tip to the International Drive area, about $10 more to the U.S.–192 area. Depending on the number of people in your party, this will cost more or less than paying by the head for an airport shuttle.

By Car To get to the hotel areas used by theme park guests, catch the Beeline Expressway (Rte. 528) west to International Drive, and exit at Sea World. Or stay on the Beeline to I–4, and head either west to Walt Disney World and U.S. 192/Kissimmee or east to downtown Orlando. Call your hotel for the best route.

By Train, Bus, and Car

By Train **Amtrak** (tel. 800/USA–RAIL) operates the *Silver Star* and the *Silver Meteor* to Florida. Both stop in Winter Park (150 Morse

Blvd.), in Orlando (1400 Sligh Blvd.), and then, 20 minutes later, in Kissimmee (416 Pleasant St.).

By Bus Contact **Greyhound Lines** (555 N. Magruder Ave., Orlando, tel. 407/843–7720 or 800/231–2222).

By Car If you want to have your car in Florida without driving it there, board the **Auto-Train** in Lorton, Virginia (tel. 703/690–3355), near Washington, D.C. Its southern terminus is Sanford, Florida (tel. 407/323–4800), some 23 miles north of Orlando.

Staying in Orlando

Getting Around

By Car The most important artery in the Orlando area is **I–4.** This interstate highway, which links the Atlantic Coast to Florida's Gulf of Mexico, ties everything together, and you'll invariably receive directions in reference to it. The problem is that I–4, though considered an east–west expressway in our national road system (where even numbers signify an east–west orientation and odd numbers a north–south orientation), actually runs north and south in the Orlando area. So when the signs say east, you are usually going north, and when the signs say west, you are usually going south. Think north–EAST and south–WEST.

Another main drag is **International Drive,** a.k.a. I-Drive, which has many major hotels, restaurants, and shopping centers. You can get onto International Drive from I–4 Exits 28, 29, and 30B.

The other main road, **U.S. 192,** cuts across I–4 at Exits 25A and 25B. This highway goes through the Kissimmee area and crosses Walt Disney World property, taking you to the Magic Kingdom's main entrance. U.S. 192 is sometimes called by its former names, Spacecoast Parkway and Irlo Bronson Memorial Highway. Irlo Bronson was a prominent local developer.

By Bus If you are staying along International Drive, in Kissimmee, or in Orlando proper, you can ride public buses to get around the immediate area. To find out which bus to take, ask your hotel clerk or call the **Tri-County Transit Authority Information Office** (tel. 407/841–8240) during business hours. Fares are 75¢, with 10¢ extra for transfers.

By Taxi Taxi fares start at $2.45 and cost $1.40 for each mile thereafter. Call **Town and Country Cab** (tel. 407/828–3035) or **Yellow Cab Co.** (tel. 407/699–9999).

Sample Fares **To WDW's Magic Kingdom:** about $20 from International Drive, $11–$15 from U.S. 192. **To Universal Studios:** $6–$11 from International Drive, $25–$30 from U.S. 192. **To Church Street Station,** downtown: $20–$25 from International Drive, $30–$40 from U.S. 192.

From the Hotels to the Attractions Scheduled service and charters linking just about every hotel and major attraction in the area are available from **Gray Line of Orlando** (tel. 407/422–0744), **Mears Transportation Group** (tel. 407/839–1570), **Phoenix Tours** (tel. 407/859–4211), and **Rabbit**

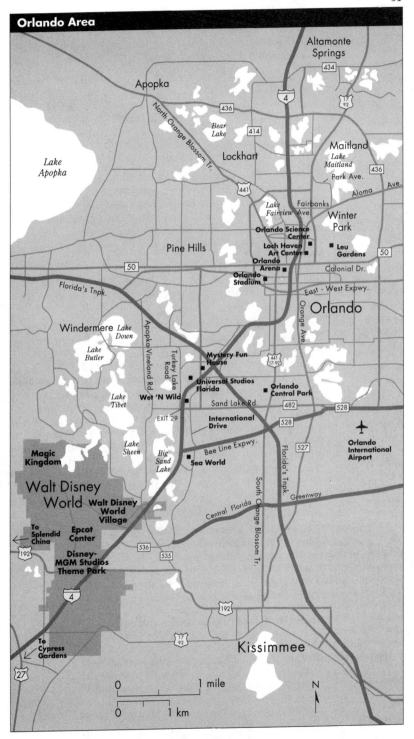

Bus Lines (tel. 407/291–2424). In addition, many hotels run their own shuttles especially for guests; to arrange a ride, all you have to do is ask your hotel's concierge, inquire at the front desk, or phone the operator directly.

When making your plans, remember that the bus schedule may not always coincide with your schedule: They may not run to the places you want to see on the days or at the times you prefer, whether that's back to your hotel at midday or out to the theme parks in late afternoon. Some buses also pick up or drop off guests at several hotels, adding to your ride time and delaying your arrival at your destination.

One-way fares are usually $6–$7 per adult, a couple of dollars less for children 4–11, between major hotel areas and the Disney parks. Excursion fares to Busch Gardens and Cypress Gardens, which are more than a half-hour's drive, are $27 per person, including admission as well as round-trip fare.

Guided Tours

In the Theme Parks Guided tours are available in all the area's major theme parks (*see* Essential Information in the individual theme-park sections of Chapters 3 and 4).

Around Orlando
Balloon Rides Quick, look up! Any morning in Orlando chances are fair to good that you'll spot a bright-colored hot-air balloon floating through the skies. You don't have to have your own gear to experience these silent, beautiful craft. Several operators offer trips, which usually include a Continental-breakfast picnic with champagne or a gala restaurant meal. They'll take children as well as adults (though most discourage parents from bringing babies and toddlers, who may be frightened by the experience). The cost is about $150 per adult at **Balloons by Terry** (3529 Edgewater Dr., Orlando, tel. 407/422–3529); **Rosie O'Grady's Balloon Flights** (also 3529 Edgewater Dr., Orlando, tel. 407/841–UPUP); and **Rise & Float Balloon Tours** (5767 Major Blvd., opposite Universal Studios at the Mystery Fun House, Orlando, tel. 407/352–8191), whose hot-air balloon is decorated with two hot-pink flamingos and a giant palm tree.

Helicopter Rides Seven different area tours, ranging from $20 to $399, are available from **Falcon Helicopter Service** (8990 International Dr., next to Caruso's Palace, Orlando, tel. 407/352–1753; at the Hyatt Hotel at I–4 and U.S. 192, no tel.; at the Howard Johnson's, 5071 W. Irlo Bronson Memorial Hwy., Kissimmee, tel. 407/397–0228; and at Universal Studios, no tel.).

Important Addresses and Numbers

Tourist Information The main source is the Orlando/Orange County Convention and Visitors Bureau's **Visitor Information Center** in the Mercado Mediterranean Village (8445 International Dr., tel. 407/363–5871). **Kissimmee–St. Cloud Convention and Visitors Bureau** (1925 E. Irlo Bronson Memorial Hwy., tel. 407/847–5000 or 407/423–6070) is 2½ miles east of I–4 on U.S. 192.

You can get **Walt Disney World** information from ticket windows and at Guest Services and Guest Relations, which have desks in the Disney hotels and theme parks as well as an information line (tel. 407/824–4321).

Emergencies   **Police** or **ambulance** (tel. 911). All of the area's major theme parks have first-aid centers.

Doctors   Hospital emergency rooms are open 24 hours a day. The most accessible hospital is the **Orlando Regional Medical Center/Sand Lake Hospital,** in the International Drive area (9400 Turkey Lake Rd., tel. 407/351–8500).

For minor medical problems, contact **Housemed** (2901 Parkway Blvd., Kissimmee; tel. 407/648–9234 or 407/846–2093), which runs a clinic open 9–9 daily and a mobile minor emergency service that offers hotel room visits by physicians for minor medical care and dispenses nonnarcotic medicine. Closer to Orlando, a block west of Kirkman Road, is the **Family Treatment Center** (6001 Vineland Rd., Orlando, tel. 407/351–6682; open weekdays 8–8, weekends 8–6). Near WDW, in Lake Buena Vista, the most convenient facility is the **Buena Vista Walk-in Medical Center,** next to the Walt Disney World Village entrance (Rte. 535, tel. 407/828–3434), open daily 9–8; shuttle service from any of the Disney theme park's first-aid stations costs $15 round-trip.

24-Hour Pharmacies   **Eckerd Drugs** (908 Lee Rd., Orlando, tel. 407/644–6908) is just off I–4 at the Lee Road exit, and **Walgreen's** (6201 International Dr., tel. 407/345–8311 or 407/345–8402) is opposite Wet 'n' Wild.

Dentists   **Emergency dental referral** (tel. 407/847–7474).

Road Service   **AAA Emergency Road Service** (tel. 407/877–2266 or 800/824–4432). In Walt Disney World, there is a **Car Care Center** (*see* Essential Information in Chapter 3).

24-Hour Markets   There are three **Gooding's Supermarkets** off I–4, one a few blocks from International Drive (7600 Dr. Phillips Blvd., tel. 407/352–8851), one on I-Drive proper (8255 International Dr., tel. 407/352–4215), and the other at the Crossroads of Lake Buena Vista, outside Disney Village Marketplace at Exit 27 (12521 Rte. 535, tel. 407/827–1200).

Credit Cards

The following credit card abbreviations are used throughout this guide: AE, American Express; D, Discover; DC, Diners Club; MC, MasterCard; V, Visa.

2 Portrait of Walt Disney World®

The Mouse and the Virgin

By Andrew Holleran

Books authored by Andrew Holleran include Dancer from the Dance *and* Ground Zero

I couldn't sleep the night before I went to Disney World. Fear, loathing, a clammy dread—all combined to produce what I call red-alert insomnia: the sensation that someone is pouring battery acid through your brain. A Floridian for more than 20 years, living two hours away by car, till this year I had patriotically avoided going near the place. It wasn't like the Statue of Liberty, which the New Yorker doesn't feel rushed to visit. No, Disney World was everything I preferred to ignore about Florida. My family went. My neighbors went. (One of them, a 75-year-old man, has gone every year for the past 15 to see what's new.) I didn't have to. Disney World meant plastic, kitsch, southern California, mobs of people, crushing traffic, and the utter ruin and devastation of the once sleepy city of Orlando, Florida.

I was further depressed by what its staggering success ($703 million profit in 1989 on revenues of $4.6 billion) said about my country, culture, and time. The Egyptians gave us the Pyramids, the Greeks the Parthenon, the French the cathedral of Chartres, and our contribution is . . . a celluloid mouse? Despair deepened when I heard that France was building a Disney theme park in Marne-la-Vallée, a mere 20 miles from Paris, directly connected by the Métro. The new Versailles! That France—France, the most critical of cultures—should *ask* for a theme park built around a fiberglass imitation of a European castle was like Sarah Ferguson, Duchess of York, buying her clothes at Ralph Lauren in New York. Who's imitating whom? But then Disney has always earned a good share of its revenues abroad. Disneyland is one of the only things that Japanese have asked to import, and Tokyo Disneyland is a smash. Walt Disney World is now the single most successful commercial attraction of its kind in the world. One of every four visitors in Florida comes to see it. Even two hours to the north, you feel a ripple effect.

The morning I drove to Orlando, I was making the sort of pilgrimage people used to make to Mont-Saint-Michel or Jerusalem. "You know, he almost put it in St. Louis," I said to my sister as we drive south on Route 19 through Ocala National Forest. "But Adolph Busch, the beer baron, stood up at a dinner they gave for Disney and said anyone who built a theme park and did not sell beer inside was crazy. So, on the plane back to California, Disney said, "Forget about St. Louis."

"Why?"

This essay originally appeared in the August 1990 issue of Wigwag *magazine.*

"Because, he had no intention of selling beer. He disliked the odor of beer on hot days in amusement parks—the parks in southern California he used to take his daughter to in the '30s and '40s. He said they were all dirty, disgusting places run by tough and phony people. This is how it all started."

I could have told her more. After reading Richard Schickel's *Disney Version,* John Taylor's *Storming the Magic Kingdom,* and an article by John McAleenan in the Orlando *Sentinel* about the actual building of Disney World, I was bursting with tidbits like that. The fact that Disney went ahead in 1954 with the building of Disneyland is chiefly because he could promote it on his weekly television show. That amusement parks were dying in the '50s, and the manufacturers of rides refused to build Disney the new ones he had in mind. That on the day Disney World opened, the people who built it actually wondered if anyone would come. That Disney himself had come up against obstacles throughout his career, and ended up one of the most tenacious, determined, and resilient men in the history of American business. In fact, I was more fascinated by Disney's career (with these low points that people seem to have forgotten) than by his amusement parks. But I didn't mention any of this. I dropped my sister off in Apopka, a small town 10 miles from Orlando, where she was playing golf in a community built entirely for golfers—as strange as anything I was likely to see in the Magic Kingdom. Then I drove to Orlando.

Walt Disney World is not in Orlando exactly but sits 20 miles southwest of downtown. It lies on both sides of a busy highway called I–4, on 28,000 acres of what used to be pinewoods, cattle pastures, and swampland, between two cities in two counties: Orlando, in Orange County, and Kissimmee, in Osceola County. Actually, Disney World exists in a world of its own—a separate entity, both physically and legally. Bill Donegan, an Orange County commissioner, likes to compare it to the Vatican.

The reason there's a lot of space between Disney World and the two cities it lies between is that Walt Disney wanted it that way. When Disney decided to put his second theme park in Florida, he wanted enough land around it to form a buffer against the sort of commercial crud that had marched up Harbor Boulevard in Anaheim to the very edge of Disneyland, and to enable him to build his own hotels to house the guests who were staying outside Disneyland. So, where Disneyland sits on 180 acres, Disney World occupies 28,000—roughly the area of Boston. ("If he had it his way," says Joe Fowler, an ex-admiral who helped construct Disney World, "we would have bought 50,000 acres.")

In the mid-'60s, big parcels were easy to find in central Florida; it was still mostly rural. In his first flight over the unbroken pinewoods in 1965, Disney saw an island in the middle of a lake down below and, imagining the fun he could have with it, said, "This is great. Buy it." (It later became Discovery Island, a bird sanctuary and zoological park.) He bought the land—for about $180 an acre—without letting the real estate agent and lawyer who worked for him know his identity. The publisher of the Orlando *Sentinel* learned the truth only by agreeing to keep it a secret; if the news got out, the deal was off. He kept the secret. In those days, everybody wanted growth. Forty-eight hours after the news that 28,000 acres had been acquired by Disney, land adjacent to his went up to $80,000 an acre. Anyone who studies Walt Disney's remarkable career will discover this: He was a sharp businessman.

But he was not—and this is what's so strange, driving down I–4 in the middle of this boom—always the success we see today. His pedigree was one of failure. His father, one of 11 children born in Ontario and raised in Kansas, went south to Florida as a young man to grow citrus. (He met Walt's mother, a schoolteacher on vacation, there.) A freeze wiped out his grove, and he went north to Chicago, where he got work as a carpenter on the Columbian Exposition of 1893. For the next 10 years he worked as a small contractor. "My mother used to go out on a construction job and hammer and saw planks with the men," said Walt, who was born in Chicago in 1901, the youngest of four sons. His first name was that of the Congregational minister who christened him; his second, Elias, that of his father. When he was five, his father moved again, acquiring a farm near Marceline, Missouri. Four years later, the failure of the farm forced Walt's father to auction off the livestock and move once more, to Kansas City. There Walt worked a predawn newspaper route, in blizzards so bitter they gave him nightmares as an adult. He also took art classes. Right after the armistice in 1918, he went to France, where he sold fake German helmets as souvenirs to American G.I.s and painted the Croix de Guerre on their jackets for 10 francs apiece (his first paying art job). Back home, a job waited for him in a Chicago jelly factory his father had bought. But he returned instead to Kansas City to get newspaper work, and ended up starting an animation business. It was not a success at first. Business was so poor, in fact, he had to tell his one big customer (a dentist who wanted an educational film for kids) that he couldn't meet him to discuss the project because he had no shoes: His only pair was being fixed. In 1923, at the age of 21, he gave up, like his father—but this time Disney went west, to Hollywood.

Each venture he pursued came, after some small success, to a dead end. When the banks lent him money—after the success of *Snow White and the Seven Dwarfs*—to build a studio, they insisted it be constructed so that if it failed it could be converted into a hospital (which is why the hallways are wide enough for a bed to be rolled down the middle). In 1939, *Snow White* won an Academy Award (a big statue for Snow White, seven tiny ones for the dwarfs). In 1940, *Pinocchio* was such a bomb that bankers cut off credit to his company. But each time he reached a dead end, he came up with something. Mickey Mouse was invented near bankruptcy, on a train to Los Angeles from New York, where Disney had just learned that his Eastern distributor had lured his best people away. He started making nature movies only because his feature-length animation-film career petered out in 1959 with *Sleeping Beauty* (another flop). He survived because he plowed whatever profits he did make into his own company (Walt Disney Productions), lived modestly in a town where other studio heads aped the English aristocracy, always drove a hard bargain (on actors, the saying went: "Disney gets you on the way up or the way down"), and never surrendered the rights to a single one of his films or to the merchandising connected with them. This strategy made him one of the few moguls to survive into the '60s with his studio intact.

Intact and insular: The Disney organization was always a family enterprise. All four brothers ended up living in Los Angeles—they played croquet together at Roy's house on summer Sundays—but the company consisted of only Walt and Roy. Roy handled the finances. Walt was the creative half, though Richard Schickel says he could barely draw the images for which his studio became famous, and another man, Ub Iwerks, was responsible for much of the animation that has burned itself into the national consciousness.

Not only was Walt Disney Productions the creation of two brothers—so close-knit that Walt decided to marry soon after Roy did—but in the early days the employees were sort of an extended family as well. Loyalty was very important to Walt Disney. (When Iwerks left to start his own firm and later returned to Disney, Walt could never really look him in the eye again.) Families, of course, have fights. When his employees went out on strike in 1941, Disney was so offended he refused to talk with them; the altercation was finally settled by someone else, while Disney was on a State Department–sponsored tour of South America. In 1953, Disney alienated Roy by forming a private company called Retlaw (Walter spelled backward) to control the merchandising rights to the name Walt Disney. Because the name Walt Disney was on just about everything connected to the studio, and Retlaw's income went to Walt and his two daughters, Roy was furious. The feud went on for nearly a decade, during most of which they refused to speak to each other. Telling people his side of the story, Roy would explain that when he and Walt were growing up in Kansas City, Walt would often wet the bed they shared. "He'd pee all over me," Roy would say, "and he's still doing it." (Walt would confirm the story and add, "I pissed on him then, and I'm pissing on him now.") The feud ended up dividing the company into "Walt men" (marketing, studio, theme parks) and "Roy men" (finance, legal, administrative), and the schism lasted long after the brothers' deaths—Walt's in 1966 and Roy's in 1971.

While the brothers were living, however, even their feud couldn't alter the united front the Disney company presented to outsiders. Not only did Walt retain the rights to every film he made (something other studios surrendered, especially when TV came along) and control the merchandise associated with his characters, but he also formed a company to distribute the movies. Yet even this was not enough. When the banks cut off his line of credit in 1940, Disney was forced to issue stock to raise enough money to complete *Fantasia*, and issuing stock meant the

Disney company was no longer his. Eventually, the stock would be bought by pension funds, institutional investors, and tycoons like Sid Bass, Irwin Jacobs, and Ivan Boesky. Disney did not live to see the struggle that ended with raiders almost dismembering the company. He did live, however, to see his studio finally hit it big with *Mary Poppins* (for a time, the sixth biggest-grossing movie ever) and, before that, to realize another of the many ideas everyone told him was crazy: Disneyland.

By the time Disney came to Orlando, looking for a place to build a second theme park, he had become a shrewd and canny businessman, and he had also been burned. He had learned the importance of controlling his product. Disney World was his second child, and he meant to avoid all the mistakes he'd made with the first. Those mistakes—the reason Disney World is 20 miles from downtown Orlando on its own tract of 28,000 acres—all involved the same thing: letting others have control. When he was building Disneyland, for instance, a local utility group appealed to his belief in private enterprise, and persuaded him to let the company supply him with electricity. (Disney was such a staunch Republican that when L.B.J. decorated him with a medal in 1964, he wore a Goldwater button on his lapel.) Then one day he went down to the park and was horrified to see high-tension wires converging on his domain. The company refused to bury them unless he paid for it. (He did.) When security guards from another outside firm failed to show the right attitude toward his guests (never "customers"), Disney fired them, hired his own, and sent every Disney employee (actually, people who work at Disney World and Disneyland are never called employees but, rather, "cast members") to the University of Disneyland, in Anaheim, to make sure they remained friendly, no matter how tired they were. What Disney wanted was to do things his way.

Florida let him. After he'd obtained everything he could through private means, he got the rest of what he wanted through the Florida legislature: control over the land. The bill Florida passed in 1967 to welcome Disney is called the Reedy Creek Improvement District Act. To read it is to gape at the powers given therein: It's like a land grant from the king of Spain. What the act did was set up a special taxing region called the Reedy Creek Improvement District (after a small stream on the property), which was authorized to provide its own pest and flood control, waste-removal systems, fire protection, and building codes. The last provision was especially important to Disney. The Disney company says it asked for the Reedy legislation to remove from Orange and Osceola counties the burden of supplying an infrastructure, and allow Disney to build its own state-of-the-art structures. But according to an Orange County official, Disney really wanted Reedy Creek so it could avoid the lengthy process of obtaining building permits from the county. This is how Disney continues to beat its competitors to the punch. Its new Disney-MGM Studios, for instance, opened months before Universal's theme park, 15 miles to the north, even though Universal broke ground a year before Disney did.

Disney has always been faster than people thought possible. When the construction firm originally hired to build Disney World said it would not be able to finish on time, Disney fired them and hired its own team, headed by a former general who'd overseen the Normandy invasion and a former admiral—both graduates of M.I.T.—and met the deadline by working 24-hour shifts.

Indeed, Reedy Creek is not only immune to local building codes and permits; it is also free of having to pay impact fees, which Orange County now levies on developers over the cost of building and maintaining roads. The impact fee on the average house built in Orange County today is $4,400. The fee for a Disney hotel with 7,000 rooms, Bill Donegan figures, would come to more than $18 million.

On the other hand, Reedy Creek contributes a lot of money to the local county governments. Besides levying taxes within its boundaries (Disney paying for Disney), it pays property taxes to Orange and Osceola counties as well. To date, Disney has paid $181 million in taxes to Orange County alone, half of which has been allocated to its schools. (Disney contributes more to the Orange County education budget than the nine next largest corporate contributors combined.) So, despite comparisons to the Vatican, Reedy Creek is not quite independent. Moreover, Phil Smith, a lawyer who helped draft and shepherd the act through the legislature in 1967, says the bill was really nothing new; it merely set up a taxing district that combined different powers found at the time in other limited-purpose taxing districts. Still, Disney values its status enough to energetically cultivate good relations with Tallahassee—it used to sponsor an annual Legislator's Day, on which state lawmakers and their families are guests of the park. And while there may be other special taxing districts, none of them are as famous, rich, or spectacularly successful as Reedy Creek.

In fact, the very success of Disney World has become its particular problem. Disney likes to point out that the phenomenal growth that has quadrupled the population of Orlando since 1960 would have occurred with or without Disney. One of the reasons Walt Disney chose the Orlando area was that growth was forecast. Disney is proud of the fact that it's the area's largest employer (over 31,500 jobs). It also points out that the average visitor to central Florida spends only four of 13 days at Disney World. And yet—because of Disney World's hotel-building boom (Orlando already has more hotel rooms than Manhattan, but the area's occupancy rate is 81%, which is very high); its addition of a third theme park (the Disney-MGM Studios); its water parks (Typhoon Lagoon, River Country), campgrounds, and nightclubs; and its avowed intention to make Disney World the center of convention business in the Southeast—it appears to folks beneath the castle that Disney wants to create a resort so all-inclusive that a guest never needs to leave it for anything but the plane home. This makes perfect sense for Disney, but it makes everyone around Disney World, particularly the hotels and attractions that live on Disney's spillover, nervous.

All this growth raises the question of who should pay for Disney World's astonishing success. The obvious problem is Orange County traffic. Because Disney does not have to pay impact fees, Orange County persuaded it in 1988 to chip in $1.3 million to improve the roads that feed into the highway leading to the Magic Kingdom (the infamous I-4); in exchange, Orange County made a matching grant and promised not to sue Reedy Creek for the next seven years. This was called the Interlocal Agreement. Bill Donegan, who says he'd have signed the original Reedy Creek Improvement District Act, voted no on the Interlocal Agreement. "It's a matter of balance. Quality of life," he says. "Disney-bashing is now a way of life."

It seems inevitable that it would be: Disney is so famous and successful that its sins are part of the public discourse down here. Not only has Disney World been fined by the E.P.A. for sewage violations and for the improper storage of toxic waste, but it recently made headlines when vultures began to peck out the eyes of tortoises on Discovery Island. Attempts to discourage the birds apparently included beating some of them to death. The state charged Disney with 16 counts of animal cruelty, so Disney gave $95,000 to local conservation groups and the charges were dropped.

Driving to Disney World from Apopka, anyone can see why. I-4 goes right through Orlando, which used to be a quiet central Florida city dotted with lakes and orange groves and is now a car-clogged central Florida city with lakes and postmodern skyscrapers. Downtown is still oddly bucolic and gentle, but everything that surrounds it is not. Orange County, Florida, now looks like Orange County, California. It has the same landscape of one- and two-story buildings, interspersed with trees, crisscrossed by viaducts and freeways seen from the window of a moving car. In fact, the only thing that's different is that the cars move here. On the second day of my visit, I saw an accident on I-4—an accident that halted a line of cars stretching all the way to the skyscrapers of downtown Orlando on the horizon—but I was going the other way and experienced no delay. Orlando has the sort of traffic that turns into gridlock instantly when the slightest thing goes wrong—an accident, a closed lane—but so long as everything keeps moving, well, it keeps moving. (In 1990, the federal government announced an experimental program in which 100 cars in Orlando will be equipped with special computers to predict traffic and to program driving as they move about the area. A very Disney idea, in a way—the car of tomorrow, the car that drives itself.) Driving to Disney World through Orlando, I saw exactly why Orange County is leading a peasant's revolt: all that money, all that success, off in the lazy distance, while outside the castle gates, beneath the hot Florida sun, the cars, concrete, and crowds turn Orlando into another version of L.A. It's a relief to leave the city behind.

And it's a thrill to realize that you are finally coming to, yes, Walt Disney World! The first signs of Disney World are two huge hotels, looming above the highway, from whose pediments two gigantic swans, two gigantic dolphins, and several gigantic seashells look down like Ozymandias on the passing scene. Even before learning that they are the work of Michael Graves (Disney has hired some very fancy architects for its hotels), I thought, Now, this is fun.

It's even more fun to get off I–4 and turn up a winding road into Disney's green domain (containing not only theme parks, hotels, campgrounds, lakes, and 7,200 acres of wilderness preserve, but also a tiny village where a few Disney employees live). The road curves through dense woods to a sort of turnpike toll station (where you get a $4 parking ticket), ending in one of three immense parking lots (one for each park), where a cheerful Disney employee—I mean, cast member—directs you to a parking space. Then you get into a long train of what look like linked golf carts and are taken to the entrance of whichever park you're visiting: Epcot, the Magic Kingdom, or the Disney-MGM Studios.

Of the three theme parks in Disney World—the Magic Kingdom, opened in 1971, Epcot Center in 1982, and the Disney-MGM Studios in 1989—the newest is the smallest. Its parking lot holds 4,500 cars, while Epcot Center and the Magic Kingdom each have parking spaces for 12,000. (This is why the Disney-MGM Studios closed as early as 8:30 AM recently—when the parking lot fills up, the doors close.) There are lines everywhere, though people seldom complain about them, I'm told, because they keep moving. (A more cynical view was expressed by a friend, that she has met only one person, on a plane, who dared to say she would never go back to Disney World because of the crowds. Her theory is that people who spend a lot of money and travel that far for their vacation are not likely to voice any disappointment when they get back home. Also, there is something suspicious about someone who does not like Mickey Mouse.) The truth is, the moment you enter Disney World you have the sensation that you're in the hands of invisible engineers. The experience is always fluid. The lines do keep moving, and every line has a sign beside it saying how long the wait is.

What you wait in line for varies from park to park. The Studios are a re-creation of a Hollywood back lot, including directors who ask you if you want to be in their movie. (There are also stuntmen, a fact that drives people at Universal crazy. Jay Stein, who has been in charge of Universal's theme park since the project was conceived in 1973, claims that he showed his plans to Disney chairman Michael Eisner in the '70s when Eisner was still president of Paramount. Disney spokesmen deny this. But when Eisner announced plans in 1985 for a studio at Walt Disney World, Sid Sheinberg, the president of MCA, Universal's parent company, said, "The mouse has become a ravenous rat." And to this day Stein calls the Disney-MGM Studios "a rip-off of Universal.") Epcot consists of corporate showcases clustered near the entrance and a chain of 11 national pavilions ringing a lagoon. The pavilions are clever pastiches of indigenous landmarks (the Eiffel Tower, a Japanese teahouse, a Moroccan Casbah), most of which contain shops, restaurants, and theaters where films about each country are shown. The films are free; the shops and restaurants are not, and the feeling that you are in the hands of expert people-movers is surpassed only by the feeling that an awful lot of money is changing hands rapidly.

Another cynical friend had warned me that Epcot Center is basically a big shopping mall, but it's really more than that. For one thing, it's full of performers, and the performers at all three parks are as important an element of the experience as the physical plant itself; acrobats, singers, comedians, and storytellers are constantly assembling, dispersing, and reappearing as you walk from one attraction to the next. The Magic Kingdom, in fact, has a famous subterranean system of corridors so that the cowboys, for instance, don't have to walk through the audience to stage their gunfights. Nor, for that matter, do the people who supply the restaurants; Disney didn't want his guests seeing Coke being delivered. The Magic Kingdom is, after all, an illusion.

I t's also curiously small, and smallness is part of the strategy—to make it toylike. Frontierland blends imperceptibly into Fantasyland, which is just around the corner from Tomorrowland, which leads you to Main Street, U.S.A., at the end of which is Cinderella Castle, where Cruella de Ville is singing a torch song on the castle steps while cowboys are having a shootout in Frontierland, a Mississippi steamboat is coming round the bend of a tiny river, and a brass band is playing near the Liberty Oak. The Magic Kingdom is the most intimate, shopworn, and emotionally charged of the three theme parks. Though they share the same cleanliness and the same extraordinary cleverness—Disney World, like God, is in the details— the Magic Kingdom is the most Disney of the parks. Only twice was the illusion shattered, when I noticed very small things: a broken door handle on the monorail, an attendant telling a man that his daughters weren't allowed to stand on the railing to watch Cruella de Ville—odd moments when reality (decay, authority) intruded for just a second.

Mostly, though, the illusion holds as you walk around. And you walk around a lot. Indeed, the paradox of Disney World is that once you arrive, the chief cause of Orlando's troubles with Disney—the traffic that has filled county roads to the brim— completely vanishes. In Disney World you go by foot, monorail, or boat. (There are lots of lakes here; water was an important part of Disney's dream. Ironically, the big lake he admired from the air proved, on close inspection, to have brown water, which, the Disney people feared, visitors would think was dirty. So they drained the lake, dug up the muck, replaced it with sand, and filled it back up again.) You walk in and continue to walk—all day, into the night. "Do people faint?" I asked someone the second day of my visit. "No," she said, "but they do get sunburnt."

The sun here is so strong that just before opening, the Magic Kingdom had to be repainted because the colors that created the desired mood in Anaheim were all wrong in Orlando's clear glare. In Disney's original plan Epcot lay beneath a glass dome to keep out excess heat and humidity, but the dome never materialized. So, entering Epcot, I was out under the big blue Florida sky in a large park of broad lawns, impeccable flower beds, architectural fantasies, and fountains—a sort of permanent World's Fair. Epcot, actually, is an acronym that stands for Experimental Prototype Community of Tomorrow. Disney, who thought of his parks as always changing, always improving—who got pleasure from knowing that the trees he planted would get bigger and more beautiful—wrote: "Epcot . . . will never cease to be a living blueprint of the future, where people actually live a life they can't find anywhere else in the world today." Besides a dome, it was to have had schools, churches, offices, apartments, stores, parks, golf courses, marinas, a monorail, a vacuum-tube trash-disposal system, a central computer controlling everything from streetlights to hotel reservations, and petless residents who behaved—as visitors to Disneyland were expected to—"properly." But Epcot has turned out to be what Star Wars was for Reagan: only a dream.

In a small theater off the town square of the Magic Kingdom, you used to be able to see a film about Disney, narrated by Walt himself. In it was a sketch of his proposal for Epcot. Set in a flat plain surrounded by the glowing circles of what might be monorails, its skyscrapers rise into the sky exactly as we thought they would, back in the '50s, in cities of the future. The reality could hardly be more ironic. Epcot has pinewoods, manicured flower beds, and perfectly circulating lakes and streams; Orlando provides the skyscrapers—off in the distance, on a broad flat plain, sans monorail. It's an environmental prototype of nothing, except the problems that plague all Florida cities in the last decade of the century: where to put the cars, how to provide housing for the poor, how to control sprawl. (Bill Donegan says that after he voiced his complaints about all this at an urban affairs conference at Harvard, an official from Cleveland told him he envied Orlando's problems.) These are the problems of every place that is not an amusement park.

For that, to my astonishment when I finally got there, is all Disney World really is: an amusement park. A very nice amusement park. About an inch deep. *Very* well done, but still, for all the brouhaha—the symbolism that politicians, intellectuals, and commentators find irresistible; the staggering financial success; the brilliant engineering and problem solving—just an amusement park. (In fact, there were so many English accents the day I went that I felt I was at Brighton. England surpassed Canada in 1989 as the country that sent the most visitors, followed by Germany, Brazil, and Mexico.) It's a place to spend the day walking from one exhibit to another, buying postcards and souvenirs, eating ice cream, watching movies about France or China in circular theaters surrounded by giant screens, looking at masses of other people (mostly young, white, middle-class, and nicely dressed; strangely self-edited, as if Disney had chosen them, too), strolling past small children (and adults) being photographed with Pluto. ("How does he breathe?" I asked the attendant. "The way a dog breathes," he answered. "I mean the person inside," I said. "That's not a person," he explained. "That's Pluto.")

It's a place where litter is picked up immediately if anyone is so disreputable as to drop something on the ground, and where, standing on a Venetian bridge watching a crowd watch a juggler in the street by Doge's Palace, I tapped on the balustrade and wondered, What is all this made of? (Fiberglass.) It's a place where you see kids in crazy hats (my favorite: the Donald Duck baseball cap, with a brim that quacks when squeezed) and where you'll overhear a boy standing next to you in line suddenly gasp, "Quick! Run! There's my parents!" And its the sort of place where, after several hours, everyone's face assumes a blank, zombielike expression, as if anesthetized by entertainment. It's—this comes as a shock—a big amusement park.

And yet it's not *really* just an amusement park—we all know that. The phrase Walt Disney concocted is "themed entertainment experience," which is actually a much more accurate description. There are no bumper cars here. This is a three-dimensional representation of the art world Disney created, and its appeal is subconscious and finally irresistible. (Emperor Hirohito of Japan used to wear, on informal occasions, a Mickey Mouse watch.) Schickel says that Disney removed the "secrets and silences" from childhood—subjected us all to the same sentimental kitsch. And it's true that Disney has a hold on childhood; one mother I know complained that a trip to Disney World seems to have become an American child's *right.* The Disney company knows this. The reason that Disney releases its classic animation features every seven years is that seven years is time enough for a new crop of children to grow up. And one of the factors in Disney's revival after the doldrums and confusion following Walt's death was the simple desire of a new generation of parents to take their kids to the Disney productions *they* had seen as children. Some product! Disney deals in family, childhood, nature, fairy tales, and the sort of timeless America that a lot of people feel vanished with *Son of Flubber.* (Until the mid-'70s, women were discouraged from wearing halter tops in Disneyland, and alcoholic drinks have been served here only recently, after dark, at large corporate parties.) The cleanliness, the sexlessness of Disney's world, is part of its appeal. The joke around the company—when Disney was alive, in fact—was that Walt himself could never have worked at Disneyland. He had a mustache, liked a stiff drink at the end of the day, and swore. To this day, cast members are forbidden to have facial hair.

During the uncertain years following Disney's death, when company executives still felt him looking over their shoulders, everyone was aware that while the country itself had changed, Disney had to remain true to itself or lose its identity altogether. Faced with the fact that a hit movie for kids was now *Porky's,* Walt's son-in-law, Ron Miller, launched a new company in 1983—Touchstone Pictures—to enable Disney to keep up with the changing times without surrendering its special place in the American mind. (Even so, its first picture was *Splash.* Today, under Jeffrey Katzenberg, there are some far less Disneyesque films on the market.) Everyone realized that Disney stood, ineluctably, for certain things. Things that give you goose bumps. Listening to the Voices of Liberty—a superb choral group—perform in the American Pavilion at Epcot, I heard such unabashed, sentimental, and piercing patriotism that I didn't know whether to stay or run. (I ran.) The Disney company is so closely identified with a certain American gentility that when Saul Steinberg, the Wall Street investor, held a meeting of his staff in 1984 to consider a buyout of the company (with the backing of Michael Milken, the onetime junk-bond king), he was warned that news of a Jewish raider acquiring Disney and selling off the pieces might produce an anti-Semitic backlash. The raid proceeded anyway, and fending it off caused a shakeup in the Disney organization that not only reunited the two sides of the feuding family but also resulted in the hiring of Michael Eisner and Frank Wells as chairman and president. The rest, as they say, is history. On January 29, 1987, Snow White and the Seven Dwarfs paraded onto the floor of the New York Stock Exchange to dramatize Disney's highest-ever first-quarter earnings.

Each year, Dick Nunis, president of Walt Disney Attractions, gives Orange and Osceola counties a "State of Our World" address, outlining what Disney is considering over the next five or 10 years. There is still a lot of the 28,000 acres to be developed. Some of it is bog, but even so, what remains can't be covered with theme parks alone. Disney is thinking about a major new shopping mall, an office development, and in 10 years perhaps, another park. ("No one really knows what Disney is thinking," one local official says.) In the meantime, its neighbors try to deal with their own future.

The feeling in the surrounding area seems often to be one of paranoia—that Disney is smarter, faster, and bigger than anyone else, and it is trying to duplicate in Reedy Creek anything a tourist might leave Disney to find. Reedy Creek comptroller Ray Maxwell scoffs at this idea. "There is plenty for everyone," he says. Indeed, he points out, Orlando makes so much money selling to Disney World itself that even if tourists *were* shuttled directly from the airport to Disney World and back, it would mean just as much business for Orange County, with none of the wear and tear. As far as the roads go, he says that most of the highways around Disney World are funded by the federal and state governments, not by the county. When Orange County refused to improve Route 535, a road Disney employees use to get to work, the state repaved it, believing that the public would benefit from improving the access of Disney's employees to their workplace. The geographical boundaries of Reedy Creek are easy to ascertain—they're fixed with a surveyor's exactitude—but the political boundaries are not.

To a commissioner like Donegan, Disney World is an arrogant city-state escaping its fair share of the costs of growth around Orlando. To Ray Maxwell, this is sheer jealousy: Disney is the reason for the incredible prosperity. (The assessed value of Osceola County was $500 million in 1974 and $5 *billion* in 1990.) The growth of Orlando, he says, is no greater than the growth in other parts of the state. The infrastructure Disney built when it arrived in Reedy Creek was infrastructure Orange and Osceola counties could not have provided themselves.

But the squabbles between Disney and central Florida are over something less tangible than money: culture. Disney executives were amazed when they came here to buy land in 1965 and one of the largest property owners sold them 7,500 acres on a handshake (a handshake he did not renege on when he learned the identity of his buyer). That was the way things were done in Florida in those days; the property owner only wanted permission to graze his cattle on the land till Disney opened. Florida—central Florida, certainly—was then a culture of ranchers, farmers, sleepy county courthouses, and timber companies. Now Disney sells 30 million tickets a year (an estimate for 1989; the company no longer gives out attendance figures, because they affect the price of its stock), and people come here from all over America, and the world, to spend vacation time. (Summer, Christmas, and spring break are the busiest times; Monday is the busiest day, when people begin their vacations with fresh energy.) These people have caused change. Change would have come to Orlando anyway, no doubt, but Disney World has become its embodiment. A friend who has lived in Orlando since 1946 explains it this way: "Disney put us on the map. But I'm not sure I want to be on the map."

I know just what he means. I'm glad that I live two hours away from Disney World, with the Ocala National Forest between us—a buffer even larger than the one Disney wanted for his theme parks. At the same time, having finally come here, I'm impressed. Disney World is so well run and so well thought out—so technologically and environmentally sophisticated—that after I'd been here awhile I began to think the problem was with Orange County, not Reedy Creek: that maybe Disney should run Orlando, too. (A thought that also occurred to Ray Bradbury, who was so dazzled by Disneyland, he asked Walt Disney to run for mayor of Los Angeles. Disney thought it over, then replied, "Why should I run for mayor when I'm already king?") But as smart and innovative as the Disney operation is, it's not going to run Orlando or Kissimmee. It's a corporation run for the benefit of its stockholders—a testament to the ability of private enterprise. Here is everything technology, expertise, and energy can bring to bear on a large piece of property surrounded by the chaos of millions of people in pursuit of money, retirement, power, and golf. In fact, the golfing community of Apopka and Disney World are two of the neatest, cleanest, and best-landscaped places I've seen in Florida. The trouble is, they're both theme parks. I guess it's only when we lose the theme that we mess things up.

That is why I lingered in the Magic Kingdom longer than I thought I would—mesmerized in particular by the town square—and finally went upstairs in City Hall to ask a Disney publicist, Pam Parks, about Disney's relationship with the real world.

"Disney-bashing waxes and wanes," she said, smiling. "I would be astonished if the local politicians supported Disney without reservation."

Feeling that I was not going to get any more out of her about the political nuances of the situation, I inquired about two stories I'd heard outside the gates. Even though it was rather *noir*, I had to ask: "Is Disney World a mecca for kidnappers?"

"That's a rumor that pops up periodically," she said, still smiling. "Some woman in Scandinavia claims her sister's son was stolen here. We always track the rumor down. It always comes to nothing. No, kids do not get stolen here." (One, in fact, was on a leash down in the square as we spoke—which, when the child is six or seven, seems a *bit* paranoid.)

The second rumor I half believed myself: that Walt Disney, lover of technology and the future, believed in cryogenics (freezing the dead so that if a cure for what killed them is developed years from now they can be thawed out and brought back to life). "I must ask you another crazy question," I said. "Is Disney frozen?"

"His nephew Roy was here with his daughter awhile ago," Parks replied, "and that's one of the things *he* said: 'Can you believe people actually think he's freeze-dried and lying in the castle?' "

"In the castle!" I said. The idea was immediately appealing: Disney up in one of the turrets with Cinderella, frozen in a futuristic fridge. This park, as Richard Schickel points out, is so much the ultimate expression of one man's ideas and taste that a frozen Disney would not be entirely out of place. I went downstairs and sat on a bench beneath the portico of City Hall to examine my Mickey Mouse hat (a yarmulke with two ears sticking out; you can have your name embroidered on the back, for free), write postcards (Snow White and Dopey), and watch the Whitmanesque spectacle of all these healthy, well-built families walking by in tasteful all-cotton sports clothes. (Shirts and shoes must be worn at all times, but there are no fat people in too-tight shorts, which an anti-Disney friend, a professor at the University of Florida in Gainesville, sneeringly predicted there would be. It's amazing the emotions this place stirs up among the intelligentsia.) I sat there for a long time, strangely happy. It was spellbinding: a sort of *Volkfest*, a huge swarm of European and American families—the people who came here to escape

Europe, settled Australia, and would like to go next to the moon, no doubt, or Mars.

To be honest, I'd expected something different. I'd even re-read *The Education of Henry Adams* before coming, to prepare myself for a cultural epiphany, if not apocalypse. I reread *The Education* because, after seeing the Chicago Exposition of 1893—the one Walt's father helped put up—and the Paris Exposition of 1900, Adams titled a chapter in his autobiography "The Dynamo and the Virgin." The Dynamo was the symbol of the new, modern, industrial state—the one we've been living in since 1900. The Virgin was the symbol of Eve, the feminine principle, the presiding spirit of his beloved Middle Ages. Had Adams been alive to see Disney World, he would have had to rename his chapter "The Mouse and the Virgin." But Disney World wasn't exactly apocalyptic, now that I was here to see for myself. It was just a very nice amusement park that families can come to together. (So important to family life, the family vacation.) It was also more old-fashioned than new. The future wasn't what impressed me here. The space rides and deep-sea laboratory seemed sort of corny, what might excite a 10-year-old. It was what I was looking at now that cast a spell: the past. Specifically, this charming replica of a square in some midwestern town at the beginning of the century—not far from Marceline, Missouri, perhaps. (Every brick, shingle, and gas lamp on Main Street, U.S.A., Disney had explained, is only five-eighths of its true size. "This costs more," he said, "but made the street a toy, and the imagination can play more freely with a toy. Besides, people like to think their world is somehow more grown-up than Papa's was." Shrewd man!)

The lights came on and twinkled in the trees. The stores were jammed. The recorded waltzes played, while poor Pluto—whoever was inside it—continued to stand in the garden to one side of City Hall, hugging small children, who sometimes beamed and sometimes panicked at his embrace. (When asked why he was trying to take over Disney, Saul Steinberg replied, "I have a special fondness for children.") It was a set for *The Music Man*. It was the whole sentimental dream of Victorian life, of the American Midwest, that deepened and deepened its spell, there in the central Florida dusk. And its final irony is that this place, this wholly artificial town square, provided before my eyes the street life—the human interaction, the mingling—that our car-cities of the present have completely erased from contemporary existence. One gets in a car or flies in a plane many miles to come here to find the gemütlichkeit that cars and planes have obliterated. Disney World, which specializes in the past (Main Street, steamboats, cowboys, castle) and the future (Voyage to Mars, George Lucas, lasers, Tomorrowland), leaves the present to Orange County. Which is why I sat there, wondering how I was going to get back to the parking lot, get in the car, and drive home.

3 Exploring Walt Disney World®

By Catherine Fredman

Updated by Marianne Camas

Millions of visitors, even those who place Pirates of the Caribbean and Space Mountain among the wonders of the world, can't accurately define Walt Disney World. When you take a Walt Disney World exit off I-4 or U.S. 192 and begin traveling across empty land devoid of billboards or any other promotional materials, you're already on the grounds, even though there's no Cinderella Castle in sight. It's a very big place. And it's crammed with pleasures: from swooping above a starlit London in the Magic Kingdom's Peter Pan's flight to just sitting under the shade of a Callary pear tree frosted with blooms in Epcot Center.

The sheer size of the property—27,400 acres near Kissimmee, Florida—suggests that WDW is more than a single theme park with a fabulous castle in the center and the most dazzling rides on earth. The property's acreage translates to 43 square miles—twice the size of Manhattan or Bermuda, 60 times larger than Monaco, and just a shade smaller than Nantucket or Liechtenstein. If you were to drive at 60 miles per hour from one side of the property to the other, it would take close to three-quarters of an hour. On a tract that size, 98 acres is a mere speck, yet that is the size of the Magic Kingdom. When most people imagine Walt Disney World, they think only of those 98 acres, but there is much, much more.

More than 2,500 acres of the property is occupied by hotels and villa complexes, each with its own theme and each equipped with recreational facilities such as swimming pools and golf courses. Epcot Center, a little more than twice the size of the Magic Kingdom, is the second major theme park. A combination of a science exploratorium and a world's fair, Epcot offers visions of the future and celebrations of the world's cultural diversity. In 1989, the Disney-MGM Studios Theme Park, devoted to the doings of the film business, opened nearby. In addition, there are thousands of acres of undeveloped land—grassy plains and pine forests patrolled by deer, and swamps patched by thickets of palmettos and fluttering with white ibis—even now, almost 25 years after opening day.

As Disney himself decreed, WDW has never been completed; as one new confection welcomes its first guests, another begins construction and still others are under study. So read up before you go, call ahead to find out what's new, and make a plan. Then relax—and have a wonderful time.

Essential Information

Important Numbers

Information

For **general information,** contact Guest Relations or Guest Services in any hotel or Disney theme park (tel. 407/824-4321). For **accommodations and shows,** call WDW Central Reservations (tel. 407/W-DISNEY). To inquire about **resort facilities,** call the individual property (*see* Disney Hotels in WDW and Other Hotels in WDW in Chapter 9).

Walt Disney World

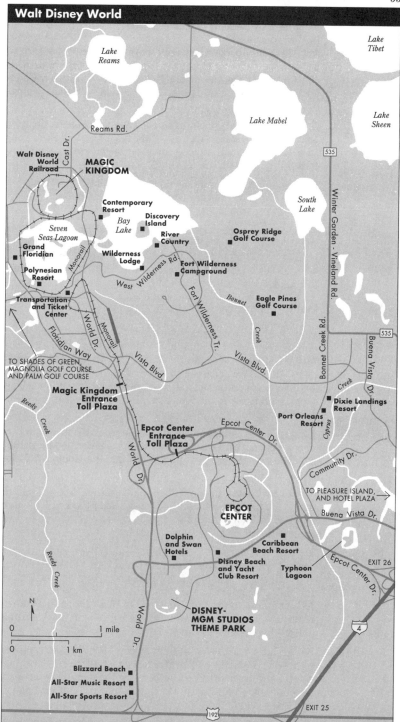

Lake Reams

Lake Tibet

Lake Mabel

Lake Sheen

Reams Rd.

Cast Dr.

Walt Disney World Railroad

MAGIC KINGDOM

535

Winter Garden - Vineland Rd.

South Lake

Contemporary Resort

Discovery Island

Bay Lake

Seven Seas Lagoon

River Country

Osprey Ridge Golf Course

Grand Floridian

Wilderness Lodge

Fort Wilderness Campground

Polynesian Resort

Monorail

West Wilderness Rd.

Fort Wilderness Tr.

Bonnet

Eagle Pines Golf Course

Transportation and Ticket Center

World Dr.

Monorail

Vista Blvd.

Vista Blvd.

Creek

Bonnet Creek Rd.

535

Buena Vista Dr.

Floridian Way

TO SHADES OF GREEN, MAGNOLIA GOLF COURSE, AND PALM GOLF COURSE

Reedy Creek

Magic Kingdom Entrance Toll Plaza

Creek

Epcot Center Entrance Toll Plaza

World Dr.

Epcot Center Dr.

Port Orleans Resort

Cyprus

Dixie Landings Resort

Community Dr.

TO PLEASURE ISLAND, AND HOTEL PLAZA

EPCOT CENTER

Buena Vista Dr.

Reedy Creek

Dolphin and Swan Hotels

Caribbean Beach Resort

EXIT 26

Disney Beach and Yacht Club Resort

Typhoon Lagoon

Epcot Center Dr.

N

0   1 mile

0   1 km

World Dr.

DISNEY-MGM STUDIOS THEME PARK

I-4

Blizzard Beach

All-Star Music Resort

All-Star Sports Resort

192

EXIT 25

To get very specific information, call the attraction or depart-ment directly: **Discovery Island** (tel. 407/824–3784), **Disney Village Marketplace** (tel. 407/828–3058), **Fort Wilderness** (tel. 407/824–2900), **KinderCare** child care (in-room, tel. 407/827–5444; drop-off, tel. 407/827–5437), **learning programs** (tel. 407/354–1855), **Pleasure Island** (tel. 407/934–7781), **River Country** (tel. 407/824–2760), **Disney-MGM Studios TV-show tapings** (tel. 407/560–4651), **Typhoon Lagoon** (tel. 407/560–4141).

Reservations On-site Disney hotel guests can make advance reservations for **Epcot Center restaurants** (tel. 407/824–4321); you'll need your reservation number. Anyone can reserve **golf tee times and lessons** (tel. 407/824–2270).

Financial Services Fulfill your banking or money wiring needs at the **Sun Bank** (tel. 407/824–5767) or **Western Union** at the Contemporary Resort (tel. 407/824–3456).

Lost and Found There are same-day lost-and-found offices at **Epcot Center** (tel. 407/560–6105 or 407/560–6236), in the **Magic Kingdom** at City Hall (tel. 407/824–4521), and in **Disney-MGM Studios** (tel. 407/560–4668). After one day, all items are sent to the **Main Lost & Found** office (tel. 407/824–4245).

Getting There by Car

Walt Disney World has three exits off I–4. For the Magic King-dom, Disney-MGM Studios, Fort Wilderness, and the rest of the Magic Kingdom resort area, take the one marked **Magic Kingdom–U.S. 192.** From here, it's a 4-mile drive along Disney's main entrance road to the toll gate, and another mile to the parking area; be prepared for serious bumper-to-bumper traffic both on I–4 nearing the U.S. 192 exit and on 192 itself.

For access to Disney Village Marketplace, Pleasure Island, Ty-phoon Lagoon, the Crossroads Shopping Center, and the estab-lishments on Hotel Plaza Boulevard, use the **Route 535–Lake Buena Vista** exit.

The **Epcot Center–Disney Village** exit is the one to use if you're bound for those destinations or for hotels in the Epcot Center and Disney Village resort areas; you can also get to Disney Vil-lage Marketplace and Disney-MGM from here.

Parking Every theme park has a parking lot—and all are huge. Always write down exactly where you park and take the number with you. Although in theory Goofy 13 is unforgettable (sections of the Magic Kingdom lot are named for Disney characters), a day full of unforgettable experiences in the Disney parks may prove otherwise. Trams make frequent trips between the parking area and the parks' turnstile areas.

Parking Fees For each lot, admission is $5 for cars, $6 for RVs and campers (or free for Walt Disney World resort guests with ID). Save your receipt; if you want to visit another park the same day, you won't have to pay to park twice. Parking is free at Typhoon Lagoon and River Country.

Auto Needs   Emergency road service is provided by the **Disney Car Care Center** (tel. 407/824–4813)—an AAA facility near the Magic Kingdom Toll Plaza. Repair service is available weekdays 7 AM–6 PM. The gas islands are open daily until 90 minutes after the Magic Kingdom closes. If you drop off your car for service, the management will shuttle you to the park of your choice.

Getting Around

Walt Disney World has its own transportation system that can get you wherever you want to go. It's fairly simple once you get the hang of it.

By Monorail   The elevated **monorail** serves many important destinations. It has two loops: one linking the Magic Kingdom, an area known as the Transportation and Ticket Center (TTC), and a handful of resorts, including the Contemporary, the Grand Floridian, and the Polynesian Village, and the other looping from the TTC directly to Epcot Center. Before pulling into the station, the elevated track circles through Future World—Epcot Center's northern half—and circles the giant silver geosphere housing the Spaceship Earth ride to give you a preview of what you'll see.

By Boat   Motor **launches** connect WDW destinations located on waterways. Specifically, they operate between the Epcot Center resorts (except the Caribbean Beach) and Disney-MGM Studios and between Discovery Island—in Bay Lake—and the Magic Kingdom, Fort Wilderness, and the Polynesian, Contemporary, and Grand Floridian resorts (Discovery Island admission ticket, WDW resort ID, or multiday admission ticket required).

By Bus   In addition, **buses** provide direct service from every on-site resort to both major and minor theme parks, and express buses go directly between the major theme parks. To Typhoon Lagoon, you can go directly from (or make connections at) the TTC, Disney Village Marketplace, Epcot Center, and the Epcot Center resorts (the Beach and Yacht Clubs, the Caribbean Beach Resort, the Swan, and the Dolphin).

By Tram   From the Epcot Center resort area, **trams** operate to the International Gateway of the park's World Showcase.

Hours   Monorail, launches, buses, and trams all operate from early in the morning until at least midnight. (Hours are shorter during early closing periods.) Check on the operating hours of the service you need if you plan to be out later than that.

Fees   All of this transportation is free if you are staying at an on-site resort or if you hold a three-park ticket. If not, you can buy yourself unlimited transportation within Walt Disney World for $2.50 a day.

Admission Fees

Visiting Walt Disney World is not cheap, especially if you have a child or two along. Everyone 10 and older pays adult price;

reductions are available for children 3–9. No discounted family tickets are available.

Tickets In Disneyspeak, "ticket" refers to a single day's admission to the Magic Kingdom, Epcot Center, or the Disney-MGM Studios. If you want to spend two or three days visiting the attractions, you have to buy a separate ticket each day. A ticket is good in the park for which you buy it only on the day you buy it; with tickets, you can't park-hop. If you buy a one-day ticket and later decide to extend your visit, you can apply the cost of it toward the purchase of any passport (but only before you leave the park). Exchanges can be made at City Hall in the Magic Kingdom, at Earth Station in Epcot Center, or at Guest Relations at Disney-MGM.

Passports If you want to spend more than three days, you have several options. The **Four-Day Value Pass** allows admission to each of the three parks on any three days. You can then visit one of the parks again on one more day. You cannot visit more than one park on one day. There is a way to avoid this restriction: In the spring of 1994, the Disney folks introduced the **Four-Day Park Hopper**, a personalized photo ID pass which allows unlimited visits to the three parks on any four days. The **Five-Day World Hopper** is also a photo ID; it includes unlimited visits to the three theme parks over five days, plus 7 days' admission to WDW's minor parks—Pleasure Island, Typhoon Lagoon, River Country, and Discovery Island. (Once the newest Disney water park, Blizzard Beach, opens in mid or late 1995, it will also be included in the World Hopper, so expect a corresponding price increase for this multipark passport.) Disney says it introduced the photo IDs as a way to prevent counterfeiting; however, these new park-hopping passes were introduced after Disney weathered a storm of controversy over its decision to allow park-hopping only to guests registered at hotels on Disney property.

These three passes can save you money. In fact, if you plan to visit the minor parks or go to Typhoon Lagoon more than once, it may pay to buy a Five-Day World Hopper Pass even if you're staying only four days. Each time you use a passport, the entry date is stamped on it; remaining days may be used even years in the future. A variety of annual passes are also available, at a cost only slightly more than a World Hopper Pass; if you plan to visit twice in a year, these are a good deal.

Prices Disney changes its prices at least once a year and without any notice. At press time, WDW admission prices (including 6% tax) were as follows, but call as close as possible to the time of your trip for the most current information.

	Adults	Children
One-day ticket	$38	$30.60
Four-Day Value Pass	$130.95	$102.45
Four-Day Park Hopper	$141.55	$113.05
Five-Day World Hopper	$189.15	$151.10

River Country	$15	$12
Discovery Island	$10	$6
Combined River Country/ Discovery Island	$18	$13
Typhoon Lagoon	$23	$17.50
Pleasure Island	$16	$16

Where to Buy Tickets and Passports Tickets and passports to Walt Disney World, Epcot Center, and Disney-MGM Studios Theme Park can be purchased at admission booths at the TTC, in all on-site resorts (if you're a registered guest), and at the Walt Disney World kiosk on the second floor of the main terminal at Orlando International Airport. American Express, Visa, and MasterCard are accepted, as are cash, personal checks (with ID), and traveler's checks.

By Mail If you buy your admission media by mail, you'll be waiting at the turnstiles, ready to get a jump on the day, while everyone else is lining up at Guest Services in the Disney hotels or at the ticket booths at the theme parks. Send a check or money order to Admissions, Walt Disney World, Box 10000, Lake Buena Vista, FL 32830. Allow four to six weeks for processing.

Hand Stamps If you want to leave the Magic Kingdom, Epcot Center, and Disney-MGM and return on the same day, be sure to have your hand stamped on the way out. You'll need your ticket *and* the hand stamp to be readmitted.

Opening and Closing Hours

Major Theme Parks Operating hours for the **Magic Kingdom, Epcot Center,** and **Disney-MGM Studios** theme parks vary widely throughout the year and change for school and legal holidays. In general, the longest days are during the prime summer months and over the year-end holidays, when the Magic Kingdom is open until midnight (later on New Year's Eve); Epcot Center is open until 11 PM; and Disney-MGM is open until 9 PM.

At other times, Epcot Center and Disney-MGM are open until 8 and the Magic Kingdom until 7—but there are variations, so call ahead.

Note that though the Magic Kingdom, Epcot Center, and Disney-MGM officially open at 9 AM, visitors may enter at 8:30, and sometimes at 8. The parking lots open at least an hour before the parks do. Arriving at the Magic Kingdom turnstiles before the official opening time, you can breakfast in a restaurant on Main Street, which opens before the rest of the park, and be ready to dash to one of the popular attractions in other lands at "rope drop," the park's official opening time. Arriving in Epcot Center or Disney-MGM Studios, you can make dinner reservations before the crowds arrive and take in some of the attractions and pavilions well before the major crowds descend, which is usually at about 10.

Guests staying on-site can sneak in an hour earlier every other day starting with Sunday (the information is usually included with the passport).

Minor Parks   Hours at **Discovery Island, River Country,** and **Typhoon Lagoon** are 10–5 daily (until 7 in summer). Hours at **Blizzard Beach** had not yet been determined at press time.

Dining

Walt Disney World is full of places to snack and eat. The theme parks are chockablock with fast-food spots; all have full-service, sit-down restaurants, and in Epcot Center's World Showcase, these eating-and-drinking spots are part of the show. On-site hotels offer still other options, including buffeterias as well as full-service restaurants.

This book does not describe and rate every eating spot. Best bets for quick meals are described as Time Out in the theme park sections of this chapter, and top options for meals in full-service restaurants are in the theme parks' Dining sections. For reviews of restaurants in Disney hotels and at Epcot Center, *see* Chapter 8.

Fresh fruits, salads, steamed vegetables, and low-fat foods are more widely available than you might expect. In full-service restaurants, for instance, you can usually get skim milk, and many fast-food operations have low-fat milk.

Beer, Wine,   The Magic Kingdom's no-liquor policy does not extend to the
and Spirits   rest of Walt Disney World, and in fact, most restaurants and watering holes, particularly those in the on-site hotels, mix elaborate fantasy drinks based on fruit juices or flavored with liqueurs.

Important Tips for Your Visit

The order in which you tour each of the Disney parks has everything to do with your priorities, the time of year you visit (which is in turn related to the opening and closing hours and the size of the crowds), how long you're staying in Walt Disney World, and whether you're staying on or off WDW property. The "Strategies for Your Visit," covering various Disney theme parks in the pages that follow, assumes that you want to see that park in a single day and that you're traveling during a period of good-size crowds and long hours. The italicized "Crowds" and "Strategies" information that follows each attraction's review should help you draw up alternative plans. No matter where you go, you will have a smoother time of it if you follow certain basic rules.

- Arrive in the theme parks early—well ahead of the published opening times—so that you can check belongings into lockers, rent strollers, and otherwise take care of business before everyone else.

- See the three-star attractions either first thing in the morning, during a parade, or at the very end of the day.

- Whenever possible when you're visiting the theme parks, eat in a restaurant that takes reservations, or have meals before or after mealtime rush hours (from 11 AM to 2 PM and again from 6 to 8 PM). Or leave the theme parks altogether for a meal in one of the hotels. Early meals are particularly advantageous; you'll be resting up and cooling off while the rest of the world is waiting in line; while they're all waiting to order, you'll be walking right into many attractions.

- Spend afternoons in high-capacity sit-down shows or catching live entertainment—or leave the park entirely for a swim in your hotel pool.

- If you plan to take in Typhoon Lagoon, go early in your visit (but not on a weekend). You may like it so much that you'll want to go again.

- If a meal with the characters is in your plans, save it for the end of your trip, when your youngsters will have become accustomed to these large, looming figures.

- If a meal in a World Showcase restaurant is in your plans, make your reservations in advance if you're staying at a Disney hotel (*see* Chapter 8).

- Familiarize yourself with all age and height restrictions—and don't let your younger children get excited about rides they're too short or too young to experience.

Entertainment

Live entertainment adds texture to visits to the Disney theme parks. Although the jokes may be silly, the humor broad, and the themes sometimes excessively wholesome, the level of professionalism is high and the energy of the performers unquestionable. Be sure to pick up a performance schedule on your way into the theme parks.

Ratings

Every visitor leaves the Magic Kingdom, Epcot Center, and Disney-MGM Studios with a different opinion about what was "the best." Some attractions get raves from all visitors, whereas others are enjoyed most by young children or older travelers. To take this into account, our descriptions rate each attraction with ★ , ★★ , or ★★★ , depending on the strength of its appeal to the visitor group noted by the italics preceding the stars. A three-star attraction, standing out for its imaginative qualities or technical wizardry, elicits the most enthusiastic responses in that group; see it even if your time is limited.

At Epcot Center's World Showcase, the national pavilions are enjoyable by audiences of all ages; however, young children may consider such cultural fare less exciting than the fantasy-oriented attractions in the Magic Kingdom, and they may be exhausted by all the walking required.

Access for Travelers with Disabilities

Attractions in all the Disney parks typically have both a visual element that makes them appealing without sound and an audio element whose charm remains even without the visuals; many are accessible by guests using wheelchairs, and most are accessible by guests with some mobility. Guide dogs and service animals are often permitted.

At many rides and attractions, guests with mobility, hearing, and visual impairments do not use the main entrance and sometimes even bypass lines; to find out where to enter or if you have specific questions, ask any host or hostess.

WDW's *Guidebook for Guests with Disabilities* details many specific challenges and identifies the special disabled-guest entrances. In addition, story notes, scripts, or song lyrics are covered in the *Guidebook for Guests with Hearing Impairments.* Both publications are available at the main visitor information locations in every park, along with **cassette tapes** and **portable players** that provide audio narration for most attractions (no charge, but refundable deposit required). There are also **wheelchair rentals** in every park.

Magic Kingdom

For most people, the Magic Kingdom *is* Walt Disney World. Certainly it is both the heart and soul of the Disney empire. The Magic Kingdom is comparable to California's Disneyland; it was the first Disney outpost in Florida when it opened in 1972, and it is the park that traveled, with modifications, to France and Japan.

For a park that wields such worldwide influence, the Magic Kingdom is surprisingly small: At barely 98 acres, it is the tiniest of Walt Disney World's Big Three. However, the unofficial theme song—"It's a Small World After All"—doesn't hold true when it comes to the Magic Kingdom's attractions. Packed into six different "lands" are nearly 50 major crowd-pleasers, and that's not counting all the ancillary attractions: shops, eateries, live entertainment, cartoon characters, fireworks, parades, and, of course, the sheer pleasure of strolling through the beautifully landscaped and manicured grounds.

Many of the rides are geared to the young, but the Magic Kingdom is anything but a kiddie park. The degree of detail, the greater vision, the surprisingly witty spiel of the guides, and the tongue-in-cheek signs that crop up in the oddest places (for instance, in Fantasyland, the rest rooms are marked "Prince" and "Princess") all contribute to a delightful sense of discovery that's far beyond the mere thrill of a ride.

Essential Information

Getting Around Once you're in the Magic Kingdom, distances are small, and the best way to get around is on foot; the Walt Disney World Rail-

road, the Main Street Vehicles, the Skyway between Fantasyland and Tomorrowland, and the Tomorrowland Transit Authority (formerly the WEDway PeopleMover) do help you cover
some territory and can give your feet a welcome rest, but they're
primarily forms of entertainment, not transportation.

Tourist **City Hall** (tel. 407/824–4521) is the principal information center.
Information Here you can pick up the *Magic Kingdom Guide Book* and a
schedule of daily events (if you haven't requested one by mail in
advance), search for misplaced belongings or companions, and
ask questions of the omniscient staffers.

Other cast members throughout the park can be helpful, too. In
fact, providing information for visitors is part of the job description of the young men and women who sweep the pavement and
faithfully keep litter in its place.

Reservations One of the most frequently asked questions at City Hall is
whether this is the place to make reservations for the Diamond
Horseshoe Jamboree. (The answer is no. That's done across
Town Square at Disneyana Collectibles.) Reservations for the
handful of other full-service restaurants must be made at the
individual establishment.

Services The Magic Kingdom's soothing, quiet Baby Care Center is next
Baby Care to the Crystal Palace at the end of Main Street. Furnished with
rocking chairs, it has a low lighting level that makes it comfortable for nursing. There are toddler-size toilets, and the cast
members have supplies such as **formula, baby food, pacifiers,** and
disposable diapers for sale. You'll find **changing tables** here, as
well as in all women's rooms and some men's rooms. You can also
buy disposable diapers in the Emporium on Main Street. The
Stroller Shop near the entrance to the Magic Kingdom (on the
east side of Main Street) is the place for **stroller rentals** ($5 fee;
$1 deposit required).

Barbershop Tucked in a corner just off Main Street, where the Emporium
ends, the Harmony Barber Shop isn't just for show—it's a for-
real place to get a **haircut** from Disney cast members dressed in
19th-century costumes.

Cameras and Kodak's disposable Fun Saver cameras are widely available. Or,
Film at the Camera Center on Main Street, you can borrow a Kodak
disk camera (you just have to buy the film) or rent **35mm cameras**
or **video camcorders** ($5 and $40, respectively; refundable $100–
$800 deposit required). Multiple-day rentals of camcorders are
available. Be advised that camcorders are full-size models.

For **minor camera repairs,** the Camera Center is the place.

For **two-hour film developing,** look for the Photo Express sign
throughout the park; drop your film in the container, and you
can pick up your pictures at the Camera Center as you leave the
park. Instant (almost) gratification.

First Aid The Magic Kingdom's First Aid Center, staffed by registered
nurses, is alongside the Crystal Palace.

Guided Tours A good way to get a feel for the layout of the Magic Kingdom and what goes on behind the scenes is to take one of the 3½-to 4-hour guided orientation tours ($5 per adult, $3.50 per child, plus park admission). Tours include visits to some of the rides, but don't expect to go to the head of the line—you still have to wait your turn. Tours leave at 10:15 AM, so reserve early in the day.

Lockers You'll find them in an arcade underneath the Main Street Railroad Station (50¢). If what you need to store won't fit in the larger lockers, inquire at City Hall.

Lost Children and Adults If you're worried about your children getting lost, you can get them **name tags** at the Magic Kingdom (at City Hall or at the Baby Center next to the Crystal Palace). If your fears are realized, immediately ask any cast member and try not to panic; obviously lost children are usually taken to City Hall or the Baby Care Center, where lost children's logbooks are kept, and everyone is well trained to effect speedy reunions.

City Hall also has a computerized **Message Center,** where you can leave notes for your traveling companions, both those in the Magic Kingdom and those in other parks.

Lost and Found City Hall is the place to report losses and finds (or call 407/824–4521). If nobody claims what you turn in, you may get to keep it.

Money For cash or currency exchange, go to the Guest Relations window in the turnstile area, to City Hall, or to the Sun Bank branch in Town Square (open 9–4 daily), with an ATM nearby.

Package Pickup Ask the shop clerk to send any large purchase you make to Guest Relations in the Entrance Plaza so you won't have to carry it around all day. (Allow three hours.)

Wheelchair Rentals Go to the gift shop to the left of the ticket booths at the Transportation and Ticket Center or at the Stroller and Wheelchair shop inside the main entrance to your right ($5 plus $1 deposit); the latter also has motor-powered chairs ($25 plus $20 deposit). Electric scooters are available by reservation ($25 plus $20 deposit; tel. 407/824–4321). If your rental needs replacing, ask a host or hostess.

Strategies for Your Visit

Arriving at least 30 minutes before rope drop is essential so that you can make reservations for the Diamond Horseshoe Jamboree, get your bearings, and explore the shops on Main Street. If you are staying at a Disney resort, check your passport to see whether you are entitled to early admission; this is vital, especially for parents with small children, who will be able to visit most of the Fantasyland rides before the park officially opens, thereby offering the option of an afternoon trip to Discovery Island.

Blitz Tours Go directly to Fantasyland and start with a ride on **Dumbo, the**
With Small **Flying Elephant.** Then ride **Cinderella's Golden Carrousel** and,
Children moving clockwise, the other attractions. Leave **It's a Small World**
until last; its continuously moving lines keep crowds shuffling
along and it's a nice end to a Fantasyland visit.

Proceed to Liberty Square and have an early lunch at Liberty
Tree Tavern. Take a postprandial tour of **Tom Sawyer Island** and
follow it up with the next show at Frontierland's **Country Bear
Jamboree.** By now it should be about time to find a place on the
pavement to watch the three o'clock parade—Frontierland is
one of the best places in the park in which to do it.

Upon exiting the Country Bear Jamboree, turn right (most people go left, to Splash Mountain and Big Thunder Mountain Railroad). Then make another right at Frontier Woodcarving at the
end of the row of false-fronted shops and take the shortcut to
Adventureland.

Proceed directly across the Adventureland plaza to the **Jungle
Cruise.** If your arms and legs are up to it, scramble around the
Swiss Family Treehouse. We don't really recommend the **Tropical Serenade** unless you're in need of an air-conditioned place to
sit down or want to inoculate your children against terminal
kitsch.

Now stroll through the rest room arch next to Plaza del Sol
Caribe by the **Pirates of the Caribbean** back to Frontierland,
round the corner of Splash Mountain to the **Walt Disney Railroad** station. Take the train to **Mickey's Starland.** From here,
depending on your stamina, either proceed to Tomorrowland for
Carousel of Progress or hop back on board the train to Main
Street.

If you're really determined to eke out every penny, leave the
park (for Discovery Island, perhaps, or your hotel). Come back
for dinner at the **Crystal Palace.** Many kids want to repeat the
rides in Fantasyland, so now is a good time to do that. At about
eight o'clock, claim a piece of pavement to watch the nine o'clock
SpectroMagic parade.

For Upon entering the gates of the Magic Kingdom, go right over to
Everyone **Disneyana Collectibles** on the right side of Town Square and
Else make reservations for a late-morning show of the **Diamond
Horseshoe Jamboree.** Position yourself for the rope drop at the
southwestern spur off the Hub that leads to Adventureland.
Then sprint right over to **Splash Mountain** via the Adventureland plaza (it's marginally shorter than going through Frontierland, which is what everyone else is doing). From Splash
Mountain, everyone naturally goes to **Big Thunder Mountain
Railroad;** buck the trend and go instead to Adventureland. Here
you can visit **Pirates of the Caribbean, Jungle Cruise,** and the
Swiss Family Treehouse before the crowds, as well as knock off
this relatively remotely located land.

Proceed to Frontierland through the exit near the **Tropical Serenade.** You should have just enough time to get oriented before going to the **Diamond Horseshoe Jamboree** (to your left as you enter Frontierland). Have a snack here—you'll be having a late lunch. At this point, everyone else is beginning to think about lunch—so it's a good time to visit the **Haunted Mansion.** If the lines look too daunting, backtrack to the **Hall of Presidents** and try again later.

From the Haunted Mansion or Hall of Presidents it's a quick slide over to Fantasyland. Hit one or two of the more accessible attractions while those with younger kids are at the feeding trough—you'll be back. When it looks as though the postlunch crowd is swelling, head out through **Cinderella Castle** and take a right to the Crystal Palace for your own relaxed, late lunch. You'll also be perfectly positioned to grab a piece of pavement for viewing the three o'clock parade.

Head straight across the Hub to Tomorrowland. Again, count on the fact that everyone else had an early lunch and therefore will need an early dinner—which is when you can ride **Space Mountain** and **Alien Encounter.** Whet your appetite in the meantime, and take a little break on the **Tomorrowland Transit Authority, AstroOrbiter,** or **Carousel of Progress,** and at the **Metropolis Science Centre.**

Hop on the **Skyway** right outside of Space Mountain for a journey back to Fantasyland. By now, it should be getting on in the day—a good time to visit some more attractions, now that tired children are being taken home. Wander back to Liberty Square for dinner at the Liberty Tree Tavern, give yourself time to digest—the **Country Bears Jamboree** is a good spot for this—and then head over to **Big Thunder Mountain Railroad** for a nighttime ride. After that, it's time to find a place to watch the **SpectroMagic** parade, which wends its way up Main Street, around the Hub and—how fortuitous!—into Frontierland.

You've still got about an hour or so before the fireworks. This is a good time to visit attractions that were just too mobbed earlier (like Alien Encounter or Space Mountain, if you missed one during your first pass) or attractions that are easy on the adrenaline and light on the mood (like **Cinderella's Golden Carrousel** or **It's a Small World**). Again, you'll want to stake out a place to view the fireworks about 30 minutes before ignition—the southwest corner of the Hub is good because you can see over the trees and get a great view of Tinkerbell as she wafts along her wire to tomorrow and tomorrow and Tomorrowland. (Or try the central court of Fantasyland, where you can watch sitting down, nursing a soft-ice-cream sundae from one of the stands).

Rainy Days If you visit during a busy time of year, pray for rain. Rainy days dissolve the crowds here. Unlike those at Disney-MGM and Epcot Center, however, many of the Magic Kingdom's attractions are outdoors. If you don't mind getting damp, pick up a bright yellow poncho on Main Street ($4.50 adults, $4 children) and soldier on.

Exploring the Magic Kingdom

Numbers in the margin correspond to points of interest on the Magic Kingdom map.

The park is laid out on a north-south axis, with Cinderella Castle at the epicenter and the various lands surrounding it in a broad circle. Upon passing through the entrance gates, you immediately discover yourself in Town Square, a central connection point containing City Hall, Sun Bank, Tony's Town Square Café, and Disneyana Collectibles. Town Square directly segues into Main Street, a boulevard filled with Victorian-style stores and dining spots. Main Street runs due north and ends at the Hub, a large tree-lined circle in front of Cinderella Castle. Rope drop, the ceremonial stampede that kicks off each day, occurs at various points along Main Street and the Hub.

As you move clockwise from the Hub, the Magic Kingdom's different lands start with Adventureland—home of Pirates of the Caribbean, the Jungle Cruise, and the Swiss Family Robinson Treehouse. Next come Frontierland and Liberty Square, containing Splash Mountain, Big Thunder Mountain Railroad, and the Haunted Mansion. Fantasyland is located directly behind Cinderella Castle, in the castle's courtyard, as it were. Mickey's Starland is set off the upper right-hand corner (that's northeast, for geography buffs) of Fantasyland. And Tomorrowland, directly to the right of the Hub, rounds out the circle.

Main Street With its pastel Victorian buildings, antique automobiles oohga-oohga-ing as they stop to offer you a lift, sparkling sidewalks, and atmosphere of what one writer has called "almost hysterical joy," Main Street is more than a mere conduit to the other enchantments of the Magic Kingdom. It is where the spell is first cast.

Like Dorothy waking up in a technicolor Oz or Mary Poppins jumping through the pavement painting, you emerge from the tunnel beneath the Walt Disney World Railroad Station into a realization of one of the most tenacious American dreams. The perfect street in the perfect small town in a perfect moment of time is burnished to jewellike quality thanks to a ⅘-scale reduction, nightly cleanings with a firehose, and constant repainting; neither life-size nor so small as to appear toylike, the carefully calculated size is meant to make you feel as though you're looking through a telescope into another world.

Everyone's always happy in this world, their spirits kept sunny thanks to outpourings of music: Dixieland jazz, barbershop quartets, brass band parades, and scores of Disney films and American musicals played over loudspeakers. Old-fashioned horse-drawn trams and omnibuses—horns a-tootle—chug along the street. Street vendors in Victorian-era costumes sell balloons and popcorn. And to complete the illusion of the perfect dream, Cinderella's Castle floats at the end of Main Street: the Holy Grail that is for once within reach.

The Magic Kingdom

Fort Sam
Clemens

Rivers of America

WDW
Railroad
Frontierland
Depot

Columbia
Harbour
House

Aunt
Polly's
Landing

FRONTIERLAND

Liberty Tree
Tavern

LIBERTY

SQUARE

Caribbean
Plaza

Adventureland
Bazaar

Crystal
Palace

First Ai
Station

ADVENTURELAND

Automatic
Teller

Newssta

KEY

Restaurants
Restrooms
Rail Line
Skyride
Monorail

Monorail

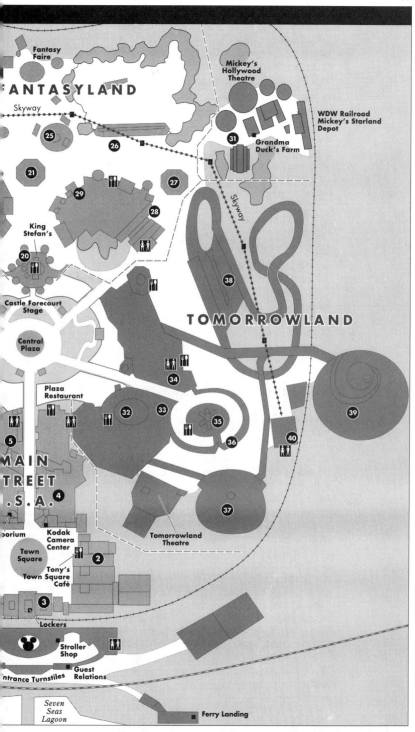

Fantasy
Faire

FANTASYLAND

Skyway

Mickey's
Hollywood
Theatre

WDW Railroad
Mickey's Starland
Depot

25

26

31

Grandma
Duck's Farm

21

27

29

Skyway

28

King
Stefan's

20

38

Castle Forecourt
Stage

TOMORROWLAND

Central
Plaza

Plaza
Restaurant

34

32

33

35

5

36

40

MAIN

39

STREET

U.S.A.

4

37

Emporium

Kodak
Camera
Center

Tomorrowland
Theatre

Town
Square

2

Tony's
Town Square
Café

3

Lockers

Stroller
Shop

Guest
Relations

Entrance Turnstiles

Seven
Seas
Lagoon

Ferry Landing

1 On your left as you enter Town Square is **City Hall,** information central, and opposite, in the bright yellow, Victorian gingerbread building that used to house the Walt Disney Story, is the **2** home of **Disneyana Collectibles,** a trivia buff's delight of animation art and other memorabilia.

Although attractions with a capital "A" are minimal on Main Street, there are plenty of inducements to spend more than the 40 minutes most visitors usually take. The stores that most of the structures contain range from the **House of Magic,** complete with trick-showing proprietors; to the **Harmony Barber Shop,** where you can have yourself shorn; to a milliner's emporium stocking Cat-in-the-Hat fantasies; to all sorts of snacks and souvenirs. (If the weather looks threatening, head for the **Emporium** to purchase those signature mouse-eared umbrellas and bright yellow ponchos with Mickey emblazoned on the back.) The best time to shop is midafternoon, when the lines at the rides resemble a malevolent anaconda taking a nap; if you go at the end of the day, you'll be engulfed by the rush-hour crowds.

Main Street is also full of in-jokes for those in the know. For instance, check out the proprietors' names above the shops: Crystal Arts honors Roy Disney, Walt's brother; the Shadow Box—nod, nod, wink, wink—is the domain of Dick Nunis, chairman of Walt Disney Attractions; at the House of Magic, Card Walker—the "Practioner of Psychiatry and Justice of the Peace"—is the company's former chairman of the Executive Committee. At last glance, today's Head Mouseketeer, Michael Eisner, still doesn't have his own shop.

Step right up to the elevated platform above the Magic Kingdom's entrance for a ride on living history, the **Walt Disney World** **3** **Railroad.** Walt Disney was a railroad buff of the highest order— he constructed a ⅛-scale train in his backyard and named it *Lilly Belle,* after his wife. Another *Lilly Belle* rides the rails here, as do *Walter E. Disney, Roy O. Disney* (named for Walt's brother), and *Roger Broggie* (named for a Disney Imagineer and fellow railroad aficionado). All the locomotives date from 1928, coincidentally the same age as Mickey Mouse. Disney scouts tracked them down in Mexico, where they were used to haul sugarcane in the Yucatán, brought them back, and completely overhauled them to their present splendor. And splendid they are, with their striped awnings, brightly painted benches, authoritative choo-choo, and hissing plume of steam. They are also quite useful. Their 1½-mile track runs along the perimeter of the Magic Kingdom, through the woods and past Tom Sawyer Island and other attractions; stops are in Frontierland and Mickey's Starland. It's a great introduction to the layout of the park and a much-welcome relief for tired feet and dragging legs. The four trains run at five- to seven-minute intervals. *Duration: 21 min. Crowds: Can be substantial beginning in late morning through late afternoon. Strategy: Go in midafternoon if you don't see a line; otherwise, skip on a first-time visit. Audience: All ages. Rating:* ★

Six screens run continuous vintage Disney cartoons in the cool,
❹ air-conditioned quiet of the **Main Street Cinema,** halfway up
Main Street on the right. It's a great opportunity to see the genius of Walt Disney and to meet the endearing little mouse that
brought Disney so much fame. *Steamboat Willie,* the first sound
cartoon, was also the first chance America had to meet Mickey
Mouse, who, in his silver-screen debut, meets Minnie and is inspired to serenade her by using a cow's udder. Disney said that
he loved his creation more than any woman (one wonders how
Lilly Belle felt about this, especially since it was she who convinced her husband to change the character's name from Mortimer). Standing room only and the lure of other attractions
farther inside the park keep Main Street Cinema from ever
being too crowded, and in fact you can sit on the raised platform
in the center of the screening room and still see all the films—all
of them silents, without dialogue, screened with organ music.
*Duration: Stay as long as you like. Crowds: Negligible. Strategy:
A refuge on hot, crowded afternoons. Audience: All ages. Rating:*
★★

Electronic-games rooms are de rigueur, it seems, at most theme
parks and even the Magic Kingdom is not immune. Located on
the left side of Main Street, just before you reach Central Plaza,
❺ the **Penny Arcade** is nonetheless a game room with history.
Sure, there are a few contemporary quarter-eaters, but most
are the sort of amusements that parents in *The Music Man*
would have worried about if they hadn't been so concerned about
the dangers of pool. There are manual Mute-o-scopes and their
automatic successors, Cail-o-scopes, an early version of a moving picture in which images are drawn on a stack of cards that
is quickly flipped to animate the image. (Interestingly, the
Disney animation department produces its films based on the
same principle.) Most of the short stories are slapstick comedy,
of the sort later popularized by Mack Sennet and his Keystone
Kops: In "Yes, We Have No Bananas," a suitor slips on a fateful
banana peel; "Oh Teacher" describes the antics of a teacher's
pet; and "Expecting" details the trials and tribulations of people
waiting in line—something you should expect to do a lot of during the course of a visit. There are also several fortune-telling
machines with marionette-like seers—the type that got Tom
Hanks into such *Big* trouble. *Duration: Up to you. Crowds: Moderate but seldom oppressive except at parade time. Strategy: A
good place to while away the busy part of a day, but bring a pocketful of change. Audience: All ages. Rating:* ★★

Adventure- From the scrubbed brick, manicured lawns, and meticulously
land pruned trees of the Central Plaza, an artfully dilapidated
wooden bridge leads to Adventureland, Disney's version of jungle fever. The landscape artists went wild here: South African
Cape honeysuckle droops, Brazilian bougainvillea drapes, Mexican flame vines cling, spider plants clone, and three different
varieties of palm trees sway, all creating a seemingly spontane-
ous mess. The bright, all-American, singalong tunes that fill the
air along Main Street and Central Plaza are replaced by the
recorded repetitions of trumpeting elephants, pounding drums,

and squawking parrots. The architecture is an eclectic mish-mash of the best of Thailand, the Caribbean, Africa, and Poly-nesia, arranged in an inspired disorder that recalls comic-book fantasies of far-off places. The message is that though the na-tives may be restless, the kids are all right.

Adventureland surrounds its own oblong central plaza. To the right as you cross the bridge is the **Adventureland Bazaar,** whose six shops have names like Bwana Bob's, Traders of Timbuktu, Zanzibar Shell Company, and Elephant Tales; they sell exotic—and generally quite affordable—safari-theme clothing, sharks'-teeth jewelry, elephant-hair bracelets, and other trinkets from the erstwhile Dark Continent as well as a menagerie's worth of life-size tropical critters. To the left are the spreading branches of the Swiss Family Robinson's banyan tree. Continuing around the plaza are the entrances to the Jungle Cruise, the Pirates of the Caribbean, and the Polynesian greathouse containing the Enchanted Tiki Birds.

In the far end of the plaza is another conglomeration of shops, the **Caribbean Plaza,** selling treasures inspired by the Pirates of the Caribbean: tropical clothing, costume jewelry (how about some pineapple earrings?), pirate's swords, hats embroidered with skull and crossbones, and in a surprising lapse in kitsch, delicate crystal and blown glass. (Be advised that many of these crystal items are also for sale in the King's Gallery inside the archway of Cinderella's Castle.) At **Lafitte's Portrait Deck,** you can stick your head through a pirate cutout and bring home a picture of yourself as the Scourge of the Spanish Main.

❻ Few New York City apartments can boast the light, the airiness, the number of rooms, and all the services of the **Swiss Family Treehouse,** the first attraction on your left (the camouflaged en-trance is *way* over to the left). In fact, the only thing lacking is an elevator. Based on the classic novel by Johann Wyss about the adventures of a family shipwrecked on the way to America, the treehouse shows what you can do with a big banyan and a lot of imagination. The rooms are furnished with patchwork quilts and mahogany furniture. Disney detail abounds: The kitchen sink is made of a giant clamshell; the boys' room, strewn with clothing, has two hammocks instead of beds; and an inge-nious system of rain barrels and bamboo pipes provides running water in every room (German visitors seem especially fascinated by this). Small wonder that in the 1960 film, when offered the chance to leave their island, all but one Robinson decided to stay on. As you clamber around the narrow wooden steps and rope bridges that connect the rooms in this split-level dwelling, take a look at the Spanish moss. It is real, but the tree itself—some 90 feet in diameter, with more than 600 branches—was con-structed by the props department. The 800,000 leaves are made of vinyl and cost $1 per leaf in the early 1970s. It all adds up to a species of tree unofficially called *Disneyodendron eximus,* or "out-of-the-ordinary Disney tree." *Duration: Up to you. Crowds: Artfully camouflaged so you may not see them—and the lines move slowly. Strategy: Go first thing in the morning or after dark.*

Audience: All ages; toddlers unsteady on their feet may have trouble with the stairs. Rating: ★★

Register your geographical switch from the Caribbean to the jungle by playing bongo drums on the grinning fetish statues that separate the Robinsons' idyllic condo and the **Jungle Cruise.** During this ride, you cruise through three continents and along four rivers: the Congo, the Nile, the Mekong, and the Amazon. The canopied launches pack in visitors tighter than sardines, the safari-suited guides make a point of checking their pistol, and the *Irrawady Irma* or *Mongala Millie* is off for another "perilous" journey. The guide's spiel is surprisingly funny, with just the right blend of cornball humor and the gently snide; unfortunately, some guides' tendency to imitate the unintelligible Chuck Yeager drawl patented by airline pilots is all too successful, and you can't understand half of what they're saying. Nitpicking aside, you'll encounter animals of the African veldt, elephants bathing, slinky pythons, an irritated rhinoceros, a bunch of hyperactive hippos (good thing the guide's got a pop pistol), and a tribe of hungry headhunters. Then there's Old Smily, the crocodile, who's always waiting for a handout—or, as the guide quips, "a foot out." Kids who might be terrified by the Pirates of the Caribbean will love this ride, and adults love the patter and all the detail (listen for what's playing on the radio of the overturned jeep). *Duration: 10 min. Crowds: Huge, from late morning until suppertime. Strategy: Go first thing in the morning or during the daily parade, but not after dark—you'll miss a lot. Audience: All ages. Rating:* ★★★

Time Out Among the fast munchies here, some of the best are the fresh pineapple spears at Adventureland's **Aloha Isle.**

"Avast, ye scurvy scum!" is the sort of greeting your kids will proclaim for the next week—which gives you an idea of the impact of the stellar **Pirates of the Caribbean.** This boat ride is Disney at its best: memorable vignettes, incredible detail, a gripping story, and catchy music whose relentless "Yo! Ho-ing" can only be eradicated by "It's a Small World."

The gracious arched entrance soon gives way to a dusty dungeon, redolent of damp and of a spooky, scary past. Lanterns flicker as you board the boats and a ghostly voice intones, "Dead men tell no tales." (Usually, at this point, a much higher, younger voice quavers, "Mommy, can we get off?") A deserted beach, strewn with shovels, a skeleton, and a disintegrating map indicating buried treasure, is the preface to this story of greed, lust, and destruction.

Emerging from a pitch-black time tunnel, you're literally in the middle of a furious battle. A pirate ship, cannons blazing, is attacking a stone fortress. Cannonballs splash into the water just off your bows, and AudioAnimatronic pirates hoist the Jolly Roger while brave soldiers scurry to defend the fort—to no avail. Politically correct nerves may twinge as the women of the town are rounded up and auctioned. "Strike your colors, ye brazen wench, no need to expose your superstructure!" shouts one pirate, but the scene is terrific: pirates chasing chickens, ducking the town mayor in the well, and collapsing into a snoring stupor with a couple of pigs. Check out the hairy legs of the two carousers straddling the wall. The wild antics of the pirates result in a conflagration, the town goes up in flames, and all goes to their just reward amid a chorus of "Yo-ho! Yo-ho! A pirate's life for me." There's a moral in there somewhere, if you want to look for one—or you can just enjoy the show. *Duration: 10 min. Crowds: Waits seldom exceed 30 minutes, despite the ride's popularity. Strategy: A good destination even during the busy afternoon hours. Audience: All ages. Rating:* ★★

❾ Don't expect much when your preshow host is a mechanical toucan called Claude Birdbrain. Inside the blessedly air-conditioned Polynesian longhouse that houses the **Enchanted Tiki Birds,** the avian intelligence quotient doesn't improve markedly, and ethnic stereotyping runs rampant. Four parrots run the joint—Pierre, José, Fritz, and Michael (the Irish one—need we add that his plumage is green?)—each of which has an appropriately ethnic accent. "Tropical Serenade" is sung and whistled by hundreds of AudioAnimatronic figures: exotic birds, swaying flowers, and Tiki god statues with blinking red eyes. Toddlers love the repetition of the song "In the Tiki, Tiki, Tiki, Tiki, Tiki Room." Older folks tend to roll their eyes along with the statues. This was Disney's first AudioAnimatronic attraction and the animatronics still hold up fine, but the audio could use an update. *Duration: 17 min. Crowds: Waits seldom exceed 30 minutes. Strategy: Go when you need to sit in an air-conditioned room. Audience: All ages. Rating:* ★.

From Adventureland, you can go on to Frontierland or to Liberty Square. For the latter, continue around to the left as you exit the Tiki House, into the passageway between the Sunshine Tree Terrace and the Tiki Tropic shop. For Frontierland—and a shortcut to Splash Mountain—look for the rest rooms in the Caribbean Plaza as you exit the Pirates of the Caribbean. They open onto a tiled arcade that divides the two lands. Note, however, that rest room patrons get easily confused upon exiting and end up in the wrong land. In other words, this is a prime place to misplace your children or your partner, so station someone *right* outside the rest rooms in the arcade to keep watch.

Frontierland Frontierland, in the northwest quadrant of the Magic Kingdom, invokes the American frontier. The period seems to be the latter half of the 19th century, and the West is being won by Disney staffers dressed in checked shirts, leather vests, cowboy hats, and brightly colored neckerchiefs. Banjo and fiddle music twang from tree to tree.

The screams that periodically drown out the string-sawing are not the result of a cowboy surprising an Indian. They come from one of the Magic Kingdom's big guns, Splash Mountain, an elaborate water flume. Opened in October 1992, it quickly eclipsed all the other attractions in popularity. Big Thunder Mountain Railroad, one of the park's two roller coasters, also gives vocal cords a workout. Other Frontierland attractions are somewhat tamer: Tom Sawyer Island, an enormous landscaped playground perfect for games of hide-and-go-seek; the Frontierland Shooting Arcade, an electronic shooting arcade that pleases even the sulkiest adolescent; and two musical revues—the Country Bear Jamboree and the Diamond Horseshoe Jamboree.

The rust-red rock spires of Thunder Mountain and Splash Mountain serve as local landmarks and set a landscaping tone best described as "Arid, Extra Dry." In contrast to the lush vegetation of Adventureland, Frontierland is planted with mesquite, twisted Peruvian pepper trees, slash pines, and many varieties of cactus. The unpainted buildings and wooden sidewalks have a ramshackle quality, and even though you know that no dust is allowed in Walt Disney World, the setting evokes dusty thoughts.

Shops and eateries are along the avenue bordering the southern curve of a lake that, because it variously represents the Mississippi and Missouri rivers and their tributaries, is called Rivers of America. (It still looks like a lake.) Emporia here are generally referred to as "posts," as in the Frontierland Trading Post and Prairie Outpost, which sell sheriff badges, leatherwork, cowboy hats, and Southwestern, Indian, and Mexican crafts. Then there's Big Al's, for genuine Davy Crockett coonskin hats. Yee-haw!

The Walt Disney World Railroad makes a stop at Frontierland. It tunnels through Splash Mountain and drops you off between Splash Mountain and Thunder Mountain.

⑩ At rope drop, the hordes hoof it to **Splash Mountain.** Based on the animated sequences in Disney's 1946 film *Song of the South*, it features AudioAnimatronic creations of Brer Rabbit, Brer Bear, Brer Fox, and a menagerie of Brer beasts (including Brer Frog and a Heckle-and-Jeckle duo of Brer Crows). As you settle into the eight-person hollowed-out logs, Uncle Remus's voice growls, "Mark mah words, Brer Rabbit gonna put his foot in Brer Fox's mouth one of these days." And this just might be the day.

As the boat carries you through a lily pond (just bopping with Brer Frogs merrily singing the ride's theme song, "Time to Be Moving Along") past signs for Brer Fox's lair and Brer Bear's den, Brer Rabbit's silhouette hops along in front, always just ahead of you. Every time some critter makes a grab for the bunny, the log boats drop out of reach. But Brer Fox has been studying his book *How to Catch a Rabbit,* and our lop-eared friend looks as if he's destined for the pot. Things don't look so good for the flumers either, as the boats creak up and up the mountain, past a pair of pessimistic crows. You get one heart-stopping pause at the top—just long enough to grab the safety bar—and then the boat plummets down the world's longest and sharpest flume drop right into a gigantic briar patch. (In case you want to know what you're getting into, the drop is 52½ feet tall—that's about five stories—at a 45-degree angle, enough to reach speeds of 40 miles per hour and make you feel weightless.) From the boat—especially if you are in the front seat—it looks truly as if you are going to be impaled on those enormous spikes. Try to smile through your clenched teeth: As you begin to drop, a flashbulb pops, so you can purchase a photographic memento of the experience before exiting the ride. Brer Rabbit escapes— and so do you, wet and exhilarated—to the tune of "Zip-a-Dee-Doo-Dah," whose bouncy melody has become something of a Disney theme song. Knowing how much we all like to watch people getting the pants scared off them, Disney constructed the flume so that spectators can see the plunge into the briar patch from the footbridge between Splash Mountain and Thunder Mountain. In an especially neat touch, it looks as if the log boats disappear into the pond below the briar patch with a giant splash—leaving only bubbles in their wake. *Duration: 11 min. Crowds: Yes! Strategy: If you're not in line by 9:45, your only hope is during meals or a parade. Audience: All except very young children. No pregnant women or guests wearing back, neck, or leg braces; minimum height 42 inches. Rating:* ★★★

Now that your blood is up, scoot across the footbridge to another **⑪** classic Disney ride, **Big Thunder Mountain Railroad.** As any true roller-coaster lover can tell you, this three-minute ride is a tame one; despite the posted warnings, you won't stagger off, you won't throw up, and you won't vow to never subject yourself to the experience again. The thrills are there, however, thanks to the intricate details and stunning scenery along every inch of the 2,780-foot-long wooden track.

Set in gold-rush days, the runaway train rushes and rattles past 20 AudioAnimatronic figures—including donkeys, chickens, a goat, and a grizzled old miner surprised in his bathtub— $300,000 of genuine antique mining equipment, tumbleweeds, a derelict mining town, hot springs, and a flash flood.

The ride was 15 years in the planning and took two years and close to $17 million to build (a price tag that, give or take a few million, equaled the entire cost of California's Disneyland in 1955). The 197-foot mountain is based on the monoliths of Utah's Monument Valley, and thanks to 650 tons of steel, 4,675 tons of cement, and 16,000 gallons of paint, it closely resembles the real thing. *Duration: 4 min. Crowds: Large. Strategy: Thunder Mountaineers swear that the ride is even better at night, when you can't anticipate the curves and the track's rattling sounds as if something's about to give. But then you'd miss the scenic details. The solution—go twice. Audience: All except young children. No pregnant women or guests wearing back, neck, or leg braces; minimum height 40 inches. Rating:* ★★★

Head back across the footbridge past Splash Mountain, and bear left along Frontierland's main drag to the landing stage for the **⑫** rafts to **Tom Sawyer Island.** (These rafts are not to be confused with the Mike Fink Keel Boats or the Liberty Square Riverboat, both of which also ply Rivers of America but dock in Liberty Square.)

An artfully misspelled sign, signed by Tom Sawyer, conveys the island's attractions: "If'n you like dark caves, mystry mines, bottomless pits, shakey bridges 'n' big rocks, you have came to the best place I know." Aunt Polly would have walloped Tom for his orthography, but she couldn't have argued with the truth. The 6-mile-long island—actually two islands connected by an old-fashioned swing bridge—is a natural playground, all hills and trees and rocks and shrubs. Other guidebooks suggest that parents sit this one out on the porch of Aunt Polly's Landing, sipping lemonade; we say, why let the kids have all the fun?

Most of the attractions are on the main island, where the boats dock and where Aunt Polly's Landing and the rest rooms are. These include the mystery cave, a pitch-black (almost) labyrinth where the wind wails in a truly spooky fashion; Injun Joe's cave, all pointy stalactites and stalagmites and endowed with lots of columns and crevices from which to jump out and startle younger sisters and brothers; Harper's Mill, an old-fashioned grist mill (nothing scary here); and, in a clearing at the top of the hill, a rustic playground. As you explore the shoreline on the dirt paths, keep an eye out for the barrel bridge—every time someone takes a step, the whole contraption bounces.

On the other island is Fort Sam Clemens, a log fortress from which you can fire air guns (with great booms and cracks) at the soporific passengers on the Liberty Square Riverboat. It's guarded by an equally soporific AudioAnimatronic sentry, loudly snoring off his last bender. Both islands are sprinkled with lookouts for great views to Thunder Mountain and Frontierland, as well as nice natural niches—often furnished with benches and water fountains. *Duration: Up to you. Crowds: Seldom overwhelming, but it wouldn't matter—here, the more the merrier. Strategy: Try it as a refreshing afternoon getaway. Audience: All ages. Rating:* ★★

Back on the main street, a row of barns, false-fronted buildings, and other structures straight out of Dodge City house shops, eateries, and two theaters. The first one on your right is home
⑬ to the **Country Bear Jamboree,** a stage show in which wisecracking, cornpone AudioAnimatronic bears joke, sing, and play country music and 1950s rock and roll. The show stars Henry, the massive but debonair master of ceremonies; the robust Trixie, the Tampa Temptation, who laments a love lost while perched in a swing suspended from the ceiling; Bubbles, Bunny, and Beulah, harmonizing on "All the Guys that Turn Me Down Turn Me On"; and Big Al, a cult figure who has inspired postcards, stuffed animals, and his own shop next door. *Duration: 16 min. Crowds: Large, considering the relatively small theater. Strategy: Visit before 11 AM, during the daily parade, or after most small children have left for the day. Stand to the far left in the anteroom where you wait to end up in the front rows; to the far right if you want to sit in the last row, where small children can perch on top of the seats to see better. Audience: All ages. Rating:* ★★★

⓮ The **Frontierland Shootin' Arcade** is a classic shooting arcade but with laser beams subbing for bullets and an 1850s frontier-town theme. Genuine Hawkins 54-caliber buffalo rifles have been refitted to emit electronic beams. When they strike, tomb-stones spin and epitaphs change, ghost riders gallop out of clouds, and skulls pop out of graves, accompanied by the sounds of howling coyotes, creaking bridges, and the cracks of the rifles blasted over the digital audio system. *Cost: 25¢ per 5 shots. Strategy: Bring a pocketful of change. Audience: Older children and adults. Rating:* ★★

"Knock, knock." "Who's there?" "Ya." "Ya who?" "Yaaahooo!" And they're off, with another riproaring, raucous, corny, non-stop, high-kicking, elbow-jabbing song-and-dance-and-fiddling **⓯** **Diamond Horseshoe Jamboree,** staged in a re-creation of an Old West saloon. The show features a sextet of dance hall girls and high-spirited cowboys, Sam, the stagestruck and lovelorn saloon keeper, and Lily, a shimmying, feather-boa-toting reincarnation of Mae West, whose throaty version of "A Good Man Is Hard to Find" brings down the house. (At other times, Lily switches around the hall, tickling noses with her boa and uttering such lines as "Watch it, honey, this is Frontierland, not Fantasyland!"). The cowboys leap from the balconies and swing around columns, Lily's Girls perform an exuberant cancan, and everyone has a hand-clapping good time. Seating begins half an hour before curtain time, and snacks and light refreshments may be purchased at your table. *Showtimes: 10:45, 12:15, 1:45, 3:30, and 4:45; reservations essential. Duration: 30 min. Crowds: Full house for most performances. Strategy: Book in early morning at Disneyana Collectibles (12:15 show fills up first) or show up 30 minutes before showtime to wait for cancellations. But give it a miss if you're on a tight schedule and have plans to see the Hoop-Dee-Doo Revue in Fort Wilderness. Audience: All except young children. Rating:* ★★

Liberty Square The weathered siding gives way to neat clapboard and solid brick, the mesquite and cactus are replaced by stately oaks and masses of azalea, and the rough-and-tumble western frontier gently slides into Colonial America. Liberty Square picks up where Frontierland leaves off, continuing around the western shore of Rivers of America and forming the eastern boundary of Fantasyland.

The theme is Colonial history, which Northerners will be happy to learn is solid Yankee. The small buildings, topped with weather vanes and exuding comfortable prosperity from every rosy brick and every spiffy shutter, are pure New England, and in a delightful literary wink, the silversmith shop lists as its pro-prietor J. Tremaine (hero of the Esther Forbes novel about the Revolutionary War that's required reading in most junior high schools). There's even a **Liberty Tree,** a 130-year-old live oak ac-tually found on Walt Disney World property and moved to the Magic Kingdom. Just as the Sons of Liberty hung lanterns on trees as a signal of solidarity after the Boston Tea Party, the

Liberty Tree's branches are decorated with 13 lanterns representing the 13 original colonies.

After the crowds in Frontierland, Liberty Square seems relaxed and peaceful—perhaps because its attractions tend to be sedentary. There's the Hall of Presidents, an AudioAnimatronic view of the history of the United States; Mike Fink Keel Boats and Liberty Square Riverboat—two ways to waste time on the Rivers of America; and the Haunted Mansion, Disney's ne plus ultra spook show. The shops in this area tend to sell more arts than kitsch; in addition to the silversmith shop, there's Olde World Antiques's one-of-a-kind objects and reproductions as well as custom-blended perfumes; the Yankee Trader's gourmet food and cooking items; the Silhouette Cart's profiles, hand-cut and framed while you wait; and the Umbrella Cart, whose personalized products are sure to come in handy during the daily summer afternoon thundershower. There are plenty of tree-shaded tables for picnicking and plenty of carts and fast-food eateries supplying the goods. Liberty Tree Tavern, a gracious, table-service restaurant that could have been airlifted from Colonial Williamsburg, is one of the best at the Magic Kingdom; reservations are essential.

Disney could probably patent its winning combination of movie and computerized robots and sound-and-light show, for Disney ⓰ invented it, refined it, and has kept it state-of-the-art. The **Hall of Presidents,** a multimedia tribute to the Constitution, caused quite a sensation when it opened, because it was here that the first refinements of the AudioAnimatronic system could be seen. Now surpassed by Epcot Center's American Adventure, it's still well worth attending, as much for the two-part show as for the spacious, air-conditioned theater.

It starts with a film, narrated by writer Maya Angelou, that discusses the Constitution as the codification of the spirit that founded America. Visitors learn about threats to the document, ranging from the 18th-century Whiskey Rebellion to the Civil War, and hear such famous speeches as Benjamin Franklin's plea to Continental Congress delegates to ratify it and Abraham Lincoln's fear that "a house divided cannot stand." The shows conveying Disney's brand of patriotism may be ponderous, but they're always well researched and lovingly presented; this film, for instance, was revamped in 1994 to replace a lingering subtext of Cold-War paranoia with the more progressive assertion that our democracy is a work in progress, that liberty and justice still do not figure equally in the lives of all Americans.

The second half is a roll call of all 42 U.S. presidents. Each chief executive rises and responds with a nod—even those who blatantly attempted to subvert the Constitution. The detail is lifelike, right down to the brace on Franklin Delano Roosevelt's leg. And because Disney humor will out, the robots can't resist nodding, fidgeting, and even whispering to each other while waiting for their name to come up. The last to be called is William Jefferson Clinton, who, unlike other contemporary presidential robots, has a speaking part. AudioAnimatronic Clinton's speech was written for Disney by *Aladdin* lyricist Tim Rice (he of *Jesus Christ Superstar* and *Evita*) in collaboration with the President's chief speechwriter; the audio was provided—in one take—by Human Bill Clinton himself. *Duration: 30 min. Crowds: Usually moderate. Strategy: Go in the afternoon, when you'll appreciate the air-conditioning. Audience: Older children and adults. Rating:* ★★

Time Out   **Liberty Square Market** carts sell fresh fruit—a welcome change from the Magic Kingdom's ubiquitous french fries and burgers.

A real old-fashioned steamboat, the *Richard F. Irvine* (named for a key Disney designer) is authentic, from its calliope whistle and the gingerbread trim on its three decks to the boilers that produce the steam that drives the big rear paddlewheel. In fact, **⑰** this **Liberty Square Riverboat** misses authenticity on only one count: There's no mustachioed captain to guide it during the ride around the Rivers of America. That task is taken care of by an underwater rail. The trip is slow and not thrilling, except, perhaps, to the kids getting shot at by their counterparts at Fort Sam Clemens on Tom Sawyer Island. But it's a relaxing break for all concerned, and parents can take a load off on the few chairs scattered around the upper deck while their offspring explore the boat. *Duration: 15 min. Crowds: Moderate, but capacity is high so waits are seldom trying. Strategy: Go when you need a break from the crowds. Audience: All ages. Rating:* ★

⑱ The **Mike Fink Keel Boats,** plying the same waters as the Liberty Square Riverboat, are short and dumpy and you have to sit on a bench, wedged tightly between fellow visitors, and listen to a heavy-handed, noisy spiel about those roistering, roustabout days along the Missouri. And the Tom Sawyer Island crowd doesn't even bother to shoot you. Just for that we're going to tell you the answer to the guide's extraordinarily lackluster joke: "Firewood." So there—make our day. *Duration: 10–15 min. Crowds: Lines move slowly because of boats' low passenger capacity. Strategy: Skip this on your first visit. Audience: All ages. Rating:* ★

⑲ The repository of special effects known as the **Haunted Mansion** is a howl. Or do we mean a scream? You are greeted at the creaking iron gates of this Hudson Gothic mansion by a lugubrious attendant (this must be the only job at Walt Disney World for which smiling is frowned upon, except, of course, for the occasional sinister smirk) and ushered into a spooky picture gallery. A disembodied voice echoes from the walls: "Welcome, foolish mortals, to the Haunted Mansion. I am your ghost host." A scream shivers down and you're off on one of the best attractions at Walt Disney World.

Part walk-through, part ride on a "doom buggie," the Haunted Mansion is scary but not terrifying, and the special effects are phenomenal. Catch the glowing bat's eyes on the wallpaper—a riveting twist in interior decorating; the suit of armor that comes alive; the shifting walls in the portrait gallery—are they moving up or are you moving down; the strategically placed gusts of damp, cold air; the marble busts of the world's greatest ghost writers in the library; the wacky inscriptions on the tombstones; the spectral xylophone player who enlivens the graveyard shift with bones instead of mallets; and, of course, the chattering head of the woman in the crystal ball (psst, she's a hologram). Just when you think the Imagineers have exhausted their bag of ectoplasmic tricks, along comes another one. They've saved the best for last, as you suddenly discover that your doom buggie has gained an extra passenger. As you approach the exit, your ghoulish guide intones, "Now I will raise the safety bar and the ghost will follow you home." Thanks for the souvenir, pal.

An interesting piece of Disney trivia: One of the biggest jobs for the maintenance crew here is not cleaning up but keeping the 200-odd trunks, chairs, harps, dress forms, statues, rugs, and other knickknacks appropriately dusty. Disney buys its dust in 5-pound bags and scatters it throughout the mansion from a special gadget resembling a fertilizer spreader. According to local lore, enough dust has been dumped since the park's 1971 opening to completely bury the mansion. Where does it all go? Perhaps the voice is right in saying that something will follow you home. *Duration: 8 min. Crowds: Substantial, but high capacity and fast loading usually keep lines moving. Strategy: Go early or late; at any other time, check line and go back later if it's long. Audience: All except young children, who may be frightened. Rating:* ★★★

Photographers will want to take advantage of one of the least-traveled byways in the Magic Kingdom. Just before exiting Liberty Square, turn left at the Sleepy Hollow snack shop. Just past the outdoor tables you'll find a shortcut to Fantasyland that provides about the best unobstructed ground-level view of Cinderella's Castle. It's a great spot for a family photo.

Fantasyland   You know you're in Fantasyland because the rest rooms are designated "Prince" and "Princess." And even though the thrones are plebeian and the crowds pedestrian, you can't help feeling special in this area. Walt Disney called this "a timeless land of enchantment," and Fantasyland does have the aura of having been sprinkled with pixie dust. Perhaps that's because Fantasyland's fanciful gingerbread houses, gleaming gold turrets, and, of course, its rides based on Disney-animated movies, are what the Magic Kingdom is all about.

With the exception of the slightly spooky Snow White's Adventures and Mr. Toad's Wild Ride, the attractions here are imaginative rather than thrilling. Like the animated classics on which they are based, rides that could ostensibly be classified as kiddie rides are, in fact, packed with enough delightful detail to engage adults. While the kids are awed by the bigger picture, their parents are amused by the road signs at Mr. Toad's Wild Ride or enchanted by the view of moonlit London in Peter Pan's Flight.

You can enter Fantasyland on foot from Frontierland or by skyway from Tomorrowland, but the classic introduction is through the Cinderella Castle. To set yourself up for the magic—and to provide yourself with a cooling break—turn left immediately after you exit the castle's archway. Here you'll find one of the most charming and most overlooked touches in Fantasyland: Cinderella Fountain, a lovely brass casting of the castle's namesake, who's dressed in her peasant togs and surrounded by her beloved mice and bird friends. Water splashing from the fountain provides a cooling sensation on a hot day—as do the very welcome brass drinking fountains at the statue's base. Don't forget to toss in a coin and make a wish; after all, you're in Fantasyland, where dreams do come true. Straight ahead from the castle you'll find Cinderella's Golden Carrousel. The land's other attractions are arranged around it in a somewhat bulging circle.

Fantasyland is always the most heavily trafficked area in the park, and its rides are almost always crowded. Luckily, its rides sometimes open early for guests at WDW-owned resorts. Or you can take your chances during the afternoon parade. Visitors without children should save Fantasyland for evening, when a sizable number of the little ones will have departed for their own private dreamland.

20 The royal blue turrets, gold spires, and glistening white towers of the **Cinderella Castle** are every child's fairy-tale castle come true. It was inspired by the castle built by the mad Bavarian King Ludwig at Neuschwanstein as well as by drawings prepared for Disney's animated film of the classic French fairy tale. Although often confused with Disneyland's Sleeping Beauty Castle, at 180 feet this castle is more than 100 feet taller, and with its elongated towers and lacy fretwork, it is immeasurably more graceful. It's easy to bypass the elaborate murals on the walls of the archway as you rush toward Fantasyland, but they are worth a stop. The five panels, measuring some 15 feet high and 10 feet wide, were created by Disney artist Dorothea Redmond and realized in a million bits of multicolored Italian glass, real silver, and 14-karat gold by mosaicist Hanns-Joachim Scharff. Following the images drawn for the Disney film, the mosaics tell the story of the little cinder girl from pumpkin to prince and happily ever after.

The fantasy has feet, if not of clay, then of solid steel beams, fiberglass, and 500 gallons of paint. Instead of dungeons, there are service tunnels for the Magic Kingdom's less-than-magical quotidian operations (the same tunnels that honeycomb the ground under the entire park). And upstairs does not hold, as rumor has it, a casket containing the cryogenically preserved body of Walt Disney, but instead mundane broadcast facilities, security rooms, and the like.

Within castle's archway, on the left as you face Fantasyland, is **The King's Gallery,** one of the Magic Kingdom's finest (and priciest) shops. Here you'll find exquisite hand-painted models of carousel horses, delicate crystal castles, and other symbols of fairy-tale magic, including Cinderella's glass slipper in a variety of colors and sizes.

㉑ The whirling, musical heart of Fantasyland—and maybe ~~o~~ the entire Magic Kingdom—the antique **Cinderella's Golden Carrousel** encapsulates the Disney experience in 90 prancing horses and then hands it to you on a 60-foot platter. Seventy-two of the dashing steeds date from the original carousel built in 1917 by the Philadelphia Toboggan Company; 12 additional mounts were made of fiberglass. All are meticulously painted—at a rate of about 48 hours per horse—and like real horses, each one is completely different. One steed sports a collar of bright yellow roses, another a quiver of Indian arrows, and yet another, for some completely mysterious reason, a portrait of Eric the Red. They gallop ceaselessy beneath a wooden canopy, gaily striped on the outside and muraled on the inside with 18 panels depicting scenes from Disney's 1950 film *Cinderella.* As the platter starts to spin, the mirrors sparkle, the fairy lights glitter, and the rich notes of the band organ—no calliope here—play favorite tunes from Disney movies. If you wished upon a star, it couldn't get more magical than this. *Duration: 2 min. Crowds: Lines during busy periods. Strategy: Go early, during the daily parade, or in the evening. Audience: All ages. Rating:* ★★

The first attraction on the left as you enter Fantasyland has been, in Disneyspeak, "refurbished for your enjoyment." The former site of the 3-D film *Magic Journeys* is now home to a

㉒ stage show, ***Legend of the Lion King.*** It brings to life the characters from Disney's 32nd animated feature, *The Lion King,* which debuted in the summer of 1994. *Duration: 15 min. Crowds: Rendered insignificant by large theater capacity. Strategy: Save this for mid- or late afternoon, when you want to sit down and cool off. Audience: All ages. Rating:* ★★

㉓ Moving clockwise through Fantasyland brings you to **Peter Pan's Flight,** a truly fantastic indoor ride inspired by Sir James M. Barrie's story about the boy who wouldn't grow up (Disney animated it in 1953). You board two-person magic sailing ships, whose brightly striped sails catch the wind and soar into the skies above London en route to Never-Never-Land. Along the way, you watch as Wendy, Michael, and John are sprinkled with pixie dust while Nana barks below, wave to Princess Tiger Lily, meet the evil Captain Hook, and cheer for the tick-tocking, clock-swallowing crocodile who's breakfasted on Hook's hand and is more than ready for lunch. Adults will especially enjoy the dreamy views of London by moonlight, a galaxy of twinkling yellow lights punctuated by Big Ben, London Bridge, and a moonlighted Thames River. There's so much to see that the ride seems much longer than it is. *Duration: 2¹/₂ min. Crowds: Heavy except in the evening and early morning. Strategy: Go early, during the daily parade, or in the evening. Audience: All ages. Rating:* ★★

㉔ Visiting Walt Disney World and *not* stopping for **It's a Small World**—why, the idea is practically un-American. Disney raided the remains of the 1964–65 New York World's Fair for this exhibit (sponsored, as anyone over 35 will remember, by Pepsi-Cola long before soft drinks were "It" or "The Right One, Baby,

...uh"), and then appropriated the theme song of interna-
...al brotherhood and friendship for its own.

This ride strains the patience more than the adrenal glands.
Moving somewhat slower than a snail, the barges inch through
several barnlike rooms, each crammed with musical moppets,
all madly singing the theme song, "It's a Small World After All."
It's the revenge of the Audio-Animatrons, you think, as rather
simplistic dolls differentiated only by their national costumes—
Dutch babies in clogs, Spanish flamenco dancers, German oompah bands, Russian balalaikas, sari-wrapped Indians waving
temple bells, Tower of London guards in scarlet beefeater uni-
forms, yodelers and goatherds, Japanese kite fliers, and juvenile
cancan dancers, to name just a few—parade past, smiling away
and wagging their heads in time to The Song. But somehow by
the time you reach the end of the ride, you're grinning and wagging too. You just can't help it—and small children can't wait to
ride it again. By the way, there is only one verse to The Song and
it repeats incessantly, tattooing itself indelibly into your brain.
Now all together: "It's a world of laughter, a world of tears. It's
a world of hope and a world of fears . . ." *Duration: 11 min.*
*Crowds: Steady, but lines move fast. Strategy: Look for the line to
the left—it's usually the shorter of the two. Go anytime but
mid-afternoon. Audience: All ages. Rating:* ★★

㉕ A tribute to the 1941 Disney animated film *Dumbo,* **Dumbo the
Flying Elephant** is one of Fantasyland's most popular rides.
While the story has one baby elephant with gigantic ears who
accidentally downs a bucket of champagne and learns he can fly,
the ride has 16 jolly Dumbos flying around a central column,
each pachyderm packing a couple of kids and a parent. A joys-
tick controls each of Dumbo's vertical motions, so you can make
him ascend or descend at will. Alas, the ears do not flap. *Duration: 2 min. Crowds: Perpetual, except in early morning. Strategy:
If accompanying small children, make a beeline here at rope drop;
otherwise, skip it, especially on a first visit. Audience: Young children. Rating:* ★

㉖ Yet another ride inspired by a literary work rendered into cartoon animation, Disney's 1954 film **20,000 Leagues under the Sea**
is based on the explorations of Jules Verne's nefarious Captain
Nemo. Verne imagined the reptilian shape of Nemo's subma-
rines, here faithfully rendered as 61-foot, bug-eyed, otherworldly vehicles, but he couldn't have conceived the long lines
of people waiting for one of the damper, more claustrophobic
experiences of their lives. It's like playing sardines in a can with
37 other people in the can—and then having the can dropped
into water. The ride through the 11½-million-gallon pool explores a world of kelp and sea grass, fantastic fish and clams,
coral and icebergs, and a grasping, tentacled squid. Unfortunately, despite a 1991 makeover, this attraction is no match for
two other, more recent Disney creations, namely, Epcot Center's Living Seas and Disney-MGM's The Little Mermaid. *Duration: 9 min. Crowds: Steady, with slow-moving lines. Strategy:*

Skip this on your first Magic Kingdom visit. Audience: All ages. Rating: ★

A staple in carnivals (where it's known as "Tubs o' Fun"), the **⓲ Mad Tea Party** is for the vertigo addict looking for a fix. The Disney version is based on the 1951 film *Alice in Wonderland*, in which the Mad Hatter hosts a tea party for his un-birthday. You hop into oversize, pastel-colored teacups and whirl around a giant platter. Add your own spin to the teacup's orbit with the help of the steering wheel in the center. If the centrifugal force hasn't shaken you up too much, check out the soused mouse that pops out of the teapot centerpiece and compare his condition to your own. *Duration: 2 min. Crowds: Steady from late morning on, with slow-moving lines. Strategy: Skip this on your first Magic Kingdom visit. Rating:* ★

⓲ Mr. Toad's Wild Ride, based on the 1949 Disney release *The Adventures of Ichabod and Mr. Toad* (itself derived from Kenneth Grahame's classic children's novel *The Wind in the Willows*), puts you into the jump seat of the speed-loving amphibian's flivver as he floors the accelerator on a jolting, jarring jaunt through the English countryside. At the entrance, notice the ride's two lovingly adhered-to mottoes (*Toadi Acceleratio* and *Semper Absurda*), and inside keep an eye out for such whimsical touches as signposts indicating "Worcestershire" and "Notsoshire" as well as your own destination, "Nowhere in Particular." Along the way you'll crash through walls, scatter chickens, nearly get clobbered by a falling suit of armor, go hurtling through haystacks, and end up on a collision course with a freight train. *Duration: 3 min. Crowds: Steady from late morning until evening. Strategy: Go very early, during the daily parade, or after dark. Audience: All ages. Marginally less scary than Snow White's Adventures; may startle young children. Rating:* ★★

What was previously an unremittingly scary three-minute indoor spook-house ride reopens in December 1994 as a kinder, **⓲ gentler Snow White's Adventures.** Where once the dwarves might as well have been named Anxious and Fearful, the new ride—now with six-passenger cars and a mini-version of the movie—has been tempered. There's still the evil queen, her nose wart, and her cackle, but joining the cast at long last are the prince and Snow White herself. The trip is still packed with plenty of scary moments, but an honest-to-goodness kiss followed by a happily-ever-after ending might even get you heigh-ho-ing on your way. *Duration: 3 min. Crowds: Steady from late morning until evening. Strategy: Go very early, during the daily parade, or after dark. Audience: All ages; may frighten young children. Rating:* ★★

⓳ The **Skyway to Tomorrowland** takes off on its one-way aerial trip to Tomorrowland from an enchanted attic perched above the trees in the far left corner of Fantasyland (this is also the terminus for those taking the Skyway from Tomorrowland to Fantasyland). You soar above the turquoise lagoon dotted with Captain Nemo's weird boats, the striped canopy of Cinderella's

Golden Carrousel, the crowds thronging around Fantasyland, the Grand Prix Raceway at the edge of Tomorrowland, and the extraordinarily mundane tar-paper rooftops of the buildings that house the magic. Although this is a quick shortcut to Tomorrowland, it's actually more fun to take it in the other direction. That way you'll preview the sights of Fantasyland, hear the happy music ascending, and then alight in the attic terminus, in the mood for magic. *Duration: 5 min. Crowds: Moderate from late morning until evening but usually not a problem. Strategy: Bypass this on a first visit until you've seen the major attractions. Audience: All ages. Rating:* ★

For a company that owes its fame to a certain endearing big-eared little fellow, Walt Disney World is astonishingly mouse **❸¹** free. Until, that is, you arrive at **Mickey's Starland,** a concentrated dose of adulation built in 1988 to celebrate Mickey Mouse's 60th birthday. Rarely crowded, the 3-acre niche set off to the side of Fantasyland is like a scene from a cartoon, and everything is child size. The attractions are in the imaginary town of Duckburg (yes, Donald and Huey, Dewey, and Louie are all here, along with a cast of other Disney characters), whose pastel houses are positively Lilliputian, with miniature driveways, toy-size picket fences, and signs scribbled with finger paint. The best way to arrive is on the Walt Disney World Railroad, the old-fashioned choo-choo that also stops at Main Street and Frontierland.

It looks as if the Mickster himself has just left mustard-colored clapboard **Mickey's House** (note the whimsical address). Sad to say, despite Minnie's ministrations, her mate is a slob—to say nothing of a pack rat. Mickey's red pants are carelessly tossed over a chair, his slippers and golf clubs lie nearby, he leaves the radio on when he's not here (tuned to Disney songs), and his diet, to judge from the shopping list tacked to the fridge, is decidedly one-dimensional. Check out the mouse-ear-shaped andirons in the fireplace.

You can visit with Minnie in the kitchen, then slip out the back to tour her own neat and separate dwelling, as well as Donald Duck's houseboat and Goofy's ramshackle abode. Though this is primarily a children's attraction, adults will get a kick out of the imaginative architecture and the Disney attention to detail.

Mickey's Starland Show and Hollywood Theater, held under a yellow-and-white-striped big top, presents the television stars of "The Disney Afternoon" in a cheerful sing-along musical comedy that kids adore. There are Chip and Dale, Scrooge McDuck, the ever-bumbling Launchpad McQuack, and Gadget of the "Rescue Rangers." A video cartoon of pop star Cyndi Lauper singing "Hey Mickey, you're so fine" kicks off the performance in high gear. Afterward, all the kids dash around backstage to **Mickey's Dressing Room,** where the star graciously signs autographs and poses for pictures with his adoring public.

Diagonally across the street from Mickey's House you'll find a delightful play area. Here the kids can climb, jump, slide, explore, and have a plain good old time in **Mickey's Treehouse** and **Minnie's Doll House** while Mom and Dad take a rest on benches that have a clear view of the climbing areas. For toddlers and preschoolers, there's the **Mouse-Ka-Maze,** a scaled-down version of the maze from *Alice in Wonderland.*

Next to the play area at **Grandma Duck's Farm**—a petting zoo with real live animals—the star is Minnie Moo, a placid Holstein cow whose distinctive black splotches just naturally arranged themselves into Disney's mouse logo. Like the rest of Mickey's Starland, the animals are pint-size, too, and a more cuddly bunch of baby chicks, sheep, calves, rabbits, pigs, and goats couldn't be imagined. How Walt Disney World manages to keep this imaginative barnyard so spick-and-span is completely beyond us. *Duration: Up to you. Crowds: Moderate and seldom a problem. Strategy: Go anytime. Audience: Young children, mainly. Rating:* ★★

Tomorrow- A brand-new Tomorrowland has made its long-awaited debut.
land The stark, antiseptic future forecasted by the original design had become embarrassingly passé: Bare concrete and plain white walls, plus such outdated rides as Star Jets and Mission to Mars, said more about Eisenhower-era aesthetics (or lack thereof) than third-millennium progress. To revitalize what had become the least appealing area of the Magic Kingdom, Disney artists and architects created new facades, restaurants, and shops for an energized Future City, which is more similar in mood to the themed villages of other lands. And this time around the creators showed that they had learned their lesson: Rather than predict a tomorrow destined for obsolescence, they focused on "the future that never was"—the future envisioned by sci-fi writers and moviemakers in the '20s and '30s, when space flight, laser beams, and home computers belonged in the world of fiction, not fact.

With two completely new attractions—Alien Encounter and Transportarium in the Metropolis Science Centre—an overhauled version of the Starjets (now reincarnated as AstroOrbiter) and an updated Carousel of Progress, Tomorrowland is certain to be high on the list of returning Disneyphiles as well as first-timers. Eateries here have also been revamped inside and out; however, while the menus and decor may have changed, they're still heavy on the fast-food side of things. In addition to all the new goodies, this land is home to one of the park's perennial favorites, the Space Mountain roller coaster, so count on lines at just about all hours of the day and night.

❸❷ Disney Imagineers have pulled out the stops on the **Transportarium in the Metropolis Science Centre.** Combining CircleVision 360 filmmaking with Audio-Animatronic figures, this attraction, which replaces the Circlevision 360 "American Journeys," takes visitors on a time-traveling adventure to the past and on into the future. Along the way, time-travelers meet famous inventors and visionaries of the machine age. *Duration: 20 minutes. Crowds: Moderate; moves steadily since theater seats nearly 900. Strategy:*

Go when the lines at Alien Encounter are long. All ages. Rating: ★★★

③③ There's almost never a wait at **Delta Dreamflight,** which should put your suspicions on red alert. It's in the same building complex as the Transportarium, and, in fact, the entrances can be easily confused—Dreamflight is farther along and to the right. Sponsored by Delta Airlines, this ride takes a look at the adventure of flying by showing a series of scenes of pop-up figures and photos of Delta's destinations. The idea is cute, but the execution—surprising given Disney's experience with special effects—falls far short of thrilling. At its best, the attraction screens special 70mm film segments showing barnstorming wing walkers performing such stunts as hanging off the wing and picking a ribbon off the ground and then sends you through a jet engine (you can ride past the rest of the plane's body at Disney-MGM's Backstage Studio Tour). At its worst, the photography looks as if it came from the local tourist information bureau. *Duration: 4¹/₂ min. Crowds: Light. Strategy: Go in the afternoon when everything else is crowded. Audience: All ages. Rating:* ★

Certain to become one of the Magic Kingdom's most popular—
③④ and frightening—new attractions is **Alien Encounter.** The show's innovative use of special effects provides a welcome change from its predecessor, the stodgy Mission to Mars. Playing on Tomorrowland's new Future City theme, guests enter the city's convention center to watch a test of a new teleportation system. Representatives from the device's manufacturer, an alien corporation called XS-Tech, try to transport the company's CEO from their planet to Earth to demonstrate the product. The attempt fails, however, and the catastrophic result for visitors is a close encounter with a frightening alien creature. . . . *Duration: 20 minutes. Crowds: Expect lines. Strategy: Go first thing in the morning, during the afternoon parade, or during the evening fireworks. Audience: Not suitable for small children. Rating:* ★★★

③⑤ At the center of Future City is the **AstroOrbiter,** whose gleaming superstructure of revolving planets will most likely come to symbolize the new Tomorrowland as much as Dumbo represents Fantasyland. The ride itself, however, hasn't changed much from its previous life as Starjets. Ride vehicles—now looking more like Buck Rogers toys than Space Shuttles—sail past the whirling planets during a swing through space where you control the altitude if not the velocity. *Duration: 2 minutes. Crowds: Humongous, and line moves slowly. Strategy: Skip on your first visit if time is short, unless there's no line. Audience: All ages. Rating:* ★★

③⑥ Just past AstroOrbiter, you'll find the **Tomorrowland Transit Authority** (TTA). A reincarnation of the WEDway PeopleMover, the TTA takes a nice, leisurely ride around the perimeter of Tomorrowland, circling the AstroOrbiter and eventually gliding through the middle of Space Mountain. (Some faint-hearted

TTA passengers have no doubt chucked the notion of riding the roller coaster after being exposed first-hand to the screams emanating from mountain—sounds worse than it is, though.) Disney's version of future mass transit is smooth and noiseless, thanks to an electromagnetic linear induction motor that has no moving parts, uses little power, and emits no pollutants. *Duration: 6 min. Crowds: Not one of the park's popular attractions, so lines are seldom long. Strategy: Go to preview Space Mountain, but skip on a first-time visit until you've been through all the major attractions. Audience: All ages. Rating:* ★

37 Walt Disney's **Carousel of Progress** has only been in Tomorrowland since 1974, but it was the first attraction to be given a major face-lift in the recent renovation. Originally seen at the 1964–65 World's Fair in New York, this revolving theater traces the impact of technological progress on the daily lives of Americans from the turn of this century into the near future. In each decade, there's an AudioAnimatronic family that sings the praises of the new gadgets that technology has wrought. A new preshow, seen on overhead video monitors while you're waiting to enter the theater, details the design of the original carousel and features Walt himself singing the theme song. Speaking of which, gone is the irritating theme of years' past, "The Best Time of Your Life"; it's been replaced by the ride's original ditty, "There's a Great Big Beautiful Tomorrow"—very fitting for the new Tomorrowland. *Duration: 20 min. Crowds: Moderate. Strategy: Skip on a first-time visit. Audience: All ages. Rating:* ★

Set off to the extreme left corner of Tomorrowland opposite the **38** land's main block of shops and restaurants, **Grand Prix Raceway** is one of those rides that incite instant addiction among kids and instant antipathy among parents. The reasons for the former are easy to figure out: the brightly colored Mark VII model gasoline-powered cars that swerve around the four 2,260-foot tracks with much vroom-vroom-vrooming. Like real sports cars, the vehicles are equipped with rack-and-pinion steering and disc brakes; unlike the real thing, these run on a track. However, the track is so twisty that it's hard to keep the car on a straight course— something the race car fanatics warming the bleachers love to watch. If you're not a fanatic, the persistent noise and pervasive smell of high-test can quickly rasp your nerves into the danger zone. Furthermore, there's a lot of waiting: You wait to get on the track (it can take up to an hour), you wait again for your turn to climb in a car, then you wait one more time to return your vehicle after your lap. All this for a ride in which the main thrill is achieving a top speed of 7 miles per hour. *Duration: 5 min. Crowds: Steady and heavy from late morning to evening. Strategy: Go in the evening or during a parade; skip on a first-time visit until you've been through all the major attractions. Must be at least 52 inches to drive. Audience: Older children. Rating:* ★

39 The needlelike spires and gleaming white concrete cone of **Space Mountain** are almost as much of a Magic Kingdom landmark as Cinderella's Castle. Towering 180 feet high, the structure has been called "Florida's third-highest mountain." Inside is arguably the world's most imaginative roller coaster. Although there are no loop-the-loops, gravitational whizbangs, or high-speed curves, the thrills are amply provided by Disney's masterful brainwashing as you take a trip into the depths of outer space—in the dark.

The mood for your space shot is set in the waiting area (long lines are inevitable, so milk the mood for all it's worth). A dim blue light reflects off the mirror-and-chrome walls, while above planets and galaxies and meteors and comets whirl past, strobe lights flash, and the fluorescent panels on the six-passenger rockets streak by leaving phosphorescent memories. Screams and shrieks echo in the chamber, piercing the rattling of the cars and the various otherworldly beeps and buzzes. Meanwhile, you can't help overhearing gossip about how earrings have been known to be ripped out of earlobes by the centrifugal force, pocketbooks shaken open and upended, and so on. Although it's a good idea to stow personal belongings securely, Disney staffers in a control booth constantly monitor the ride on a battery of closed-circuit televisions; at the first sign of any guest having trouble, the ride can be stopped.

That rarely happens. Instead, you wedge yourself into the seat. The blinking sign in front switches from "boarding" to "blast off," and you do. The ride lasts only 2 minutes and 38 seconds and attains a top speed of 28 miles per hour, but the devious twists and invisible drops, and the fact that you can't see where you're going, make it seem twice as long and many more times as thrilling. People of all ages adore this ride; there is, however, a bail-out area just before boarding in case you have second thoughts. *Duration: 3 min. Crowds: Large and steady, with long lines from morning to night despite high capacity. Strategy: Go either at the end of the day, during a parade, or at rope drop (in which case wait at the Plaza Restaurant rather than at the top of Main Street to get a 120-yard head start on the crowd). No pregnant women or guests wearing back, neck, or leg braces; minimum height 44 inches. Audience: All but young children. Rating:* ★★★

40 The brightly colored cable cars of the one-way **Skyway to Fantasyland** can be picked up at the station right outside Space Mountain for the commute to the far western end of Fantasyland. Not only a great shortcut, the open-air cars offer magnificent views of Cinderella's Castle and many of the Fantasyland rides; that is, you can scope out the lines from above and plan your strategy accordingly. Last but not least, those aerial tramlets provide one of the few opportunities for a little peace and quiet among the madding crowd. *Duration: 5 min. Crowds: 10- to 20-min waits except in early morning and during parades. Strategy: Skip this on your first visit. Audience: All ages. Rating:* ★

Dining

Alas, the gustatory offerings are mostly fast food—and mundane fast food at that. Every land has its share of restaurants flipping burgers, hot dogs, and nachos, with chef's salad thrown in as the token "health food" for the on-the-go crowd. In addition, the walkways are peppered with carts dispensing popcorn, ice cream, lemonade, and soda.

Full-Service Restaurants There are three full-service restaurants in the Magic Kingdom; reservations are essential and can be made at all restaurants.

Liberty Square Liberty Square's **Liberty Tree Tavern** is hands-down the best of the group. Decorated in lovely Williamsburg colors, with Early American antiques and lots of brightly polished brass, it's a pleasant place even when jammed to the gills. The menu is all-American, with the oversize salads and assorted sandwiches a good bet at lunch, and fresh fish, prime rib, and chicken the best choices at dinner. You can also order a full Thanksgiving turkey feast with all the trimmings—even in July. But then you'd miss out on the idiosyncratic garnish that decorates the sandwiches: a slice of watermelon cut to resemble Mickey Mouse's profile, ears and all.

Fantasyland No Magic Kingdom visitor can consider dining in the park without contemplating **King Stefan's Banquet Hall.** The food covers the basic choices of seafood salad or roast beef sandwiches at lunch, with chicken or seafood or prime rib at dinner. But the real attraction is that you get to eat inside Cinderella Castle in an old mead hall, where Cinderella herself is sometimes on hand and serving wenches whisk around in long medieval gowns and 13th-century-style wimples. How they prevent their veils from dragging in the mayonnaise is one of those secrets revealed only to the adepts.

Main Street The third full-service restaurant of the trio is **Tony's Town Square Café,** named after the Italian restaurant in *Lady and the Tramp* where Disney's most famous canine couple share their first kiss over a plate of spaghetti. (The video plays on a TV in the restaurant's waiting area.) Lunch and "Da Dinner" menus offer pasta, of course, along with seafood, steak, and chicken.

Cafeteria The cafeteria service at the **Crystal Palace,** just to the left of the Hub, makes for as pleasant a dining experience as the full-service places do. The offerings in this glass-roofed conservatory are varied, generous, and surprisingly good (the black bean soup is especially noteworthy, as are the burritos and the herb-roasted chicken), and there's a sizable choice of pasta dishes and hearty salads. The place is huge, but its barn-size dimensions are softened by numerous nooks and crannies, comfortable banquettes, cozy cast-iron tables, and lots of sunlight. It's also one of the few places in the Magic Kingdom that serves breakfast.

Entertainment

Daytime Particularly along Main Street, you'll come upon all sorts of shows and happenings: a **barbershop quartet, ragtime pianist, brass bands, banjo pickers.** Every day just after 5, homing pigeons wing their way to Cinderella Castle from Town Square as part of a **flag ceremony.** There are usually **song-and-dance revues**

in the Cinderella Castle forecourt and in Fantasyland and To-morrowland as well.

Still, **Disney characters** are the main event, especially if you're traveling with children (but even if you're not). They sign autographs and pose for snapshots throughout the park—line up at City Hall for your turn to pose for a picture, or snag Mickey's autograph in the star's own dressing room in the Hollywood Theater in Mickey's Starland. You can get another eyeful at the 30-minute-long **daily parade** that proceeds down Main Street through Frontierland beginning at 3; it shows off floats, balloons, cartoon characters, dancers, singers (usually lip-synching to music played over the public-address system), and much waving and cheering. It's as good as the Macy's Thanksgiving Day Parade—and the streets are cleaner. There's usually some thematic rubric attached; recently, it's been billed as Mickey's Surprise Celebration Parade—although when one little girl inquired about the nature of the surprise, her father, glancing at a lowering sky preparing to deliver the daily afternoon thundershower, replied, "The surprise is that at three o'clock it's going to pour like hell." Note that the lines at popular attractions often disappear during the parade.

After Dark The former Main Street Electrical Parade was shipped overseas to EuroDisney and replaced by **SpectroMagic,** a 30-minute extravaganza of battery-lighted floats, sequined costumes, sparkling decorations, and twinkling trees. There are staffers dressed as dragonflies, carrying battery packs that light up their emerald-and-sapphire wings. Shimmering, oversize Christmas-tree ornaments roll down the street. Mickey Mouse and Minnie—in silver sequins—ride an ornate peacock, and Cinderella's coach is outlined in hundreds of fairy lights.

Speaking of fairies, let's not forget **Fantasy in the Sky,** the Magic Kingdom fireworks display. Heralded by a dimming of all the lights along Main Street, the camouflaged loudspeakers play "When You Wish upon a Star." A single spotlight illuminates the top turret of the Cinderella Castle and—poof!—Tinkerbell emerges in a shower of pixie dust. Thanks to an invisible guy wire, she appears to fly over the treetops and the crowds, on her way to a Never-Never-Land touchdown located, appropriately enough, in Tomorrowland. Her disappearance signals the start of the fireworks, which fill the sky with some pixie dust of their own. It's a magical way to end an enchanted idyll.

Shopping

Everywhere you turn there are shops and stalls urging you to take home a little piece of the magic. Here are some of the all-time best Magic Kingdom souvenirs: pirate hats, swords and plastic hooks-for-hands sold at the **House of Treasure** just outside Pirates of the Caribbean in Adventureland; creepy-crawly rubber snakes and lizards, just the sort of thing to spook a younger sibling, sold at **Bwana Bob's** kiosk next to the entrance to the Jungle Cruise in Adventureland; Davy Crockett coonskin hats, personalized sheriff badges, and Big Al memorabilia at **Big**

Al's across from the Country Bear Jamboree in Frontierland; a fairy princess upside-down-ice-cream-cone hat with a gauze veil, at **The King's Gallery** inside Cinderella Castle; children's clothing with Disney characters at **Tinkerbell's Treasures** in Fantasyland; and last but not least, distinctive canary yellow umbrellas with black mouse ears on top and the signature yellow ponchos adorned with a smiling Mickey on the back—a bargain at $4.51.

Access for Travelers with Disabilities

Attractions
Main Street
To board the **Walt Disney World Railroad** at the Main Street Station, you must transfer from your wheelchair, which can be folded to ride with you or left in the station. Alternatively, board at Frontierland or Mickey's Starland. The **Main Street Cinema** is barrier free for guests using wheelchairs—a definite miss for visually impaired guests, since the cartoons are silents, played without dialogue, and set to theater organ music. The **Main Street Vehicles** can be boarded by guests with limited mobility who can fold their wheelchair and climb into a car. In the **Penny Arcade,** the machines may be too high for guests using wheelchairs and not of much interest for some guests with visual impairments. There are curb cuts or ramps on each corner.

Adventure-
land
The **Swiss Family Robinson Treehouse,** with its 100 steps and lack of narration, gets low ratings among those with mobility and visual impairments. At the **Jungle Cruise,** boarding requires that a guest step down into the boat; those who can lip-read will find the skippers' punny narration, delivered with a handheld mike, difficult to follow, though you can try (ask for a seat up front). Boarding **Pirates of the Caribbean** requires transferring from a nonfolding to a folding wheelchair, available at the entrance; the flume drop may make the attraction inappropriate for those with limited upper-body strength or who wear neck or back braces, and because of gunshot and fire effects, service animals should stay behind. The theater-style **Enchanted Tiki Birds** is barrier free for guests using wheelchairs.

Frontierland
To ride **Big Thunder Mountain Railroad** and **Splash Mountain,** you must be able to step into the ride vehicle and walk short distances (in case of emergency evacuation); those with limited upper-body strength should assess the situation on site, and those wearing back, neck, or leg braces should not ride. (Ditto for service animals.) **Tom Sawyer Island,** with its stairs, bridges, inclines, and narrow caves is not negotiable by those using a wheelchair. The **Diamond Horseshoe Jamboree** and the **Country Bear Jamboree** are completely wheelchair accessible; if you lip-read, ask to sit up front (especially at the Diamond Horseshoe, whose script is not in the guide for guests with hearing impairments). The **Frontierland Shootin' Gallery** has two guns at wheelchair level. Frontierland is the only area of the park, aside from Main Street, that has sidewalk curbs; there are ramps by the Mile Long Bar and east of Frontierland Trading Post.

Liberty
Square
The **Hall of Presidents** is completely barrier free for guests using wheelchairs. The **Liberty Square Riverboat** is completely wheelchair accessible; to ride the **Mike Fink Keel Boats,** guests must

negotiate two steep steps. At the **Haunted Mansion,** guests using wheelchairs must transfer to the "doom buggies" and take one step; however, if you can walk as much as 200 feet, you will enjoy the great preshow as well as the sensations and eerie sounds of the rest of the ride. **Mickey's Starland** is completely accessible.

Fantasyland Boarding the **Skyway** is impossible for guests who use a wheelchair unless they can transfer to the ride cabins. Go for the round-trip, because stairs are a chief feature of the Tomorrowland Station. And if you're visually impaired, don't waste your time; there's no narration, and the panoramic view is the ride's chief raison d'être. The stage show **Legend of the Lion King** has wheelchair seating; for guests with visual impairments, the chief attraction is the music by Elton John. **It's a Small World** can be boarded without leaving your wheelchair, but only if it's a standard-size one; guests using a scooter or an oversize chair must transfer to one of the attraction's standard chairs, available at the ride entrance. To board **Peter Pan's Flight, Dumbo the Flying Elephant, Cinderella's Golden Carrousel, the Mad Tea Party, Mr. Toad's Wild Ride,** and **Snow White's Adventures,** guests using wheelchairs must transfer to the ride vehicles. Mr. Toad's, Dumbo, and Peter Pan's are inappropriate for service animals. To board **20,000 Leagues under the Sea,** you must be able to descend and ascend nine steps.

Tomorrow- **Alien Encounter, Transportarium,** and **Carousel of Progress** are
land barrier free for those using wheelchairs. To board **Delta Dreamflight, AstroOrbiter,** and the **Tomorrowland Transit Authority**, you must be able to walk several steps and transfer to the ride vehicle. The TTA has more appeal to guests with visual impairments, Dreamflight greater charm for those with hearing impairments. To drive **Grand Prix Raceway** cars, you must have adequate vision and be able to steer, press the gas pedal, and transfer into the low car seat. The cautions for Big Thunder Mountain Railroad and Splash Mountain (*see* Frontierland, *above*) also apply to **Space Mountain.**

Shops and All restaurants and shops throughout the park have level en-
Restaurants trances or are accessible by ramps.

Information *See* Hints for Travelers with Disabilities in Chapter 1 and Access for Travelers with Disabilities at the beginning of this chapter.

Epcot Center

Walt Disney World was created because of Walt Disney's dream of EPCOT, an "Experimental Prototype Community of Tomorrow." Disney envisioned a future in which nations co-existed in peace and harmony, reaping the miraculous harvest of technological achievement. He suggested the idea as early as October 1966, saying, "EPCOT will be an experimental prototype community of tomorrow that will take its cue from the new ideas and new technologies that are now emerging from the creative centers of American industry." He wrote of the never completed, always improving Epcot, "Epcot...will never cease to be a living blueprint of the future . . . a showcase to the world for the ingenuity and imagination of American free enterprise."

But with Disneyland hemmed in by development, Disney had to search for new lands in which to found his new world. He found it in central Florida. Many of the technologies incorporated into the Walt Disney World infrastructure were cutting-edge at the time. But the permanent community that he envisioned has not yet come to be. Instead, we have Epcot Center—which opened in 1982, 16 years after Disney's death—a showcase, ostensibly, for the concepts that would be incorporated into the EPCOTs of the future. Then, as now, it was composed of two parts: **Future World,** where the majority of its 10 pavilions are sponsored by major U.S. corporations and demonstrate their technological advances, and **World Showcase,** where 11 exhibition areas each represent a different country.

Epcot Center today is both more and less than Walt Disney's original dream. Less because some of the Future World pavilions are stuck in a 1965 World's Fair mentality, their driving vision, like the companies that sponsored them, eerily out of touch with today's values. Less because World Showcase presents idealized views of its countries, as an Epcot guide put it: "as Americans perceive them." Less because the missionary zeal that infuses the park backfires occasionally; young children get bored and adults start to wonder if they have to take a short test at the exit.

But these are minor quibbles in the face of the major achievement: Epcot is that rare paradox—an educational theme park—and a very successful one, too. The amount of imagination concentrated in its 230 acres is astounding and can't help rubbing off on the visitors. Through ingenious architecture, intriguing exhibits, amusing movies, and lively rides, Epcot Center inspires curiosity, rewards discovery, and encourages the creative spark in each of us.

Although rides have been added over the years to amuse young 'uns, the thrills are mostly in the mind. Consequently, because it helps to have a well-developed intelligence that one can exercise, Epcot is best for older children and adults.

Essential Information

Getting Around It's a big place; a local joke suggests that Epcot is an acronym for "Every Person Comes Out Tired." But still, the most efficient way to get around is to walk. Just to vary things, you can cruise across the lagoon in one of the air-conditioned, 65-foot water taxis that depart every 12 minutes from World Showcase Plaza at the border of Future World. There are two docks: Boats from the one on the left zip to the Germany pavilion, from the right to Morocco. In World Showcase, you can board the slow-moving double-decker buses that depart every 5–8 minutes and stop in front of every other pavilion.

If you think the huge distances involved may be a problem, start out by renting a stroller or wheelchair (*see below*).

Tourist Information   **Earth Station,** underneath Spaceship Earth, is the principal information center, the place to pick up schedules of live entertainment, park brochures, and the like. The computerized WorldKey Information System kiosks, in Earth Station and in World Showcase near Germany, are another resource. Using the touch-sensitive screens, you can obtain detailed information about every pavilion, leave messages for companions, and get answers to almost all of your questions. If the computer can't give you the answer, you can request the assistance of a host or hostess.

Reservations   At press time, lunch or dinner reservations for Epcot Center full-service restaurants could be made at WorldKey terminals in Earth Station only on the day of the meal, unless you're staying on-site, in which case you may be able to reserve one to three days in advance. Lunch reservations can also be made at the restaurants themselves. For up-to-date information that applies to you, call Guest Relations (tel. 407/824–4321).

Services
Baby Care   Epcot Center has a Baby Care Center as peaceful as the one in the Magic Kingdom; it's near the Odyssey Restaurant in Future World. Also furnished with rocking chairs, it has a low lighting level that makes it comfortable for nursing, and cast members have supplies such as **formula, baby food, pacifiers, and disposable diapers** for sale. You'll find **changing tables** here, as well as in all women's rooms and some men's rooms. You can also buy disposable diapers near the park entrance at Baby Services. For **stroller rentals** ($5 a day; $1 deposit required), look for the special stands on the east side of the Entrance Plaza and at World Showcase's International Gateway.

Cameras and Film   Kodak's disposable Fun Saver cameras are widely available. Or you can borrow a Kodak **disk camera** (you just have to buy the film) or rent **35mm cameras** or **video camcorders** ($5 and $40, respectively; refundable $100–$800 deposit required); sources include the Kodak Camera Center, in the Entrance Plaza; the lagoon's-edge World Traveler, at the end of the promenade between Future World and World Showcase; and Cameras and Film at Journey into Imagination.

For **two-hour film developing,** look for the Photo Express sign throughout the park (at the Kodak Camera Center and Cameras and Film at Journey into Imagination in Future World, and in World Showcase at Northwest Mercantile in Canada, World Traveler at International Gateway, Heritage Manor Gifts in the American Adventure, at the booth on the right as you enter Norway, and Artesanias Mexicanas in Mexico); drop your film in the container, and you can pick up your pictures at the Kodak Camera Center as you leave.

First Aid   The park's First Aid Center, staffed by registered nurses, is near the Odyssey Restaurant in Future World.

Guided Tours   Reserve up to three weeks in advance for the two 4-hour behind-the-scenes tours, led by knowledgeable Disney cast members and open to guests 16 and older ($20 plus park admission; tel. 407/345–5860). Both offer up-close views of the phenomenal detail involved in the planning and maintenance of Epcot Center.

Hidden Treasures of World Showcase (Sun., Wed., and Fri. 9:30–1:30) tells you everything, from the provenance of the boulders in Japan's garden to the number of bricks in the U.S. pavilion. **Gardens of the World** (Mon.–Wed. 9–1) explains World Showcase's realistic replicas of exotic plantings.

Lockers You'll find them to the west of Spaceship Earth; outside the Entrance Plaza; and in the Bus Information Center by the bus parking lot (50¢). If what you need to store won't fit into the larger lockers, go to Guest Relations in the Entrance Plaza or at Earth Station.

Lost Children and Adults If you're worried about your children getting lost, get them name tags at either Earth Station or the Baby Care Center. If the worst happens, immediately report it to any cast member and try not to panic; the staff here is experienced at reuniting families, and there are lost-children logbooks at Earth Station and the Baby Care Center.

Earth Station also has a computerized Message Center, where you can leave notes for your traveling companions, both those in the Magic Kingdom and those in other parks.

Lost and Found Go to the west edge of the Entrance Plaza. If nobody claims what you turn in, you may get to keep it.

Money For cash and currency exchange, go to the Sun Bank branch at Epcot Center (open 9–4 daily), the Guest Relations window, or Earth Station. There is an American Express ExpressCash machine on the left side of the Entrance Plaza.

Package Pickup Ask the shop clerk to forward any large purchase you make to Guest Relations in the Entrance Plaza so that you won't have to carry it around all day. (Allow three hours.)

Wheelchair Rentals You'll find them inside the Entrance Plaza on the left; and to the right of the ticket booths at the Gift Stop; and at World Showcase's International Gateway. Standard models are available ($5 plus $1 deposit); you can also reserve an electric scooter (tel. 407/824–4321; $25 plus $20 deposit).

Strategies for Your Visit

Epcot Center is now so vast and varied that a dedicated visitor really needs two days to explore it all. However, if you want to attempt the whole thing in a day, the first rule is: Don't sleep late. Not only are there so many attractions, but you'll want to arrive early to beat the lines and make reservations at the restaurants. The second rule is: Don't spend time eating. Instead, have a big breakfast and tote a snack to tide you over so that you can have a late lunch. The third rule is: Walk fast, see the shows when the park is empty, and slow down and enjoy the shops and the live entertainment when the crowds thicken.

Blitz Tour When you arrive at Epcot Center, your first task is to send the speediest member of your party ahead to the WorldKey Information System terminals in **Earth Station** to make reservations for a 5:30 dinner, because after your marathon day, you'll be ready to sit down. Thus, dining early will give you time to zip through the attractions you've missed while everyone else is dawdling over dinner. Reservations made, you can smugly proceed to **Spaceship Earth** with nothing more on your mind than to have it expanded. Everyone else will also be lining up at Spaceship Earth, but the first-thing-in-the-morning lines move along snappily, and this attraction really is the best introduction to Future World.

Upon saying good-bye to Walter Cronkite, everyone else will head for the first pavilion they see: either Universe of Energy or the Living Seas. Skip 'em, we say, and go directly to the **Wonders of Life.** Once here, stay to your left; if the lines are minimal, you can segue from Body Wars to *The Making of Me* to Cranium Command with barely a pause.

Then head to Future World's western pavilions. Visit **Journey into Imagination** first; while most other visitors are breathing Mesozoic fog at Universe of Energy, you can meet Dreamfinder on the ride and then walk right into *Honey, I Shrunk the Audience*. Don't linger in the Image Works—you can always come back.

Now enter **The Land**; take the boat ride and see Symbiosis and Food Rocks. By this time there may be a line at Living Seas, but if there isn't, go on in and stay as long as you like. Outside, things should be getting crowded. Head counterclockwise into World Showcase, toward **Canada.** (Everyone else will be hoofing it toward Mexico.) Then see **France** and the **American Adventure.** If there are lines at **Norway** by the time you get there, head for **Innoventions** and the **Image Works.**

After dinner, see any World Showcase attractions you missed, plus the **Universe of Energy, Horizons,** and **World of Motion;** lines are practically nonexistent then, and because rides are continuous at the last two pavilions, you can literally run from one to another, detouring at the **Wonders of Life** for a fruit-yogurt smoothie. World Showcase empties after 5, and there's a truly magical quality to the lush plantings at dusk.

If you have a day and a half or two days, plan to do just the opposite of what most visitors do: Explore World Showcase in the morning, Future World in the afternoon.

Exploring Epcot Center

Epcot Center is divided into two distinct areas separated by the 40-acre World Showcase Lagoon. The northern half, which is where the monorail drops you off and which is considered the official entrance, comprises Future World, whose pavilions honoring technological achievements are sponsored by major U.S. corporations. The southern half, at whose International Gateway the trams from the Dolphin and Swan hotels and Disney's Yacht Club and Beach Club resorts drop you off, comprises World Showcase, whose 11 exhibition areas, each spotlighting the culture of a different country, are sponsored by foreign governments and corporations.

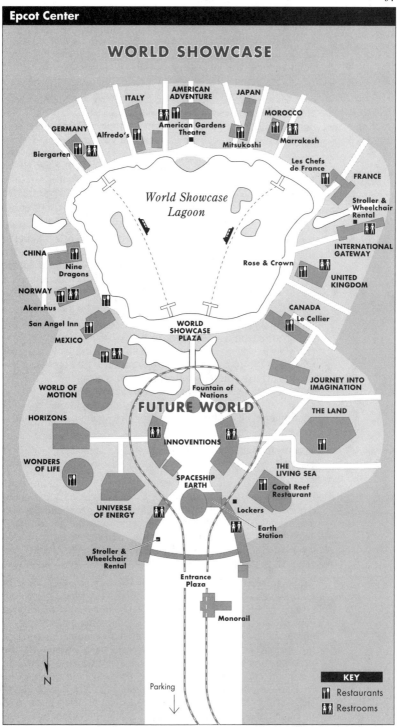

Future Future World is made up of two concentric circles of pavilions.
World The inner core is composed of the Spaceship Earth geosphere
and, just beyond it the new Innoventions exhibit and Innoventions plaza. The large Fountain of Nations serves as a dividing point between the inner core and the pavilions beyond.

Seven pavilions compose the outer ring of the circle. On the east side they are, in order, Universe of Energy, Wonders of Life, Horizons, and World of Motion. With the exception of the Wonders of Life, the pavilions present a single, self-contained ride and an occasional postride showcase; a visit rarely takes more than 30 minutes, but it depends on how long you spend in the post-ride area. On the west side there's the Living Seas, The Land, and Journey into Imagination. Like the Wonders of Life, these blockbuster exhibits contain both rides and interactive displays; count on spending at least 1½ hours per pavilion—and wanting to stay longer.

Spaceship Balanced like a giant golf ball waiting for some celestial being
Earth to tee off, the multifaceted silver geosphere of Spaceship Earth
is to Epcot Center what the Cinderella Castle is to the Magic Kingdom. As much a landmark as an icon, it can be seen on a clear day from an airplane flying down either coast of Florida.

Everyone likes to gawk at the golf ball, but here are some truly jaw-dropping facts: It weighs 1 million pounds, measures 164 feet in diameter and 180 feet in height (aha! you say, it's not really a sphere!), and encompasses more than 2 million cubic feet of space. It's balanced on six pylons sunk 100 feet into the ground. The anodized aluminum sheath is composed of 954 triangular panels, not all of equal size or shape. And, last, because it is not a geodesic dome (which is only a half sphere), the name "geosphere" had to be invented; no other like it existed when it was built.

Spaceship Earth contains both the Spaceship Earth ride and Earth Station, the principal source of Epcot Center information.

Hands-down the most popular ride at Epcot Center, as much for its subject matter and execution as for its proximity to the entrance, Spaceship Earth explores human progress and the continuing search for better forms of communication. Scripted by science fiction writer Ray Bradbury and narrated by Walter Cronkite, the journey begins in the darkest tunnels of time, proceeds through history, and ends poised on the edge of the future.

AudioAnimatronic figures present in astonishing detail Cro-Magnon man daubing mystic paintings on cave walls, Egyptian scribes scratching genuine hieroglyphics on papyrus, Roman centurions building roads, Islamic scholars mapping the heavens, and 11th- and 12th-century Benedictine monks hand-copying ancient manuscripts in order to preserve the wisdom of the past (one monk, not as tireless as history would have us believe, is conked out at his carrel, his candle smoking in the gusts of his snores). As you move into the Renaissance, Michelangelo paints the Sistine Chapel, Gutenberg invents the printing press, and in rapid succession, the telegraph, radio, television, and computer come into being. The pace speeds up, you're bombarded with images from our communication age, and, just as you begin to think you can't absorb another photon, you're shot through a tunnel of swirling lights into serene space, its velvety darkness sparkling with thousands of stars, and in one corner, hanging like the jeweled toy envisioned by Milton in *Paradise Lost*, is our own Earth as photographed by the astronauts on one of the *Apollo* moon shots. It's breathtaking. A dazzling new finale debuts in late 1994: Toward the conclusion of the ride, visitors arrive in a "Global Neighborhood" that ties all of the peoples of the earth together through an interactive global network. Special effects, animated sets, and audience-enclosing laser beams are used to create the experience. *Duration: 15 min. Crowds: Longest during the morning and shortest just before park closing time. Strategy: Ride first thing in the morning or just before leaving. Audience: All ages. Rating:* ★★★

Innoventions   Disney's latest addition to Future World is **Innoventions,** a 100,000-square-foot attraction situated at the center of the complex. Live stage demonstrations, interactive hands-on displays, and exhibits highlight new technology that affects daily living. Innoventions visitors get a first look at new electronic games and toys, new computers, advanced home appliances, special televisions, and other major innovations of the near future. Each of the 15 major exhibit areas is presented by a leading manufacturer.

Time Out   Two large fast-food emporiums dominate the Innoventions Plaza area. If you're facing World Showcase, the **Stargate Restaurant** is to the left, and the **Sunrise Terrace** is to the right. With its pink, blue, and dark purple color scheme (and blessed air-conditioning), Stargate has a relatively soothing atmosphere despite the hordes it feeds. The menu consists of burgers, chicken nuggets, and chef and fruit salads. **Sunrise Terrace** lists pasta and pizza as its offerings; it's also one of the few places in Epcot that serves breakfast. Morning fare includes omelets and the Sunrise Scramble, a tasty Egg McMuffin clone. Adjacent to the Sunrise Terrace is **Fountainview Expresso,** a café with freshly ground coffees, scrumptious croissants, fruit tarts, crême brulée, and éclairs. You can eat at the circular counter or perch at one of the high chairs and tables. There's also a patio with tables and umbrellas that offers a fine view of the fountain. In the afternoon, this is a great place to sip wine and watch the fountain show without having to stand in the blazing sun and crane your neck.

Universe of   Two large topiary dinosaurs stand guard over Universe of En-
Energy   ergy. The first of the pavilions on the left, or east, side of Future World, it occupies a large, lopsided pyramid, sheathed in thousands of mirrors, which serve as solar collectors to power the ride and films within. One of the most technologically complex shows at Epcot Center, the exhibit combines one ride, two films, the largest Audio-Animatronic animals ever built, 250 prehistoric trees, and enough cold, damp fog to make you think you've

been transported to the inside of a defrosting refrigerator. "We don't want to go through that fog again," one child announced after emerging from a particularly damp vision of the Mesozoic era. About the rest of the ride, however, he had few qualms.

The 10-minute preshow film about the different forms of energy—nuclear, solar, electric, mechanical, and thermal—takes place in an enormous, standing-only (or sitting-on-the-floor) antechamber. There's a twist, however: The 14-by-90-foot projection surface is made up of 100 separate screens, which rotate according to complicated computerized directions to form what their creator, Czech filmmaker Emil Radok, described as a "kinetic mosaic." Here you are also serenaded for the first of many times with the jingle peculiar to this particular pavilion: "Hear the flow, see it grow, it's the Universe of Energy." If you say so.

Everyone then files into an adjoining area, which resembles a drive-in theater, complete with seats arranged in blocks. This is the setting for a five-minute animated film depicting the eras in which today's fossil fuels originated. No cute Disneyesque dinosaurs populated this earth; these animals are hulking, shadowy figures, lumbering across a steamy landscape of volcanoes, lush plants, and eerie insects. Even more eerie is the moment at the conclusion of the movie when the blocks of seats shift and rotate, then break up, and move forward into the ride.

The ride lurches into the forest primeval—and do we ever mean primeval. Huge trees loom out of the mists of time, ominous blue moonbeams waver in the fog, sulfurous lava burbles up, and the air smells distinctly of Swamp Thing. Through this unfriendly landscape brontosauruses wander trailing mouthfuls of weeds, a tyrannosaurus fights it out with a triceratops, pterodactyls swoop through the air, and a truly nasty sea snake emerges from the swamp to attack the left side of the tram. It's a view of the past that makes you glad to live in the present. In fact, it's almost a relief to hear the familiar "Hear the flow, see it grow . . ."

The ride concludes with another film, this one a 12-minute description of the search for alternative forms of energy. Dramatic shots of North Sea drilling platforms and a space-shuttle blast-off sequence so unusual that even NASA requested a copy serve to underline rather than mask the message. An interesting fact here: The 96-passenger, 30,000-pound "traveling theaters" are guided along the concrete floor by a wire only 1/8-inch thick and are powered by the 80,000 solar cells on the roof so that you have been, as they say, "riding on sunshine." *Duration: 1/2 hour. Crowd: Steady but never horrible; 600 people enter every 15 minutes. Stragegy: To be at the front of the ride (and have your experience of the primeval landscape unspoiled by rows of modern heads in front of you), sit in the seats to the far left and front of the theater. Audience: All ages. Rating:* ★★★

Wonders of Life   A towering statue of a DNA double helix outside the gold-crowned dome of the Wonders of Life welcomes you to one of Epcot Center's most popular attractions. Truly one of the wonders of Epcot Center, it takes an amusing but serious and educational look at health, fitness, and modern lifestyles. One improvisational theater revue, two films, and dozens of interactive gadgets that whiz, bleep, and blink make up the Fitness Fairground. Walt Disney World's first flight simulator—Body Wars—takes visitors on a bumpy platelet-to-platelet ride through the human circulatory system. And the entertaining multimedia presentation, Cranium Command, reveals the workings of the mind of a typical 12-year-old boy during the course of an ordinary day.

The flight-simulator technology that is used to train commercial and military pilots adapts perfectly to thrill rides. By synchronizing the action on a movie screen with the movement of the capsule, the simulator tricks your mind into thinking that you're experiencing a wild ride without your ever leaving your seat. Probably the mildest flight simulator in central Florida, **Body Wars** still offers a thrilling ride, thanks to the fascinating film and the ingenious idea. You and your fellow scientists enter a capsule (the simulator chamber) that, like something out of *Honey, I Shrunk the Kids*, will be miniaturized and injected into the body's bloodstream. "How's the weather in there?" calls out one of the specialists on the screen. "Clear and warm, temperature about 98.6," comes the reply from within. And in a couple of seconds, you experience it yourself: shooting through the heart, wheezing through the lungs, and picking up a jolt of energy in the brain.

Length: 5 min. Crowds: Sometimes discouraging, with occasional 45-min waits. Strategy: Go as soon as the park opens, during the hour before closing, or between 6 and 7 PM, the peak dinnertime in World Showcase. Not recommended for pregnant women or guests who have neck or back injuries, heart problems, or motion sickness. Audience: All but young children. Rating: ★★★

Showtimes are staggered to pick up as soon as another lets out, so with a little luck you can segue right into *The Making of Me,* a valuable film on human conception and childbearing. Starring Martin Short as a man who, in search of his origins, journeys back in time to his parents' childhood, youth, marriage, and, eventually, their decision to have him, the film uses both animation and actual footage from a live birth to explain where babies come from. Some scenes are explicit, but all the topics are handled with gentle humor (as when the sperm race for the egg to the tune of "The Ride of the Valkyries") and (as when his parents make the big decision) with great delicacy. Children tend to be dumbstruck; many adults find the film affecting enough to get out the handkerchiefs for a quick swipe at overflowing eyes. *Length: 14 min. Crowds: Long lines all day because the theater is so small. Strategy: Save this one for after 6 PM. Audience: All ages. Rating: ★★★*

Luckily the theater housing **Cranium Command** seats 200 at a shot. Combining a fast-paced movie with an elaborate set, this engaging show looks at how the cranium manages to make the heart, the uptight left brain, the laid-back right brain, the stomach, and an ever-alert adrenal gland all work together as their host, a 12-year-old boy, surmounts the slings and arrows of a typical day. The star is Buzzy, a bumbling AudioAnimatronic Cranium Commando for whom adolescent boys are the last chance before being consigned to run the brain of a chicken. Buzzy's is not an easy job; as the sign on the way to the theater warns, you are entering "The Home of the Flying Endorphins." As Buzzy's 12-year-old wakes up late, dashes off without breakfast, meets the new girl in school, fights for her honor, gets called up before the principal, and, finally, returns home (and has a much-needed snack), Buzzy attempts to coordinate a heart (operated by "Saturday Night Live's" muscle-team Hans and Franz), a stomach (run by George Wendt, late of "Cheers," in a sewer worker's overalls and rubber boots), and all the other body parts. He succeeds—barely. And the show is so well done that we'd almost like to see Buzzy fail, so we could watch him run the life of a typical chicken. *Length: 20 min. Crowds: Long lines, but the big theater can quickly erase 'em. Strategy: Go when everyone else is at Body Wars. Audience: All ages. Rating:* ★★★

The rest of the Wonders of Life pavilion is taken up by the **Fitness Fairground,** an educational playground that teaches both adults and children about good health. There are games in which you can test your golf and tennis prowess, pedal around the world on a stationary bicycle while watching an ever-changing view on video, and guess your stress level at an interactive computer terminal. "Goofy about Health," an 8-minute multiscreen montage, follows Goofy's conversion from a foul-living dog to a fun-loving guy. The Anacomical Players Theater, seating 100 people, is a corny but funny improvisational show with lots of audience participation. The Frontiers of Medicine, the only completely serious section of the pavilion, demonstrates leading-edge developments in medicine. *Duration: Up to you. Crowds: Shifting, but they don't affect your visit. Strategy: Hang loose and take turns. Audience: All ages. Rating:* ★★★

Time Out — **Pure & Simple,** a food stall offering healthful snacks and full meals, proves that nutritious can also be delicious. While cholesterol addicts pig out on basic burgers and fries, those who take the Wonders of Life message to heart can sample the venison chili spiked with fresh herbs, the salads with a choice of zippy dressings (including the beta-carotene salad with tomato-basil vinaigrette), and sandwiches that for once are better than what you'd make at home, all followed by a slice of angel food cake or a fruit or yogurt smoothie. The whole-wheat waffles with berry toppings are somewhat overrated, but a nice touch. The prices won't give you a heart attack either, although overhearing the Anacomical Players ask—and answer—as you eat, "Why do some people pick their nose?" may give you pause.

Horizons — **Horizons** is a relentlessly optimistic look at the once and future future. After being enjoined to "live your dreams," you ride a tram past visions of the future, where former great minds imagine what the world might have been like in a hundred years or so. There's the 19th-century French artist Albert Robida's vision of Paris in the 1950s, with dirigible taxis, and Jules Verne's picture of spaceships as bullets with microscopic portholes. Visitors slathered with sunscreen will get a kick out of the 1930s view of the 1990s home, which includes personal tanning centers where you could choose between Hawaiian, Florida, or Bahamas shades of brown. The tram then moves past a series of tableaux of life in a future space colony. This pavilion was built more than a decade ago, and the magnetic levitation trains it envisioned are now being tried out in Japan. Who knows whether the holographic telephones will soon be marketed? Visitors who have already gone through Living Seas and The Land will find Mesa Verde's future farming sequence and the Sea Castle section especially interesting; at Horizons you get the idea of what innovations are being imagined and then you see them being tested in other pavilions. The Omega Centuri tableau, portraying a free-floating space colony, prefigures virtual reality, with its games of zero-gravity basketball and simulated outdoor sports. *Length: 15 min. Crowds: Often large because of its location near Innoventions, but the only time the wait exceeds 15 min is when the megaride at the nearby Universe of Energy lets out, and usually swift-moving trams keep wait times down. Strategy: Keep an eye on the line, and if it's long, just go back later. Audience: All ages. Rating:* ★★

World of Motion Shaped like a wheel, World of Motion features the Trans-Center—a 33,000-square-foot exhibit and auto showroom displaying new models from General Motors—and the **World of Motion ride,** which is essentially a dippy, feel-good frolic through scenarios depicting the history of human attempts to get somewhere else faster. Despite the 20-odd elaborate sets and more than 140 Audio-animatronic characters, sophisticated this ain't. Broad humor rules as humanity tries out ostrich-power and zebra-power before harnessing horse-power, invents the wheel, rolls up the magic carpet, and experiments with flying machines, balloons, steam carriages, riverboats, stagecoaches, airplanes, automobiles, and a host of Rube Goldberg contraptions. Genuine antiques, such as old-fashioned autos and a 150-year-old Wells Fargo stagecoach, lend verisimilitude. Kids love this, as well as the addictive jingle, "It's Fun to Be Free." Adults may feel the same way when the ride ends. *Length: 15 min. Crowds: Large, but this high-capacity, continuously loading ride can handle the numbers. Strategy: Go anytime, and don't be daunted by lines—they move quickly. Audience: All ages. Rating:* ★★

What's fascinating about the **TransCenter** is not just the latest models from GM, or the assembly line robot, or even the wind tunnel demonstrating the principles of aerodynamic drag, but the display of all the experimental automobiles that provide faster, cheaper, more ecologically sound alternatives to what clogs up our roads nowadays. You also see short presentations on milestones in 20th-century transportation and the quality tests GM uses to ensure it doesn't raise lemons.

Time Out   Handsome, hexagonally shaped **Odyssey** restaurant looks like a pleasant sit-down eatery, but the food comes a lot faster. Disney characters put in appearances at breakfast time.

Living Seas   On Epcot Center's western outer ring is the first satellite pavilion, Living Seas, a favorite among children. Epcot Center is known for its imaginative fountains; the one at Living Seas flings surf in a never-ending wave against a rock garden beneath the stylized marquee. Time and technology have caught up with the 5.7-million-gallon aquarium at the pavilion's core, thrilling when it first opened, so that what was once revolutionary has now been equaled by top aquariums around the country and at Sea World. Still, the three-minute **Caribbean Coral Reef Ride** encircling the acrylic tank may be too short. Sometimes you'll catch sight of a diver, testing out the latest scuba equipment, surrounded by a cloud of parrot fish while scattering a mixture of dry dog food, chicken's laying pellets, amino-acid solution, and B-complex vitamins or carefully placing a head of lettuce within reach of a curious sea turtle.

After the ride, you may want to circumnavigate the tank at your own speed on an upper level, pointing out barracudas, stingrays, parrot fish, sea turtles and even sharks, before exploring the two levels of **Sea Base Alpha,** a prototype undersea research facility that is a typical Epcot Center playground. Each of its six modules is dedicated to a specific subject: the history of robotics, ocean exploration, ocean ecosystems, dolphins, porpoises, and sea lions. Fully interactive, these contain films, touchy-feely sections, miniaquariums, and video quizzes; there's even a deep-sea diving suit that visitors can try on. *Duration: 45 min. and up, including the 3-min ride, depending on how long you leer at angelfish and play Diver Dan at the modules. Crowds: Large, all day long. Strategy: Stop in first thing in the morning or after 5. Audience: All but young children. Rating:* ★★★

The Land   Shaped like an intergalactic greenhouse, the enormous skylighted The Land pavilion dedicates 6 acres and a host of different attractions to everyone's favorite topic: food. You can easily spend two hours exploring here. The main event is the **Listen to the Land** boat ride. Piloted by an informative, overalls-clad guide, you cruise through three biomes (rain forest, desert, and prairie ecological communities) and into an experimental greenhouse that demonstrates how food sources may be grown in the future, not only on Earth but also in outer space. Sunshine bass, tilapia, pacu—the piranha's vegetarian cousin—and shrimp are raised in controlled aquacells, and tomatoes, peppers, and squash thrive in the Desert Farm area through a system of drip irrigation that delivers just the right amount of water and nutrients to their roots. Gardeners will be interested in the section on integrated pest management, which relies on "good" bugs like ladybugs to control insect predators. Many of the growing areas are actual experiments-in-progress, in which Disney and the U.S. Department of Agriculture have joined forces to produce, say, a sweeter pineapple or a faster-growing pepper. Interestingly, while the plants and fish in the greenhouse are all quite real—and are regularly harvested for use in The Land's restaurants—those in the biomes are artful fakes, manufactured by Disney elves out of flexible, lightweight plastic. The grass is made out of glass fibers and is implanted into rubber mats—a useful deterrent to barefooted trespassers, perhaps. *Length: 14 min. Crowds: Large all day. Strategy: Go during mealtimes. Audience: Teens and adults. Rating:* ★★★

The terminally cute singing fruits and vegetables of the Kitchen Kaberet Revue have been replaced with a new musical extravaganza, **Food Rocks.** It's a rowdy concert where recognizable rock 'n' roll performers take the shape of favorite foods and sing about the joys of nutrition. There are performances by the Peach Boys, Chubby Cheddar, and Neil Moussaka, among others. *Length: 20 minutes. Crowds: A large theater erases them. Strategy: Go when the line at Listen to the Land is too long. Audience: children. Rating:* ★

The **Harvest Theater** is home to a *National Geographic*–like film called *Symbiosis*, a heavy title for a fascinating flick about humanity's interaction with nature. We're not saying that this is all fun with the Philippine rice researchers who are featured. In fact, there are some definite horror stories about our misuse of the land, but they are balanced by reassuring rescue stories about forest management in Sweden, Germany, and the American Pacific Northwest. All in all, it's an intelligent look at how we can profit from the earth's natural resources while ensuring that the earth benefits, too. Filmed in 30 countries, it has some terrific scenery, especially in the opening shots of the hillside rice terraces near Banaue in the Philippines. *Length: 20 min. Crowds: Generally not a concern. Strategy: Go anytime. Audience: Breathtaking for adults, a nap opportunity for toddlers, and too relentlessly educational for older grade schoolers. Rating:* ★★

Still hungry? Guided **Greenhouse Tours** of the greenhouses and aquacell areas cover the same topics as the boat ride but in much more detail—and you have the chance to ask questions. Reservations are essential and can be made on the lower floor, in the corner opposite the boat ride entrance, behind Broccoli and Co., a delightful shop stocking hydroponic plants, gardening books, vegetable refrigerator magnets, place mats, and cheerful aprons. *Length: 45 min; available daily every $^1/_2$ hr 9:30–4:30. Strategy: Reserve ahead. A good activity for busy times of day— late morning through afternoon. Audience: Adults and budding horticulturists. Rating:* ★★

Time Out Talk about a self-contained ecosystem: The pavilion grows its own produce and houses the **Farmer's Market** food court, composed of a dozen or so stands: a soup-and-salad stand, bakery (with great jumbo-size cinnamon rolls and corn muffins before 11 AM and brownies and cheesecake afterward), barbecue store, sandwich stand, ice cream stand, potato store, and beverage house, which bolsters the usual soft drinks with milk shakes, buttermilk, vegetable juice, and exotic fruit nectars. The brownies are legendary, and Epcot staffers have been known to make a special trip to pick up some of the bakery's chocolate chip cookies. Just remember that at this pavilion, you must eat all your vegetables.

Journey into Imagination

The last of the big three pavilions on the west side, Journey into Imagination, sets your mind spinning. We'd say that it's a fitting climax to an Epcot Center visit except for the fact that you want to be as alert and sparkling as possible to enjoy the clever Journey into Imagination ride through the creative process, the 3-D film *Honey, I Shrunk the Audience,* and the Image Works, a computer-enhanced creative playground. Don't miss the quirky fountains outside: the Jellyfish Fountains, which spurt streams of water that flatten at the top into their namesake shape, and the Serpentine Fountains, whose random squirts arc from one garden bed to another, over paths and—most of the time—over the people standing on them. Count on spending at least 1½ hours here, more if you become addicted to the Stepping Tones section of the Image Works.

The stars of the pavilion are a jolly red-headed, full-bearded, top-hatted professorial type called Dreamfinder and his sidekick, the ever-inquisitive, pop-eyed purple dragon, Figment (who often show up outside the pavilions to welcome visitors). They also guide you on the **Journey into Imagination Ride,** a dreamy exploration of how creativity works. It begins with Dreamfinder's creating this Figment of his imagination, by combining a lizard's body, a crocodile's nose, a goat's horns, two big yellow eyes, two small wings, and an ineffable sense of wonder. Your most important stop is the Dreamport, which stores data collected by the senses for use by the imagination. Subsequent scenes show the data being spun into dreams that influence all areas of life, from science and technology to literature and the performing arts. Laser beams zing back and forth, lightning crackles, letters leap out of a giant typewriter, and an iridescent painting unfolds across a wall. Smile when you see flashing lights (about ¾ of the way through the ride)—you're on candid camera. You'll see the results at the end of the ride. *Length: 13 min. Crowds: Steady during crowded periods. Strategy: Go early or late. Audience: All ages. Rating:* ★★★

No other theme park has anything that compares with the **Image Works,** an electronic funhouse crammed with interactive games and wizardry that will give your imagination a real workout. There's the Electronic Philharmonic (best done with a partner), in which you can take turns conducting an orchestra; you wave your hands over a console to increase or decrease the sound of an indicated batch of musical instruments. These, in turn, are spotlighted on a giant screen so that everyone can tune in. At the Magic Palette, you can use an electronic paintbrush to paint video images and washes of color that resemble psychedelic northern lights. Jumping up and down on the magic carpet at the Stepping Tones produces lights and music; each hexagonal splotch of colored light corresponds to a sound—a drumroll, a harp throb, a choral blast—and with a little bit of fancy dancing, you can create an étude. Though it's lots of fun to try out all the activities, it's equally entertaining to watch other people, too. *Allow at least 1/2 hour. Crowds: Thick in late morning and afternoon, but there's plenty of room. Strategy: Go during busy periods; because there's a separate entrance, you don't have to enter through the Journey into Imagination ride. Audience: All ages. Rating:* ★★★

Late last year, *Honey, I Shrunk the Audience* replaced *Captain EO,* the longtime favorite featuring Michael Jackson. The new 3-D thriller utilizes the futuristic shrinking technologies demonstrated in two hit films with Rick Moranis. The auditorium is filled with special in-theater effects, moving seats, and 3-D film technology developed by Walt Disney Studios. *Duration: 14 min. Crowds: It's a new attraction, so expect to wait. Strategy: Go early or late. Audience: All but the youngest children. Rating:* ★★

World Showcase The 40-acre World Showcase Lagoon is 1⅓ miles around, but in that space, you circumnavigate the globe, or at least explore it, in pavilions representing 11 different countries in Europe, Asia, North Africa, and the Americas. In these, native food, entertainment, art and handicrafts, and usually a multimedia presentation showcase the culture and people; architecture and landscaping re-create well-known landmarks. France has a scaled-down model of the Eiffel Tower, America's display is housed in Liberty Hall, Japan glories in a pagoda, Italy has a reproduction of Venice's Piazza San Marco, and Morocco's minaret is practically a landmark of its own. Impressive as they are by day, the structures are truly fantastical at night, when they are outlined in literally miles of tiny lights. Instead of amusement park rides, you have breathtaking films at the Canadian, Chinese, French, and Norwegian pavilions; several art exhibitions; and the chance to chat in the native language of the friendly foreign staff, all of whom are part of a Disney exchange program. Live entertainment is an integral part of the pavilions' presentations.

The focal point of World Showcase is the American Adventure. The pavilions of other countries fan out from both sides, encircling the lagoon. Counterclockwise from World Showcase Plaza as you enter from Future World are Canada, the United Kingdom, France, Morocco, Japan, the American Adventure, Italy, Germany, China, Norway, and Mexico.

Canada "Oh, it's just our Canadian outdoors," said a typically modest native guide upon being asked the model for the striking rocky chasm and tumbling waterfall that represent just one of the high points of Canada. The beautiful formal gardens do have an antecedent: Butchart Gardens, in Victoria, British Columbia. And so does the Hôtel du Canada, a French Gothic mansion with spires, turrets, and a mansard roof; anyone who's ever stayed at Quebec's Château Frontenac or Ottawa's Château Laurier will recognize the imposing style favored by architects of Canadian railroad hotels. Like the size of the Rocky Mountains and the Great Canadian North, the scale of the structures seems immense; unlike the real thing, it's managed with a trick called forced perspective, which exaggerates the smallness of the distant parts to make the entire thing look humongous. Another bit of design legerdemain: The World Showcase Rockies are made of chicken wire and painted concrete mounted on a movable platform similar to a parade float. Ah, wilderness!

The top attraction is the CircleVision film *O Canada!* And that's just what you'll say after the stunning opening shot of the Royal Canadian Mounted Police literally surrounding you as they circle the screen. From there, you whoosh over waterfalls, saunter through Montreal and Toronto, sneak up to bears and bison, mush behind a husky-pulled dog sled, and land pluck—or, should we say, puck—in the middle of a hockey game. This is a standing-only theater, with lean rails. *Duration: 17 min. Crowds: Can be thick in late afternoon. Strategy: Go in the morning or evening. Audience: All ages (but no strollers permitted and toddlers have to be held aloft to see). Rating:* ★★★

Canada also contains shops selling maple syrup, lumberjack shirts, and other trapper paraphernalia to help you survive in the Far North or even the Deep South.

Time Out Le Cellier, a buffeteria with some style—vaulted stone ceilings and a cozy subterranean air—serves hearty fare such as pork pie, poached fresh salmon, and bread custard with maple sauce.

United Kingdom Never has it been so easy to cross the English Channel. A pastiche of there-will-always-be-an-England architecture, the United Kingdom rambles between the elegant mansions lining a London square to the bustling, half-timbered shops of a village High Street to the thatched-roof cottages from the countryside (their thatch made of plastic broom bristles in consideration of local fire regulations). And of course there's a pair of the scarlet phone booths that used to be found all over the United Kingdom, now on their way to being historic relics. The pavilion has no single major attraction. Instead, you can wander through shops selling tea and tea accessories, Welsh handicrafts, Royal Doulton figurines, and woolens and tartans from Pringle of Scotland; Lords and Ladies sells fragrances, bath accessories, and heraldic plaques (only the British would see a connection between these three). Outside, the strolling Old Globe Players coax audience members into participating in their definitely low-brow versions of Shakespeare.

Time Out Revive yourself with a pint of the best—although you'll be hard put to decide among the offerings—at **Rose & Crown Pub,** which also offers traditional afternoon tea on the outside terrace. The adjacent dining room serves more substantial fare (reservations required; *see* Chapter 8).

France You don't need the scaled-down model of the Eiffel Tower to tell you that you've arrived in France, specifically Paris. There's the poignant accordion music wafting out of concealed speakers, the trim sycamores pruned in the French style to develop signature knots at the end of each branch, and the delicious aromas surrounding the Boulangerie Pâtisserie bakeshop. This is the Paris of dreams, a Paris without the problems of parking, the numerous dogs, and all those irascible French people. (We can understand how Disney remedied the parking situation but still can't figure out where they found such a collection of pleasant, helpful, English-speaking natives who retain their inherited pertness.) It's a Paris of La Belle Epoque, "the beautiful age" just before World War I, when solid mansard-roofed mansions were crowned with iron filigree, when the least brick was drenched in romanticism. Here's a replica of the conservatorylike Les Halles—the iron-and-glass-barrel-roofed market that no longer exists in the City of Light; there's an arching footbridge, and all around, of course, there are shops. You can inspect artwork, Limoges porcelain, and crystal sold in the exquisite Plume et Palette, buy decorated writing paper Proust would have envied and a pen to match at La Signature, pick up a baking pan to make those famous madeleine cookies at Tout pour le Gourmet, and acquire a bottle of Bouzy Rouge to wash it down with at La Maison du Vin, where wine tastings are frequently held (there's a small charge).

The intimate Palais du Cinema, inspired by the royal theater at Fontainebleau, screens the film *Impressions de France,* a homage to the glories of the country. Shown on five screens spanning 200° in an air-conditioned, sit-down theater (no uncivilized lean bars here!), the film takes you to vineyards at harvesttime, Paris on Bastille Day, the Alps, Versailles, Normandy's Mont-St.-Michel, and the stunning châteaus of the Loire Valley. The musical accompaniment also hits high notes, with familiar segments from Offenbach, Debussy, and Saint-Saëns, all woven together by longtime Disney musician Buddy Baker. *Duration: 18 min. Crowds: Considerable from late morning through late afternoon. Strategy: Come before noon or after dinner. Audience: Adults. Rating:* ★★★

Time Out Stop in for a snack at **Boulangerie Pâtisserie** or **Au Petit Café,** a Parisian-style sidewalk café that serves sandwiches and omelets. *See also* Chapter 8.

Morocco You don't need a magic carpet to be instantaneously transported into an exotic culture—just walk through the pointed arches of the Bab Boujouloud gate into Morocco. A gift from the kingdom of Morocco, they are ornamented with beautiful wood carvings and encrusted with intricate mosaics made of 9 tons of handmade, hand-cut tiles; 19 native artisans were sent to Epcot Center to install them and to create the dusty stucco walls that seem to have withstood centuries of sandstorms. Look closely and you'll see that every tile has a small crack or some other imperfection, and no tile depicts a living creature—in deference to the Muslim belief that only Allah creates perfection and life.

Koutoubia Minaret, a replica of the prayer tower in Marrakesh, acts as Morocco's landmark. Traditional winding alleyways, each corner bursting with carpets, brasses, leatherwork, and other North African craftsmanship, lead to a beautifully tiled fountain and lush gardens. You can take a guided tour of the pavilion (inquire of any cast member), check out the ever-changing exhibit in the **Gallery of Arts and History,** and entertain yourself examining the wares at such shops as **Casablanca Carpets, Jewels of the Sahara, Brass Bazaar,** and **Berber Oasis.**

Japan A brilliant vermilion torii gate, derived from the design of Hiroshima Bay's much-photographed Itsukushima shrine, frames the World Showcase Lagoon and epitomizes the striking yet serene mood that pervades Japan. Disney horticulturists deserve a hand here for their achievement in constructing out of all-American plants and boulders a very Japanese landscape, complete with rocks, pebbled streams, pools, and hills. At sunset, or during a rainy dusk, the sharp edges of the evergreens and twisted branches of the corkscrew willows frame a perfect Japanese view of the five-story winged pagoda that is the heart of the pavilion. Based on the 8th-century Horyuji Temple in Nara, the brilliant blue pagoda has five levels, symbolizing the five elements of Buddhist belief—earth, water, fire, wind, sky. As you wander along the twisting paths, listen for the wind chimes and the soothing clack of the water mill, and watch a fiery sunset— Walt Disney World seems 5,000 miles away.

The peace is occasionally disturbed by performances on drums and gongs by the **Genroku Hanamai players.** Other entertainment is provided by demonstrations of traditional Japanese crafts such as kite making or snipping brown rice toffee into intricate shapes; these take place outdoors on the pavilion's plaza or in the **Bijutsu-Kan Gallery,** where there are also changing art exhibitions. **Mitsukoshi Department Store,** an immense three-centuries-old retail firm known as "Japan's Sears," carries everything from T-shirts to kimonos and row upon row of Japanese dolls.

Time Out Westerners with a yen for Japanese tastes will be satisfied here at **Yakitori House,** which serves broiled chicken and beef on skewers (a sort of Japanese shish kebab) and batter-fried seafood and vegetables, respectively, as well as such Japanese specialties as clear soup and pickled ginger. Despite the fact that this is basically a gussied-up fast-food place, the food tastes authentic and is reasonably priced. *See also* Chapter 8.

American At the American Adventure, housed in a scrupulous reproduc-
Adventure tion of Philadelphia's Liberty Hall, Disney's Imagineers prove that their kind of fantasy can beat reality hands-down. The 110,000 bricks, made by hand from soft pink Georgia clay, sheathe the familiar structure, which acts as a beacon for Epcot Center visitors across the lagoon. Talk about symbolism. And when those colored lights start flashing and the lasers zing from Spaceship Earth to Liberty Hall during the sound-and-light-and-fireworks IllumiNations show after dark, it's difficult not to feel patriotic.

The pavilion's superlative attraction is a 100-yard dash through history called the **American Adventure.** To the music of a piece called the "Golden Dream," performed by the Philadelphia Orchestra, it combines evocative sets, the world's largest rear-projection screen (72 feet in width), enormous movable stages, and 35 AudioAnimatronic players, which are some of the most life-like ever created—Ben Franklin even climbs up stairs. Beginning with the arrival of the Pilgrims at Plymouth Rock and their grueling first winter, Ben Franklin and a wry, pipe-smoking Mark Twain narrate the episodes—both praiseworthy and shameful—that have shaped the American spirit. Disney detail is so painstaking that you never feel rushed and, in fact, each speech and each scene seems polished like a little jewel. You feel the cold at Valley Forge and the triumph when Charles Lindbergh flies the Atlantic; are moved by Nez Perce Chief Joseph's forced abdication of Native American ancestral lands and by women's rights campaigner Susan B. Anthony's speech; laugh with Will Rogers's aphorisms and learn about the pain of the Depression through an affecting radio broadcast by Franklin Delano Roosevelt; and recognize such popular figures as John Wayne, Lucille Ball, Muhammed Ali, and, yes, Mickey Mouse, epitomizing the American spirit.

Duration: 30 min. Crowds: Large, but the theater is huge, so you can almost always get into the next show. Strategy: Go when everything else is busy and you want to sit down and cool off. Audience: All ages. Rating: ★★★

While waiting for the show to begin, be sure to read the quotes on the walls of the Hall of Presidents. They include thought-provoking comments from Wendell Wilkie, Jane Addams, Charles Lindbergh, Ayn Rand, Archibald MacLeish, and Thomas Wolfe, and they offer far from standard patriotic pablum. Directly opposite the pavilion, on the edge of the Lagoon, is the **American Gardens Theatre.** Until recently this was the venue for concerts and shows of the Yankee Doodle Dandy variety; it now hosts **The Magical World of Barbie,** a high-spirited song-and-dance-review about the world's most famous doll and her travels and adventures around the world (aha! the Epcot connection!). Barbie and her pals Ken and Skipper also make a daily appearance near the entrance to World Showcase.

Time Out   **Liberty Inn,** a counter-service restaurant, serves burgers, sandwiches, apple pie, and other all-American fare.

Italy   Saunter around the corner into the replica of Venice's Piazza San Marco and it's as if you've moved to the land of la dolce vita. In Italy, the star is the architecture: a reproduction of Venice's Doge's Palace that's true right down to the gold leaf on the ringlets of the angel perched 100 feet atop the Campanile; the seawall stained with age to whose barbershop-striped poles two gondolas are tethered; and the Romanesque columns, Byzantine mosaics, Gothic arches, and stone walls that have all been carefully "antiqued" to look historical. Mediterranean plantings such as cypress, kumquat, and olive trees add to the verisimilitude. Inside, shops sell Venetian beads and glasswork, leather purses and belts, Perugina cookies, and the company's signature chocolate "kisses."

Germany   Germany, a make-believe village that distills the best folk architecture from all over that country, is so jovial that you practially
expect the Seven Dwarfs to come heigh-ho-ing out to meet you.
Instead, you'll hear the hourly chimes from the specially
designed glockenspiel on the clock tower, musical toots and
tweets from multitudinous cuckoo clocks, folk tunes from the
spinning dolls and lambs sold at Der Teddybär, and the satisfied
grunts of hungry visitors chowing down on hearty German cooking. Other than the four-times-a-day oompah band show in the
Biergarten restaurant (*see* Chapter 8), Germany doesn't offer
any specific entertainment, but it does boast the most shops of
any pavilion. Our favorites: Die Weinachts Ecke, for nutcrackers
and other Old World Christmas ornaments; Süssigkeiten, for
cookies and not-to-be-believed animal crackers; and Volkskunst,
whose folk crafts collection includes cuckoo clocks that range
from hummingbird scale to the size of an eagle.

Time Out   The **Sommerfest** pretzel-and-bratwurst cart is one of the rare
snacking options in this part of the World.

China   At China, a shimmering red-and-gold, three-tiered replica of
Beijing's Temple of Heaven towers over a serene Chinese garden, an art gallery displaying treasures from the People's Republic, a spacious emporium devoted to Chinese goods, and two
restaurants. The garden, planted with rosebushes native to
China, a 100-year-old mulberry tree, and water oaks (whose
twisted branches look Asian but are actually Florida home-
grown), is one of the most peaceful spots in the World Showcase,
with its piped-in traditional Chinese music.

Think of the Temple of Heaven as an especially fitting movie
theater for showings of the ***Wonders of China***, a sensational
panorama of the land and people dramatically portrayed on a
360° CircleVision screen. The only drawback is that the theater
has no chairs; lean rails are provided. *Duration: 19 min. Crowds:
Steady from late morning through late afternoon, but the theater's
high capacity means you can usually get into the next show. Strategy: Go anytime. Audience: All ages (but no strollers permitted
and small children have to be held aloft to see). Rating:* ★★★

Time Out   **Lotus Blossom Café** has egg rolls and stir-fries that you can
wash down with cold TsingTao beer. The food is a nonthreaten-
ing introduction for Occidental tastes, but more sophisticated
palates will find it bland—and overpriced at that.

Norway   In Norway there are rough-hewn timbers and sharply pitched
roofs (so the snow will slip right off), softened and brightened
by bloom-stuffed window boxes, figured shutters, and lots of
smiling, blond and blue-eyed young Norwegians, all eager to
speak English and show off their country. The pavilion complex
contains a 14th-century stone fortress that mimics Oslo's Akershus, cobbled streets, rocky waterfalls, and a wood stave church,
modeled after one built in 1250, with wood dragons glaring from
the eaves. The church houses an exhibit called "To the Ends of

the Earth," which tells the story of two early 20th-century polar
expeditions by using vintage artifacts. It all puts you in the mood
to handle beautifully embroidered woolen sweaters (which sell
briskly despite Florida's heat), wood carvings, and glass art-
works in the pavilion's shops.

Norway also has a dandy boat ride: **Maelstrom.** Visitors pile into
16-passenger, dragon-headed longboats for a voyage through
time that, despite its scary name and encounters with evil trolls,
is actually more fascinating than frightful. The journey begins
in a 10th-century village where a boat, much like yours and the
ones used by Eric the Red, is being readied for a Viking voyage.
You glide steeply up through a mythical forest populated by
trolls, who cause the boat to plunge backward down a mild waterfall, then cruise amid the grandeur of the Geiranger fjord,
experience a storm in the North Sea, and, as the presence of oil
rigs signals a return to the 20th century, end up in a peaceful
coastal village. Disembarking, you proceed into a theater for a
quick and delightful film about Norway's scenic wonders, culture, and people. *Duration: 10 min. Crowds: Steady, with slow-
moving lines from late morning through early evening. Strategy:
Go in the evening. Audience: All ages. Rating:* ★★

Time Out Open-face sandwiches can be washed down with Norwegian
Ringnes beer at **Kringla Bakeri og Kafe.** Go early or late for
speediest service. (*See also* Chapter 8 Dining.)

Mexico Housed in a spectacular Mayan pyramid surrounded by a tangle
of tropical vegetation, Mexico contains the El Río del Tiempo
boat ride, an exhibit of pre-Columbian art, a restaurant, and, of
course, a shopping plaza, where you can unload many, many
pesos.

True to its name, **El Río del Tiempo** takes you on a trip down the
river of time. Your journey from the jungles of the Yucatán to
modern-day Mexico City is enlivened by video images of feathered Toltec dancers, by Spanish-colonial AudioAnimatronic
dancing puppets, and by film clips of the cliff divers in Acapulco,
the speed boats in Manzanillo (ah, progress!), and snorkeling
around Isla Mujeres. The puppets are garish and reprise "It's a
Small World," the brain-numbing ditty. But this ride is
still one of the major attractions in World Showcase. *Duration:
9 min. Crowds: Long, slow-moving lines from late morning
through late afternoon. Strategy: Skip this one on a one-day first-
time visit. Audience: All ages. Rating:* ★

Modeled on the *mercado* (market) in the town of Taxco, **Plaza de
los Amigos** is well named: There are lots of friendly people—the
women dressed in off-the-shoulder ruffled peasant blouses and
bright skirts, the men in white shirts and dashing sashes—all
eager to sell you trinkets from a cluster of canopied carts. The
perimeter is rimmed with stores with tiled roofs, wrought-iron
balconies, and window boxes drooling flowers. What to buy?
Brightly colored paper blossoms, sombreros, baskets, pottery,

leather goods, and colorful papier-mâché piñatas, which are so popular that Epcot Center imports them by the truckload.

Time Out For burritos and margaritas, go outside to the counter-service **Cantina de San Angel.** (*See also* Chapter 8 Dining.)

Dining

In World Showcase every pavilion sponsors at least one and often two or even three eateries. Where there's a choice, it is between a full-service restaurant with commensurately higher prices, a more affordable ethnic fast-food spot, and carts and shops selling snacks ranging from French pastries to Japanese ices—whatever's appropriate to the pavilion. Reservations are essential at the formal restaurants (*see* Visitor Information and Reservations, *above*, and Chapter 8).

Future World is not bursting with eateries. You won't starve here, but you do need to plan ahead. In addition to the counter-service spots, your options include **The Land Grille Room** in the Land pavilion, a revolving restaurant that serves solid American food, and **Coral Reef,** a seafood restaurant in the Living Seas with a windowed wall onto the pavilion's enormous aquarium. For other Epcot Center sit-down dining options, *see* Chapter 8.

Entertainment

Above the Lagoon **After Dark** First there are the all-out spectaculars we've come to expect at the Disney parks. Figuring "Why waste a perfectly good lagoon," Walt Disney World uses its watery stage for the spectacular **IllumiNations** show every night a half hour before closing. Be sure to stick around. Lasers, lights, fireworks, fountains, and music from every host nation fill the air over the lagoon; the show is so over the top that it's got to be seen to be believed. Although there's generally good viewing from all around the lagoon, the best spots are on the bridge between France and the United Kingdom, the promenade in front of Canada and Norway, and the bridge between China and Germany, which will give you a clear shot, unobstructed by trees. A sweet touch after the show: Concealed loudspeakers play the theme from "It's a Small World" manipulated into salsa, polka, waltz, and even—believe it or not—Asian rhythms. Talk about a total experience.

In the Day In its never-ending attempt to widen the audience appeal at Epcot Center, Disney is experimenting with Magic Kingdom–like entertainment shows. At press time, **Splashtacular,** a musical extravaganza featuring fireworks, jet-powered cannons that spray water 150 feet high, and 50 dancers and characters including Mickey Mouse, had just debuted. Spaceship Earth serves as the backdrop for the 20-minute show, which is performed five times a day.

At the Pavilions Some of the most enjoyable entertainment takes place outside the national pavilions in their courtyards and along the promenade by the lagoon. Live shows with actors, dancers, singers, mime routines, and demonstrations of folk arts and crafts are presented at varying times of day; get times from the WorldKey terminals in Earth Station or look for signs posted outside the pavilions. Italy's farcical **Commedia di Bologna,** France's **Theatre du Fromage,** and the United Kingdom's **Old Globe Players** each enlist audience members as heroes and villains, princes and princesses, to the hilarity of all. Near American Adventure, on the new America Gardens Stage, the **Magical World of Barbie** is a 30-minute musical that follows Barbie and her friends on a whirlwind tour of four continents. The humorous show features 18 singers and dancers and is performed five times a day, Wednesday through Sunday.

Shopping

Frankly, it's difficult to spend money at Future World. True, there are all sorts of kitchen- and garden-related knickknacks at The Land's **Green Thumb Emporium** and marine merchandise at Living Seas, but after that the pickings are slim indeed. The standard range of Epcot Center logo souvenirs is available at the **Centorium**, and you can pick up an aid to healthy living, including sweats emblazoned with Disney characters working up a sweat, at **Well & Goods Limited** in the Wonders of Life. But we suggest you save your shekels for the souks of World Showcase.

World Showcase is nothing if not crammed with souvenirs, because each pavilion shelters shops galore (most of them described in the pavilion's text). Many of their wares are also sold in shop branches and department stores around the United States. But among the more exotic items are leather belts and purses from Morocco's **Tangier Traders**, beautiful writing paper from **Plume et Palette** in France, heraldic plaques at **Lords and Ladies** in the United Kingdom, Inuit and Native American crafts at **Northwest Mercantile** in Canada, nutcrackers at **Die Weinachts Ecke** in Germany, piñatas at **Plaza de los Amigos** in Mexico, and kimonoed and obi-sashed dolls at **Mitsukoshi** in Japan.

Access for Travelers with Disabilities

Accessibility standards in this park are high. Many attractions and most restaurants and shops are fully wheelchair accessible. Not only does the *Guidebook for Guests with Hearing Impairments* give scripts and story lines for all Epcot Center attractions with sound tracks, but also personal translator units can be rented ($4 plus $40 deposit) to amplify sound in some of the theater shows.

Attractions To ride the **Spaceship Earth ride,** you must be able to walk four
Future World steps and transfer to a ride vehicle; in the unusual case that emergency evacuation may be necessary, it is by way of stairs. Service animals are not appropriate. Although much of the enchantment is in the visual details, the Walter Cronkite narration is interesting as well. The Epcot Outreach resource center here is wheelchair accessible. **Universe of Energy** is accessible to guests using standard wheelchairs and those who can transfer to them; especially because this is one of the attractions whose

sound track is amplified by rental personal translator units, it is slightly more interesting to those with hearing impairments than to those with visual impairments. In **Wonders of Life,** Cranium Command, the *Making of Me*, Goofy about Health, and the Anacomical Theater are all totally wheelchair accessible, with special seating sections for guests using wheelchairs. Guests with visual impairments may wish to skip Goofy about Health; Cranium Command and the *Making of Me* are both covered in the guidebook for guests with hearing impairments. To ride the turbulent Body Wars, you must transfer to a ride seat; those who lack upper-body strength should request extra shoulder restraints. It's inappropriate for service animals. **Horizons** is accessible by guests who can walk three paces and step up one step. Service animals should not ride. **World of Motion** requires guests using oversize wheelchairs or scooters to transfer to Disney chairs; lock your brakes. In **Living Seas,** guests using wheelchairs typically bypass the three-minute ride and move directly into the SeaBase Alpha and aquarium area—the best part of the pavilion. In **The Land,** the Harvest Theater, Food Rocks, and the Greenhouse Tour are completely wheelchair accessible. Rental personal translator units amplify sound in the Harvest Theater film *Symbiosis*, and those who can read lips will enjoy the Greenhouse Tour. As for the Listen to the Land boat ride, guests using an oversize wheelchair or a scooter must transfer to a Disney chair. At **Journey into Imagination,** the ride requires guests to take three steps and step up into a ride vehicle. The Magic Eye theater, where *Honey, I Shrunk the Audience* was being screened at press time, is completely accessible. The hands-on activities of Image Works are wheelchair accessible; there's something for everyone in here.

World Showcase   Most people stroll about Epcot Center, but there are two forms of transportation here: Friendship boats, which require guests using oversize wheelchairs or scooters to transfer to Disney chairs, and the omnibuses that chug along the promenade, which require guests to walk up four steps and have a folding wheelchair. The **American Adventure, France, China,** and **Canada** are all wheelchair accessible; personal translator units amplify the sound tracks here. **Germany, Italy, Japan, Morocco,** and the **United Kingdom** all have live entertainment, most with strong aural as well as visual elements; the plaza areas where the shows are presented are wheelchair accessible. In **Norway,** you must be able to step down into and up out of a boat to ride the Maelstrom, and an emergency evacuation would require the use of stairs; service animals should not ride. In **Mexico,** the El Río del Tiempo boat ride is accessible to guests using wheelchairs, but those using a scooter or oversize chair must transfer to a Disney model.

Entertainment   Certain areas along the lagoon's edge at Showcase Plaza, the United Kingdom, and Italy are reserved for guests using wheelchairs during Splashtacular shows and IllumiNations.

Shops and Restaurants   With a few exceptions, all are wheelchair accessible. In both the Land Grille Room and Living Seas' Coral Reef Restaurant, only one level is accessible to guests using wheelchairs, and France's Bistro de Paris is accessible only via staircase.

Information *See* Hints for Travelers with Disabilities in Chapter 1 and Access for Travelers with Disabilities at the beginning of this chapter.

Disney-MGM Studios Theme Park

When Walt Disney company chairman Michael Eisner opened Disney-MGM Studios in May 1989, he welcomed visitors to "the Hollywood that never was and always will be." Inspired by southern California's highly successful Universal Studios tour (an even more successful version of which is just down I–4), Disney-MGM combined Disney detail with MGM's motion-picture expertise in an amalgamation that blends theme park with fully functioning movie and television production center, breathtaking rides with instructional tours, nostalgia with high-tech wonders.

The rosy-hued view of the moviemaking business takes place in a dreamy stage set from the 1930s, amid sleek art moderne buildings in pastel colors, funky diners, kitschy decorations, and sculptured gardens populated by roving actors playing, well, roving actors. Thanks to a rich library of film scores, Disney-MGM is permeated with music, all familiar, all happy, all evoking the magic of the movies and all constantly burbling through the camouflaged loudspeakers at a volume just right for humming along. And watching over all, like the penthouse suite of a benevolent genie, is the Earfful Tower, a 13-story water tower adorned with a mousketeer hat.

Although some of the attractions will interest young children, Disney-MGM is really best for teenagers old enough to watch old movies on television and catch the cinematic references. Not quite as fantasy oriented as the Magic Kingdom or as earnestly educational as Epcot Center, Disney-MGM could almost be said to have attitude. Not a lot, mind you, but enough to add a little sizzle to the steak.

Lights, camera, aaaaand action!

Essential Information

Getting Around Inside Disney-MGM Studios Theme Park, distances are small and walking is the optimal way to get around.

Tourist Information The **Crossroads of the World** kiosk in the Entrance Plaza dispenses maps, entertainment schedules, brochures, and the like. Take specific questions to **Guest Relations**, inside the turnstiles on the left side of the Entrance Plaza.

The **Production Information Window** (tel. 407/560–4651), also in the Entrance Plaza, is the place to find out what's being taped when and how to get into the audience.

At the corner where Hollywood Boulevard intersects with Sunset Boulevard is the **Studios Tip Board**, a large chalkboard with constantly updated information about attractions' wait time—reliable except for those moments when everyone follows the "See It Now!" advice and the line immediately triples. Studio staffers are on hand.

Reservations Make dining reservations at the Hollywood Junction kiosk, located just to the right of the Studio Tip Board at the intersection of Hollywood and Sunset boulevards. If you're staying at one of the Disney hotels, you can make reservations one to three days in advance (tel. 407/824–4321). Reservations are also required for the popular Aladdin's Breakfast Adventure, held each morning from 8:30 AM to 10:30 AM at Aladdin's Soundstage Restaurant (tel. 407/824–4321). Disney resort guests can reserve seats through their hotel's guest services desk.

Services
Baby Care At the small Baby Care Center, you'll find facilities for nursing as well as **formula, baby food, pacifiers,** and **disposable diapers** for sale. There are **changing tables** here and in all women's rooms and some men's rooms. You can also buy disposable diapers in the Guest Services building. Oscar's, just inside the entrance turnstiles and to the right, is the place for **stroller rentals** ($1 rental fee; $5 deposit required).

Cameras and Film If you want something more than a disposable Kodak Fun Saver camera, walk through the aperture-shaped door of the Darkroom on Hollywood Boulevard, and borrow a Kodak **disk camera** (you just have to buy the film) or rent a **35mm camera** or **video camcorder** ($5 and $40, respectively; refundable $100–$800 deposit required).

For **minor camera repairs,** the Darkroom is the place.

Drop off your film at the Darkroom for **one-hour film developing** or at any Photo Express container (look for signs) for two-hour film developing; you can pick up your pictures at the Darkroom or have them delivered to your hotel if you're staying on-site.

First Aid It's in the Entrance Plaza adjoining Guest Services.

Lockers You'll find them alongside Oscar's Classic Car Souvenirs, to the right of the Entrance Plaza after you pass through the turnstiles.

Lost Children and Adults If you're worried about your children getting lost, get them name tags at Guest Services. If you do get separated, ask any cast member before you panic; lost children's logbooks are kept (at Guest Services).

Guest Services also has a computerized Message Center, where notes can be left for traveling companions not only at Disney-MGM but also at other parks.

Lost and Found Report your loss or find at Guest Services in the Entrance Plaza. If nobody claims what you turn in, you may get to keep it.

Money There is an ATM near the Production Information Window, outside Disney-MGM's Entrance Plaza. Currency exchange is available at the Guest Relations window.

Package Ask the shop clerk to forward any large purchase you make to
Pickup Guest Services in the Entrance Plaza so you won't have to carry
it around all day. (Allow three hours.)

Wheelchair Go to Oscar's, to your right in the Entrance Plaza ($5 plus $1
Rentals deposit); Oscar's also has motor-powered chairs ($25 plus $20
deposit). No electric scooters are available in this park. If your
rental needs replacing, ask a host or hostess.

Strategies for Your Visit

Blitz Tour Pick up an entertainment schedule on your way into the park.
Then run, do not walk, right up Hollywood Boulevard, hang a
right at Sunset Boulevard, and dash to MGM's newest attraction, the 13-story **Twilight Zone Tower of Terror.** (You won't be
the only one with this plan, so if the lines look too awful, consider
swinging back during the quieter evening hours.) Next, head
back to the Chinese Theater for the **Great Movie Ride.** It'll put
you in the mood for a day at the Disney-MGM Studios like nothing else—and help you brush up on the songs pouring out of the
hidden speakers. There's nothing like having a bunch of tunes
to whistle while standing in line. So suitably armed, head to the
Backstage Studio Tour and spend the rest of the morning backstage and **Inside the Magic.**

Beat the crowds to an early lunch at one of the lakeside beaner-
ies. Keep your eyes tuned to the Indiana Jones Epic Stunt Spectacular and SuperStar Television schedules. As soon as they
have magnetized enough people, take your cue and zip over to
the **Monster Sound Show.** Nothing like some simple arithmetic
to realize that 2,000 seats in the Indiana Jones amphitheater and
1,000 seats at SuperStar Television won't fit into the 270 seats
at the Monster Sound Show without one humongous line, right?
This way, you avoid it. *Then* you can go to **SuperStar Television.**
However, save Indiana for later—it's especially dramatic at
night.

Instead, amble over to **Jim Henson's Muppet*Vision,** checking
the lines at **Star Tours** on the way. If you can't see a line, nip in
now. If the line looks appalling, the Muppets are a great conso-
lation prize. Especially because Muppet*Vision lets out in a back
corner and while everyone is milling around and thinking of
wandering up New York Street, *you* can whip right back to Star
Tours for a second try.

You'll need a little downtime after Star Tours. Take the opportunity to explore **Hollywood Boulevard** (don't save the shops
until closing time because they'll be mobbed), grab an ice cream
at Gertie's, and catch the show at the **Theater of the Stars.** That
will put you in the right mood for the **Magic of Disney Animation,**
and the time will be right, too—the crowds here will have begun
to thin but the animators won't have gone home yet. Spend all
the time you want but make sure that you catch the last show at
the **Indiana Jones Epic Stunt Spectacular.** We love the way the
idol's eyes glow in the dusk, and the gobs of flame from the ex-
ploding truck make you understand just why this attraction is

called "spectacular." Then there's the music, which will carry you all the way back to the parking lots. Remember to turn at the gate for one last look at the Earfful Tower, whose perky appendages are outlined in gold lights.

Exploring Disney-MGM Studios Theme Park

Disney-MGM Studios is divided into six sightseeing clusters. Hollywood Boulevard is the main artery to the heart of the park: the glistening red-and-gold, multiturreted replica of Grauman's Chinese Theater, home of the Great Movie Ride. Encircling it in a roughly counterclockwise fashion are Sunset Boulevard and the Twilight Zone of Terror; the Studio Courtyard, which houses the entrance to the Backstage Studio Tour, the Inside the Magic special effects and production tour, and the Magic of Disney Animation; the Backlot, which has Jim Henson's Muppet*Vision 3-D, and *Honey, I Shrunk the Kids* Movie Set Adventure playground; the Backlot Annex, containing the Indiana Jones Epic Stunt Spectacular and Star Tours; and—adjoining Hollywood Boulevard—Lakeside Circle, whose principal attractions include SuperStar Television and the Monster Sound Show.

Surprisingly, the entire park is rather small—only 110 acres, one-quarter the size of Universal Studios—with barely a dozen major attractions, as opposed to 45 in the Magic Kingdom and 23 in Epcot Center. When the lines are minimal, the park can be easily covered in a day with time for repeat rides. And even when the lines seem to stretch clear to Epcot Center, a little careful planning should allow you to see everything on one ticket.

Numbers in the margin correspond to points of interest on the Disney-MGM Studios map.

Hollywood Boulevard With its palm trees, pastel buildings, and flashy neon, Hollywood Boulevard paints a rosy picture of Tinseltown in the 1930s and 1940s. The sense of having walked right onto a movie set is enhanced by the art-deco storefronts, strolling brass bands, and roving actors dressed in costume and playing everything from would-be starlets to nefarious agents. They are frequently joined by characters from Disney movies new and old, who pose for pictures and sign autographs. *Beauty and the Beast*'s Belle is a favorite, as are Jafar, Princess Jasmine, and the Genie from *Aladdin.*

Hollywood Boulevard, like Main Street, is crammed with souvenir shops and memorabilia collections. Oscar's Classic Car Souvenirs & Super Service Station is crammed with fuel pump bubble-gum machines, photos of antique cars, and other automotive knickknacks. At Sid Cahuenga's One-of-a-Kind antiques and curios, you might find (and acquire) Brenda Vaccaro's shawl, Liberace's table napkins, or autographed stars' photos. Down the street at Cover Story, don the appropriate costume and have your picture put on the cover of a major magazine.

Time Out For a sweet burst of energy, snag a cinnamon swirl at **Starring Rolls,** a stand in the alley between the Brown Derby and Theater of the Stars. Or try the croissants, the turnovers, or the almost-authentic bagels.

At the head of Hollywood Boulevard is the fire-engine-red, pagodaed replica of Grauman's Chinese Theater, which houses the ❶ **Great Movie Ride.** Disney-MGM pulls out all the stops on this tour of great moments in film.

The lobby, really an ingenious way to spend time standing in line, slots you past such icons as Dorothy's ruby slippers from *The Wizard of Oz*, a carousel horse from *Mary Poppins*, and the piano played by Sam in *Casablanca*. You then shuffle into the preshow area, an enormous screening room with continuously running clips from *Mary Poppins*, *Raiders of the Lost Ark*, *Singin' in the Rain*, *Fantasia*, *Footlight Parade*, and, of course, *Casablanca*. (As the segment from *Raiders of the Lost Ark* comes on, kids who have already caught the Indiana Jones Epic Stunt Spectacular but not the original movie can be heard to say, "Say, that's the guy we saw today, right?") The line continues snaking through the preshow, which itself is so much fun that you almost resent that you'll miss favorite clips once the great red doors swing open and it's your turn to ride.

Disney cast members dressed in 1920s newsboy costumes usher you onto open trams and you're off on a tour—through AudioAnimatronics, scrim, smoke, and Disney magic—of cinematic climaxes. First comes the world of musical entertainment, with Gene Kelly clutching that immortal lamppost in one hand and a useless umbrella in the other as he sings the title song from *Singin' in the Rain* and Mary Poppins (with *her* umbrella) and her sooty admirers reprising "Chim-Chim-Cher-ee" among others. The lights dim and you move into gangsterland, with James Cagney snarling in *Public Enemy*. Then it's on to a western shootout à la John Wayne as Calamity Jane tries to rob the Miners' and Cattlemen's Bank and hijack the tram—and succeeds.

Nothing like a little time warp to bring justice. With pipes streaming fog and alarm klaxons whooping, the tram meets some of the slimier characters in *Alien* (look up for truly scary stuff) and then eases into the cobwebby, snake-ridden (and slithering) set of the Temple of Doom, where Calamity Jane attempts to bluff an idol threat—and gets vaporized.

Each time you think you've seen the best scene, the tram moves into another set: Tarzan yodels and swings on a vine overhead, then Bogey toasts Bergman in front of the plane to Lisbon. The finale has hundreds of robotic Munchkins cheerily enjoining you to "Follow the Yellow Brick Road," despite the cackling imprecations of the Wicked Witch of the West (check out Dorothy's tornado-tossed house—those on the right side of the tram can just spot the ruby slippers). The tram follows the Yellow Brick Road and there it is: Emerald City.

As icing on the cake, there's one more movie presentation with three screens all going at once to display yet more memorable

Disney-MGM Studios Theme Park

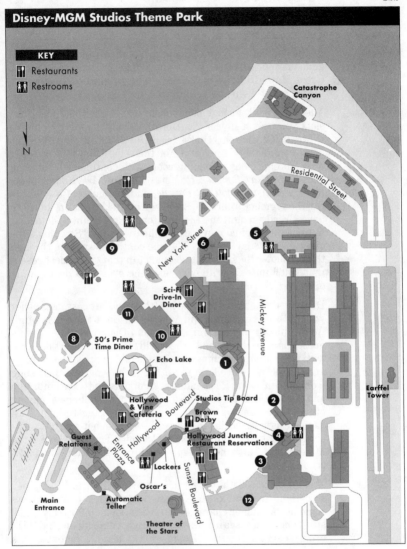

KEY

🚻 Restaurants

🚻 Restrooms

N

Catastrophe Canyon

Residential Street

New York Street

Sci-Fi Drive-In Diner

50's Prime Time Diner

Echo Lake

Hollywood & Vine Cafeteria

Hollywood Boulevard

Studios Tip Board

Brown Derby

Hollywood Junction Restaurant Reservations

Mickey Avenue

Earffel Tower

Guest Relations

Entrance Plaza

Lockers

Oscar's

Main Entrance

Automatic Teller

Theater of the Stars

Sunset Boulevard

Backstage Studio Tour, **5**

Great Movie Ride, **1**

Honey, I Shrunk the Kids Movie Set Adventure, **7**

Indiana Jones Epic Stunt Spectacular, **9**

Inside the Magic Special Effects and Production Tour, **6**

Jim Henson's Muppet*Vision 3-D, **8**

Magic of Disney Animation, **4**

Monster Sound Show, **12**

Star Tours, **10**

SuperStar Television, **11**

Twilight Zone Tower of Terror, **2**

Voyage of the Little Mermaid, **3**

moments, including great kisses ranging from Rhett Butler and Scarlett O'Hara embracing to Roger and Jessica Rabbit engaging in an animated smooch. Then the lights come up and the announcer calls you for the final scene: The Exit. *Duration: 22 min. Crowds: Steady and large all day long; when the inside lines start spilling out the door, expect at least a 25-min wait. Strategy: Go first thing in the morning or at the end of the day (then if the lines still look long, ask before you slink away discouraged—Disney staffers often "stack" people up outside to clear up the crowds inside and to prepare for closing). Audience: All but young children (for whom it may be too intense). Rating:* ★★★

Sunset Boulevard This newest of Disney-MGM's theme avenues pays tribute to famous Hollywood monuments with facades derived from the Carthay Circle, the Beverly Wilshire Theatre, and other City of Angels landmarks. The Theater of the Stars, for example, is reminiscent of the famed Hollywood Bowl; rather than hosting rock acts, however, the 1,500-seat covered amphitheater is home to a musical production called *Beauty and the Beast–Live on Stage*. As guests turn onto Sunset Boulevard from Hollywood Boulevard, first stop for the hungry hordes is Hollywood Junction Station, where reservations can be made for restaurants throughout the park. Starstruck shoppers should find something to feed their fandom at Legends of Hollywood, which brims with books, videos, and posters of classic films, while the young at heart should stop by Once Upon A Time, which showcases displays of vintage character toys.

Time Out For a lengthy lineup of fast-food items, try the **Sunset Ranch Market**. Headliners include fresh fruit from a farmer's stand, Rosie's red hot dogs, and Catalina Eddie's frozen yogurt.

All the crowds, however, are most likely looking for the park's **❷** newest excuse for an adrenaline rush: the **Twilight Zone Tower of Terror,** due to open in late 1994. Ominously overlooking Sunset Boulevard is a 13-story structure that's reputedly the now-deserted Hollywood Tower Hotel. You take an eerie stroll through the dimly lighted lobby and decaying library to the boiler room before boarding the hotel's giant "elevator." As you head upward past seemingly deserted hallways, ghostly former residents appear around you, until suddenly—faster than you can say "where's Rod Serling?"—the creaking vehicle abruptly plunges downward in a terrifying, 130-foot free-fall drop! *Duration: 10 min. Crowds: Since it's a new attraction, expect some horrendous lines; the last major Disney thrill ride to open, Splash Mountain, saw 1¹/₂–2 hr waits in its first months. Strategy: Go early or, even better, wait until the evening dinner hours when the crowds thin out. Audience: Older children and adults; no pregnant women or guests with back, neck, or heart problems. Rating:* ★★★

Studio Courtyard As you exit Sunset Boulevard, veer right through the high-arched gateway to the Studio Courtyard. You're now at one end of Mickey Avenue and straight ahead are the Voyage of the Little Mermaid, the Magic of Disney Animation, and the Backstage Studio Tour, often combined with Inside the Magic at the other end of Mickey Avenue for a two-hour whiz-bang revelation of cinematic secrets.

Time Out   The Studio Courtyard also houses **Catwalk Bar** and **Soundstage Restaurant,** a food court in an aptly named barn of a building with an attic's worth of furniture dangling from the ceiling. This stuff would be a great source of conversation—if you could hear anything. Burgers, fajitas, chef's salads, and the like are on the menu.

A boxy building on the left invites you to join Ariel, Sebastian, **❸** and the underwater gang in the **Voyage of the Little Mermaid** stage show, which condenses the movie into a marathon presentation of the greatest hits. In an admirable effort at verisimilitude, a fine mist sprays the stage; visitors sitting in the front rows will get refreshed. *Duration: 15 min. Crowds: Steady all day. Strategy: Go first thing in the morning or wait until the stroller brigade's exodus after 5. Audience: All ages. Rating:* ★★★

❹ The **Magic of Disney Animation,** a self-guided tour through the Disney animation process, is one of the funniest and most engaging attractions at the park. More than any backstage tour, more than any revelation of stunt secrets, this tour truly takes you inside the magic as you follow the many steps of animation from concept to charisma.

Although you can move at your own pace, the staff tries to keep crowds to a minimum, so groups assemble in a lobby. Take the opportunity to check out the collection of drawings and original cels, which are the clear celluloid sheets on which the characters were drawn for *Snow White, Fantasia,* and other Disney classics. Here too are the Academy Awards that Disney has won for its animated films.

From the lobby, you segue into the Disney Animation Theater for a hilarious eight-minute film in which Walter Cronkite and Robin Williams explain animation basics. A *Peter Pan* sequel called *Back to Neverland*, with Walter Cronkite as Walter Cronkite and Robin Williams as a Little Lost Boy (the irrepressible Robin really wants it to be called *Peter Pan: First Blood*), it was almost impossible to film because the steadfast, avuncular Cronkite kept cracking up. You might too, if you suddenly discovered Tinkerbell in your jacket pocket. Robin Williams discovers the potential range of animation ("Hey," he proclaims as he's redrawn into a familiar rodent, "I can be a corporate symbol!") while we learn about cel making, layout artists, background artists, cleanup artists, sound effects, and more.

From the theater, you follow walkways with windows overlooking the working animation studios, where you see salaried Disney artists at their drafting tables doing everything you just learned about. Their desks are strewn with finished drawings of Aladdin, Genie, and other famous characters, and you can peer over their shoulders at soon-to-be-famous characters. This is better than magic—this is real.

Meanwhile, Robin and Walter continue their banter on overhead monitors, explaining the processes as you saunter from story room, where animators develop story lines; to the drawing boards, where ideas metamorphose from sketch to colorful characters; to the cleanup room, the special effects area, and the special camera that transfers drawings to cels. To produce one 24-minute film, the 70-plus members of the animation team must create 34,650 drawings and add scenes from at least 300 background paintings. No wonder everyone wears headphones, although one doubts they're listening to "Whistle While You Work."

The penultimate stop is a continuously running video, *Animators on Animation.* "You believe the character *is* alive," confesses one of the geeky-looking animators who so identify with their characters that they can take on their personalities. Watching a low-key, pleasant Asian man become the blowsy, evil Ursula from *The Little Mermaid* right before your eyes makes you wonder if pixie dust is in the air.

Disney knows how to make an exit, and with a valedictory quip from Robin Williams, you head into the Disney Classics Theater for a presentation of the best moments from animated films. It's fascinating to see the evolution of the art from the bright colors and straightforward drawings in *Snow White* and *Pinocchio* to the rainbow hues and complex panoramas of *Beauty and the Beast* and *Aladdin.* Best of all, you know that here the characters always will live happily ever after. *Duration: Usually around 30 min. Crowds: Steady all day. Strategy: Go in the morning or late afternoon, when you can get in with less waiting and still see the animators at work (they leave by 6 and are not always around on weekends). Audience: All but toddlers. Rating:* ★★★

❺ The **Backstage Studio Tour,** a combination tram ride and walking tour, takes you on a tour of the back-lot building blocks of movies: set design, costumes, props, lighting, and the de rigueur Catastrophe Canyon. Disney-MGM outdoes Universal Studios on this ride because it's got an ace in the hole: a real moviemaking environment. You literally ride through working offices, peering through windows as Foley artists mix sound, lighting crews sort cables, costumers stitch seams, and so on. The motor pool boasts the usual bunch of beat-up automobiles, including a series of old blue Plymouths from *Who Framed Roger Rabbit?* The greens department is a gardener's delight, with its elephant topiaries, trellised roses, and the faux tree trunk used in *Honey, I Shrunk the Kids;* most of the greens are used to camouflage unsightly parts of movie sets, so the next time you see a particularly verdant tree on film, think about what's behind it.

The residential street gives new meaning to the term "open house," as the tram winds past false fronts in styles ranging from Frank Lloyd Wright to generic suburban. New Yorkers will get the usual kick out of seeing the litter-free, graffiti-free depiction of their fair city on New York Street. The tram rumbles past the boneyard, where the helicopter from *Blue Thunder* and the orange-and-red Pacific Electric trolley car used in *Who*

Framed Roger Rabbit? are permanently parked; an egret (live, not animated) now uses the trolley car as its perch.

Then it's on to Catastrophe Canyon. The tram's announcer swears that the film that's supposedly shooting in there is taking a break. Not! The next thing you know, the tram is bouncing up and down in a simulated earthquake, an oil tanker explodes in gobs of smoke and flame, and a water tower crashes to the ground, touching off a flash flood, which douses the oil tanker but threatens to drown the tram. Although the earthquake is more like a shimmy, the water and fire provoke genuine screams. As the tram pulls out, you see the backstage workings of the catastrophe: The canyon is actually a mammoth steel slide wrapped in copper-colored cement, and the 70,000 gallons of flood water—enough to fill 10 Olympic-size swimming pools—is recycled 100 times a day, or every 3½ minutes.

Let your heartbeat slow down as the tram takes another pass through the Big Apple. This time you're close enough to see that brownstones, marble, brick, and stained glass are actually expertly painted two-dimensional facades of fiberglass and Styrofoam. Grips can slide the Empire State and Chrysler buildings out of the way anytime. Note the storefronts carefully; you'll encounter them again in a Bette Midler film on the Inside the Magic tour.

Hop off the tram and walk through the **Studio Showcase,** an exhibit of film and television memorabilia, including models from *The Nightmare Before Christmas* and the set from the "Tonight Show." Then follow Roger Rabbit's pink footsteps to the **Loony Bin,** where kids can have their picture taken in front of the directional signs indicating Thisaway and Thataway, or open all the Pandora's boxes of such sound effects as boinks, toots, squeaks, chugs, clunks, and speeding trains. Roger Rabbit souvenirs are sold here, as are palm buzzers and other magic tricks.

Duration: 25 min. Crowds: Steady through the afternoon, but lines seem to move quickly. Strategy: As you enter the tram, remember that people sitting on the left get seared and wet; people on the right get crushed as the people on the left leap into their laps. Go early. Closes at dusk. Audience: All but young children. Rating: ★★★

Time Out   The **Studio Catering Company Commissary** here will provide you with sustenance for the next tour: hot dogs, burgers, pizza, and fries.

❻   The **Inside the Magic Special Effects and Production Tour,** a walking tour, explains how clever cameramen make illusion seem like reality through camera angles, miniaturization, matte backgrounds, and a host of other magic tricks. While you're waiting in line, Goldie Hawn and Martin Short appear on overhead video screens. They host a humorous overview of the processes you're about to see. Then you're off to the first stop, an outdoor special-effects water tank. Here two willing-if-unwary members of the audience don bright yellow slickers. One gets to play the skipper of the ill-fated *SS Miss Fortune,* while the other unsuspecting soul assumes the role of submarine commander "Captain Duck," about to pilot his craft into battle. As the audience watches, the skipper nearly gets drowned in a thunderstorm, and the doughty Duck gets strafed, torpedoed, and doused with 400 gallons of water from a depth charge while a video records the scenario and plays it back with music and background.

To show how miniature props are filmed to look life-size, two children from the audience climb up on a hairy bumblebee to shoot a scene from *Honey, I Shrunk the Kids.* A matte, blue screen background is used to combine their scene with realistic shots of the bee's flight, and the audience sees the end result on overhead videos.

Three soundstages are used for filming the "Mickey Mouse Club," "Ed McMahon's Star Search," and assorted movies. Specially soundproofed catwalks let visitors eavesdrop as overhead video monitors explain what goes on. It takes five hours to shoot a 30-minute episode of the Mickey Mouse Club; most of the taping takes place in the afternoon and evening. "Star Search," on the other hand, tapes two or three shows a day from summer through Thanksgiving.

Then it's on to the sets of a complicated and hilarious sequence from *The Lottery,* a short film in which Bette Midler chases a pigeon that has stolen her winning $1-million lottery ticket. (Now New Yorkers can feel aggrieved at the graffiti-covered subway car, since no one else around the country realizes that the subways are now mostly graffiti free.) The actual sequence is subsequently shown on overhead video screens. The 2½-minute scene took five days and 100 people to create; the work was done exclusively at Disney-MGM Studios, and you may recognize many of the scenes from the Backstage Studio Tour.

In the Post-Production area, George Lucas, aided by R2D2 and C3PO, explains how computers are used for editing, and Mel Gibson and PeeWee Herman switch voices in a lecture on sound tracks. As a finale, you stop in at the Walt Disney Theater to rest your feet while Michael Eisner previews upcoming Disney and Touchstone films.

Duration: 1 hr. Crowds: Large but constantly moving. Strategy: Don't assume that crawling into the tour guide's back pocket will give you the best view. Stay in the middle to remain in the center of the action, and aim for the right if you want a front-row view and the left if you want to stay dry. Audience: Older children and adults. Rating: ★★★

The Backlot   A rather amorphous area built around New York Street, the Backlot merges so seamlessly into the Post-Production area that it's almost easier to consider it a post-post-production area rather than a separate section. In addition to New York Street sets that can be toured on foot as long as crews aren't filming—and that are worth it, for the wealth of detail to be seen in the store windows—the Backlot also comprises a stage show by the Teenage Mutant Ninja Turtles, another by the Muppets, Jim

Henson's Muppet*Vision 3-D, and the *Honey, I Shrunk the Kids* Movie Set Adventure, a playground.

❼ Take a left at the corner of Mickey Avenue and New York Street and let the kids run free in the ***Honey, I Shrunk the Kids Movie Set Adventure,*** a state-of-the-art playground based on the movie about Lilliputian kids in a larger-than-life world. They can slide down a gigantic blade of grass, crawl through caves, climb a mushroom mountain, inhale the scent of a humongous plant (and have it spit water back in your face), and dodge sprinklers set in the resilient flooring, which is made of ground-up tires. All the requisite playground equipment is present: net climbs, ball crawls, ingenious caves and slides, and so on. Because this is an enclosed area, there's often a line to get in, which seems rather restrictive for a playground. *Duration: Up to you. Crowds: Steady. Strategy: Come early or come back when there's no line. Audience: Children and those who love them. Rating:* ★★★

❽ You don't have to be a Piggyphile to get a kick out of **Jim Henson's Muppet*Vision 3-D,** a combination of 3-D movie and musical revue. In the waiting area, Muppet movie posters advertise Miss Piggy in *Star Chores* ("She swore she'd never sign another autograph") and *To Have and Have More* ("Here's looking at you, pig"), and Kermit the Frog in an Arnold Schwarzenegger parody, *Kürmit the Amphibean* (starring Kürmit der Frög, "so mean, he's green"). The theater was constructed especially for this show, with special effects built into the walls. All the Muppet characters make an appearance, with Miss Piggy in the role of the Statue of Liberty. Guided by a new character, Waldo the spirit of 3-D, the technology is at its best here. In fact, the 3-D effects are coordinated with other sensory stimulation so you're never sure what's coming off the screen and what's being shot out of vents in the ceiling and walls. An equal-effect theater, the house has no bad seats. *Duration: 10-min preshow, 20-min show. Crowds: Steady from morning through late afternoon, and because the waiting area is carefully hidden, you don't know how long the line is until you've waited for too long. Strategy: Go early or late. Audience: All ages. Rating:* ★★★

Look for the candy pink Mercedes a few yards from the Miss Piggy Statue of Liberty. It's parked across from the **Studio Arcade,** Disney-MGM's collection of video games, which replaced the collection of movie and TV props now in the Studio Showcase. Older kids will enjoy a stop here, perhaps while adults browse in nearby shops.

Backlot Annex Segue from the Backlot into the Backlot Annex, more of an offshoot of Lakeside Circle. You can be sure the crowds are not swarming for the fast-food Backlot Express, which is nothing special. No, the attractions are two of the park's most high-powered: the Indiana Jones Epic Stunt Spectacular and Star Tours.

❾ The rousing theme music from the Indiana Jones movies blares out like a clarion call, summoning visitors to see the **Indiana Jones Epic Stunt Spectacular,** featuring the stunt choreography of veteran coordinator Glenn Randall (*Raiders of the Lost Ark,*

Indiana Jones and the Temple of Doom, E.T., and *Jewel of the Nile* are among his credits). Presented in a 2,200-seat amphitheater, the show starts with a series of near-death encounters in an ancient Mayan temple. Clad in his signature fedora and looking cute enough for front-row viewers to consider painting "Love You" on their eyelids just like Professor Jones's adoring student did in *Raiders of the Lost Ark*, Indiana slides down a rope from the ceiling, dodges spears that shoot up from the floor, avoids getting chopped by booby-trapped idols, and snags a forbidden gemstone, setting off a gigantic boulder that threatens to render him two-dimensional.

It's hard to top that opener, but Randall and his pals do just that with the help of 10 audience participants ("Okay, I need some rowdy people," the casting director calls). While the lucky few demonstrate their rowdiness, behind them the set crew casually wheels off the entire temple (two people roll the boulder like a giant beach ball) and replaces it with a Cairo street, circa 1940. Nasty Ninja-Nazi stuntmen roll out a mat and bounce around performing flips and throws in the background. This is one of those times when it's better to be in the audience.

The scene they're working up to takes place on a busy Cairo street, down which saunter Indy and his redoubtable girlfriend, Marian Ravenwood, portrayed by a Karen Allen lookalike. She is to be kidnapped and tossed in a truck while Indy fights his way free with bullwhip and gun and bad guys tumble from every corner and cornice. Motorcycles buzz around, the street becomes a shambles, and as a stunning climax, the truck carrying Marian flips and bursts into flame. Viewers sitting up front can feel the heat.

Randall et al. do a great job at explaining the stunts. The audience sees how they are set up, watches the stars practice them in slow motion, and learns how cameras are camouflaged behind imitation rocks for trick shots. Only one stunt remains a secret: How do Indy and Marian escape the explosion? That's what keeps 'em coming back.

Duration: 30 min. Crowds: Large, but the theater's high capacity means that everyone who wants to get in usually does. Strategy: Go at night, when the idols' eyes glow red. Audience: All but young children. Rating: ★★★

Time Out At the **Backlot Express**, you don't need a reservation to chow down on the burgers, fajitas, and chef's salads.

While everyone else is heading to the stunt show, make tracks ❿ for **Star Tours,** the hands-down showstopper flight simulator. Flight simulators, on which many of the latest theme park rides are based, were once used simply to train military and commercial airline pilots. But when their film is synchronized to movement, as of a ride vehicle in theme parks, guests truly feel what they see. Guarded by an otherworldly metallic monster, Star Tours is inspired by the *Star Wars* films. "May the force be with you," says the attendant on duty, " 'cause I won't be!" Piloted by

Star Wars characters R2D2 and C3PO, the 40-passenger Star-Speeder that you board is supposed to take off on a routine flight to the moon of Endor. But with R2D2 at the helm, things quickly go awry: You shoot into deep space, dodge giant ice crystals and comet debris, innocently bumble into an intergalactic battle, and attempt to avoid laser-blasting fighters as you whiz through the canyons of some planetary city before coming to a heart-stopping halt.

Although the technology is the same as that of Body Wars in Epcot Center's Wonders of Life pavilion, the presentation is wittier and the ride is wilder. You don't "go" anywhere, as you do on a roller coaster; however, because your imagination and vision are engaged as you are tossed around, the experience is all-encompassing. Simply put, there's nothing like it—until, we have to say, you go on Back to the Future . . . The Ride, at Universal Studios. But that's almost too much for a first-timer, and this is just right.

Duration: 7 min. Crowds: Legendary, with near-perpetual 40–60 min waits. Strategy: Try shortly before closing time. Although you can always get in first thing in the morning, it'll spoil you for the rest of the park. When you line up to enter the simulation chamber, keep to the right to sit in the back rows (where you'll get a rougher ride), to the far left to sit up front (closer to the screen and therefore getting more realistic sensations). No pregnant women, children under 3, or guests with motion sickness or neck, back, or heart problems; children under 7 must be accompanied by an adult. Audience: Older children and adults. Rating: ★★★

Lakeside Circle Set off to the left, or west side, of Hollywood Boulevard, Lakeside Circle is an idealized California. In the center is cool blue Echo Lake, an oasis fringed with trees and benches and ringed with landmarks: pink and aqua restaurants trimmed in chrome (with sassy waitresses and television sets at the tables); Min and Bill's Dockside Diner, which offers fast food in a shipshape atmosphere; and Gertie, a Sinclair gas station dinosaur that dispenses ice cream, Disney souvenirs, and the occasional puff of smoke in true magic-dragon fashion. Look for Gertie's giant footprints in the sidewalk. On the north side of the pond are Lakeside Circle's two attractions: SuperStar Television and the Monster Sound Show.

⑪ "I need a woman over 21 who can tell a guy off," the **SuperStar Television** casting director proclaims, and at least 25 candidates scream for attention. Twenty-eight are chosen and through judicious dubbing appear to play the starring roles on shows from "I Love Lucy" to "Gilligan's Island."

While the volunteers are led off to makeup and costume, the audience files into a 1,000-seat theater reminiscent of the days of live television broadcasting. Most important, eight 6-foot-wide monitors hang in front of a stage that has three movable sets. Through blue-screen electronic techniques, the onstage action appears on the screen to have merged with clips from classic shows.

The pace is fast and furious, and a good director can make all the difference, coaching the volunteer actors with words and body language, then running on to the next skit. Soap opera fans get a special kick from a particularly sensational love-triangle scene in "General Hospital." Then a woman volunteer, outfitted in white apron and tall white chef's hat, desperately tries to wrap chocolates on an ever-speedier assembly line in one of the best-known episodes from "I Love Lucy." Other scenes include the "Vonzells" singing "Da Doo Run Run" on "The Ed Sullivan Show," an extremely young New York Yankee (this role almost always goes to cute little kids, especially girls with pigtails) getting interviewed by Howard Cosell after hitting a grand slam homer, and Neil Armstrong landing on the moon and reading his famous "One step for a man, one giant step for mankind" line from a placard held by yet another volunteer.

Each show is flavored differently by the volunteer cast. It's not easy to get chosen—only about 12 out of 1,000 make it. To even the odds, arrive 15–30 minutes before starting time, go to the front of the waiting area, and let a staffer know that you would *love* to be in the show. Dressing outrageously and having a loud cheering section helps. By the way, unlike Indiana Jones volunteers, SuperStar actors can watch the action on monitors.

Duration: 30 min. Crowds: Large, but the large theater keeps waiting minimal. Audience: All but young children. Rating: ★★

Time Out　**Min & Bill's Dockside Diner** is the spot for sandwiches—step right up to the counter. Be sure to save room for "Ice Cream of Extinction" at **Gertie's.**

⑫　Despite its name, the **Monster Sound Show** is anything but scary. Rather, it's a delightful, multifaceted demonstration of the use of movie sound effects. The show features many of the gadgets created by soundmaster Jimmy Macdonald, who became the voice of Mickey Mouse during the 1940s and invented some 20,000 sound effects during his 45 years at Walt Disney Studios. Most qualify as gizmos—a metal sheet that, when rattled, sounds like thunder; a box of sand for footsteps on gravel; and other noises made from nails, straw, mud, leather, and other ordinary components.

The 270-seat theater is small enough for volunteer Foley artists (the movie name for sound effects specialists, named for Jack Foley, the man who created the system) to be seen as they dash around trying to coordinate their sound effects with the short movie being shown simultaneously. The audience sees the scene—a hilariously klutzy Chevy Chase playing an insurance man on a visit to a haunted house—three times: once with the original sounds, once without any sound as the Foleys-for-a-day try to fill in, and then once more with the volunteer product. Somehow the boinks and bangs never seem to come in on time. Gonnng!

The postshow is a treat consisting of hands-on exhibits called **SoundWorks.** There are buttons that go boing and knobs you push to alter your voice. Earie Encounters lets you imitate fly-ing-saucer sounds from the 1956 film *Forbidden Planet*. At Movie Mimics, you can try your chords at dubbing Mickey Mouse, Roger Rabbit, and other Disney heroes.

Soundsations is a "3-D audio" experience in which you enter a soundproofed room, don a pair of earphones, and . . . you're a movie executive on the first day of work at Walt Disney Studios. A face-to-face chat with Mickey Mouse is just one thrill; wait until you meet the studio barber. It's literally hair-raising. *Duration: as long as you're interested. Crowds: steady. Audience: all ages.* ★★★

Dining

Full-Service Restaurants Although the glow often gets tarnished at mealtime, Disney-MGM's full-service restaurants are so much fun that the magic continues. Once you're inside, that is. Unfortunately, visitors never seem to want to leave their tables—after all, would you if you could watch television monitors airing '50s sitcoms while chowing down on veal-and-shiitake-mushroom meatloaf? Consequently, the lines can be enormous and reservations are routinely late.

With its staff in black tie and its airy, palm-fronded room positively exuding suave, the 235-seat **Brown Derby** is one of the nicest places to eat in the park. (It's also one of the most expensive.) The Cobb Salad, a conglomeration of salad greens, tomato, bacon, turkey, egg, blue cheese, and avocado—invented at the restaurant's Hollywood namesake—is alive and well here, as you can see from the numerous orders getting tossed tableside. The all-California wine list is wide-ranging enough to keep an oenophile happy. And the butter comes in molds shaped like miniature derby hats. Patrons seated in booths can even have a '40s-style dial telephone brought to their tables.

You'll certainly want to spend a leisurely lunch at the **'50s Prime Time Café,** whose video screens constantly show sitcoms, whose place mats pose television trivia quizzes, and whose waitresses play "Mom" with convincing enthusiasm. The menu is what your own mom might have made were she a character on one of those video screens—meatloaf, broiled chicken, pot roast, hot roast beef sandwich—all to be washed down with root beer floats and ice cream sodas. Don't go to Star Tours immediately afterward—the time warp might be too much to endure.

If you don't mind zombies leering at you while you slurp up sloppy joes, more meatloaf, chef's salad, and the like, then head for the **Sci-Fi Dine-In Theater,** a re-creation of an actual drive-in. All the tables face a large screen, where a 45-minute reel of the best and worst of science fiction trailers plays in a continuous loop. Only here would popcorn be considered an appropriate appetizer.

To replace the energy you've no doubt depleted by miles of theme park walking, load up on carbs at the Studio's newest full-service restaurant. **Mama Melrose's Ristorante Italiano** offers pasta, chicken, steak, and seafood dishes, as well as pizza baked in a gourmet brick oven.

Reservations   Reservations are required at all the full-service restaurants, and for popular seating times, must be made in person at the restaurant or first thing in the morning at Hollywood Junction Restaurant Reservations, just to the right of the Studios Tip Board, at the intersection of Hollywood and Sunset Boulevards.

Cafeteria   The usual menu of upscale fast foods—baby back ribs, roasted chicken, and tortellini at lunch, prime rib, veal chops, and mesquite-grilled pork chops at dinner—constitutes the fare at **Hollywood & Vine Cafeteria of the Stars.** The usual complement of downscale fast-food spots is also available.

Entertainment

Parades? Disney characters? Eccentric actors? You never know what will turn up around the next bend, so pick up an entertainment schedule on your way into the park.

The Theater of the Stars, which used to be where Sunset Boulevard now merges with Hollywood Boulevard, has a new home on Sunset Boulevard. Like its predecessor, it's modeled after the famed Hollywood Bowl; unlike its predecessor, it has more seats. At press time, the Theater of the Stars was presenting the extremely popular Beauty and the Beast—Live on Stage, a skillful condensation of the animated film. The show is almost always crowded; queue up at least 30 minutes prior to show time for good seats, especially if you're with children.

About 12 times a day, a bright-yellow buggy comes roaring up Mickey Avenue on the Backlot, and out scramble the **Teenage Mutant Ninja Turtles**—Raphael, Michelangelo, Leonardo, and Donatello—to be welcomed by a horde of screaming kids. They deliver a 15-minute song-and-dance show, shout "Cowabunga, dude!" every 90 seconds or so, and sign autographs. If you want a good view, get to the staging area about 15 minutes before showtime. Usually by the time you hear the first "Cowabunga!" it's too late.

Aladdin's Royal Caravan, a parade that marches down Hollywood Boulevard each day at 1 PM, is one of this park's most popular attractions. Parade-goers start staking out spots on the curb along the route up to 45 minutes before the parade begins. Prince Ali, the Genie, and their friends come to life in oversize characters complemented by marching bands, dancers in brightly colored costumes, and imaginative floats depicting scenes from the hit movie. Watch out for the water-spitting candles.

The **fireworks** here may be Disney's best. Revisiting Mickey as he appeared in the "Sorcerer's Apprentice" in *Fantasia*, they feature a giant balloon of the great star, floating amid the starbursts and chrysanthemums raining down on Grauman's Chinese Theater. Traditionally these are presented on Friday and Saturday nights (nightly in summer).

Shopping

Budding animators can hone their talents with Paint-a-Cel, a kit with two picture cels ready to be illustrated. It's sold at the **Animation Gallery** in the Animation Building. Genuine Indiana Jones bullwhips and fedoras are sold at the **Indiana Jones Adventure Outpost** next to the stunt amphitheater. All sorts of Roger Rabbit magic tricks are just waiting to buzz, explode, squish, and trick you at the **Loony Bin.** At the conclusion of Star Tours, **Endor Vendors** stocks Darth Vader and Wookie masks as well as other out-of-this-world paraphernalia. For Disney-theme Christmas ornaments, try **It's a Wonderful Shop,** which is tucked in a corner near the Muppets on Location. **The Costume Shop,** near one of the entrances to the New York Street, features getups of Disney villains and villainesses, including favorite outfits of *Sleeping Beauty's* wicked Maleficent and *101 Dalmatian's* Cruella DeVille. And who could resist a pair of Mickey Mitts, an easy-to-pick-up last-minute gift sold at **Legends of Hollywood** on Hollywood Boulevard. Use them to wave at the Earfful Tower on your way out.

Access for Travelers with Disabilities

Almost everything in this park is wheelchair accessible.

Attractions Disney-MGM attractions are wheelchair accessible, with the single exception of the Star Tours thrill ride. At press time, the facts were not yet in on Twilight Zone Tower of Terror on the new Sunset Boulevard; check with Guest Relations for restrictions.

Hollywood The **Theater of the Stars** is completely accessible to guests in
Boulevard wheelchairs. To board the **Great Movie Ride,** you must transfer to a Disney wheelchair if you use an oversize model or a scooter; the gunshot, explosion, and fire effects make the attraction inappropriate for service animals.

Studio The **Voyage of the Little Mermaid** show and the **Magic of Disney**
Courtyard **Animation** are both wheelchair accessible, with terrific entertainment value for all guests with disabilities. The **Backstage Studio Tour** is also wheelchair accessible. Guests with hearing impairments who lip-read should request a seat near the tour guide. The earthquake, fire, and water effects of the Catastrophe Canyon scene make the attraction inappropriate for some service animals. The **Inside the Magic Special Effects and Production Tour** are similarly accessible by those in wheelchairs.

The Backlot The *Honey, I Shrunk the Kids* **Movie Set Adventure** is barrier free for most guests using wheelchairs, although the uneven surface may make maneuvering difficult. **Jim Henson's Muppet*Vision 3-D** is also completely wheelchair accessible. Guests with hearing impairments may request a personal audio link that will amplify the sound here.

Backlot The **Indiana Jones Epic Stunt Spectacular** is completely wheel-
Annex chair accessible. Explosions and gunfire may make it inappropriate for service animals. **Star Tours,** a turbulent ride, is

accessible by guests who can transfer to a ride seat; those lacking upper-body strength should request an extra shoulder restraint. Service animals should not ride.

Lakeside Circle **SuperStar Television** is completely wheelchair accessible. So is the **Monster Sound Show.** However, the entertainment value there is derived from the timing of different sound effects, so guests with hearing impairments may decide to skip this one.

Entertainment Live entertainment locations, including those used at press time for the **Teenage Mutant Ninja Turtles** show and **Beauty and the Beast—Live on Stage,** are completely wheelchair accessible. Certain sections of parade routes are always reserved for guests with disabilities. **Tapings** of television shows are wheelchair accessible, but none of the sound stages currently have sign-language interpreters.

Restaurants and Shops All are fully wheelchair accessible, but there are no braille menus or sign-language interpreters.

Information *See* Hints for Travelers with Disabilities in Chapter 1 and Access for Travelers with Disabilities at the beginning of this chapter.

Discovery Island

Originally conceived as a re-creation of the setting of Robert Louis Stevenson's *Treasure Island,* complete with wrecked ship and Jolly Roger, Discovery Island evolved gradually into its contemporary status as an animal preserve and member of the American Association of Zoological Parks and Aquariums, where visitors can see and learn about some 100 different species of exotic birds and animals amid 11½ lushly landscaped acres. Its long, white-sand beaches, its hills, and its hidden groves were sculpted and planned by Disney Imagineers, who brought in 15,000 cubic yards of sandy soil, added 1,000 tons of boulders and trees, and planted 20 types of palm trees, 10 species of bamboo, and dozens of other plants whose original habitats ranged from Argentina, Trinidad, and Costa Rica to the Himalayas and South Africa. Despite all that work, Discovery Island remains the least artificial attraction in Walt Disney World. Although it is barely a 15-minute boat ride from the dock at the Magic Kingdom, surprisingly few visitors take the time to explore it.

Although it's possible to "do" Discovery Island in less than an hour, anything more than a stop-and-start saunter would do it injustice. You can wander along the shady boardwalks at your own pace, stopping to inspect the bougainvillea or visit with a rhinoceros hornbill. You can picnic on the beach or on one of the benches in the shade and watch trumpeter swans glide by. You can simply sit and read without being disturbed by the ecstatic screams of thrill riders. The only thing you may not do is go swimming—the Water Sprites and motor launches on Bay Lake come just too close for safety.

Essential Information

Getting
Around

Boardwalks and well-beaten paths wind through the island's lush vegetation.

Tourist
Information

Disney hosts and hostesses at the entrance kiosk can answer most questions you may have and can give you maps and show schedules.

Guided Tours

Reserve ahead for **Discovery Island Kidventures,** four-hour guided tours for children aged 8–14 (tel. 407/824–3784; $32, including lunch, transportation, craft materials, and a souvenir photo), offered Wednesday and Sunday in summer, but Wednesday only the rest of the year.

Access

All paths and boardwalks are accessible by wheelchair. No signage is in braille, and no signing is available.

Wheelchairs

Available for rent throughout Walt Disney World, wheelchairs are available here on loan—with no charge.

Exploring Discovery Island

Pick up a map and a schedule of bird shows at the entrance kiosk and then start exploring. It's truly impossible to get lost, because the boardwalks, however twisty and no matter how many detours, essentially trace a circle around the island. It may take a while, but you'll always get back to your starting place.

Just past the first right-hand bend in the boardwalk is the **Discovery Island Bird Show,** where aviary "Animal Encounters" shows are presented in an open amphitheater equipped with benches and numerous perches. "Feathered Friends" features macaws and cockatoos, including the tricky green trio of Larry, Curly, and Moe. "Birds of Prey" demonstrates the behaviors of such predatory birds as owls, hawks, and king vultures. There's usually a show every hour from 11 to 4; most last about 15 minutes.

Large and airy enclosures holding additional birds and animals are set along the boardwalk throughout the island. More animals are allowed to roam free, so you're likely to surprise a male peacock spreading his iridescent fan in an attempt to woo an unimpressed female or you can watch 500-pound Galápagos tortoises inch along the beach. Informative signs explain the animal's characteristics and point out particularly interesting plants.

The island menagerie also contains areas dedicated to specific species. **Monkey Point** is home to a family of golden-lion tamarins from South America. **Avian Way,** one of the largest walkthrough aviaries in the world, houses both a colony of scarlet ibis, whose brilliant color is enhanced by a special carotene-rich diet, and a bunch of blush-colored roseate spoonbills. It's especially amusing to watch the spoonbills scoop up fish in their lagoon—as well as to eavesdrop on the peanut gallery. More carotene helps the Caribbean flamingos in **Flamingo Lagoon** keep their characteristic tropical coral color. Dainty demoiselle and gold-crested, African crowned cranes delicately pick their way around **Crane's Roost** while alligators loll about in slothful splendor in the **Alligator Pool.** The pool also hosts another Animal Encounter: "Reptile Relations" looks at the habits of snakes and alligators. And what would Florida be without pelicans? You don't have to imagine, thanks to a protected flock in **Pelican Bay.**

Time Out Sandwiches, hot dogs and burgers, ice cream sandwiches and bars, frozen juice bars, and both beer and soft drinks are sold at the **Thirsty Perch,** at the entrance dock.

Typhoon Lagoon

According to Disney legend, Typhoon Lagoon was created when the quaint, thatched-roof, lushly landscaped Placid Palms Resort was struck by a cataclysmic storm. It left a different world in its wake: Surfboards sundered trees, once-upright palms imitated the Leaning Tower of Pisa, a great buoy crashed through the roof of one building, a small boat was blown through the roof of another, and part of the original lagoon was cut off, trapping thousands of tropical fish—and a few sharks. Nothing, however, topped the fate of *Miss Tilly*, a shrimp boat from "Safen Sound, Florida," which was hurled high in the air and became impaled on Mount Mayday, a magical volcano that periodically tries to dislodge *Miss Tilly* with huge geysers of water.

Ordinary folks, the legend continues, would have been crushed by such devastation. But the resourceful residents of 56-acre Placid Palms were made of hardier stuff—and from the wreckage they created Typhoon Lagoon, the self-proclaimed "world's ultimate water park."

Four times the size of River Country, Typhoon Lagoon offers a full-day's worth of activities: bobbing in 4-foot waves in a surf lagoon the size of two football fields, speeding down arrow-straight water slides and around twisty storm slides, bumping through rapids, and snorkeling. More mellow folks can float in inner tubes along the 2,100-foot Castaway Creek, rubberneck from specially constructed grandstands as human cannonballs are ejected from the storm slides, or merely hunker down in one of the many hammocks or lounge chairs and read a book. A children's area replicates adult rides on a smaller scale. It's Disney's version of a day at the beach—complete with lifeguards in spiffy red-and-white-striped T-shirts.

Essential Information

Tourist The **Guest Relations** window just outside the entrance turn-
Information stiles, to your left, can answer many questions. Inside, a chalk-board gives water temperature and surfing information, and all rides and attractions are marked with red nautical pennants indicating the thrill level: one pennant equals "laid back," two means "radical," three means "hot stuff," and four equals "awe-

some." Because the semantical differences between "radical" and "awesome" are minimal, assume that one and two pennants means you can keep your sunglasses on, and three or four pennants suggests that you should hand them to someone for safekeeping and then secure the knot on your swimsuit.

Services and Facilities
Dressing Rooms, Lockers, and Rest Rooms

Men's and women's thatch-roofed **dressing rooms** and two sizes of full-day **lockers** ($5 and $7) are in two areas—to the right of the entrance and near Typhoon Tilly's Galley & Grog Shop. The latter area is usually less crowded. You can also rent **towels** (50¢ at the stand to the right of the main entrance), but they're a little skimpy; bring your own beach towel or buy one at Singapore Sal's (*see below*). The Typhoon Lagoon Imagineers thoughtfully placed **rest rooms** in every available nook and cranny. Most are equipped with showers, and they are much less crowded for clothes-changing than the main dressing rooms are.

First Aid

The small first-aid stand is left of the entrance, not far from the Leaning Palms food stand.

Inner Tubes, Rafts, and Snorkels

The rental **rafts** concession, the building with the boat sticking through the roof to the left of the entrance, past the Leaning Palms food concession, rents **inner tubes.** You need to rent tubes only for the lagoon; they are provided for Castaway Creek and all the white-water rides. You can borrow **snorkels and masks** at Shark Reef, and **life vests** are available at High and Dry Towels (25¢ deposit). You may not bring your own equipment into Typhoon Lagoon.

Lost Things or People

Ask after your misplaced people or things at the Guest Relations window just outside the entrance turnstiles, to your left.

Supplies

Singapore Sal's, to the right of the main entrance, is the place to acquire sunscreen, hats, sunglasses, and other beach paraphernalia.

Access

Wheelchair rentals are available in the entrance turnstile area (free with ID). All of the paths that connect the different areas of Typhoon Lagoon are wheelchair accessible. Guests who use a wheelchair can also float in Typhoon Lagoon and on Castaway Creek, provided it's possible to transfer to a raft or inner tube. The park is head and shoulders above River Country in the accessibility department.

Picnicking

Picnicking is also permitted. Tables are set up at Getaway Glen and Castaway Cove, near Shark Reef. Bring a box lunch from your hotel—and you'll eat well without having to line up with the masses.

Strategies for Your Visit

There's really only one problem with Typhoon Lagoon—it's popular. In the summer and on weekends, the park often reaches capacity (7,200 people) by midmorning, by which time Castaway Creek is a bank-to-bank carpet of tangled arms and legs, Typhoon Lagoon resembles the Times Square subway station at rush hour, and the lines for Humunga Kowabunga, the storm slides, and Shark Reef can top an hour. In that time, you could have driven to the Atlantic Ocean.

If you must go during the summer, go for a few hours during the dreamy late afternoons or when the weather clears up after a thundershower. (Typically, rainstorms drive away the crowds, and lots of people simply don't come back.) If you plan to make a whole day of it, avoid weekends—Typhoon Lagoon is big among locals as well as tourists. Instead, visit on a Monday, or on Sunday morning, when the locals are in church. Arrive 30 minutes before opening time so you can park, buy tickets, rent towels, and snag inner tubes before the hordes descend. Set up camp and hit the slides, white-water rides, and Shark Reef first. Then bobble along Castaway Creek and save the lagoon itself for later.

If you're visiting at a relatively unpopulated time of year, go in the afternoon, when the day will have warmed up a bit. Do Castaway Creek first to get a sense of the park.

There are plenty of lounge chairs, a number of hammocks, and definitely not enough beach umbrellas. If you crave shade, commandeer a spot in the grassy area around Getaway Glen on the left side of the park just past the raft-rental concession. If you like lots of action, people-watching, and sand in your face, go front and center at the surf pool. For sand and relative quiet, head for the coves and inlets on the left side of the lagoon.

Exploring Typhoon Lagoon

Numbers in the margin correspond to points of interest on the Typhoon Lagoon map.

The layout is so simple that it is truly impossible to get lost—trust us. The eponymous wave and swimming lagoon is at the center of the park; the waves break on the beaches closest to the entrance and are born in Mount Mayday at the other end of the park. Castaway Creek encircles the lagoon. Anything requiring a gravitational plunge—storm slides, speed slides, and raft trips down rapids—starts around the summit of Mount Mayday. Shark Reef and Ketchakiddie Creek flank the head of the lagoon, to Mount Mayday's right and left, respectively.

❶ The heart of the park is, of course, **Typhoon Lagoon,** a swimming area that spreads out over 2½ acres and contains almost 3 million gallons of clear, chlorinated water. It's scalloped by lots of little coves, bays, and inlets, all edged with white-sand beaches—spread over a base of white concrete, as body surfers will soon discover when they try to slide into shore. Ouch! The main attraction is the waves. Twelve huge water-collection chambers hidden in Mount Mayday dump their load with a resounding "whoosh" into trap doors to create waves large enough for Typhoon Lagoon to host amateur and professional surfing championships. A piercing hoot from *Miss Tilly* signals the start and finish of wave action: Every even hour, for 10 minutes on and 10 minutes off, 4-foot-plus waves issue forth every 90 seconds; every odd hour is devoted to moderate bobbing waves.

Even during the big-wave periods, however, the waters in Blustery Bay and Whitecap Cove are protected enough for timid swimmers.

❷ Circular, 15-foot-wide, 3-foot-deep **Castaway Creek** is everyone's water fantasy come true. Snag an inner tube and float along the creek that winds around the entire park, a wet version of the Magic Kingdom's Walt Disney World Railroad. You pass through a rain forest that showers you with mist and spray (don't think you can put your ankles up and read a book, tempting though it may sound), you slide through caves and grottos, you burble by overhanging trees and flowering bushes, and you get dumped on at the Water Works (whose "broken" pipes the Typhoon Lagooners never got around to fixing). The current ambles at 2½ feet per second; it takes about 30 minutes to make a full circuit. There are exits along the way, where you can hop out and dry off or do something else—and then pick up another inner tube and jump right back in.

Follow Castaway Creek up toward Mount Mayday, and at the head of the lagoon, veer right for **Shark Reef.** Anyone who ❸ wanted to leap out of the boat in the Magic Kingdom's 20,000 Leagues under the Sea or jump into the tank at Epcot Center's Living Seas will make tracks for this 360,000-gallon snorkeling tank. The coral reef is artificial, but the 4,000 tropical fish—including black-and-white striped sergeant majors, sargassum trigger fish, yellowtail damselfish, and amiable nurse and bonnet-head sharks—are quite real. So are the southern stingrays that congregate in the warmer, shallower water by the entrance (to prevent algae growth, Shark Reef is kept at a brisk 72°, which is 18° colder than the rest of Typhoon Lagoon). A sunken tanker divides the reef; its portholes give landlubbers access to the underwater scene and lets them to go nose to nose with snorkelers. Unless the reef is practically deserted—almost never—you are supposed to swim in a counterclockwise circle around the tanker; one circuit takes about 15 minutes. Go first thing in the morning or at the end of the day if you want to spend more time. Chilly air and water temperatures close the reef from November through April.

❹ There's no time to scream on **Humunga Kowabunga,** but you'll hear just such vociferous reactions as the survivors emerge from the catch pool opposite Shark Reef. The basic question is: Want to get scared out of your wits in three seconds flat—and like it enough to go back for more? "Do that?" asked one observer. "I'm not crazy!" The two side-by-side Humunga Kowabunga speed slides rightly deserve their four-pennant designation, as they drop more than 50 feet in a distance barely four times that amount. (For nonmathematicians, that's *very steep.*) Oh yes, and then you go through a cave. In the dark. Awesome, indeed. The average speed is 30 miles per hour; however, you can really fly if you lie flat on your back, cross your ankles, wrap your arms around your chest, and arch your back. Just remember to smile for the rubberneckers on the grandstand at the bottom—and to readjust your bathing suit before leaving the water. *No pregnant*

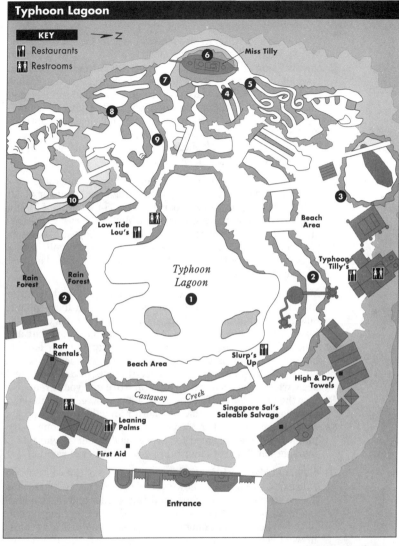

women or guests with back or heart problems or other physical limitations.

It's a long and twisty-turny schlep up the right side of Mount Mayday and a short but even more twisty-turny ride down on
❺ the **Jib Jammer, Rudder Buster, and Stern Burner storm slides.** Each of these three body slides is about 300 feet long and snakes in and out of rock formations, through caves and tunnels, and under waterfalls, but each has a slightly different view and offers an idiosyncratic twist (we'll only say that the one in the middle has the longest tunnel; the others' secrets you'll have to discover for yourself). Maximum speed is about 20 miles per hour and the trip takes about 30 seconds.

What goes down can also go up—and up and up and up and up. "It's like climbing Mount Everest," wailed one teenager about
❻ a climb that seems a lot steeper than the 85-foot peak of **Mount Mayday** would warrant. However, it's Mount Everest with hibiscus flowers, a shivering rope bridge, stepping-stones set in plunging waters, and—remember that seminal typhoon?—a broken canoe scattered over the rocks near the top. The view encompasses the entire park.

Mayday Falls, Keelhaul Falls, Gangplank Falls—white-water raft rides that you experience in oversize inner tubes—plunge down the left side of Mount Mayday. Like the storm slides, they feature caves and waterfalls and intricate rock work but add
❼ some extra elements. The 460-foot slide over **Mayday Falls,** in blue inner tubes, is the longest and generally acclaimed the bumpiest; it's a straight slide over the falls into a catchment area, which gives you just enough time to catch your breath be-
❽ fore the next plunge. The spiraling, 400-foot **Keelhaul Falls** ride, in yellow inner tubes, takes a more roundabout trip, and the
❾ speed seems faster than the purported 10 miles per hour. **Gangplank Falls** was designed for groups and families, who ride in four-person, 6½-foot inner tubes down 300 feet of rapids.

❿ **Ketchakiddie Creek,** located just to the right of the white-water ride exits, sports scaled-down versions of the big people's rides. There are slides, minirapids, squirting whales and seals, bouncing barrels, waterfalls, sprinklers, and all the other ingredients of splash heaven. The bubbling sand ponds, in which kids can sit in what seems like an enormous Jacuzzi, are special favorites. *All adults must be accompanied by a child under 4 feet (and vice versa).*

Time Out Standard fast-food beach fare—burgers, dogs, chef's salads, and, of course, ice cream and frozen yogurt—is what's cooking at **Leaning Palms,** to the left of the entrance, and **Typhoon Tilly's Galley & Grog Shop,** on the right just south of Shark Reef. Tilly's grog is mostly carbonated, but she also sells Davy Jones lager. **Let's Go Slurpin',** a beach shack on the edge of Typhoon Lagoon, dispenses frozen margaritas as well as wine and beer. Food carts purveying lemonade, soda, ices, and snow cones are scattered around the park.

River Country

Imagine a mountain in Utah's red-rock country. Put a lake at the bottom, and add a verdant fuzz of maples and pines here and there on the sides. Then plant some water slides among the greenery, and call it a "good ole fashion swimmin' hole." That's River Country.

It was the first of Walt Disney World's water parks. Whereas larger, glitzier Typhoon Lagoon is balmy and tropical, this one is rustic and rugged. Some of the activities are the same, but the mood is different. River Country is smaller and in many ways has more charm. If you have plenty of time, you should cover both.

Essential Information

Tourist Information The **Guest Services** window, at the entrance turnstiles, can answer most of your questions. It's also the spot to take finds and report losses.

Services and Facilities
Dressing Rooms and Lockers
There are **dressing rooms** for men and women near the entrance, with coin-op **lockers** (50¢) and **towel rentals** ($1). Bring quarters to avoid having to wait in line for change, and bring your own towel (the ones here are skimpy). You'll also need your own beach towel.

First Aid It's in the white building next to the guest pay phone, but it's open only during Easter break and in summer. At any other time, go to Guest Services.

Lost Children Obviously lost youngsters are usually taken to the towel window and then walked around until they spot their folks. River Country is small enough for that system to work fine.

Access Wheelchairs are available at Guest Services at no charge (with ID as deposit), but very little of the park is wheelchair accessible; you're better off at Typhoon Lagoon.

Tips Go early in the morning to avoid the crowds that sometimes close River Country altogether on busy days. Alternatively, in summer, wait until 4, and take advantage of the reduced-price admission ticket.

Exploring River Country

Walking from the dressing rooms brings you to the 330,000-gallon swimming pool, bright blue and concrete paved, like something out of a more modern Midwest. There are a couple of short, steep water slides here. Beyond that is **Bay Cove**, the roped-off corner of Bay Lake that's the main section of River Country. Rope swings hang from a rustic boom, and there are various other woody contraptions from which kids dive and cannonball. The main event, however, consists of the two big water slides— 100 and 260 feet long—that descend from **Whoop 'n' Holler Hollow** down the side of the mountain. Look for the boardwalk and stairway. A more leisurely trip down can be taken via **White**

Water Rapids, a series of short chutes and swirling pools that you descend in a jumbo inner tube. Laughs, not thrills, are what this one is all about, as your tube gets caught in the pool's eddies, and you spin around, stuck, until someone slides down and bumps you out.

Off to the edge of the property is a **nature trail** that skirts the shore of Bay Lake.

Time Out   You can pick up burgers, hot dogs, and fries at **Pop's Place** or, in summer and over Easter break, buy nachos, ice cream, soda, and beer at the **Watering Hole.** Picnicking is permitted.

Elsewhere in the World

Walt Disney World is much more than theme parks. You can play tennis or golf, go boating or fishing, ride a bike, take a hike, or even work out in a health club (*see* Chapter 7). Colorful restaurants and dinner shows abound, and children love having breakfast, lunch, or dinner with the Disney characters (*see* Chapter 8). And far from shutting down at night, this family entertainment spot gets a second wind when the sun goes down: You can sip a drink and listen to music in any number of night spots, take in a movie in a state-of-the-art theater, watch fireworks, and lots more (*see* Chapter 10).

4 Sea World, Universal Studios, and Beyond

By Catherine
Fredman

Updated by
Mary
Meehan

Theme parks grow so well in the sandy central Florida soil that
one might almost imagine a handful of seeds, scattered across
the fertile I–4 belt, waiting for the right combination of money
and vision to nurture them into the next . . . Walt Disney World.
WDW is, in fact, something of an upstart latecomer. Long before
the strains of "It's a Small World" echoed through the palmetto
scrub, other theme parks tempted visitors away from the
beaches into the scruffy interior of central Florida.

None was anywhere near the scale of today's megaparks. I–4
hadn't even been built when Dick and Julie Pope created Cypress Gardens, which now holds the record as central Florida's
oldest continuously running attraction. Busch Gardens was
founded a quarter-century later, in 1959, as an exotic-animal
sideshow attached to a brewery and beer garden.

But when the Magic Kingdom opened on October 1, 1971, and
was immediately successful, the central Florida theme park
scene went from mom-and-pop operations to big business. Sea
World filled its tanks two years later. Epcot Center debuted in
1982. Disney-MGM Studios Theme Park threw down the movie
gauntlet in 1989; Universal Studios answered the challenge one
year later. Splendid China joined the fray in 1993. And meanwhile, Busch Gardens has steadily expanded, spawning the
Busch Entertainment Corporation (BEC), which, with the 1989
acquisition of Cypress Gardens and Sea World, became the second-largest theme park owner and operator in the world. Its
neighbor down the interstate remains number one.

Growth engendered more growth. Whereas it used to be that
you could do a whole park—any park—in about six hours, a thor-
ough visit now can barely be contained in a day—and a full day,
too. As competition sharpened and tastes grew more sophisticated, a sort of me-too mentality became prevalent. If one park
has a flight simulator, then all parks must have one (the best are
Disney-MGM's Star Tours and Universal Studios' Back to the
Future . . . The Ride). Ditto Broadway-style music-and-dance
shows, distinguished for their professional presentation, snazzy
costumes, high-kicking dancers, and completely forgettable
plots. A blessing for parents, every park now has a sophisticated
children's play area; ball crawls, four-story net climbs, bouncing
rooms, water tricks, and twisty slides—all designed to match a
preconceived theme—are de rigueur. So, too, thankfully, are
lighter gustatory offerings that, though not exactly heart
healthy, are a welcome alternative to the usual greasy burnt offerings.

Prices have risen accordingly, with Universal Studios and Walt
Disney World topping the scales at nearly $40 for a full-day adult
ticket. Busch Gardens, Sea World, and Cypress Gardens match
Walt Disney World's combined pass system with discounts
on tickets to BEC parks that are purchased at another BEC
attraction.

The problem for visitors with a tight schedule or a slim wallet is
that each of the parks is worth a visit. But if you're staying in

the Orlando area, a decision can be made on the basis of distance. Busch Gardens is 75 miles away, a good 90-minute commute each way; Cypress Gardens is a little closer, but the 60-minute drive through the dusty citrus groves seems to take forever. Coincidentally, these two parks offer few high-tech, gasp-producing spectacles. If you want to take in a park that has more cultural substance than blockbuster style, try Splendid China; this new attraction is only a few miles from WDW, but the emphasis here is on expert craftsmanship, not astounding effects. In any case, Sea World and Universal Studios are not to be missed. Universal Studios is best seen *after* visiting Disney-MGM; it definitely gilds Mickey's lily.

Sea World

Many visitors are surprised to discover that there's a lot more to Sea World than Shamu, its mammoth killer-whale mascot. Aptly named, 135-acre Sea World is the world's largest zoological park and is devoted entirely to the mammals, birds, fish, and reptiles that live in the ocean and its tributaries. Sure, you can be splashed by Shamu and his other orca buddies, but you can also be spat at by a walrus, stroke a stingray, experience life as a manatee, and learn to love an eel (well, maybe).

What's even more astonishing is that the fun factor is closely tied to educational elements. Every attraction is designed to teach visitors about the beauty of the marine world and how that world is being threatened by human thoughtlessness. It's all very politically and environmentally correct. Yet the presentations are rarely dogmatic, never pedantic, and almost always memorable as well as enjoyable.

After a rough adolescence under previous owner Harcourt Brace Jovanovich (which included a threat of bankruptcy amid rumors that stressed-out killer whales had turned on their trainers), Sea World was purchased by Anheuser-Busch in 1989 and added to that company's stable of entertainment theme parks, whose Florida representatives now are Busch Gardens, Adventure Island, and Cypress Gardens. Sea World turns 22 in 1995 and, thanks to Anheuser-Busch's new management, is bigger and better than ever. The park rivals Disney properties for sparkly cleanliness, smiley staff, and attention to detail—the nautical flags flying over the entrance spell out "Sea World" in semaphore, and the strollers are shaped like upended dolphins (you push the tail).

It used to be you could whip through Sea World and still have time to play a few rounds of golf. No more. Count on spending an entire day—and wanting to return.

Essential Information

Tourist Information   Contact Sea World (7007 Sea World Dr., Orlando 32821, tel. 407/351–3600; no TTY).

You're given a computer-generated map at the park entrance. An especially neat and considerate touch is the recommended show schedule, personalized according to your arrival time, that's printed out on it. In the park, a large board at the entrance lists all show times.

Inside the park, the main information center is **Guest Relations,** near the park entrance.

Getting There
Sea World is just off the intersection of I–4 and the Bee Line Expressway, 10 minutes south of downtown Orlando and 15 minutes from Orlando International Airport. Of all the central Florida theme parks, it's the easiest to find. Signs direct you to Exit 28 off I–4 and guide you the short distance to the parking lot.

Parking
Parking costs $5 per car, $7 per RV or camper.

Admission
Regular one-day admission tickets cost $34.95 for adults, $29.95 for children 3–9, including tax. Two-day tickets, which must be used within one week, are $39.95 for adults, $34.95 for children. Discounted and multipark single-day tickets to Cypress Gardens and Busch Gardens may be purchased at the ticket booth at the exit. AAA members who present their membership card receive a 10% discount.

Hours
Sea World is open daily 9–7; during the summer and on holidays, the park may stay open as late as 10 PM.

Services
Baby Care
There are **diaper-changing tables** in or near most women's rest rooms, and in the men's rest room at the front entrance, near Shamu's Emporium. You can buy **diapers** at machines located in all changing areas and at Shamu's Emporium. A special area for **nursing** is alongside the women's room at Friends of the Wild gift shop, equidistant from Sea World Theater, Penguin Encounter, and Sea Lion and Otter Stadium. You will find **stroller rentals** at the Information Center ($5 for single, $10 for double; no deposit). However, **no formula or baby food** is sold on the premises; the nearest sources are a five-minute drive away at Gooding's Supermarket on International Drive, Publix supermarket and Eckerd's drugs on Central Florida Parkway, and K-Mart on Turkey Lake Road.

Cameras and Film
Disposable Kodak Funsaver cameras are for sale on the premises, as are film and blank videotapes. There were neither camera nor camcorder rentals nor camera repairs on the premises at press time.

First Aid
First Aid Centers are behind Stingray Lagoon and near Shamu's Happy Harbor. Registered nurses are on duty.

Guided Tours
Even if you already know the answer to the frequently asked question, "Do you paint Shamu?" it's worth spending the nominal extra fee to sign up for the 90-minute behind-the-scenes guided tours—"Backstage Explorations" or "Animal Lover's Adventure"—or the 45-minute "Animal Training Discoveries," in which Sea World trainers discuss animal behavior and training techniques ($5.95 adults, $4.95 children 3–9). Tours leave every 30 minutes until 3 PM. Register at the guided tour center

to the left of the Guest Relations/Information Center at the park entrance. Sign-language interpreters can be provided with advanced notice.

Lockers They're inside the park entrance and to the right, next to Shamu's Emporium. The cost is $1.

Lost Children and Adults Lost parents and lost children should rendezvous at the Information Center just inside the park entrance. All employees who see lost-looking children have been trained to take them to the Information Center. A parkwide paging system helps reunite guests.

Lost and Found Go to the Information Center to reclaim your misplaced items or to drop off somebody else's.

Money Foreign currency can be exchanged at the Special Services Window at the Main Gate (daily 10–3). An ATM linked to various bank and credit-card networks is at the exit gate.

Package Pickup When you make purchases anywhere in the park, your clerk can send them to Package Pickup, in Shamu's Emporium, on request. Allow an hour between making your purchase and your departure.

Wheelchair Rentals Both standard and electric wheelchairs are available ($5 and $25 daily with driver's license).

Strategies for Your Visit

When to Go Friday, Saturday, and Sunday are usually busier than the rest of the week, except during weeks that include Christmas, July 4, and Easter, when every day is equally busy.

Blitz Tour The recommended itinerary and show schedule printed on the park map make a lot of sense. There's only one problem: Everyone else will be following them, too. Although there's room for all at the stadiums, the other attractions—especially Penguin Encounter and the Dolphin Community Pool—can get unpleasantly crowded, and there will be lines at Mission: Bermuda Triangle.

Instead, walk straight through the park to the **Sea World Theatre** to see "Window to the Sea," both to orient yourself and to get a sense of the larger vision of the park. Then whip into **Penguin Encounter** early, to visit one of the most spectacular attractions at its least crowded. Proceed to **Terrors of the Deep.** Follow the crowds across the bridge to **Shamu Stadium**; while they're watching the first Shamu show, you can sneak into **Mission: Bermuda Triangle.** Let your stomach subside with some souvenir shopping at the nearby concession, then beat the crowds to lunch at Mango Joe's Café. Get a lakeside table and catch the early **Gold Rush Ski Show,** too.

While on this side of the lagoon, visit the sea lions at **Pacific Point Preserve,** plus **Manatees: The Last Generation?** and the **Shamu Breeding Pool and Nursery.** That should put you right in place for the afternoon Shamu show.

Wander back across the bridge and treat yourself to some interactive exhibits: There's the **Dolphin Community Pool, Stingray Lagoon,** and the **Caribbean Tide Pool,** where fondling the starfish is not to be missed; visit these exhibits during the day because the herring and smelt concessions close at dusk. Keep an eye on the time: You'll want to intersperse these with the shows at the **Whale & Dolphin Stadium** and the **Sea Lion & Otter Stadium.**

By now, you'll be feeling a little frayed. The soothing New Age music at the **Tropical Reef** strikes just the right note, especially once cranky children and their families have left for the day. The **"Water Fantasy"** is another good option. During high season, stick around for the "Sea World Fireworks Spectacular, a laser-and-fireworks show that fills the air with color and sound.

On Rainy Days Although Sea World gives the impression of open-air roominess, almost a third of the attractions are actually indoors and all the others are shielded from the elements by canopies, cantilevered roofs, or tautly stretched tarpaulins. Pick up a signature poncho—it's clear, with a black-and-white orca on the back—at one of the ubiquitous concession stands, and dive right in.

Other Tips
- When the park hours are extended, wait until midafternoon to arrive. Then you can do most of your touring during the less steamy parts of the day and have dinner in the park.

- Try to arrive early for Shamu shows, which generally fill to capacity on even the slowest days.

- Set up a specific rendezvous time and location at the start of your visit in case you and your companions get separated.

Exploring Sea World

Sea World is organized around the nucleus of a 17-acre central lake. Rather than being divided into sections or "lands," as is the case at other Florida entertainment parks, Sea World's attractions flow into each other. As you enter, the lake is to your right. The right side of the park contains Shamu Stadium, Shamu Breeding Pool and Nursery, Shamu's Happy Harbor play area, the Mission: Bermuda Triangle flight simulator, Atlantis Water Ski Stadium, and Anheuser-Busch Hospitality Center, home of the hulking Clydesdale horses. The left side of the park is considerably denser, with all the other attractions stacked one on top of another. You can orient yourself by the Sky Tower (admission: $3), whose revolving viewing platform is generally visible even above the trees; it's directly opposite Shamu Stadium.

The computerized, color-coordinated map handed out at the entrance makes the park look much larger than it is. It's actually quite compact, but artful landscaping, curving paths, and concealing greenery make it very easy to get disoriented. When that happens, don't try to figure out the sometimes confusing signs; just find an aqua-shirted staff member and ask for directions. If you're panicked about missing a Shamu performance, just remember that the key is finding the lake; Shamu Stadium is no more than a 10-minute walk away.

This guide covers the attractions as you would encounter them if you were exploring the park in a clockwise direction.

Numbers in the margin correspond to points of interest on the Sea World map.

① At the end of the entrance avenue is the first of many lagoons, this one embracing the **Tropical Reef,** an exhibit in which Sea World goes head to head with Epcot Center's older Living Seas pavilion and scores. An indoor (that is, air-conditioned) attraction, the centerpiece is a cylindrical mega-aquarium where more than 1,000 tropical fish swim around a 160,000-gallon man-made coral reef. Identification photos of Tinker's butterfly fish, black-and-white Moorish idols, bright-blue-striped yellow sergeant majors, and their piscine pals are displayed just above eye level, but because the pesky things don't stay put under their portraits, matching fish to picture is like playing connect-the-dots with moving dots. Kids especially like to run circles around the tank in search of one particular species. There are also 17 miniaquariums set in pillars and around the perimeter, displaying king crabs, moray eels, and other single species as well as vignettes of undersea life. *Crowds: Not usually a problem. Strategy: Go toward the end of the day (because it's near the entrance, most people stop here on their way in). Audience: All ages. Rating:* ★★★

② Just opposite the Tropical Reef's exit is the **Caribbean Tide Pool,** whose lagoon is a touchy-feely version of the Tropical Reef. Under the watchful eye of a Sea World guide, you can reach into the lukewarm water, pick up a starfish or a sea anemone, and ask such basic questions as "What do they do?" (Answer: "Not much.") *Crowds: Make it hard to get to the animals. Strategy: Go early or late. Audience: All ages. Rating:* ★★

③
④ Don't even bother to dry off your hands. Ringing the Caribbean Tide Pool and the Tropical Reef are the **Dolphin Community Pool,** and **Stingray Lagoon,** two separate outdoor feeding and petting pools. Smelts are sold at concession stands next to each pool at three for $1 to feed the fish. Buy a batch and stroke the stingrays as they flap up (they feel like wet crushed velvet). This is one of the most rewarding experiences in the park for all ages, and the snack-happy animals are obligingly hungry all day. *Crowds: Can make it hard to get to the animals during busy seasons. Strategy: Go early—the smelt concession stand closes at dark. Audience: All ages. Rating:* ★★★

Time Out Adjoining the Dolphin Community Pool, full-service **Bimini Bay Café** dishes up light and tasty tropical cuisine in a pale pastel setting that would be refreshing even without the air-conditioning. The veranda tables have a great view of the action "backstage" at the waterski show, the floats where the waterski tow boats pick up their next load of daredevil stuntmen and stuntwomen.

⑤
⑥ Two of the most entertaining shows at Sea World are at **Whale & Dolphin Stadium** and **Sea Lion & Otter Stadium,** two gleaming white-and-navy-blue structures that dominate the left and top

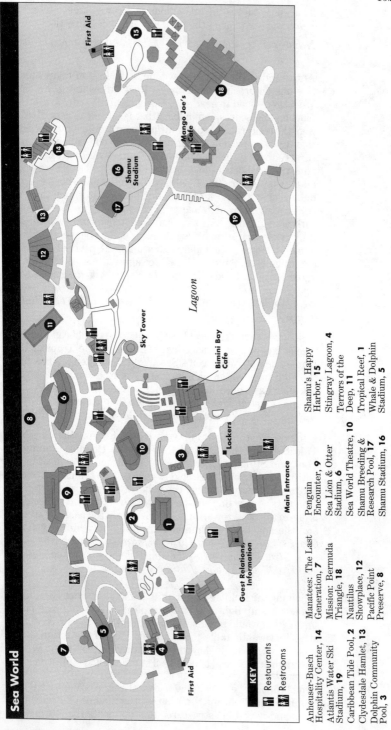

Sea World

KEY

🚻 Restaurants
🚻 Restrooms

First Aid

First Aid

Main Entrance

Guest Relations: Information

Lockers

Sky Tower

Lagoon

Shamu Stadium

Bimini Bay Cafe

Mango Joe's Cafe

Anheuser-Busch
Hospitality Center, **14**
Atlantis Water Ski
Stadium, **19**
Caribbean Tide Pool, **2**
Clydesdale Hamlet, **13**
Dolphin Community
Pool, **3**

Manatees: The Last
Generation, **7**
Mission: Bermuda
Triangle, **18**
Nautilus
Showplace, **12**
Pacific Point
Preserve, **8**

Penguin
Encounter, **9**
Sea Lion & Otter
Stadium, **6**
Sea World Theatre, **10**
Shamu Breeding &
Research Pool, **17**
Shamu Stadium, **16**

Shamu's Happy
Harbor, **15**
Stingray Lagoon, **4**
Terrors of the
Deep, **11**
Tropical Reef, **1**
Whale & Dolphin
Stadium, **5**

perimeter of this side of the park and are separated from each other by the overgrown refrigerator that houses Penguin Encounter. Whale & Dolphin Stadium, whose bright tropical colors and cheerful pink lighthouse evoke the Caribbean, is located just beyond Stingray Lagoon. Sea Lion & Otter Stadium, whose rather bland exterior conceals the wildly inventive, multilevel balconies (read: diving boards) and staircases (read: water slides) of the "Hotel Clyde and Seamore" set, is located at the top of the attractions on the left side of the park, just to the left of the spot where the central lake begins to curve.

The dolphin show spotlights one lucky child from the audience (to get yours picked, come early and ask one of the stadium attendants), six Atlantic bottle-nose dolphins, and two false killer whales. The dolphins wave, leap, and do backflips; in one sequence, the trainer rides on their backs and then gets torpedoed into the air. The child from the audience stands on the side of the tank, commands the dolphins with hand gestures, and gets splashed. *Duration: 20 min. Crowds: You'll always get in. Strategy: Sit in the first four rows if you want to get splashed. Audience: All ages. Rating:* ★★★

"Hotel Clyde and Seamore," the current show in Sea Lion & Otter Stadium, is a comedy featuring break-dancing sea lions, an environmentally sensitive otter, and a heroic walrus that lumbers in and saves the day from blundering, littering humans. Show times are staggered so that there's time to explore the attractions between the two stadiums between shows. *Duration: 40 min, including the 15-min preshow. Crowds: No problem. Strategy: Sit toward the center for the best view, and don't miss the show's opening minutes. Audience: All ages. Rating:* ★★★

Sea World's commitment to the conservation of Florida's manatees, a gentle cross between a walrus and an oil barrel, is especially striking at **Manatees: The Last Generation?** just behind Whale & Dolphin Stadium. Visitors tramp down a Plexiglas tunnel beneath the naturalistic, 3½-acre lagoon to **Manatee Theater,** where a film examines manatees' lifestyle and describes how human encroachment is threatening the species' survival. You can snoop at the lettuce-chomping giants and native fish, including tarpon, gar, and snook, in **Manatee Habitat,** a 300,000-gallon tank with a 126-foot seamless acrylic viewing panel; keep an eye out for mama manatees and their nursing calves. Other animals that share the manatee's world live in **Alligator Habitat,** a marsh display, and **Bird Habitat.** *Strategy: Go during a Shamu show, and not right after a dolphin show. Audience: All ages. Rating:* ★★★

The nonstop chorus of "aarrrps" and "yawps" leads the way to **Pacific Point Preserve,** a new 2½-acre home for California sea lions and harbor and fur seals, just behind Sea Lion & Otter Stadium. The naturalistic beaches, waves, and huge outcroppings of upturned coastal rock duplicate the rocky northern Pacific coast. (The weather, on the other hand, is distinctly Floridian.) Viewers stroll around the edge of the surf zone, a favorite hangout for fun-loving pinnipeds, and can peep at underwater activities through the Plexiglas wall at one side of the tank. Buy some smelt and watch the sea lions sing for their supper from close up. *Crowds: Not a problem. Strategy: Go anytime. Audience: All ages. Rating:* ★★★

There are 17 species of penguin, from the little crested fairy penguin to the large orange-striped king penguin, as well as puffins and murries, which scoot around a refrigerated re-creation of Antarctica at **Penguin Encounter,** a large white building between Whale & Dolphin Stadium and Sea Lion & Otter Stadium. The indoor viewing area is the chilliest spot in Sea World, but it's even colder inside the penguins' habitat; in fact, it snows daily. The birds love it, clustering under the icy precipitation, then waddling over to their frigid pool and taking the plunge. A Plexiglas wall on the viewers' side of the tank shows that the penguins are as graceful in the water as they are awkward on land. Sea World's penguin-breeding program has been so successful that it routinely supplies birds to other zoos. *Crowds: Frequently gridlocked, despite a moving walkway tactfully nudging visitors past the glassed-in habitat. Strategy: Go while the dolphin and sea lion shows are on. Audience: All ages. Rating:* ★★

The indoor **Sea World Theatre,** between Penguin Encounter and the central lagoon, screens "Window to the Sea," a brief overview of the park's research, conservation, and breeding efforts. (Sea World has emergency teams that routinely save beached whales, injured manatees, and other water animals.) The film starts out like a dreary PBS special but picks up enough to keep even children entertained. Footage of a killer-whale attack increases the gore factor that's so appreciated by some adolescents. If a behind-the-scenes tour seems more interesting now that you've had a look at the park's scientific side, skitter right back to the entrance—groups leave every half hour until 3 PM. *Duration: 20 min. Crowds: No problem. Audience: All but young children. Rating:* ★★

Later in the afternoon (usually starting at 5), the film presentation in Sea World Theatre is replaced with **Water Fantasy,** a delightfully kitschy demonstration of what you can do with a really state-of-the-art sprinkler system and some colored lights. The stage floor, a sort of giant wading pool, contains 36 revolving nozzles that spray water into fountains, waving plumes, and helices, all in time to a sound track of pop tunes. Still, this undemanding show and air-conditioned theater are a pleasant relief after all the intense animal interaction, and the youngsters will love it. *Duration: 20 min. Crowds: Not a problem. Strategy: Go when you want to sit down and cool off. Audience: All ages. Rating:* ★

Continue around the central lagoon, ignoring the lure of the bridge shortcut to Shamu Stadium, to a large and innocuous white structure housing some thoroughly nasty critters. **Terrors of the Deep** is Sea World's attempt to make you love—or at least no longer be repulsed by—dangerous sea creatures such as eels, barracuda, venomous and poisonous fish, and sharks. Each animal is profiled via a video screen and educational posters ("There is little to love about the eel," one says, backing up its point by explaining how a slimy coat of mucus makes so-called blue eels appear green). Then you walk through a series of four Plexiglas tubes—surrounded by tanks—containing the world's largest collection of such animals. Sharks slide just feet overhead and eels slither out from their hiding places. Stop to absorb this neatly contained underwater nightmare in a large viewing theater with benches. Even at its most crowded—and this is another one of Sea World's most popular attractions—the walk-through tubes and overhead videos mean that even small children can get an eyeful. *Duration: Plan to spend 40 min. Crowds: Most significant when adjacent sea lion show gets out. Strategy: Go during the sea lion shows. Audience: All ages. Rating:* ★★★

⑫ The renovated **Nautilus Showplace,** completely redone during 1994, is home to Sea World's only song-and-dance extravaganza. This seafaring-themed show is a typical combination of high-energy performers and low-down music. *Duration: 30 min. Crowds: Not a problem. Strategy: Good when you need a rest. Audience: All ages. Rating:* ★★

⑬ Again following the lakeshore, you come to **Clydesdale Hamlet**
⑭ and **Anheuser-Busch Hospitality Center.** A feature of all Anheuser-Busch parks, the walk-through hamlet houses hulking Clydesdale horses and provides a bucolic corral for their ponderous romping. A statue of a heroically endowed stallion, which youngsters are encouraged to scramble up, makes a perfect generic theme-park photo opportunity. The Clydesdales are so incongruous in this marine-oriented setting that you have to agree with one teenager, who wisecracked, "Look, Dad, surf 'n' turf." The hospitality center, far from espousing the Teutonic overtones of its Busch Gardens cousin, is light and airy, combining cafeteria-style service with a bar serving Anheuser-Busch beverages. *Crowds: Never significant. Strategy: Go anytime. Audience: All ages. Rating:* ★

Little ones can't wait to scramble along the lakeshore path to
⑮ **Shamu's Happy Harbor,** a 3-acre outdoor play area with crawlable, climbable, explorable, bounceable, and get-wetable activities, including a four-story net climb. Youngsters go wild for the "ball rooms"—two tents filled with thousands of Styrofoam balls that children can wade through (there are separate ones for toddlers and grade schoolers)—and the tent with the air-mattress floor, which is like a giant trampoline. There are pipes to crawl through and much more. Though it's not as dramatic as Disney-MGM's *Honey, I Blew Up the Kids* Movie Set Adventure and lacks the water slides of Universal's play area, Shamu's Happy Harbor is much more spacious and airy. *Crowds: Often a challenge. Strategy: Don't go first thing in the morning or you'll never drag your child away (but if you go in midafternoon, expect plenty of hubbub). No height or age restrictions. Audience: Toddlers through grade schoolers. Rating:* ★★

In fact, the only thing likely to distract your child from the net **16** climb is directly opposite: **Shamu Stadium,** home to Sea World's orca mascot and hands-down the most popular feature in the park. Several shows daily showcase the whales' acrobatic, spectator-drenching antics. Fantastic flips and jumps are combined with video footage of orcas in the wild and gently educational factoids about the care and training of the giant mammals. After an unprecedented two births in late 1993—a baby boom by orca standards—Sea World revamped the show to focus on "Baby Shamu." Because killer whales do not reach their full size for four years, the kids are likely to be part of the show for a while. At press time, even the funky, glitzy **Shamu Night Magic** evening show had been suspended in favor of another "Baby Shamu" show, but this may have changed by the time you arrive. Come about 15 minutes early just to watch the mesmerizing sight of the whales gliding around the 5-million-gallon Plexiglas-walled tank. The sides are high enough so that even viewers in the higher stadium seats can see the underwater action through the clear walls. *Duration: 25 min. Crowds: Sometimes a problem. Strategy: Go 45 min early for the early afternoon show. Close-up encounters through the Plexiglas walls are not to be missed, so trot on down. Audience: All ages. Rating:* ★★★

17 Adjoining the stadium, **Shamu Breeding & Research Pool** allows unprecedented up-close-and-personal underwater viewing of the orcas' breeding and nursery area. The outdoor tanks are on the same level as the main pool in Shamu Stadium and have similar Plexiglas walls and viewing setups. Sea World can never predict when its whales will get pregnant, but its breeding program has been astonishingly successful. There's a good chance that you'll see a miniature Shamu, looking remarkably like an inflatable pool toy, cavorting after its mother. *Crowds: Sometimes so large you'll have to edge your way to viewing areas. Strategy: Go early or late, or be patient. Audience: All ages. Rating:* ★★★

18 **Mission: Bermuda Triangle** is next to Shamu's Happy Harbor and opposite Shamu Stadium. A replication of a deep-sea dive afflicted by forces beyond its control, this flight simulator adds an extra dimension to the contraption's usual pitch, heave, surge, sway, roll, and yaw: seasickness. It shakes, rattles and rolls, but not much else. If your day is busy, stick to what Sea World does best—animals. *Duration: 10 min. Crowds: Waits of up to an hr. Strategy: Go when a Shamu show is in progress. If traveling with your offspring, one parent should supervise the children at Shamu's Happy Harbor while the other stands on line. And don't go right after lunch. No pregnant women, children under 42 inches tall, or guests with back, neck, or heart conditions. Audience: All but young children. Rating:* ★

Time Out **Mango Joe's Café,** a speedy, tropical-colored cafeteria between Shamu Stadium and Atlantis Water Ski Stadium, serves fresh fajitas, hefty salads, and delicious Key lime pie, and the place has

plenty of umbrella-shaded tables, many right on the lake. Some
tables have a great view of the waterskiing show.

⑲ The last attraction on the lagoon circuit, **Atlantis Water Ski Stadium** presents a themed waterskiing show on Sea World's central lagoon, complete with singing, dancing, and lots of stunts—a
rip-roaring, gag-filled extravaganza that is to Cypress Gardens'
performance what the Ice Capades are to Olympic figure-skat-
ing competitions. There's a sketchy theme, whose gossamer
story is important only as an excuse for the usual suspects to
present themselves: good guys (they do flips off ramps), bad
guys (they specialize in skiing barefoot and on their faces to
show how tough they are), gals (they get to show off skimpy
costumes), and a clown or two. *Duration: 35 min. Crowds: Not a
problem. Strategy: Be warned—the splash factor is significant in
the first 10 rows; the terrace at neighboring Mango Joe's Café and
the deck at the Bimini Bay Café are alternative viewing spots.
Audience: All ages. Rating:* ★★★

Dining

In addition to the standard entertainment park fare of burgers,
barbecue, and the usual burnt offerings sold at restaurants and
concessions throughout the park, Sea World has two dandy
places for lunch: **Mango Joe's Café** and **Bimini Bay Café** (*see
above*), from which you have a close-up view of the frenetic activity on the floats where the waterski show stunts are set up.

Unfortunately, the pickings are slim for dinner. Mango Joe's
closes down, alas, leaving a meager choice of barbecued chicken
and ribs at **Buccaneer Smokehouse** and sandwiches and salads
at **Anheuser-Busch Hospitality Center.**

Luau Alternatively, you can opt for entertainment in the form of the
"Aloha!" Polynesian Luau Dinner and Show at Bimini Bay Café.
In an Anheuser-Busch family version of *Blue Hawaii*, scantily
clad dancers undulate across the floor, bearing lei-draped platters of roast pig. Reservations are required and may be made
the same day either at the luau reservations counter at the information center at the entrance or by telephone (tel. 407/363–
2195 or 800/227–8048). The cost is $27.95 adults, $18.95 for
juniors 8–12, $9.95 for children 3–7, including one cocktail and
all nonalcoholic drinks.

Shopping

There are some hard-hearted souls who pass up a plush Shamu,
but they are few and far between. These are available all over
the park. Also extremely cuddly are the stuffed manatees sold
at **Manatee Cove,** near the manatee exhibit; proceeds from the
toys go to benefit a manatee preservation organization. The
Friends of the Wild shop near Penguin Encounter carries various
items, including tropical fish earrings and hair ornaments. The
coolest gift is sold at the **Mission: Bermuda Triangle Shop**—lo-
goless but genuine neoprene water shoes decorated in black and

white, à la orca. If you've left the park before realizing that your Aunt Betsy simply must have a Shamu slicker, visit the shop just outside the entrance.

Access for Travelers with Disabilities

Services   There are **TTYs for outgoing calls** at Bimini Bay Restaurant, across from Whale & Dolphin Stadium.

Attractions   Because many of the shows are in theaters and stadiums, guests using wheelchairs will have an easy day at Sea World. With reserved seating areas, the **Nautilus Showplace, Sea Lion and Otter Stadium, Sea World Theatre, Shamu Stadium,** and **Whale and Dolphin Stadium** are completely accessible, though entry usually requires an uphill climb along sloping ramps. The stadium shows usually fill to capacity, so plan to arrive 30–45 minutes before each show (45–60 minutes in peak seasons). At Shamu Stadium, the reserved seating area is inside the splash zone, so if you don't want to get soaking wet, get a host or hostess to recommend another place to sit. There is entertainment value in all of the theater and stadium shows for both hearing-impaired and visually impaired guests with a single exception: Performances in the Nautilus Showplace may be unrewarding for guests with visual impairments.

Penguin Encounter, Terrors of the Deep, and **Tropical Reef** are all wheelchair accessible. To ride the moving-sidewalk viewing areas in Penguin Encounter and Terrors of the Deep, guests must transfer to a standard wheelchair (available in the boarding area) if they do not already use one. Tropical Reef and Penguin Encounter have minimal entertainment value for guests with visual impairments. All will be enjoyable for guests with hearing impairments.

The **Anheuser-Busch Hospitality Center** is completely accessible. **Shamu's Happy Harbor** has some activities that are accessible to children using wheelchairs and anyone else who wants to climb, crawl, or slide.

The turbulent **Mission: Bermuda Triangle** is accessible only by guests using a wheelchair who can transfer into the ride seat. If you like other thrill rides, you'll like this one. Guests with back, neck, or heart problems should skip it, though. The **"Aloha!" Luau** is completely accessible.

Shops and   Restaurants are accessible, but drinking straws are not
Restaurants   provided here; this is out of concern for the safety of the animals. Bring your own. Shops are level, but many are so packed with merchandise that maneuvering in a wheelchair can be a challenge.

Universal Studios Florida

Film fans know that Disney has no copyright on movie magic. Universal Studios has worked celluloid wizardry since 1915, and it wasn't long afterward that it offered visitors behind-the-scenes tours of what was to become the world's biggest and busiest motion picture and television production studio—that of Universal Studios Hollywood. So it wasn't surprising that Orlando's entertainment park expansion should pique the interest of that other candidate from California. Universal Studios Florida opened in June 1990.

Far from being a me-too version of Disney-MGM Studios, Universal Studios Florida is a theme park with plenty of personality of its own. And its personality can be summed up in one word: attitude. It's saucy, sassy, and hip—and doesn't hesitate to invite comparisons with the competition. Where Disney-MGM has the Muppets trilling "Great Balls of Fire," Universal's Beetlejuice Graveyard Revue, a new take on the Grateful Dead, sports a transfunkified Dracula belting "I'm Gonna Wait 'til the Midnight Hour" and a miniskirted Frankenstein's Bride getting down to "You Make Me Feel Like a Natural Woman." Disney-MGM's strolling actors are pablum compared to the Blues Brothers peeling rubber in the Bluesmobile. And let's face it, even the Muppets are matched by E.T., Tickli Moot Moot, and other inventions of Steven Spielberg, Universal's genius on call. Universal's even figured out a way to keep people entertained while they wait in line: From arcade games at Nickelodeon to news shows on overhead screens in the *Jaws* line, Universal makes the most of its video connection.

In short, Universal Studios is the bad boy of central Florida entertainment parks. It's come a long way from the public relations nightmare of its opening days, when almost none of the highly touted rides functioned. Now they do, and so-called blockbuster rides such as Kongfrontation, Back to the Future . . . The Ride, E.T. Adventure, Earthquake—The Big One, and even the much-maligned Jaws (so glitch-haunted in its early days that it had to be closed for two years for repairs) are running and—judging from the delighted shrieks and groans issuing forth—running just fine. Universal Studios Florida is now the third most popular entertainment park in the United States, after Walt Disney World (with its three theme parks) and Disneyland; Universal Studios Hollywood, by the way, is a close fourth. Look forward to further expansion as Universal takes advantage of its Hollywood connections and opens rides and exhibits that tie in with hit movies. In 1994, a *Jurassic Park* exhibit opened, and park officials say a tribute to *The Flintstones,* starring John Goodman, should be in place by the spring of 1995.

The lofty adult ticket prices raise expectations very high indeed. They are met most of the time, but resentment can set in if you're confronted by too many long lines and the movie-theater-like price gouging at ubiquitous concession stands and snackeries. We know, we know, it's a free country. But as one disgruntled customer at Schwab's Drugstore groused, "I still think $1.90 for a drink this size is a little excessive."

With Disney-MGM just down the road, is Universal worth the visit? Absolutely—they're not the same thing: If Disney-MGM is the introductory course, Universal Studios is graduate school.

As such, the attractions are geared more to older kids than the stroller set. If your party is prepared for some loud and scary entertainment, then you should have a wonderful time.

Essential Information

Tourist Information

Contact Universal Studios (1000 Universal Studios Plaza, Orlando 32819-7610, tel. 407/363–8000, TTY 407/363–8265).

Stop by **Guest Relations,** in the Front Lot to the right after you pass through the turnstiles, for brochures, maps, and a schedule of the day's entertainments, tapings, and filmings.

Studio Information Boards in front of Studio Stars Restaurant and Mel's Drive-In provide up-to-the-minute ride and show operating information—including the length of lines in minutes at the Studios' major attractions.

If you want to watch a production filming or taping, consult the Production Schedule at the entrance turnstiles or stop in at Guest Relations. Attendants at the Nickelodeon studio can tell you how to get studio audience tickets.

Reservations

Reservations at the Universal Studios restaurants that accept them (*see below*) can be made as far in advance as you want to make them; just call the restaurant or go there in person first thing in the morning.

Getting There

Universal Studios is about ½ mile north of I–4 Exit 30B (Kirkman Rd., or Rte. 435), near the intersection of I–4 and the Florida Turnpike. Be warned, however, that getting from the 30B/Kirkman exit to the park is confusing—you have to drive past the entrance gates and then loop back. It's much easier to reach Universal Studios if you get off I–4 at Exit 29, which is slightly south of the park. From Exit 29, directions are as follows: If traveling westbound on I–4, make a right onto Sand Lake Road and another right onto Turkey Lake Road; if traveling eastbound, make a left onto Sand Lake Road and then a right onto Turkey Lake Road. Numerous billboards and signposts mark the way.

Parking

The cost is $5 for cars, $7 for campers. Valet parking is also available for $11.

Admission

Tickets, excluding tax, cost $36 for one day, $55 for two days; $29 and $44, respectively, for children 3–9. They're available in advance by mail through Ticketmaster (tel. 800/745–5000).

Discounts

Making your purchase at the Orlando/Orange County Convention and Visitors Bureau ticket office at the Mercado International Market (8445 International Dr.) will save you about $4 per adult ticket ($3 on children's prices). When you buy your ticket at the gate, you can save $2.50 by using the Orlando Magicard, available free on request (tel. 800/551–0181) or in person at the Mercado. Card-carrying AAA members can receive a 10% discount at the park; the discount may be higher at an AAA office.

Hand Stamps   If you want to leave the park and come back the same day, have your hand stamped when you leave, and show your hand and your Studio Pass when you return.

Ticket Upgrades   If you decide that one day is not enough, buy your next day's ticket at Guest Relations just inside the Main Entrance *before* you leave the park, and you'll pay only the two-day ticket price.

Hours   Universal Studios is open 365 days a year, from 9 to 7, with hours extended as late as 10 during summer and holiday periods.

Services   There are **diaper-changing tables** in both men's and women's
Baby Care   rest rooms; there are **nursing facilities** at Guest Relations just inside the Main Entrance and to the right, as well as at First Aid, adjoining Louie's Italian restaurant between San Francisco and New York. No **diapers** are sold on the premises; instead, they're complimentary—to guests in need—at Animal House, Doc's Candy Store, the Universal Studios Store, and other locations (ask!). You will find **strollers** (which look like Jurassic Park jeeps) for rent in Amity and just inside the Main Entrance to the right, next to the First Union National Bank (singles $6, doubles $12; no deposit required). However, **no formula or baby food** is sold on the premises; the nearest sources are K-Mart on Sand Lake Road, Walgreen's on Kirkman Road, and Publix supermarkets on Sand Lake and Kirkman roads.

Baby Exchange   All Studio rides have Baby Exchange areas, so that one parent or adult party member can watch a baby or toddler while the other enjoys the ride or show. The adults then change roles, and the former caretaker rides without having to wait in line all over again.

Cameras and Film   At the Lights, Camera, Action shop in the Front Lot, just inside the Main Entrance, you'll find **rental video cameras** ($29.95 per day; deposit or credit-card imprint required) and **loaner 35mm cameras.** You must show a valid driver's license and a major credit card.

For **minor camera repairs,** go to the Dark Room on Hollywood Boulevard.

For **one-hour film developing,** the Dark Room is the spot.

Car Care   You can fill 'er up at the '40s-vintage Texaco station at the Turkey Lake Road entrance. If you need a battery jump, raise your hood and speak to the nearest employee.

First Aid   Universal Studios' First Aid Center is between New York and San Francisco, next to Louie's Italian Restaurant.

Guided Tours   Universal offers two VIP tours, which offer what's called "back-door admission" or, in plain English, the right to jump the line. No other theme park has anything like this, which we suppose is the ultimate capitalist fantasy. In any case, they're definitely worthwhile if you're in a hurry, if the day is crowded, and if you have the money to burn—from $90 for an individual four-hour VIP tour (including park admission) to $900 for an eight-hour tour for up to 15 people (again including park admission).

Lockers   They're across from Guest Relations (*see above;* 50¢).

Lost Children and Adults   If you lose your children or traveling companions, speak up immediately at Guest Relations or at Security (behind Louie's, between New York and San Francisco).

Lost and Found   Misplaced possessions go to Guest Relations near the Main Entrance.

Money   The First Union National Bank, just inside the Main Entrance, cashes traveler's checks, makes cash advances on credit cards, and exchanges foreign currency. There's one ATM at the bank and another outside the Main Entrance, to the right of the Guest Relations Window; they're linked to Plus, Honor, and some to Cirrus.

Wheelchair Rentals   Wheelchairs ($5 a day) and electric wheelchairs ($25 a day) can be rented in Amity and just inside the Main Entrance, to the right, next to the First Union National Bank. You must leave a valid driver's license or $25 as a deposit. If the wheelchair breaks down, disappears, or otherwise needs replacing, speak to any shop attendant.

Strategies for Your Visit

When to Go   As in the Disney parks, Mondays through Wednesdays are the busiest days of the week. The pace slows down on Thursdays and Fridays and builds again over the weekend. Saturdays and Sundays are usually busy, but especially during holiday weeks.

Blitz Tour   Universal estimates that 14 hours are needed to experience the entire park. So if you want to at least attempt seeing everything in one day, arrive early so that you can take care of business and see the fabled attractions before the park gets very crowded.

Visit the **Funtastic World of Hanna-Barbera** first. Then head to the far end of the park for **Back to the Future . . . The Ride** before the lines become impossible. Round the lagoon and visit **Jaws, Earthquake—The Big One,** and **Kongfrontation**; we promise you won't feel jaded by seeing these three in a row. While you're in the neighborhood, catch **Beetlejuice's Graveyard Revue;** it's just the right chaser for having had the wits scared out of you.

Have lunch in the nearby San Francisco lot and then shift over to Production Central for the **Production Tram Tour** and the **Nickelodeon Studios Tour.** Then visit the **Gory, Gruesome & Grotesque Horror Make-Up Show, Jurassic Park: Behind the Scenes, Hitchcock's 3-D Theatre, "Murder, She Wrote" Mystery Theatre,** and **Ghostbusters.** Now's the time to explore the New York and San Francisco–Amity backlots as you wander over to the **Wild, Wild, Wild West Stunt Show.**

Round the lagoon again—this time from the other direction—and check out the lines at Back to the Future, in case you want a second go-round. **E.T. Adventure** is the perfect valedictory ride; when the extraterrestrial bids you farewell from his enchanted forest, it's a metaphor for your entire visit. And the exit places you in a good strategic location for the **Dynamite Nights Stunt Spectacular** on the lagoon.

On Rainy Except during Christmas week, rainy days are less crowded—
Days even though the park is in full operation. (Only a couple of street shows get canceled.)

Other Tips The strategies that stand you in good stead in the Disney parks also prevail here.

- Call the day before your visit to get official park hours.

- Arrive in the parking lot 30–45 minutes early and see the biggest attractions first.

- Lunch before 11 and dine at 5. Or have a filling snack at 10:30, lunch after 2, and dinner at 8 or later. Or lunch on the early side at a place that takes reservations (Lombard's Landing and Studio Stars are good bets). Be sure to make your reservations ahead of time (or, at the very least, when you enter the park).

- If you're traveling with small children, avoid backtracking. Universal is just too big.

- Set up a rendezvous point at the start of the day, just in case you and your companions get separated.

- Be sure to mark your parking location by some permanent landmark. Universal Studios' parking lots do not have overhead signs designating parking areas.

Exploring Universal Studios Florida

The 444 acres of Universal Studios are a bewildering conglomeration of stage sets, shops, reproductions of New York and San Francisco, and anonymous soundstages housing theme attractions as well as genuine moviemaking paraphernalia. On the map, these sets are neatly divided into six neighborhoods: the Front Lot, Production Central, Hollywood, New York, Expo Center, and San Francisco/Amity, which lazily wend their way around a huge blue lagoon, the setting for the Dynamite Nights Stunt Spectacular. On foot, it's a different story. There is no prominent central edifice by which to orient yourself, and the street names change depending on which "neighborhood" you're in. In other words, expect to get lost early and often. Rather than trying to figure out whether you're on Sunset Boulevard, Hollywood Boulevard, or Rodeo Drive (the answer is "yes"), look for official staffers; their snappy, surprisingly classy pink-and-white-striped oxford-cloth shirts and white walking shorts stand out.

The Front Like Disney-MGM's Hollywood Boulevard, Universal Studios'
Lot Front Lot is essentially a scene-setter, a mood manipulator, the first of many opportunities to squander the contents of your savings account on merchandise or snacks, and the place to find many services. The main drag, the Plaza of the Stars, stretches from the marble-arched entrance gateway straight down to the other end of the lot, affording a great trompe-l'oeil view of New York City's public library painted on a wall in the New York neighborhood. One thousand miles in as many yards—how's that for magic?

Hollywood Angling off to the right of Plaza of the Stars, Rodeo Drive stretches from the Front Lot to the lagoon (turning into Hollywood Boulevard along the way). The street forms the backbone of Hollywood, which contains such attractions as Lucy: A Tribute, the Gory, Gruesome & Grotesque Horror Make-Up Show, and Jurassic Park: Behind the Scenes, as well as more shops and nosheries.

Numbers in the margin correspond to points of interest on the Universal Studios map.

❶ As the first attraction you meet after promenading through the grandiose gateway, **Lucy: A Tribute** occupies a prime corner at Rodeo Drive and Plaza of the Stars. A walk-through collection of Lucy's costumes, accessories, and other memorabilia, trivia quizzes, and 20-second spots from the series shown on overhead video screens, the exhibition doesn't quite match the value of the real estate. Fans of the ditzy redhead may want to reminisce over every item, however. *Duration: Around 15 min. Crowds: Seldom a problem. Strategy: Save this for a peek on your way out or for a hot afternoon. Audience: Adults. Rating:* ★

❷ Farther along the street, just past the bend where Rodeo Drive turns into Hollywood Boulevard, the **Gory, Gruesome & Grotesque Horror Make-Up Show** is especially appreciated by young children and teens, showing as it does what goes into and oozes out of the most mangled monsters in movie history. There's a delicious irony in the fact that you settle into comfortable seats in an air-conditioned theater to find out how an actor's mouth turned into a roach motel in the movie *Creep Show*, how man-to-wolf transmogrification is effected in *American Werewolf in London*, and, of course, the secret of the famous spinning-heads scene in *The Exorcist*. The Horror Make-Up Show demystifies without disillusioning—although you never do learn the exact proportions of shrimp sauce, oatmeal, and red dye that go into making a gallon of blood and guts. *Duration: 25 min. Crowds: Not daunting. Strategy: Go in the afternoon or evening. Audience: All but young children, who may be frightened; older children eat up the blood-and-guts stories. Rating:* ★★

❸ From the makeup show, walk out front to **Jurassic Park: Behind the Scenes.** This collection of memorabilia from the largest-grossing movie ever is surprisingly small given the film's blockbuster status. Nonetheless, it's worth dropping by if only to see the triceratops lying in the entryway. The rest of the exhibit includes some Jurassic jeeps, costumes, and stills from the production process. Although park officials aren't promising anything, look for an accompanying dinosaur-themed thrill ride sometime in the next year. *Duration: 10–15 min. Crowds: Not a problem. Strategy: Go anytime. Audience: All ages. Rating:* ★★

Time Out At the corner of Hollywood Boulevard and 8th Avenue (which, just for the sake of confusion, turns into Sunset Boulevard along the bottom shore of the lagoon), is **Mel's Drive-In,** a flashy '50s eatery with a menu and decorative muscle cars straight out of *American Graffiti*. For burgers and fries, this is one of the best choices in the park. It's complete with roving doo-wop group, and—unlike at the Hard Rock Café, which serves a similar menu—the decibel level allows normal conversation.

Production Central Marked in green on the park map, Production Central spreads over the entire left side of the Plaza of the Stars and practically encircles Hollywood, too. It contains six huge warehouses with working soundstages, as well as such attractions as Hitchcock's 3-D Theatre, the Funtastic World of Hanna-Barbera, the "Murder, She Wrote" Mystery Theatre, Nickelodeon Studios, and Universal Studios' trademark Production Tram Tour.

Nickelodeon Way leads off to the left of the Plaza of the Stars opposite Lucy: A Tribute. Past the Green Slime Geyser welcoming you to Nickelodeon Studios is the embarkation point for the ❹ **Production Tram Tour,** an updated version of the old Hollywood Glamortram, that takes you on a nonstop ride around the park. The guide is full of nifty trivia about movies filmed on the giant soundstages (for instance, check out the continuity glitch in *Parenthood* when Steve Martin extols the joys of living in St. Louis while driving past a sign that reads "Florida's Turnpike, 6 miles") or props now slowly rusting in the boneyard—yes, this is where Jaws' dorsal fin washed up—but the ride neither orients you nor takes you inside any of the soundstages. *Duration: 20 min. Crowds: Ebb and flow. Strategy: Go in the afternoon as a midday respite for tired feet or in the evening. Try to nab a seat in the front; exhaust fumes perfume the rear cars. Audience: All ages. Rating:* ★

The Production Tram Tour lets you off right back where you started, where the Green Slime Geyser is still going strong, enticing visitors into **Nickelodeon Studios.** This tour, showing how ❺ a television show is produced, is akin to Disney-MGM's Inside the Magic. About 90% of Nickelodeon's original programming is produced on the soundstages you'll walk through. The banks of lights, concrete floors, and general warehouse feel go a long way toward demystifying movie magic, but it's exactly that behind-the-scenes perspective that makes the tour interesting. You'll get a peek at wardrobe and makeup studios, as well as a tour of the kitchen where Slime is made. The tour winds up in the **Game Lab,** an even wackier version of the interactive wonders in the Image Works at Epcot Center's Journey into Imagination. *Duration: 30 min. Crowds: Steady, long lines. Strategy: Skip it on a first-time visit or if no shows are taping. Audience: All ages but especially grade schoolers. Rating:* ★★

❻ The **Funtastic World of Hanna-Barbera,** a combination ride-video-interactive display at the corner of Nickelodeon Way and Plaza of the Stars, is Universal's answer to Disney-MGM's Animation Building and one of the most popular attractions at Universal Studios. Before the show, Yogi Bear appears on overhead video monitors to explain how cartoons are constructed. The "dynamically aggressive ride," as the park puts it, puts you inside a Jetsons cartoon in a hint of what you might expect at the Back to the Future . . . The Ride flight simulator. But the best

Universal Studios

NEW YORK

5th Ave.
Park Ave.
Delancey St.
42nd St.
Canal St.
South St.

57th St.

Amblin Ave.

Studio Stars Restaurant

PRODUCTION CENTRAL

8th Ave.
South St.
87th Ave.

Mel's Drive-In

HOLLYWOOD

Hollywood Blvd

Nickelodeon Way

Plaza of the Stars

Rodeo Dr.

FRONT LOT

Lockers

Stroller Rental

Automatic Teller

Guest Relations

Celebrity Circle

← TO TURKEY LAKE RD.

Main Entrance

"The Adventures of Rocky & Bullwinkle", **9**

Alfred Hitchcock's 3-D Theatre, **7**

Back to the Future...The Ride, **17**

Beetlejuice's Graveyard Revue, **12**

Dynamite Nights Stunt Spectacular, **16**

E.T. Adventure, **19**

Earthquake---The Big One, **13**

Fievel's Playland, **18**

Funtastic World of Hanna-Barbera, **6**

Ghostbusters, **10**

Gory, Gruesome & Grotesque Horror Make-Up Show, **2**

Jaws, **14**

Jurassic Park: Behind the Scenes, **3**

Kongfrontation, **11**

Lucy: A Tribute, **1**

"Murder, She Wrote" Mystery Theatre, **8**

Nickelodeon Studios, **5**

Production Tram Tour, **4**

Wild, Wild, Wild West Stunt Show, **15**

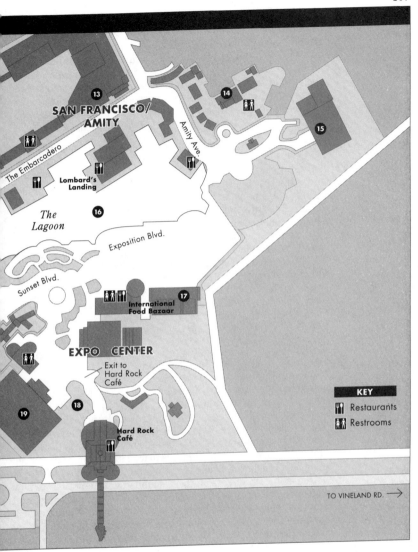

SAN FRANCISCO/ AMITY

13

14

15

The Embarcadero

Amity Ave.

Lombard's Landing

The Lagoon

16

Exposition Blvd.

Sunset Blvd.

International Food Bazaar

17

EXPO CENTER

Exit to Hard Rock Café

19

18

Hard Rock Café

KEY

Restaurants

Restrooms

TO VINELAND RD. →

part is the interactive electronic magic booths at the end of the attraction, in which you provide the studio voice for a Flintstone cartoon, paint Pebbles's hair green with a computerized brush, and twirl dials and push buttons to mix up a sound-salad of boinks, splats, and plops. *Duration: 8 min. Crowds: Usually stunning, despite high capacity. Strategy: Go as soon as the gates open or at night. No pregnant women or guests with motion sickness or heart, neck, or back problems; must be 40 inches tall to ride. Audience: All ages; frightening for some toddlers. Rating:* ★★★

"Have you ever had a premonition?" asks the superbly cultured and ever-so-slightly spooky voice of Alfred Hitchcock, the star **❼** of the high-capacity **Alfred Hitchcock's 3-D Theatre,** located across the Plaza of the Stars from Hanna-Barbera. It starts off a dandy multimedia tribute to the master of suspense, who made 53 films for Universal Studios. Thanks to 3-D glasses, you learn what it's like to be a citizen of Bodega Bay on a day of abnormal avian activity. Audience participation reveals the secret of *Psycho*'s famous shower scene as well as some previously unseen 3-D footage from *Dial M for Murder.* As in any good Hitchcock film, this attraction engages your mind as well as your adrenaline—and has a characteristic twist of an ending. *Duration: 40 min. Crowds: Sizable early in the day while visitors pass by on their way into the park. Strategy: Save it for later in the afternoon or evening. Audience: All but young children, who may be frightened. Rating:* ★★★

❽ One reason why **"Murder, She Wrote" Mystery Theatre** is so popular is that you learn that kissing the back of your hand involves more suction than a kiss on the lips and that it produces a better noise for the sound track. It's just the kind of fact that senior-citizen sleuth Jessica Fletcher would use to nail a nasty. This attraction, presented in a large sit-down theater, combines the best of Disney-MGM's "Monster Sound Show" and "Superstar Television" as the audience is placed in the role of executive producer, racing the clock to put together an episode of the show. Three manic producers on three soundstages demonstrate how a script is chosen, how sounds are mixed (hence the kissing), and what happens when everything is put together. When they ask for volunteers, raise your hand and help them make some joyful noise. *Duration: 40 min. Crowds: Substantial, but waits are seldom discouraging. Strategy: Go in the afternoon, when you feel like sitting down and cooling off. Audience: Older children and adults. Rating:* ★★★

Friends of Frostbite Falls follow the call of the moose around the **❾** back of the "Murder, She Wrote" soundstage to **"The Adventures of Rocky & Bullwinkle,"** a musical revue starring Bullwinkle the Moose, his faithful friend Rocky Squirrel, the dashing and ineffably dense Canadian Mountie Dudley Doright, and those two Russian nogoodniks, Boris Badenov and his slinky sidekick, Natasha. The action takes place on an animated set at the edge of Universal's New York back lot and involves lots of songs, corny jokes, and trademark explosions when Boris and Natasha's nefarious plot backfires. Kaboomski. *Duration: 15–20 min. Crowds: Never a problem. Strategy: Shows* *every hour, usually beginning around 11; go anytime. Audience: All ages. Rating:* ★★

New York   The New York back lot—like the San Francisco and Amity neighborhoods elsewhere in the park—has been rendered with surprising detail, right down to the cracked concrete and slightly stained cobblestones. Only two things are missing: potholes and litter. The Blues Brothers Bluesmobile regularly cruises the neighborhood, and musicians hop out to give impromptu performances at 70 Delancey. (These shows are really worth catching. Check the signs near Guest Services for performance times.) Every corner opens onto a trompe-l'oeil view of, say, Park Avenue or Gramercy Park. Designated photo-op spots place you with just the right backdrop.

⑩ New York is also home to **Ghostbusters,** those paranormal problem solvers first introduced in the 1984 movie. The preshow, which takes place in a stand-up theater designed as a cluttered store, is a sales pitch for a Ghostbusters franchise, with some hands-on lessons in slime control from volunteers from the audience. (Don't worry, the stuff slides right off your clothes without leaving any stains.) Then everyone files into the ectoplasmic containment chamber (that is, a large sit-down theater) for an equipment demonstration—suitably mismanaged to send spooks slithering through the auditorium. All the movie favorites—even the Stay Puft Marshmallow Man—are here amid ghostly explosions and arcing lasers, and the climax—we're not giving anything away when we say it involves the sprinkler system—is breathtaking. *Duration: 15 min. Crowds: Steady, but the auditorium can hold almost everyone. Strategy: A good bet for crowded periods; check show times at Guest Relations before you enter the park. Audience: Older children and adults. Rating:* ★★★

⑪ Keep up the thrill quotient at **Kongfrontation,** a Universal powerpunch just down 5th Avenue from Ghostbusters. The waiting area reproduces a New York subway station, complete with graffiti. (One former New York mayor objected to the set on the grounds that it painted a picture of a much-bruised Big Apple.) As you board the trams for the escape from the ape-threatened city to Roosevelt Island, police radios crackle with news of Kongsightings. Then you round a corner and . . . you're in the middle of mayhem. King Kong grabs the tram, helicopter gunships swoop in for a shot, everyone's screaming joyously, and the distinctive odor of banana breath fills the air. Somehow you escape, but the quavering voice of the tram operator implies that the beast still lurks, waiting for a second chance. *Duration: 5 min. Crowds: Lines ebb and flow throughout the day and move slowly because of the ride's small capacity. Strategy: Go early or late; if your time is limited, opt for Jaws and Earthquake, because they provide more thrill for the time spent in line. No pregnant women or guests with motion sickness or heart, back, or neck problems; must be 40 inches tall to ride alone. Audience: Older children and adults; Kong is too realistic for youngsters. Rating:* ★★

San Francisco/ Amity From Gotham City, it's just a few yards to San Francisco, thanks to Universal Studios' magical geography. The structures here imitate the wharves and warehouses of the Embarcadero and Fisherman's Wharf district, with the distinctive redbrick Ghirardelli chocolate factory, cable-car tracks cut through the middle of the street, and rusty "No Fishing" signs written in Chinese. It's hard to know just where San Francisco segues into Amity, the New England fishing village terrorized by the shark in *Jaws.* But suddenly, you're definitely back on the East Coast, amid Cape Cod cottages and win-a-stuffed-animal game stall honkytonks. At the center of town, a towering scaffold displays a 24-foot great white shark, complete with spiked teeth and nasty expression. One would think it would be safe to go back into the water, but . . . Universal Studios doesn't make money from movie sequels for nothing.

12 First, though, ease your transcontinental switch at **Beetlejuice's Graveyard Revue,** a live sound-and-light spectacle in an open-air amphitheater in which the ghoul with groove transfunkifies a group of scary monsters into a rhythm-and-blues band. Based on the 1991 movie starring Michael Keaton, it has a graveyard rock-and-roll call that includes a hot, earring-wearing Dracula, Frankenstein playing bass guitar, and his miniskirted bride street dancing. The amplification is enormous, and what with the noise, the smoke, and the monsters, kids often seem confused if not downright scared. But adults will enjoy the music and the high-energy performances. *Duration: 25 min. Crowds: Steady, but high capacity of amphitheater means no waiting. Strategy: Go when rides' lines are at capacity or after dark on hot days. Audience: Older children and adults. Rating:* ★★★

13 Just next door in what could easily be called Adrenaline Alley is another headliner, **Earthquake—The Big One.** The preshow is almost as good as the main attraction; using audience volunteers, matte paintings, and video cameras, it reproduces choice scenes from the movie *Earthquake.* ("This is not a happy disaster, so no smiling," cautions the staffer running the show.) Suitably glum, everyone troops onto Bay Area Rapid Transit subway cars (Universal Studios seems determined to do in the urban public transportation systems) to ride out an 8.3 Richter scale tremor and its consequences: fire, flood, blackouts. Unlike in Disney-MGM's Disaster Canyon, there are no "safe" seats on this ride; catastrophe strikes from every angle (including above and below), so everyone gets a few months shaved off his or her life. *Duration: 20 min. Crowds: Discouraging. Strategy: Go first thing in the morning or after 6, or you'll feel as if another couple of months in your life have been wasted while you wait on line. No pregnant women or guests with motion sickness or heart, neck, or back conditions; those under 40 inches must ride with an adult. Audience: All but young children. Rating:* ★★★.

14 Stagger out of San Francisco into Amity for **Jaws,** Universal's second attempt at this terror-filled boat ride (the first incarnation had an embarrassing tendency to get stuck midattack). Just when you thought it was safe to go back into the water, along comes the finny fiend attempting to turn you into saltwater taffy. This time your boat is under attack, with concomitant explosions, noise and shaking, in addition to the gnashing of sharp shark teeth. Don't think you're safe when the boat escapes into the boathouse either. The special effects on this ride really shine, especially the fire and electrical explosions. *Duration: 7 min. Crowds: Lines are long most of the day, but nothing like those at Back to the Future. Strategy: Go early or after dark for an even more terrifying experience—you can't see the attack but can certainly hear and feel it. No pregnant women or guests with motion sickness or heart, neck, or back conditions. Audience: All but young children, who will be frightened. Rating:* ★★★

⑮ Last but not least on the "can-you-top-this" parade is the **Wild, Wild, Wild West Stunt Show,** presented in a covered amphitheater at the very end of Amity Avenue. The sign "Square Dance and Hanging, Saturday Night," lets you know what kind of town you've moseyed into. Repeated playing of the theme from "Bonanza" confirms your hunch. The show involves trapdoors, fistfights, bullwhips (take that, Indiana!), water gags, explosions, shoot-outs, horseback riding, and one tough mama who proclaims, "Listen, poptart, I've been falling off barns since I was three," and then demonstrates her inimitable style by hurling herself off the ridgepole. By the end of the show, the set is in shambles and every other theme park in central Florida has been skewered in jokes and snide remarks ("Look, Ma, I'm Shamu," yells one sopping stuntman as he emerges, spitting water, from a well). The panting stuntpeople take time out from rebuilding the set for photographs, autographs, and questions. They will not, however, explain how you can replicate the stunt at home. *Duration: 16 min. Crowds: Large, but its 2,000-seat amphitheater means no waiting. Strategy: On hot days go after dark, when it will be cooler in the amphitheater. Audience: All ages. Rating:* ★★★

⑯ You're now at the end of the lagoon that's the setting for **Dynamite Nights Stunt Spectacular,** presented nightly at 7. This is a shoot-'em-up stunt show with a difference: It's performed on water skis and in motorboats and at night. As far as theme park finales go, this one pales in comparison with Disney's fireworks. There are a few noisy boats, some loud explosions, and much ado about nothing. If you're worried about getting stuck in parking lot gridlock, skip it. If you do decide to stay, amble back along the lagoon and pick your spot for the evening show. There are definitely bad and good views: The best are from the footbridge, at the opposite end of the lagoon on New York's South Street, as well as along Exposition Boulevard, the avenue along the lagoon adjoining Expo Center. Prime locations fill up at least 30 minutes before show time, so be warned. *Duration: 20 min. Crowds: Large, but there's plenty of room for all. Strategy: Bring a snack and claim your spot 30 min before show time. Audience: All ages. Rating:* ★

Expo Center Taking up the southeastern section of the park, Expo Center contains another great group of Universal Studios attractions:

Back to the Future . . . The Ride, Fievel's Playland, and E.T. Adventure.

17 If there's one ride that's on top of everyone's list it's **Back to the Future...The Ride.** This is the flight simulator to beat all others, even (probably) those yet to be built. Michael J. Fox, star of the 1985 movie, said that the ride actually delivered what the script imagined. When beleagured pop star Michael Jackson was visiting Walt Disney World, he made a special detour specifically to experience this ride—and rode it three times in a row. Even Disney-MGM's Star Tours, which easily outranks most other flight simulators, can't compare with this one. The cause of all the unbridled enthusiasm is a seven-story, one-of-a-kind Omnimax screen, which surrounds your De Lorean-shaped simulator vehicle so that you lose all sense of perspective as you rush backward and forward in the space-time continuum. It also helps that this simulator's motion is the most aggressive of all flight simulators—and there are no seat belts. Having your wallet slide out of your pocket is the least of your worries and a stiff neck is a distinct possibility. *Duration: 5 min. Crowds: Up to 2 hr in busy seasons at peak times (between 11 and 3). Strategy: Arrive in the park at opening and dash on over—or be prepared to wait (and wait... and wait); lines drop off a hair about 1/2 hour after the mad mass rope-drop rush. Or go late. For view and motion, sit smack-dab in the middle, especially Car 6 on Level II; for the best chance of getting this car, ease yourself into Row 8 in the preride area. No pregnant women, guests under 40 inches tall, or guests with motion sickness or heart, back, or neck problems. Audience: Older children and adults. Rating:* ★★★

18 For parents who are doing the baby swap on Back to the Future, or for younger children who need some time out, **Fievel's Playland,** just around the corner, is a true gift. Based on the adventures of Steven Spielberg's mighty-if-miniature mouse, this gigantic playground incorporates state-of-the-art amusements that are now de rigueur in entertainment parks: a four-story net climb equipped with tubes, ladders, and rope bridges; tunnel slides; water play areas; a harmonica slide that plays music when you slide along the openings; ball crawls; and a 200-foot water slide that you whiz down while sitting in Fievel's signature sardine can. *Duration: It's up to your preschooler. Crowds: Not significant, though waits do develop for the water slide. Strategy: On hot days, go after supper, or prepare to sweat. Audience: Toddlers, preschoolers, and their parents. Rating:*★★

Time Out The **International Food Bazaar** is an efficient, multiethnic cafeteria serving Italian, American, German, Greek, and Chinese dishes at affordable prices (most of the entrées cost either $5.95 or $6.75). The Italian Caesar salad and Greek salads are especially welcome on a muggy day.

19 Spielberg's best-known creation receives his due at **E.T. Adventure,** located in a large structure adjoining Fievel's Playland. To the hoarsely murmured mantra of "Home, home," you board bicycles mounted on a movable platform and pedal through fantastic forests floating in mists of dry-ice fumes, magic gardens populated by such whimsical new Spielberg characters as the Tickli Moot Moot, and across the moon (remember to turn to catch your shadow) in an attempt to help the endearing extra-terrestrial find his way back to his home planet. Though the ride begins like an outer-space version of Disney's It's a Small World, it picks up enough to have a thrill-ride bite. The music is as tear-jerking as ever, and so is the little surprise at the end when E.T. personally says good-bye. Another surprise—the waiting area—a pine-scented forest complete with E.T. beckoning you on—is one of the most pleasant at this park. *Duration: 5 min. Crowds: Sometimes not bad, but up to 2 hr during crowded periods. Strategy: Go early. No one suffering from motion sickness or heart, back, or neck problems; guests under 40 inches tall must ride in orbs. Audience: All ages. Rating:* ★★★

Time Out For all-American burgers and shakes in a full-service restaurant, one of the best choices is the guitar-shaped **Hard Rock Café.** The neck of the guitar extends out of the park into the parking lot, enabling area visitors to take their teenagers without buying an admission ticket. The rock music is classic but earsplitting, which makes conversation next to impossible—not always a bad thing when dining with teenagers. The walls are crammed with rock-and-roll memorabilia, a treat for hard-core fans who can recognize many of the items' obscure provenance.

Dining

Most eateries are on Plaza of the Stars and Hollywood Boulevard. And their stellar locations are often matched by astronomical prices. Several restaurants accept reservations: Production Central's **Studio Stars** (tel. 407/363–8769), which has an all-you-can-eat buffet; San Francisco/Amity's **Lombard's Landing** (tel. 407/362–9955), designed to resemble a warehouse from 19th-century San Francisco; and the **Hard Rock Café** (tel. 407/351–7625; *see above*).

Shopping

Every ride and every attraction has its affiliated theme shop; in addition, Rodeo Drive and Hollywood Boulevard are pock-marked with money pits. Choice souvenirs include the Universal Studios' trademark movie clipboard; sepia prints of Richard Gere, Mel Gibson, and Marilyn Monroe; supercool sunglasses à la Blues Brothers; and, of course, all the gak you want to eat. Check out the "Do Not Disturb" signs from the Bates Motel at the **Bates Motel Gift Shop,** as well as Bates Motel stationery and bathrobes, and little plush King Konglets at Kongfrontation. Stop by Hollywood's **Brown Derby** for the perfect topper, from fedoras à la Indiana Jones to bush hats from *Jurassic Park.* Be advised that few of the attraction-specific souvenirs are sold outside of their own shop, so if you're struck by Fred Flintstone "yabba dabba doo" boxer shorts at the **Hanna-Barbera Shop,** seize the moment—and the shorts.

Access for Travelers with Disabilities

As in Walt Disney World's major parks, each attraction has an audio portion that will appeal to those with visual impairments and a visual portion to charm those with hearing impairments. But Universal Studios has also made an all-out effort not only to make the premises physically accessible by those with disabilities but also to lift attitudinal barriers. Power-assist buttons were added to heavy, hard-to-open doors, lap tables were provided for guests in shops, bathroom facilities (already up to code) were modified with niceties such as insulating under-sink pipes and companion rest rooms. In addition, all the employees now attend disability awareness workshops to remind them that people with disabilities are people first. And you can occasionally spot staffers using wheelchairs. Parts of the park with cobblestone streets now have paved paths, and photo spots have been modified for wheelchair accessibility. Various attractions have been retrofitted, so that most attractions can be boarded directly in a standard wheelchair; those using oversize vehicles or scooters must transfer to a standard model—these are available at the ride's entrance—or into the ride vehicle.

Services Many employees have had basic sign-language training—even some of the animated characters speak sign, albeit, because many have only four fingers, an adapted version. Like Walt Disney World, Universal Studios Florida supplements the visuals with a special **guidebook** containing story lines and scripts in all of the attractions described below, unless otherwise noted. There is an **outgoing TTY** on the counter in Guest Relations, just inside the Main Entrance and to the right.

The park also publishes the **"Studio Guide for Guests with Disabilities,"** which pinpoints the special entrances available for those with disabilities (which often bypass the attraction's line). In addition, cassettes with narrative descriptions of the various attractions can be borrowed, along with portable tape players. You can get these and the various booklets at Guest Relations.

Attractions **Alfred Hitchcock's 3-D Theatre, "Murder, She Wrote" Mystery Theater, Ghostbusters, Animal Actors Stage Show,** the **Gory, Gruesome & Grotesque Horror Make-Up Show, Beetlejuice's Graveyard Revue,** and the **Wild, Wild, Wild West Stunt Show** are all completely wheelchair-accessible, theater-style attractions. Guests with visual impairments will enjoy all of these shows, but sound and special effects make all but Alfred Hitchcock's 3-D Theater and "Murder, She Wrote" inappropriate for service animals.

Hollywood **Lucy: A Tribute** is wheelchair accessible, but the TV show excerpts shown on overhead screens are not close captioned.

Production Central Guests using an oversize wheelchair or scooter must transfer to a standard wheelchair to board the **Production Tram Tour.** The information in the narrative—interesting to those with visual impairments—is written down in the guidebook for the hearing impaired. The **Nickelodeon Studios** tour is also completely accessible by guests using wheelchairs and enjoyable for guests with other disabilities. If you lip-read, ask to stay up front. The **Funtastic World of Hanna-Barbera** is completely accessible by guests using wheelchairs. However, your experience will be more intense if you can transfer to a ride seat and tolerate your vehicle's sudden sharp accelerations, climbs, stops, dives, and banked turns. If you can't, you can still experience the attraction, albeit from a stationary seat. Guests with other disabilities who enjoy other thrill rides will enjoy this one as well.

New York and San Francisco/ Amity
If you use a standard-size wheelchair or can transfer to one or to the ride vehicle directly, you can board **Kongfrontation, Earthquake—The Big One,** and **Jaws** directly. If their turbulence will be a problem for you, you shouldn't ride. Service animals should not ride. Note that guests with visual impairments as well as those using wheelchairs should cross San Francisco with care.

Expo Center
To ride **E.T. Adventure,** you must transfer to the ride vehicle or to a standard-size wheelchair if you're not already using one. Service animals are not permitted. There is some sudden tilting and accelerating, but anyone with back, neck, or heart conditions can ride in E.T.'s orbs (the spaceships) instead of the flying bicycles.

Restaurants
All restaurants are wheelchair accessible. However, you can't take into the Hard Rock Café wheelchairs or scooters rented in the park.

Entertainment
There are special viewing areas at all of the outdoor shows, including **Dynamite Nights Stunt Spectacular.**

Busch Gardens

When Anheuser-Busch opened a small hospitality center adjacent to its Tampa brewery in 1959, the company couldn't foresee the day that a couple of somnolent koalas and a ride called Kumba would be more of a draw than a draught would be. Busch Gardens, as the tropical biergarten was called, was seen as a useful place to stash the Busch family's collection of exotic animals and birds while tending to the real business: making and selling beer.

But 12 years later, the call of the wild proved so strong that Anheuser-Busch began to develop Busch Gardens into a multifaceted, Africa-themed park and zoo, with the brewery increasingly relegated to a sideshow. Rising profits demanded the creation of a separate corporate umbrella, and as a profit center spun off from the parent company, Busch Entertainment Corporation (BEC) was endowed with the mandate to expand and multiply in the field of leisure-time entertainment. Now owners of Busch Gardens; The Old Country in Williamsburg, Virginia; Adventure Island in Tampa; Sesame Place in Langhorne, Pennsylvania; the Sea World parks in Orlando, San Antonio, Texas, Aurora, Ohio, and San Diego, California; and Cypress Gardens in Winter Haven, BEC has become the second-largest theme park owner-operator in the world, right behind the Walt Disney Company.

There is little of the crowd and bustle of the Disney parks here. The animal displays and lush landscaping help to create a softer mood. The personnel are equally casual; they seem less stiff and programmed than some of the clean-shaven assembly-line workers at the home of the Mouse. Their relaxed attitude can seem disrespectful or charming depending on your point of view. Another odd note is that some of the attractions, such as the Show Jumping Hall of Fame and the Questor flight simulator, have nothing to do with the African theme that led Busch Gardens to be dubbed "The Dark Continent" (a name later dropped in the interest of political correctness); in fact, they seem like a theme park version of monkey-see-monkey-do.

But that's merely a case of smudged icing on what's still a very satisfying cake. A member of the American Association of Zoological Parks and Aquariums, Busch Gardens ranks among the top four zoos in the United States. More than 3,200 birds, mammals, and reptiles are spread out on its 300 acres; the aviary houses some 600 rare and exotic birds, and about 500 African big-game animals roam uncaged on the 60-acre Serengeti Plain. Busch Gardens participates in the Species Survival Program, lending animals to other zoos for breeding as well as recording tremendous success with breeding endangered animals on the premises. At press time, the park was negotiating to host a pair of rare Chinese pandas.

The park itself is divided into nine areas linked to the common theme of turn-of-the-century Africa, plus the brewery. Animals are exhibited wherever possible—on islands, near concession stands, in spacious cages in the middle of a maze of lines, and in displays and shows in which they are the stars. But there's more than enough for the non–animal lover to do, what with numerous roller coasters and other gut-wrenching rides (beware the Kumba), water attractions, a Skyride, and shops galore. And there's always the brewery, whose self-guided tour is rarely crowded—a nice, if ironic, touch, considering it is the park's raison d'être.

Essential Information

Tourist Information Contact Busch Gardens (Box 9158, Tampa 33674, tel. 813/987–5283, no TTY).

On-site park information is available at **Guest Relations**, near the Main Entrance in Morocco.

A large signpost at the entrance lists performances scheduled for that day; show times for each performance are also posted in front of the individual stages and theaters.

Getting There Busch Gardens is at the corner of Busch Boulevard and 40th Street, 8 miles northeast of downtown Tampa, 2 miles east of I–275, and 2 miles west of I–75. It will take you an hour and 15 minutes to drive the 81 miles from Orlando on I–4. Contrary to declarations in the brochures, Busch Gardens is *not* easy to find. The printed directions are fine until you get to Fowler Avenue, and then the signs indicating your route disappear and you are guaranteed to miss 40th Street, where you are supposed to turn. A better route is to follow the brochure directions to Fowler Avenue (Exit 54 off I–75 from Orlando; Exit 33 off I–275 from Tampa), then turn left onto 30th Street—a well-marked intersection with a bank of traffic lights. Then make another left onto Busch Avenue—another well-marked intersection with traffic lights. You will finally see Busch Gardens signs telling you to make another left onto 40th Street for the entrance to the parking lot.

Parking The cost for cars is $3.

Admission Adults pay $32.95, children 3–9 $26.55. Senior citizens receive a 15% discount, and AAA members get 10% off.

Hours The park is open daily 9–8 except during off-season and on holidays, when hours are shorter.

Services
Baby Care Facilities for **nursing** and **diaper-changing tables** are in Dwarf Village; only women's rest rooms have changing tables. You'll find **stroller rentals** at Stroller and Wheelchair Rental in Morocco ($4 for singles, $8 for doubles, including $1 deposit; doubles are safari trucks!). No **formula, baby food,** or **disposable diapers** are sold on the premises, but there are shopping centers all around the park, as well as a K-Mart and Kash 'N' Karry about 1 mile east of the Main Entrance on Busch Boulevard.

Cameras and Film Disposable **Kodak Funsaver cameras** are for sale at **Safari Foto,** near the Main Entrance, as well as at other stores throughout the park. You can rent **35mm cameras** ($6.95 per day with $50 deposit) at the **One-Hour Photo Shop,** also near the Main Entrance.

Car Service If you have car trouble, raise your hood and the parking patrol will assist you.

First Aid The infirmary is alongside the Festhaus in Timbuktu.

Guided Tours Numerous tours and programs here are designed to fan the animal conservation spark. One of the most popular is the three-hour **Behind-the-Scenes Tour,** daily at 8:30 AM, in which you ride the feeding truck and see just how many carrots those gorillas go through in one day. You can also reserve ahead to join periodic four-hour **Senior Safaris** as well as wonderful age-specific half-day, full-day, and multiday programs for children ($18–$100; tel. 813/987–5555). (*See also* Traveling with Children in Chapter 1, Essential Information.)

Lockers You'll find them in the Moroccan Village, near the Congo River Rapids; in Stanleyville, near the Tanganyika Tidal Wave; and in the Congo, at the Kumba and Congo River Rapids rides. The cost is 50¢.

Lost Children and Adults Go to Security at the Main Entrance or speak to any security officer (they wear white shirts, badges, and hats and look vaguely like sheriffs).

Lost and   Report losses and finds of material goods at the Main Entrance's
Found   Security office.

Money   For currency exchange, go to the Guest Relations window near
            the Main Entrance in Morocco. There is an ATM just inside the
            Main Entrance, in Morocco; it's linked to the Plus, Honor, and
            Cirrus networks.

Package   If you'd rather not lug around your purchases all day, have them
Pickup   sent from any store in the park to **Sahara Traders,** in the Moroc-
            can village area near the entrance. You can pick them up on your
            way out. The service is free, but do allow an hour for delivery.

Wheelchair At Stroller and Wheelchair Rental in Morocco, you can rent
Rentals   standard chairs ($4, with $1 deposit) and motorized wheelchairs
            ($20, with $5 deposit). If yours disappears and needs replacing,
            ask in any gift shop.

Strategies for Your Visit

When to Go Mondays are least crowded in summer, when local schools are
                out; weekdays are most tranquil the rest of the year.

Blitz Tour Figuring out the most efficient way of visiting Busch Gardens
                is only slightly less complicated than planning a safari. Pick up
                a list of shows at the entrance gate and loosely schedule your
                day around them; they are welcome sit-down breaks in a full day
                on your feet and some are even air-conditioned. Must-sees are
                the dolphin show, the bird show, the elephant wash, and the glitzy
                entertainment in the Moroccan Palace Theater. Also be sure to
                ride the Kumba, one of the best roller coasters around.

Make **Myombe Reserve** your first stop. Then hop on the **Trans-
Veldt Railroad** at Nairobi Station and take it all around the park
to Stanleyville. People on foot get to Stanleyville and the Congo
in the afternoon; by visiting in the morning, you'll beat the lines
on the rides—including the **Stanley Falls Log Flume,** the **Kumba,**
and the **Tanganyika Tidal Wave**—and the animals will be more
lively. Work your way north through the Congo to the **Congo
River Rapids**—a refreshing splash at midday—and then catch
the show at **Dolphin Theater.**

Busch Gardens is laid out so that the crowds tend to shuffle
counterclockwise. Now go against the flow—through Timbuktu
and back to Nairobi—to visit the **Elephant Wash** et al. You're
close enough to the **Moroccan Palace Theater** to make an afternoon show or to while away the time before the next one with a
Monorail ride. If the line's not too long, try **Questor** (otherwise,
save it until the end of the day).

Wander back through Morocco, past the brewery, and to the
Bird Gardens. Time your visit for the last bird show; remember
that the brewery tour is self-guided, so you can do that anytime.

Walk back up to Stanleyville and consider your late-afternoon
options: You can go on the tidal wave again, see the rare white
Bengal tigers get frisky at Congo's **Claw Island,** ride the **Skyride**
back to Nairobi (it'll drop you off right opposite Questor), or take

the train for a late-afternoon tour of the **Serengeti** (a worthwhile trip, although this often seems to be the time of day when the kudus get randy and ardently embrace other kudus). If you end up at Nairobi, have a restorative drink on the balcony of the **Colony Club** (Budweiser, Bud Light, and O'Douls are on tap; red and white wine are also available) before hitting the Moroccan souk on your way out.

On Rainy Days   The Skyride may close temporarily because of lightning or high winds, but otherwise it's business as usual in the park.

Other Tips
- Keep in mind that the animals nap through most of the day, and you'll see the most action first thing in the morning and in the late afternoon.

- Unlike most central Florida parks, Busch offers national fast-food restaurants literally across the street. Readmission is allowed, so you can easily duck out for a burger.

- The water rides are designed to get you wet, very wet. If it's a cold or overcast day and you don't want to freeze, purchase a thin plastic poncho for about $3.50 or bring your own.

- If you want to snap loved ones in mid-ride (mid-scream?), look for photo staging spots at Congo River Rapids, Kumba, and the Tanganyika Tidal Wave.

- As soon as you arrive in the park, set up a specific rendezvous location and time in case you and your companions get separated.

Exploring Busch Gardens

Busch Gardens' nine different areas plus brewery are laid out in two concentric circles with an occasional appendage. The center is Timbuktu, an open-air carnival and bazaar. The main entrance is through Morocco; going counterclockwise along the winding paths, you'll encounter Myombe Reserve, Nairobi, the Serengeti Plain, the Congo, Stanleyville, Bird Gardens, and the Brewery, which abuts Morocco. A sharp elbow to the right from Myombe Reserve and Nairobi is the Crown Colony. Each of the areas is distinguished by its own distinctive architectural styles as well as regional music pumped through carefully camouflaged loudspeakers.

Morocco   The park's Main Entrance leads you through the gates of the tiled and turreted Moroccan fort housing park administrative offices and into a land of swirling colors and skirling music. Morocco itself contains two eateries—the Zagora Café and the Boujad Bakery—a resident snake charmer, the Moroccan Palace Theater, and numerous souvenir stands, arranged in a replica of an Arabic souk, or open-air marketplace.

It's hard not to fall into the shekel-flinging mode; Middle Eastern music wails through the speakers, brightly colored wool tassels droop overhead, brass urns glimmer, bangles shimmer, veils waft in the wind, and mouthwatering smells issue from the Boujad Bakery. Follow the main drag past the **Sultan's Tent,** a raised platform hung about with multicolored striped curtains, where a snake charmer snuggles up to a python and wraps it around her arms, waist, and neck. Show schedules are posted next to the Sultan's Tent. The snake charmer's main audience is a group of indifferent alligators, who loll about in a pond to the right of the Sultan's Tent. No hungry audience this: The alligators are so well fed and lazy that they ignore the plump koi fish that share their pond.

Numbers in the margin correspond to points of interest on the Busch Gardens map.

❶ Note that the blue-tiled, iron-fretted **Moroccan Palace Theater** is catercorner to the alligators; this is where Busch Gardens holds the glitzy, Broadway-style shows that seem to be obligatory at theme parks these days. Song, dance, and special effects (one enterprising performance was done all on ice skates) are packed into a show that's distinguished as much by its professionalism as by its exuberance. Its air-conditioned interior and convenient water fountains are especially welcome after trekking through Timbuktu. *Duration: 30–40 min. Crowd: Sizable, but there's always enough room. Strategy: Shows four times daily; check schedules posted outside. Go when you want to sit down and cool off. Audience: All ages. Rating:* ★★

Time Out The **Zagora Café** in Morocco dishes out basic burgers, fajitas, and turkey sandwiches in an enormous open-air cafeteria. **Boujad Bakery** is the place for a cup of cappuccino and a *churro* (Mexican deep-fried sweet dough liberally dusted with confectioner's sugar). Breakfast is also available.

Crown Colony Follow the path around the Moroccan Palace, under the monorail overpass to a large cul-de-sac. This is the Crown Colony, a transportation and hospitality center with two distinctly non-African attractions that couldn't be fit in elsewhere: the home of BEC's signature Clydesdale horses—a staple at every BEC park—and the requisite flight simulator.

The **Monorail** has only one station, and this is it. The lines snake past airy cages containing curious lemurs, which sets the mood for the ride itself: a journey around the adjacent Serengeti Plain. The station is the Crown Colony terminus for a seven-minute **Skyride** above the Serengeti and through Timbuktu; except in bad weather, when it sometimes closes, it's a useful shortcut to **❷** the Congo, its other terminus. The **Clydesdale Hamlet** boasts the usual batch of oversize beasts galumphing around a corral and stables; a particularly patient one is periodically led out for photographs.

❸ Tucked away in a corner of the cul-de-sac is **Questor,** Busch Gardens' flight simulator. The gimmick here is that you are helping a mad scientist search for a magic crystal, a search that takes you to the center of the earth. As flight simulators go, the shake-up is pretty good but no competition for Disney-MGM's Star Tours or Universal's Back to the Future and certainly not worth what can be a long wait. But if the line is manageable, then give it a whirl. *Duration: 5 min. Crowds: Up to 1¹/₂ hr on crowded days.*

Strategy: In summer and holiday periods, go early or late. Must be 42 inches to ride. Audience: Older children and adults. Rating: ★★

Time Out   The **Colony Club,** done up to resemble a veddy British eatery from the good old *Out of Africa* days with portraits of top-hatted sahibs, used polo mallets, and nicely faded Oriental carpets, serves sandwiches, salad platters, and pizza in a downstairs counter-service restaurant. There's full service upstairs; *see* Dining, below.

Serengeti   Looming just north of the Crown Colony and forming the east-
Plain   ern border of Nairobi and Timbuktu is the 80-acre Serengeti Plain, an open-air zoo where about 800 animals of 30 different species are allowed to run free in a re-creation of their natural habitats—all of which look remarkably similar to Florida pastureland. You'll see zebras, camels, impalas, giraffes, lions, gazelles, Cape buffalo, and kudus (a heftier impala), among other species. Don't be dismayed if it's raining; in fact, hasten right over to the Monorail to catch sight of all the animals instinctively turning their heads up into the rain. Though the Trans-Veldt Railroad skirts the eastern edge of the Serengeti, there are basically two ways to explore it: the **Skyride** and the **Monorail.** The Skyride takes you 49 feet above the Serengeti on a 1.1-mile one-way ride to the Congo; it gives you a great overview but not much detail. The Monorail is a classic Busch Gardens experience; unlike Disney's monorail, it's suspended from an overhead rail and trundles around the veldt at eye level to a zebra. A guide tells you a little about the animals as you edge along the track. If you believe the hype about seeing the animals in their natural environments, the omnipresent fence lines will be a shock. (At one point you can see the freeway from one side of the monorail car.) Busch Gardens could take some tips from sister park Sea World about displaying animals. *Duration: Monorail 20 min, Skyride 7 min. Monorails leave every 5 min; Skyrides operate continuously. Crowds: You can always walk right on. Strategy: Go anytime. Audience: All ages. Rating:* ★★

Myombe   The **Myombe Reserve** is easily overlooked, thanks to superbly
Reserve   luxuriant rain-forest landscaping and a modest entrance opposite the Moroccan Palace Theater. Completed in 1992, it's one of the park's newer and much-heralded animal attractions. Some 3 acres have been lovingly landscaped into a home for an extended family of chimpanzees (formerly of Chimp Island in the Serengeti) and another family of Western lowland gorillas (whose scientific name is, according to an educational plaque, Gorilla gorilla gorilla). There's always a well-informed guide on hand to explain that gorillas rest 40% of the day and feed another 30% or to point out the almost infinitesimal differences and complicated relationships between Sally, Smokey, and Samantha. *Crowds: Not significant. Strategy: Visit either first thing in the morning or late in the afternoon; both are close to feeding time, when both apes and chimps are more active. Audience: All ages. Rating:* ★★★

Animal Nursery, **4**
Aviary, **25**
Bird Show Theater, **26**
Brewery, **28**
Claw Island, **18**
Clydesdale Hamlet, **2**
Congo River
Rapids, **15**
Crazy Camel, **11**
Dolphin Theater, **12**
Dwarf Village, **23**
Elephant Display, **7**
Flamingo Island, **24**
Koala House, **27**
Kumba, **14**
Monstrous Mamba, **16**
Moroccan Palace
Theater, **1**
Orchid Canyon, **21**
Parrots of the
Pacific, **22**
Petting Zoo, **5**
Phoenix, **9**
Python, **17**
Questor, **3**
Sandstorm, **8**
Scorpion, **10**
Show Jumping Hall of
Fame, **6**
Stanley Falls Log
Flume, **19**
Tanganyika Tidal
Wave, **20**
Ubanga-Banga
Bumper Cars, **13**

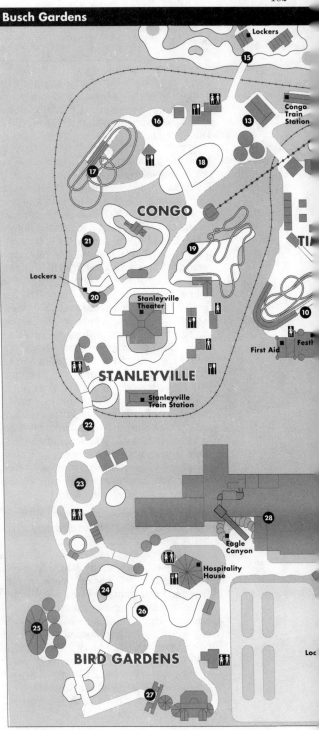

Busch Gardens

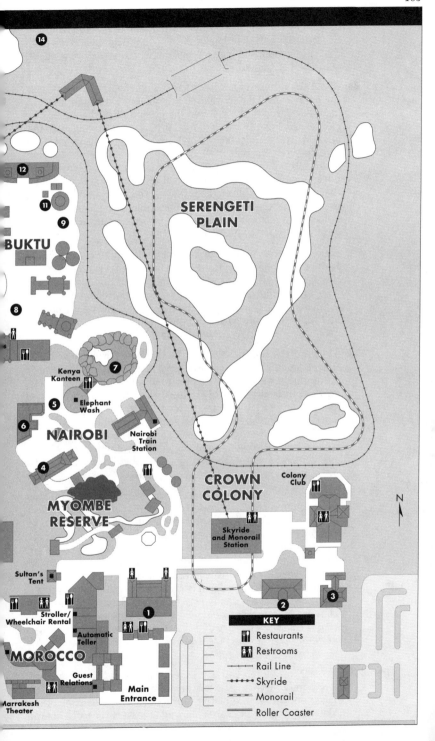

BUKTU

Kenya
Kanteen

Elephant
Wash

NAIROBI

Nairobi
Train
Station

**SERENGETI
PLAIN**

**CROWN
COLONY**

Colony
Club

**MYOMBE
RESERVE**

Skyride
and Monorail
Station

N

Sultan's
Tent

Stroller/
Wheelchair Rental

Automatic
Teller

MOROCCO

Guest
Relations

Marrakesh
Theater

Main
Entrance

KEY

⊺┰ Restaurants

⊼⊼ Restrooms

─┼─ Rail Line

•••• Skyride

═╪═ Monorail

─── Roller Coaster

Nairobi Myombe's rain-forested path leads you to Nairobi, a collection of buildings containing the animal nursery, the petting zoo, the Show Jumping Hall of Fame, the elephant display, and the Nairobi train station—a gingerbread clapboard structure straight out of *Out of Africa*.

❹ The **Animal Nursery** is a long, low building, with glass cages on the outside holding convalescing animals wrapped in nests of blankets; through the glass on the other side of the cages, you can see the laboratories and food preparation. Animals are fed
❺ at various times, so there's usually something going on. The **Petting Zoo** contains both Nubian and African pygmy goats, Barbados black-bellied sheep, ducks, rabbits, turtles, roosters, and hens. Visitors are allowed to feed only the goats and sheep (which are rotated throughout the day to keep them from being overfed); for the others, food is brought out on a tray for the twice-daily handout. *Crowds: Never significant. Strategy: Go anytime. Audience: All ages. Rating:* ★

❻ Although it has nothing to do with Africa, the **Show Jumping Hall of Fame** has everything to do with colonialism and family ties. Elizabeth Busch, a family member and a fanatic about horse jumping, needed a place to house her collection of antique riding saddles, horseshoes, ribbons, and portraits of famous horses, and this minuscule corner was found. *Crowds: Not a problem. Strategy: Go anytime. Audience: Adults. Rating:* ★

❼ The big attraction in Nairobi is the **Elephant Display,** housing 22 Asian elephants; the most attractive part of the display is their swimming pool, in which elephant parents and children snort, swim, and clean off before getting dusty again. Every couple of hours, some of the elephants troop out to the Elephant Wash area next to the Kenya Kanteen, where a schedule is posted and where they take a garden hose and give each other showers while a keeper explains elephant habits. *Crowds: Can be significant for the Elephant Wash but you can usually see. Strategy: Go anytime. Audience: All ages. Rating:* ★★★

The Kenya Kanteen is a good place to watch out for the **Trans-Veldt Railroad,** an authentic reproduction of an East African steam locomotive (with, as the tour guide points out, an American cowcatcher for those pesky impala—none of which actually can come near the tracks) that chugs around the Serengeti and then circumnavigates the park in a 2½-mile journey, making stops near the Congo River Rapids and Stanleyville (about 10 minutes to the Congo Train Station and another 10 minutes to Stanleyville). It's a dandy way to see the Serengeti. *Duration: 30 min. Crowds: Steady, but you almost always find a seat. Strategy: It comes only every 30 min, so watch the mother elephants dunking the little ones in the elephant pool until you hear the whistle, then dash for the station. Audience: All ages. Rating:* ★★

Timbuktu From Nairobi you can continue by foot through a blindingly white mud fort—rather austere compared with the fretwork-laced decorative tile of the Moroccan fort—into Timbuktu, a claustrophobic walled area housing at least three rides guaranteed to make you lose your lunch; a video arcade; the Festhaus, an incongruous little piece of Germany, with dirndled maidens and lederhosen-clad youth dancing around a beer-swilling, sausage-chomping crowd; numerous games of chance; the Crazy Camel carousel; kiddie rides; and the Dolphin Theater (if you can have lederhosen in Timbuktu, why not dolphins, too?).

8 The first ride you'll see as you exit the mud fort is the **Sandstorm,** "the number-one ride for making guests throw up," as a Busch Gardens staffer elegantly put it. It doesn't look all that menacing, but the constant rotation of both your seat and the arm it's attached to should prove the point. *Duration: 2¹/₂ min. Crowds: Not a problem. Strategy: Go anytime. Audience: Older children, teens, adults. Rating:* ★★

9 Screams issue equally from the **Phoenix,** a crescent that swings back and forth, higher and higher until it swoops sickeningly
10 over the top, and the **Scorpion,** 1,805 feet of steel roller coaster twisted into a gigantic hoop with a 65-foot drop; it reaches a maximum speed of 50 mph. *Duration: Phoenix 2 min, Scorpion 2 min. Crowds: Lines can build at midday in busy periods. Strategy: Go early or late. No riders under 48 inches on Scorpion. Audience: Older children, teens, adults. Rating:* ★★

11 Tamer diversions include the **Crazy Camel,** a delightful carousel with brightly painted camels alongside the traditional horses; carnival-type games of chance ($1 or $2 usually buys three throws); and such children's rides as Busch Flyers and a pint-size version of the Phoenix (other diminutive attractions are housed in Dwarf Village, outside Stanleyville).

12 The show at the **Dolphin Theater** is modeled on the one at Sea World, and, in fact, the dolphins and trainers are borrowed from Busch Gardens' fishy cousin. The dolphin tank is smaller than Sea World's and lacks the Plexiglas sides that let you peer at the underwater activities during the show. But the two-dolphin show is delightful. Mick and Bud more than earn their 35 pounds of raw fish, jumping and waving their flippers and thoroughly enchanting everyone, including the one lucky child chosen to come up and play with them. (If your child is between 5 and 8, outgoing, and not scared by dolphins, arrive 15 minutes early and ask an usher if your child can be picked for the show. He or she will, however, be backstage learning the proper hand signals during a dandy section of the show when the trainer plays in the water with the dolphins.) *Duration: 20 min. Crowds: Never a problem. Strategy: Go in the middle of the day, when the other animals in the park are snoozing. Audience: All ages. Rating:* ★★★

Congo and Stanleyville   Another mud fort by the Dolphin Stadium marks the exit from Timbuktu and the entrance to the Congo and adjacent Stanleyville, which is practically indistinguishable from the Congo. Unlike the open, dusty plains of the Serengeti and Nairobi, the Congo and neighboring Stanleyville are delightfully shaded by lush plantings and lofty, leafy trees, under whose branches nestle African fetish statues and piles of expedition supply boxes for that "Dr. Livingstone, I presume" touch. Hysterical shrieks from the area's several thrill rides remind you that the visitors, if not the natives, are perpetually restless.

Directly to your right after exiting Timbuktu are the aptly ⑬ named **Ubanga-Banga Bumper Cars** and, across the bridge, two of Busch Gardens' star attractions: Kumba and the Congo River Rapids. *Bumper cars' duration: About 4 min. Crowds: Never significant enough to cause a wait except in midafternoons during busy periods. Strategy: Go anytime—and if there's a line, don't bother to wait. Audience: Older children, teens, adults. Rating:* ★★

⑭ **Kumba** contains nearly 4,000 feet of turquoise steel twisting at up to 60 mph through three first-of-a-kind coaster maneuvers: a "diving loop" (plunging you from 110 feet into a loop); a camelback, with a 360° spiral and three seconds of weightlessness; and the world's largest loop, with a height of 108 feet. That's in addition to spirals, cobra rolls, and a corkscrew ride in the dark. Kumba offers a surprisingly smooth ride without the neck wrenching of most similar efforts. Catch a replay of your screaming face on three TV monitors near the exit. *Duration: 3 min. Crowds: Can mean long lines. Strategy: Go as soon as the park opens. No riders under 52 inches. Audience: Older children, teens, adults. Rating:* ★★★

⑮ Stagger on to the popular **Congo River Rapids,** one of the all-time best water rides. Visitors sit in rafts that look like enlarged inner tubes, 12 to a raft, and experience a watery version of bumper cars. As you go bumping and bucketing through nearly ¼ mile of rapids and waterfalls (and through a dark cave), be sure to wrap your camera in a waterproof bag (you will be splashed)— and remember to smile for the spectators taking pictures from the bridge. *Duration: 5 min. Crowds: There's usually a line. Strategy: Go early to avoid waits and have the best time. Audience: Older children, teens, adults. Rating:* ★★★

As you exit the Congo River Rapids, follow the screams to the ⑯ right for the **Monstrous Mamba,** another revolving octopus ride. ⑰ The **Python,** a steel roller coaster on 1,250 feet of track, hurls passengers through two hoops at 50 mph. *Duration: Monstrous Mamba 70 sec, Python 70 sec. Crowds: Significant only in busy seasons. Strategy: Go early or late in holiday periods. No riders under 47 inches; on Mamba, must be 39 inches and accompanied by adult on the Python. Audience: Older children, teens, adults. Rating:* ★★

Somehow the hysteria doesn't seem to bother the somnolent ⑱ Bengal tigers on nearby **Claw Island** (they are more active in the early morning and the late afternoon). Some particularly pleasant shady benches overlook the island and are a nice place to recuperate before hitting the next rides.

⑲ The **Stanley Falls Log Flume Ride,** which has a 40-foot drop, and ⑳ the **Tanganyika Tidal Wave,** with a 55-foot drop into a splash pool, are among the park's most popular rides, due as much to the certainty of getting wet as to their gut-turning drops. In fact, the tidal wave offers two possibilities for dunking: the ride itself and, for those who are chicken, the viewing bridge at the bottom of the drop, where a recording of Tchaikovsky's *1812 Overture* heralds the next wave. (A sign posted nearby politely reads, "This bridge is part of a water attraction. You will get soaked. Thank you.") Either huddle behind the Plexiglas shelter on the bridge or skitter off—fast. *Duration: Stanley Falls, 3¹/₂ min, Tanganyika Tidal Wave, 6 min. Crowds: Significant, with lines even on average days. Strategy: Ride early in the morning or in the evening. Audience: Older children, teens, adults. Rating:* ★★★

㉑ Just past the exit of the Tanganyika Tidal Wave is **Orchid Canyon,** a lovely 100-yard walk through 200-odd cascading orchids and bromeliads native to South Africa, the Philippines, and South America—it's a welcome respite from the sensory overload you'll get in the rest of the park. Meanwhile, placidly ignoring riders' screeches and distant pleas of "Aw, c'mon, Melissa, you *need* to go on this ride," lemurs, rhinoceroses, eland, and orangutans peacefully snooze away in spacious enclosures naturalized with rocks, trees, and, in the case of the orangutans, gymnastic equipment. A couple of thatched huts scattered throughout the Congo and Stanleyville contain snakes in wire boxes and inquisitive parrots perched in cages. Keepers are on hand to explain their behavior and hold them for you to stroke.

Stanleyville is also home to the **Stanleyville Theater,** where circus acrobats and ethnic dancers perform, and to the **Stanleyville Bazaar** and **Air Africa,** something like a Moroccan souk, with African craftspeople fashioning their wares outside.

Time Out The **Stanleyville Smokehouse** cafeteria serves slow-cooked chicken, beef, and ribs with corn on the cob and all the trimmings; the **Bazaar Café** offers hearty barbecue beef sandwiches. Between the two, the Stanleyville air is redolent of barbecue.

Move on by catching the train at the Stanleyville Train Station—a twin of Nairobi's station—located behind the Stanleyville Theater and near the orangutans' island. Or follow the path past the orangutans, onto the bridge over the train tracks, and down to Bird Gardens.

Bird Gardens This area is home to Dwarf Village, the koala habitat, and 1,883 exotic birds representing 218 species, including one of the largest managed flocks of Caribbean flamingos (fed beta-carotene supplements to maintain their bright coral color).

㉒ Just over the ramp from Stanleyville is **Parrots of the Pacific,** where multicolored parrots, macaws, and cockatoos are arranged in a circle, in cages, beneath two sprawling live oaks. A staffer is usually on hand to answer questions.

㉓ The children's play area, shady **Dwarf Village,** is well equipped with rubber safety matting, although the rides are a tad old-fashioned; you won't find the high climbing nets and snazzy sliding tunnels of the newer parks. But there are ball crawls, bouncing rooms, a miniature carousel, toy trains, and—a nice touch—storytelling. Loudspeakers merrily belt out happy kiddie songs, giving a cheerful air to the area. Several times daily, conservation specialists tell animal stories, sometimes with live animals as props. The youngsters' seats: fake toadstools. *Crowds: Seldom a problem. Strategy: Wait until later in the day, or you may never get your youngsters away; or go at midday for a respite from the heat. Audience: Young children. Rating:* ★★

㉔ The path leads right to **Flamingo Island,** whose flock of Caribbean flamingos is worth well over $1 million. The flamingos are part of a national breeding program, so the number of birds in the flock is constantly changing. *Crowds: Not a problem. Strategy: Go early or late to see birds at their most active. Audience: All ages. Rating:* ★★

㉕ To the right of Flamingo Island is the entrance to the **Aviary,** a lushly landscaped walk-through cage in which 194 species flutter freely among the trees and stalk along the ground. *Crowds: Not a problem. Strategy: Go early or late to see birds at their most active. Audience: All ages. Rating:* ★★

㉖ The **Bird Show Theater,** an open amphitheater just behind Flamingo Island, displays macaws, condors, and eagles performing natural behaviors; bird enthusiasts rate it one of the best shows anywhere. You can have your photo taken with one of the squawking stars at the adjacent posing area just after each show. *Duration: 30 min. Crowds: Sometimes significant during holiday periods. Strategy: Arrive 15 min before show time in busy seasons. Audience: All ages. Rating:* ★★

㉗ A very elaborate display with Chinese motifs down the boardwalk past the aviary once housed a pair of pandas; now it's **Koala House,** home to a breeding group of four—one male and three females. You can usually spot some joeys (baby koalas), too, although a look at the impassive parents makes it hard to imagine that any two of them ever get worked up enough to procreate. For close-up viewing by visitors, the exhibit offers a people-mover and an elevated observation gallery. Also, pay a few quarters for pellets to feed the huge decorative fish in the adjoining pool. They beg. Really. *Crowds: Not a problem. Strategy: Go in late afternoon to see the animals at their most active. Audience: All ages. Rating:* ★

Brewery
㉘ The last major attraction is the **Brewery,** a self-guided walk through a working brewery that produces 2.7 million barrels of Budweiser annually. You'll occasionally spot the big tanker cars on the freight trains that rumble out of the park bearing beer for a thirsty nation. Using automatic video and audio displays, educational placards, and labels, the tour covers every step of the process, from choosing the hops to canning the product. You don't have to be a beer fanatic to enjoy yourself, but people with a special interest in the inception of Bud Light do tend to linger. Some people gallop along, peering from the glassed-in walkways at the aging vats and bottling lines. But the written and audio displays abundantly provide beer trivia, from George Washing-

ton's favorite recipe to the secret behind how the aluminum tabs get put on top of flip-top cans. *Duration: Allot around 20 min. Crowds: Never a problem. Audience: Older children and adults. Rating:* ★★

Time Out   You won't be able to snap a cold one at the Brewery, but the **Hospitality House** right outside provides whistle-wetting wuffo on tap. After a full day at Busch Gardens, you'll need it. You can also order a delicious hero sandwich (called a Tampa Sandwich Platter). Even the outdoor setting is pleasant.

Dining

The majority of the gustatory offerings are of the red meat variety, smoked, wursted, or burgered. They are routinely washed down with Anheuser-Busch products, which are sold parkwide: Budweiser, Bud Light, Michelob, and nonalcoholic O'Doul's. Ice cream and popcorn stands are ubiquitous.

Steak, chicken, and pasta dishes are on the menu upstairs in the Crown Colony's **Colony Club,** a white-tableclothed full-service dining area whose huge windows give a great view of the Serengeti. The change in altitude affects the price only minimally, and the setting is one of the most relaxing in the park. It's also the fanciest place in the park. Unfortunately, the number of window tables is limited (so you have to eat very early or late to get one), and when the park closes early, seating may end around 4, though this varies.

Shopping

There are three must-have stuffed animals on the central Florida theme-park circuit, and two of them are here: white tiger puppets (sold at the **Stanleyville Bazaar**) and cuddly gorillas (sold at **J.R.'s Gorilla Hut,** just outside Myombe Reserve). The latter also stocks a delightfully long-limbed chimpanzee, whose Velcroed palms attach in an everlasting hug. In Stanleyville, the aforementioned Stanleyville Bazaar and **Air Africa** are chockful of pseudo-African schlock, but you can find the perfect birthday trinket or Yuletide stocking-stuffer in the form of a set of carved wooden zoo animals, perhaps, or brilliantly colored, elephant-shaped napkin rings. The **Souk** is the stop for inexpensive bangles, moderately priced brass, and exorbitantly pricey Moroccan leather, not to mention a rainbow of gauze veils to swathe your own little Salome. If all you want to do is shop, 30-minute shopping passes are available for a deposit equaling the price of admission.

Access for Travelers with Disabilities

To many wheelchair users, the Busch Gardens experience will be represented less by the wild rides than by the animals, which are on display at almost every turn. Of the rides that make up a significant part of the experience for many other visitors, almost all are accessible by guests who can transfer from their own wheelchair into the ride vehicles.

Services   The park publishes a leaflet describing each attraction's accessibility. It's available at Guest Relations.

Attractions   All attractions are wheelchair accessible in **Morocco, Myombe Reserve,** and **Nairobi.**

Crown Colony, Timbuktu   For **Questor** in the Crown Colony and for **Crazy Camel, Phoenix, Sandstorm,** and **Scorpion** in Timbuktu, you must be able to transfer from your wheelchair into the ride vehicle, and you must also be able to continuously hold on to lap bars or railings, hold yourself upright, and absorb sudden and dramatic movements. Timbuktu's other rides also cannot be boarded in a wheelchair.

Congo, Stanleyville   Guests using wheelchairs must also transfer to ride vehicles at **Congo River Rapids, Ubanga Banga Bumper Cars, Monstrous Mamba,** and **Python** in Congo and at **Stanley Falls** and **Tanganyika Tidal Wave** in Stanleyville; as at Questor (*see above*), you must also be able to hold lap bars or railings for these, as well as sit upright and absorb sudden and dramatic movements. Transferring out of a wheelchair is also required for **Congo kiddie rides.**

Bird Gardens   To play in **Dwarf Village,** children must be able to leave their wheelchair. The **Brewery** is not wheelchair accessible; the tour involves walking limited distances and several flights of stairs.

Shops and Restaurants   All shops and restaurants in Busch Gardens are wheelchair accessible.

Cypress Gardens

A botanical gardens, amusement park, and waterskiing circus rolled into one, Cypress Gardens is a uniquely Floridian combination of natural beauty and utter kitsch. It was founded during the Depression by Dick and Julie Pope; she was a Southern belle from Alabama with a green thumb, and he was a short, fast-talking real estate promoter and public relations whiz addicted to flashy jackets ("If I didn't wear the jackets," he once confided to *Life* magazine, "people would think I was a tall fire hydrant"). They created their dream in a snake- and alligator-infested cypress swamp on the shores of Lake Eloise in what are euphemistically referred to as the central Florida "highlands," and they opened for business on January 1, 1936. (Ticket receipts that day totaled $38, less than the price of a day's admission for two adults today.) Cypress Gardens has been open ever since and is central Florida's oldest continuously running attraction.

Despite Dick's self-designated status as "Swami of the Swamps" and "The Man Who Invented Florida," Cypress Gardens owes its two best-known traditions to Julie. In charge of the park during World War II while Dick was in the Armed Forces, Julie promised free water-ski shows for the soldiers at a nearby military base. What started with some stunts by Dick Jr. and his friends quickly expanded into a fully choreographed program with a bevy of "aquamaids" and stunt skiers, who originated the flips, barefoot skiing, and pyramids now a part of all waterskiing shows—both at Cypress Gardens and at other entertainment parks. When a winter storm devastated the plantings at the entrance to the park, Julie dressed the women on the staff in antebellum-style hoopskirts and had them stand in strategic locations, waving and smiling to draw visitors' attention away from the blighted blooms. These "Flowers of the South" provide photo ops to this day.

The park now encompasses more than 200 acres and contains more than 8,000 varieties of plants gathered from 75 countries. More than half of the grounds are devoted to flora, ranging from natural landscaping to cutesy-poo topiary to chrysanthemum cascades. A staff of more than 50 horticulturalists manages a 7-acre nursery complex, which turns out some 10,000 plants a week, and they produce annual chrysanthemum shows, poinsettia pageants, and a three-month spring flower extravaganza.

Essential Information

Tourist Information Contact Cypress Gardens (Box 1, Cypress Gardens 33884; 813/324–2111; in FL, 800/282–2123; outside FL, 800/237–4826; no TTY).

Within the park, the principal **information booth** is just inside the main gate.

Getting There To get here, take I–4 west to the U.S. 27S exit. From there, the route is well signed: Follow signs to Winter Haven; at Waverly, turn right (west) on Route 540, and go 5 miles. It's a 45-minute drive from Walt Disney World.

Parking The grassy parking area is divided into the North Lot and the South Lot; within these, rows are marked numerically. Parking is free.

Admission Admission costs $24.95 for adults, $16.45 for children 3–9, and $21.20 for guests over 55, excluding tax. AAA members get 10% off. Discounted tickets for Sea World and Busch Gardens can also be purchased here.

Hours The park is open daily 9:30–5:30, with extended hours during peak seasons.

Services
Baby Care You'll find **stroller rentals** at the Bazaar Gift Shop ($4 per day, with no deposit). Baby needs such as **baby food, formula, diapers,** and **wipes** can be purchased at the Winn-Dixie supermarket, across the street from the park. There are no designated facilities for nursing.

First Aid First aid is near the entrance to the Botanical Gardens.

Guided Tours Behind-the-scenes tours of the nursery, as well as botanical tours of the gardens, are available by special request. Call the main park information number (*see above*) to arrange such tours.

Lockers They're near the main office, just inside the park entrance (50¢).

Lost Things or People	Report **lost children and adults** as well as **lost possessions** at the main park office.
Money	There are no ATMs or currency exchange facilities.
Wheelchair Rentals	You can rent **standard wheelchairs** ($4 a day, with no deposit) and **motorized wheelchairs** ($5 per hour, with a $10 minimum and a $25 maximum, plus a $25 deposit).

Strategies for Your Visit

There's no sense of amusement-park anxiety at Cypress Gardens. The slow pace is partly because few people dash to gape at a banyan tree and partly due to the clientele, most of whom are older. In any case, there's no need to rush; even at a sedate pace, you can see just about everything in six hours. In summer, when the park stays open past the usual 5:30 PM closing time, you can arrive at noon and not miss anything. Lines are seldom a consideration. However, lines do build up at the Electric Boat Rides in fine weather on weekends and during winter, a favorite traveling time of the older visitors that Cypress Gardens tends to attract. Therefore, start with the boat rides and save a pedestrian perambulation of the gardens for later in the day.

Other Tips
- There are mailboxes near all exhibits, saying "Please Take One." Please do. The fliers inside contain interesting background on the attractions.

- If you have allergies, come prepared with antihistamines. The beautiful floral arrangements wreak havoc on susceptible sinuses.

Exploring Cypress Gardens

The souvenir-shop-ridden main entrance funnels visitors straight to the waterski stadiums. To the right are the Botanical Gardens; to the left are the Exhibition Gardens and the amusement area.

Numbers in the margin correspond to points of interest on the Cypress Gardens map.

❶ The **Botanical Gardens Cruise** floats through the cypress-hung canals of the Botanical Gardens, passing waving belles, flowering shrubs, 27 different species of palm, and the occasional baby alligator. Doing this first gives you a sense of Cypress Gardens' slightly schizoid history.

With luck and the right timing, you should be able to lope from disembarkation right into the **Water Ski Stadiums** for a stunt-filled waterskiing revue. Unlike Sea World's splashy song-and-dance extravaganza, the show at Cypress Gardens is purely athletic, with a nominal theme extending only to the costumes and music. Also unlike at Sea World, the front rows stay dry. But that doesn't mean it's naptime: Smiling aquamaids whiz along on one leg; the Rampmasters pivot, flip, and jump over each other at 35 mph; Corky the Clown skis backward; and the grand finale involves a four-tier pyramid with everyone waving Ameri-

Cypress Gardens

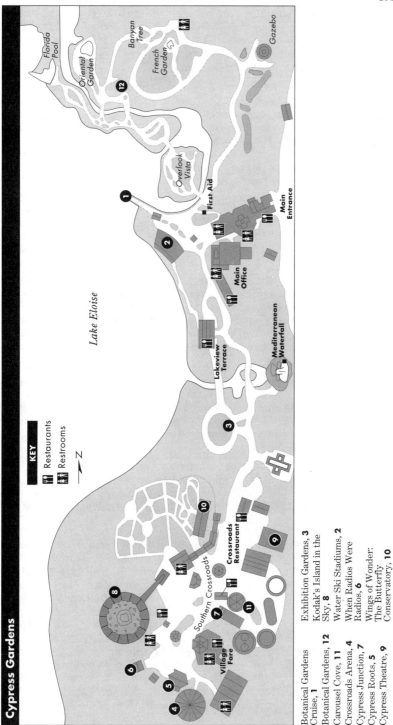

KEY

🚻 Restaurants

🚻 Restrooms

Florida Pool

Oriental Garden

Banyan Tree

French Garden

Gazebo

Lake Eloise

Overlook Vista

First Aid

Main Entrance

Main Office

Lakeview Terrace

Mediterranean Waterfall

Southern Crossroads

Village Fare

Crossroads Restaurant

Botanical Gardens Cruise, **1**
Botanical Gardens, **12**
Carousel Cove, **11**
Crossroads Arena, **4**
Cypress Junction, **7**
Cypress Roots, **5**
Cypress Theatre, **9**

Exhibition Gardens, **3**
Kodak's Island in the Sky, **8**
Water Ski Stadiums, **2**
When Radios Were Radios, **6**
Wings of Wonder: The Butterfly Conservatory, **10**

can flags. It's corny, but lively enough to keep even children entertained. *Duration: 30 min (presented every 2 hr). Crowds: Not usually a problem. Strategy: Arrive 5–10 min before show time and sit in either stadium; the view is equally good from both. Audience: All ages. Rating:* ★★★

❸ The path from the ski stadiums to Southern Crossroads, the hub of the amusement park area, meanders through the **Exhibition Gardens,** a prime belle-spotting site (the belles often sashay through here to freshen up at the Southern Mansion, a.k.a. Tara South). The landscaping philosophy is heroic in intent and hilariously vulgar in execution, especially for the special flower festivals: During the annual November Mum Festival, 2 million multicolored chrysanthemums cascade over the ledges of the 40-foot-high Mediterranean waterfall, decorate the walls of an Italian-style fountain, color four gargantuan floral hearts, and drape two topiary swans in an eye-spinning display of pink, purple, yellow, orange, and red.

❹ The **Crossroads Arena,** at the far southern end of the park, is currently home to a troupe of lively Russian acrobats and clowns. Shows at the arena do rotate, but they generally adhere to a circus theme. If you get there before the show, you can often watch the performers rehearse. *Duration: 25 min, plus 15-min preshow. Crowds: Not significant. Strategy: Try for the first or last show of the day, because the tent gets wickedly hot at midday. Audience: All ages. Rating:* ★★★

❺ As you work your way back toward Southern Crossroads, it's easy to overlook **Cypress Roots**, an unprepossessing clapboard shack chockful of fascinating memorabilia about the "Maharaja of the Marshes" and his fair bride. Save a good 20 minutes for the video interview of the Popes and the same amount of time to read all the *Life* magazine clippings of Dick Sr.'s promotional exploits.

Time Out | **Village Fare,** a conglomeration of fast-food outlets, serves pizza, salads, burgers, and roast beef on picnic tables covered with green-trellised tablecloths in an air-conditioned arena. The **Cypress Deli,** a hop and skip away, features submarine sandwiches and big salads.

❻ Nostalgia gets a firm nudge at **When Radios Were Radios,** an antique radio museum, with its collection of hundreds of 1920s Philcos, Westinghouses, and their successors dating through the **❼** 1950s. **Cypress Junction,** one of the nation's most elaborate model railroad exhibit, bridges the generation gap with its whistling freights, sleek expresses, tunnels, weather hazards, and all sorts of other knick-knacks. At any given time, you'll see nearly two dozen trains operating on its 1,100 feet of track; nearly 5,000 miniature figures of people and animals add that extra bit of detail. Oddly enough, this menagerie of miniatures was originally created as a Christmas exhibit for the *National Enquirer* **❽** in Lantana, Florida. **Kodak's Island in the Sky,** a 153-foot-high revolving platform, provides aerial views of the park's seasonal flower spectaculars and lush gardens as well as of nearby Winter Haven.

❾ One of the most popular attractions is the bird show at the **Cypress Theatre,** not the least of the reasons being that it's air-conditioned. Bird tricks are now referred to as "behaviors," although the behaviors exhibited by the parrots and macaws lean more toward such tricks as riding a bicycle or singing "Oh, What a Beautiful Morning" than the natural responses demonstrated by the raptors at the Busch Gardens bird show. Still, there's rousing audience response to "sing along with Crackles."

Anheuser-Busch Corporation's purchase of Cypress Gardens has resulted in both the installation of its signature statue of a hulking Clydesdale and a significant investment of money. The

❿ latter has been put to good use in the newest exhibit, **Wings of Wonder: The Butterfly Conservatory.** More than 1,000 butterflies representing more than 50 species flit about an enclosed Victorian-style greenhouse, whose 5,500 square feet contain three waterfalls, educational displays, and a couple of chrysalis chambers where you can watch new butterflies struggling out of their cocoon. Four new gardens surround the conservatory: a butterfly garden constructed in the shape of a butterfly wing (great for those aerial shots from Kodak's Island in the Sky); an herb and scent garden, complete with cooking demonstrations; a vegetable and fruit garden; and a rose garden.

⓫ **Carousel Cove** caters to fidgety kids who demand a reward for traipsing past antique radios and inanimate shrubbery. It's perfectly geared to grandparents and grandchildren, with none of Sea World's athletic net climbs. Most of the rides are closer to the old-fashioned, county-fair variety than to the high-tech wonders at most theme parks. There are the ball crawls and bouncing pads, where kids can work off excess energy while their weary relatives watch, as well as skee ball, ball tosses, swings, and classic kiddie rides such as the Red Baron (airplanes). Some carnival games ($1 a chance) are also available.

⓬ It's worth saving the **Botanical Gardens** for last for the same reason that you save room for dessert. Most of the plants are labeled as part of the park's education program, the plantings are naturalized, and a saunter on winding paths beneath shady live oaks or the quiet in the chamber created by a giant banyan's hanging roots provides a delicious respite from the usual entertainment park rush. Photo ops abound.

Dining

The food is fast and the service friendly, but don't expect much more than basic refueling choices on the menu. At the Southern Crossroads hub, **Crossroads Restaurant** is fairly upscale, with a sit-down restaurant and a similar salad-quiche-sandwich menu with touches of southern cooking. **Lakeview Terrace,** on the upper level of the more southerly of the pair of waterski stadiums, has a terrific view of the waterskiing show, as well as food that won't diminish your attention. Cypress Gardens is located plunk in the middle of central Florida's citrus plantations, so you can always pick up some freshly squeezed orange juice at **Baker's Dozen, Village Fare,** and most other food locations in the park.

Shopping

Before entering the park, buy a straw fan at the **Bazaar Gift Shop** at the entrance—it's invaluable for hot afternoon performances at the Crossroads Arena and on steamy days. Once inside, pick up minitopiaries and tastefully flowered T-shirts and sweatshirts (which do not turn you into a billboard for Cypress Gardens) at **Gardening, Etc.,** in Southern Crossroads. On your way out, stop in the gift shop again for pastel parasols for the baby belle in your life, a pair of flowered gardening gloves, or an all-too-apt copy of *Allergy Plants* to find out what just ambushed your sinuses.

The **Butterfly Shop,** near Wings of Wonder, has a unique collection of fluttery fancies for collectors and some nifty things for bug-loving children.

Access for Travelers with Disabilities

All of the garden attractions at Cypress Gardens are wheelchair accessible, as are all restaurants and shops. Children with disabilities may not be able to negotiate some of the rides in Carousel Cove without assistance.

Splendid China

The Orlando area's newest attraction is more a superlative open-air museum than a theme park in the Mickey Mouse tradition. Instead of standing in long lines at thrill rides and glitzy shows, visitors here stroll among painstakingly re-created versions of China's greatest landmarks. Tinkling, meditative music plays in the background, and Chinese artisans demonstrate traditional woodworking, weaving, and other crafts. Think of a park featuring scaled-down versions of the Grand Canyon, the Alamo, and the White House, plus roping shows and high school marching bands, and you'll get an idea of what a "Splendid America" might be like.

It took $100 million and 120 Chinese craftspeople working for two years to craft the 60-plus replicas, which include both manmade structures, such as the Imperial Palace, and natural phenomena, such as the rock formations of the Stone Forest. Some of the monuments are life-size, while others have been greatly reduced in scale—each brick in the Great Wall, for example, is only 2 inches long. These detailed reproductions are even more impressive when you consider that the artisans used historically accurate building materials and techniques whenever possible. Whereas Universal Studios and WDW are working to outautomate each other, Splendid China is content to stress tradition over technology; the most advanced electronics you'll see here are the tiny lights that glow inside the buildings after dark.

Park developers had planned to let the park consist solely of the miniature monuments, thereby re-creating the successful formula that has brought millions of visitors to the prototype park, Shenzhen Splendid China, which opened near Hong Kong in 1989. U.S. advisers convinced them, however, that theme-park-savvy Western visitors expected more bang for their buck, so a playground area for children and live entertainment were added. Despite the awareness that Florida's Splendid China needed to be tailored for different demographics, problems still arose that neither the Chinese creators nor their U.S. friends had foreseen.

Park officials certainly didn't figure on demonstrators, who showed up on opening day to protest China's occupation of Tibet. (The park includes a representation of Potala Palace, the official seat of the Dalai Lama, Tibet's exiled spiritual and secular leader.) And they never dreamed that early guests would trample through the displays, kick over hundreds of handmade clay figurines, or try to take home the delicately painted decorations that are cemented onto many structures. The park suffered more damage in its first few days than its cousin in Shenzhen did in six years of operation. The first stage shows were an equally uncomfortable meeting of Asian and Western sensibilities: Chinese announcers read from stilted text that seemed to describe every other performer as "breathtaking and elegant." Some parkgoers simply walked out.

Things have evened out considerably since opening day, but the difficulties are a reminder that cultural differences can be extremely powerful. They may also be the root of Splendid China's appeal. Many guests come to the park out of curiosity and find themselves fascinated by the delicate craftsmanship that went into creating the displays, the thousands of years of history that the structures represent, and the religious mythology attached to many of the re-created shrines. Splendid China turns out to be just their cup of tea.

Essential Information

Tourist Information Contact Splendid China (3000 Splendid China Blvd., Kissimmee 34747; tel. 407/397–8800 or 800/244–6226). Once you're at the park, **Guest Services** (tel. 407/397–8825) is located inside the main entrance to the right.

Getting There Splendid China is about 12 miles from Orlando, or 2½ miles west of the I–4/U.S. 192 junction. From Orlando, take I–4 west toward WDW, and get off at Exit 25B—the signs will say "Disney," "Fort Wilderness," and so on. You are now on U.S. 192; continue west past all of the exits leading to Disney. Stay in the far-left lane and look for the dragon.

Parking There's no charge for parking at Splendid China.

Auto Needs Should you experience car trouble, head for **Central Reception,** just outside the gate, and an attendant will call an auto service for you.

Admission Regular admission is $23.55 for adults, $13.90 for children 5–12. AAA members receive a 10% discount, as do senior citizens over 55.

Hours The park is open daily 9:30–8; shops and restaurants in the Suzhou Gardens area stay open until 9:30. Hours may be extended in peak seasons.

Services There are **diaper-changing tables** available in women's rest
Baby Care rooms. No **diapers** are sold on the property, but they can be purchased at Eckerd's, just off U.S. 192 near the park's entrance. **Strollers** are for rent at Guest Services (single $4, double $7, no deposit).

Cameras **Film** for most cameras is sold at Guest Services, as are **disposable 35mm cameras.** Guest Services also rents **video cameras** ($25 per day, $150 deposit).

First Aid First-aid services are immediately inside the main entrance.

Guided Tours A four-hour walking tour of the park is $5 per person. The VIP golf-cart tour whips you, a guide, and up to four friends around the park in about 90 minutes; the tour is $45, regardless of the number of people.

Lockers They're near Guest Services ($1).

Lost Things Go to Guest Services. There is a parkwide public-address sys-
or People tem that can be used for contact in an emergency.

Money You'll find an ATM at Guest Services, but no currency exchange facilities.

Package If you do your shopping before checking out the exhibits, ask
Pickup the merchant about holding the item or having it sent to Guest Services; there's no official package pickup, but most vendors will be happy to oblige.

Travel One thing Splendid China offers that's not found at any other
Agency park is a full-service travel agency. **China Travel Services** (tel. 407/397–8868), one of the largest travel agencies in China and a major investor in the park, has an office on-site. If the re-creations make you want to see the real thing, make reservations before you go home.

Wheelchair You can rent **standard wheelchairs** ($5) and **electric scooters**
Rental ($25, with $50 deposit) from Guest Services.

Strategies for Your Visit

You can probably tour every exhibit in under four hours, but once you add some time for shopping, eating, and taking in a few shows, Splendid China makes for a good one-day trip. The park is really at its most magical at night. Try not to arrive until after noon; that way you'll be in plenty of time to catch the shows, eat some dinner, watch the final parade at 6:30ish, and then wander the exhibits until closing time.

When you get to the park, go to Harmony Hall and watch the 15-minute film *This Is Splendid China*, which explains the history behind the park. Also check with Guest Services for show times and any special events. Since lines are not an issue here, there's no pressing strategy needed for touring the attractions. One thing to note: The park map numbers the exhibits counterclockwise; if you tour in that direction, you'll end up at the underwhelming mausoleum of Dr. Sun Yat-sen in the middle of the park. If you head clockwise, you'll finish up your day with the most impressive sites—the Imperial Palace and the Great Wall.

One final caveat: The passive nature of the park makes it suitable mostly for older children and adults. Young kids and even restless teens may get bored because there's plenty to see but not much to do.

Rainy Days Splendid China is very much an outdoor exhibit; once you're out among the displays there is little shelter from the elements. If rain is forecast, stay home or bring a poncho.

Exploring Splendid China

Besides the star attractions like the Great Wall and the Summer Palace, Splendid China also has reproductions of Chinese temples, pagodas, typical Chinese homes, and grottoes filled with religious statuary. Each display is accompanied by a short, written explanation or a recorded message or both, explaining its significance and history. The following text, which marks only the highlights, takes you on a clockwise tour of the park; we pause about two-thirds of the way through at the Temple of Light Amphitheater, where all of the live shows are presented; depending on what time the shows you're most interested in start, you may want to head for the theater first.

As you come through the turnstile, you enter Splendid China's version of Main Street: **Suzhou Gardens** is a re-creation of a 14th-century Chinese village. Inside the tile-roofed structures, you'll find most of the park's shops, several restaurants, and **Guest Services.**

Just adjacent to Guest Services is **Harmony Hall,** where the *This Is Splendid China* film is screened every 20 minutes. Although it contains some lovely footage of China and useful background information on the buildings and statues that the exhibits here are based on, the film does not explore the meticulous construction that went into building the park. *Duration: 15 min. Crowds: Not a problem. Strategy: See it first so you'll better understand the exhibits. Audience: All ages. Rating:* ★★

The **closing parade,** which kicks off each night at about 6:30, also starts near the main entrance and then winds through Suzhou Gardens. Featuring colorfully painted wooden floats, flotillas of traditional sedan chairs, and a slew of ornately adorned ladies, it's worth a watch. *Duration: 25 min. Crowds: Nothing significant. Audience: All ages. Rating:* ★★

Head left out of Suzhou Gardens' shopping plaza and into an area of replicated stone grottoes, the originals of which are used as temples. **Grotto 257** is a cave shrine; the interior features dark, rich colors and is authentic down to the smudges in the artwork and the missing digits on some of the statues. A number of the exhibits appear worse for wear because their prototypes were damaged during the Cultural Revolution or simply by the passage of time; the craftspeople chose to replicate these originals as authentically as possible, warts and all. Several grottoes down is the **Leshan Buddha,** a re-creation of the largest man-made statue in the world. The original, which took 90 years to build, stands 24 stories high. This version is about 35 feet high. Past the grottoes is a maze of odd obelisks, composing the **Stone Forest.** This unusual formation replicates a 200-acre park in southern Yunan Province, where pillars have been whittled out of the limestone by aeons of erosion.

At Nine Dragon Wall, head left to the **Summer Palace,** the traditional home of China's dowager empress. Aristocrats and other members of the court would come to stay during the summer to escape the heat in Beijing. As at the original, the many palace structures are reflected in a smooth pool. After the complex fell into ruins during the 19th century, the Empress Dowager Ci Xi had it rebuilt with money that was supposed to be used to expand the navy. The stone boat that you see moored at the water's edge—the prototype is made from marble—therefore takes on a certain ironic meaning. The **Temple of Heaven,** past Dr. Sun Yat-sen's Mausoleum, is a striking, blue-tiled structure. It was at this site in Beijing that the emperor, as high priest of his people, would spend time in fasting and prayer.

Now make a swing around the back of the park. Check out the Water Village—China's version of Venice—and the Lijiang River Scenery area (can you see the elephant in the rocks?). Behind the "river," in the far back corner of the park, is the controversial reproduction of **Potala Palace,** a dusty-rose-and-white structure. The original in Lhasa, Tibet's capital, is an amalgam of two palaces—the Red and the White—both commissioned by the fifth Dalai Lama (1617–82); it stands 13 stories high but seems even taller because the walls were constructed to lean inward, creating a false perspective.

Time Out | When you're ready to take a break from the miniatures, head past Jingzhen Octagonal Pavilion, Dai Village, and Manfeilong Pagoda to the **Wind and Rain Court.** Cantonese and Shanghai cuisine, along with a limited Western selection, are served in this ersatz pagoda. One park staffer said this is the place to get good hamburgers if your taste buds aren't in the mood to mu shu.

Splendid China's live-action venue is the **Temple of Light Amphitheater.** A costume show and a demonstration of music and folk dances are each presented on alternating hours. Both are slow-moving affairs, a situation that is not improved by the mumbling Chinese announcer. Without narration, the **Costume Show** amounts to a bunch of attractive young Asian women in high heels and silk who parade back and forth in time to music. The **National Art Ensemble Show** is a performance of traditional folk dances and music from across China and is considerably more interesting than the costume show. The dancers are skilled and the music intriguing, but once again, much of the symbolism of the movements is lost because the narration is hard to follow. *Duration of each: 40 min. Crowds: Not significant. Audience: All ages. Costume show rating:* ★ *Art Ensemble show rating:* ★★

Right next to the amphitheater is the **Panda Playground.** The ball crawls, slides, and maze are likely to entertain smaller children who are less than captivated by exhibits that don't move, make noise, or light up. Compared with other central Florida theme park playgrounds, however, this one is nothing to write home about. *Crowds: Not significant. Audience: Young children. Rating:* ★

An **Acrobatic Show** is held in an adjoining tent. Some cheesy magic tricks are followed by truly incredible feats of balance and flexibility. One woman stands on a bench about six feet off the ground and bends backward to pick up a coin with her mouth. This is easily the most entertaining show in the park. *Duration: 20 min. Crowds: Not significant. Audience: All ages. Rating:* ★★★

After getting your fill of Chinese entertainment, be sure to see the **1,000 Eyes and 1,000 Hands Guanyin Buddha Statue,** whose many hands are said to ease the troubles of the world. The nearby **Terra Cotta Warriors** are modeled on 7,000 life-size clay figurines unearthed by archaeologists in 1974. The original figures were realistic portraits of servants, soldiers, and cavalry in the employ of Emperor Ch'in Shih Huang Ti. When the emperor died, almost 2,000 years ago, the figures were buried with him as an honor guard. Splendid China's warriors—replicas of replicas, as it were—are housed in a cool cave.

Now take a walk along the **Great Wall,** keeping in mind that the 6.5 million tiny bricks used to make the wall were mortared into place by hand. This ¹/₂-mile-long expanse cannot begin to replicate the size of the original—the 1,500-mile-long behemoth that is the only man-made structure visible from space. As in China itself, Mongolia lies on the other side of this wall. Check to see if a wrestling demonstration is scheduled near the **Mongolian Yurt.** Mongolia's capital city, Ulan Bator, has a population of 500,000, more than half of whom live in yurts like these.

The **Imperial Palace** is the centerpiece of Beijing's famed **Forbidden City** and one of the most impressive sights at Splendid China. The compound in Beijing, built in the early 1400s as the home of the royal family, was constructed of materials brought from all over China and decorated with centuries' worth of loot; it housed so many people that as many as 6,000 cooks were needed to feed them. No commoner stepped inside the walls of its inner sanctum until the mid-20th century; some of China's emperors never stepped outside. Even the scale model here gives a sense of the immense size and the artistry that made such a lifestyle possible.

Dining

Splendid China has some splendid food. Even the cafeteria-style offerings at Suzhou Gardens' **Seven Flavors Court** are far better than normal park fare, and probably at least as good as your neighborhood take-out place. Try the nearby **Suzhou Pearl** if you're more in the mood for attentive service, elegant atmosphere, and gourmet versions of traditional Chinese dishes. (The empty room off the main area is the park owners' private dining room.) If you're out among the exhibits proper, try **Great Wall Terrace,** near the 1,000 Hands Guanyin Buddha statue; it serves Mandarin and northern Chinese cuisine and has table service. Reservations are recommended at all the sit-down restaurants and can be made at Guest Services when you first arrive. If you want just a hot dog and a soda, carts are scattered throughout the park.

Shopping

As with the food, the merchandise available at Splendid China is a cut above typical theme-park tourist souvenirs. Of Suzhou Gardens' 11 shops, only **Nine Dragon Gifts** offers pedestrian goodies like T-shirts and key chains. For more exotic offerings, check out **Ancestral Artifacts'** handcrafted Chinese furniture, the nursery at **Pen Jing Gardens** (which sells bonsai trees), and **Loomed Creations'** lovely linens. Other unusual treasures such as teas, works of calligraphy, silk embroidery, hand-painted porcelain, and jade may make you wish you had more time and money to spend.

Access for Travelers with Disabilities

There are no special programs or guides available for guests with disabilities. Most of Splendid China's attractions are wheelchair accessible, but Sun Yat-sen's Mausoleum and the Guanyin Buddha Statue have stairs. Visitors must be able to transfer to a golf-cart-like tram for the VIP guided tour. Recorded messages in both English and Spanish discuss the various exhibits but probably do not provide enough information for visually impaired guests to have a full experience. All of the shops and dining areas are wheelchair accessible, although the stone streets in Suzhou Gardens may make for some rough riding.

5 Away from the Theme Parks

Updated by
Lindy
Shepherd

When you're ready to put some distance between you and Mickey, you'll find that Orlando and the surrounding central Florida area have much more than theme parks. You'll discover an abundance of attractions—natural, unnatural, and supernatural—that are equally enjoyable and often less crowded and expensive. Call in advance for the specific directions to refine your travel plans.

Off the Beaten Track

Lesser-known attractions like those that follow, when visited together, combine to make enjoyable day trips. Both of these suggested itineraries lie to the north. Not far from I-Drive, about a half hour's drive, is tony, suburban Winter Park; farther afield is grove-filled Lake County.

Tour 1: Winter Park

Once the winter refuge of wealthy northerners, Winter Park, though part of Orlando's metro area, maintains a proud, independent, and upscale identity. A pleasant day can be spent shopping, eating, and taking in the scenery along **Park Avenue** downtown, full of trendy boutiques and restaurants. Long and narrow **Central Park** stretches through the heart of the shopping district, and benches under the ancient trees offer a respite from the bustle. Away from downtown, the moss-covered trees form canopies over brick streets, and old estates surround canal-linked lakes.

Perhaps the best way to get a feel for Winter Park is from the deck of a pontoon boat on the **Scenic Boat Tour.** The relaxing, hour-long cruise sails past 12 miles of fine old homes and around the grounds of Rollins College, on one of Winter Park's three main lakes, which are connected by 100-year-old canals. Having celebrated its 56th anniversary not long ago, this tour is one of central Florida's oldest attractions. Turn right off I–4's Fairbanks Avenue Exit. At Park Avenue, turn left and head straight into downtown Winter Park. Turn right on East Morse Boulevard; the dock is at the end of the street. *312 E. Morse Blvd., Winter Park, tel. 407/644–4056. Admission: $5.50 adults, $2.75 children 2–12. Open daily 10–4; boats leave every hr.*

Having seen it from the lake, you might want to stroll around the campus of historic **Rollins College,** a private liberal arts school at the south end of Park Avenue. It claims Mister (Fred) Rogers among its alumni—yes, this was once his neighborhood. Take time to look at the Spanish-style architecture, especially Knowles Memorial Chapel, home of the Bach Festival Society. Also on campus is the **Cornell Fine Arts Museum,** which has the largest collection of American and European art in central Florida. The permanent collection contains works ranging from the Renaissance to contemporary times. *1000 Holt Ave., Winter Park, tel. 407/646–2526. Admission free. Open Tues.–Fri. 10–5, weekends 1–5; closed major holidays.*

American Express offers Travelers Cheques built for two.

Cheques *for Two*℠ from American Express are the Travelers Cheques that allow either of you to use them because both of you have signed them. And only one of you needs to be present to purchase them.

Cheques *for Two* are accepted anywhere regular American Express Travelers Cheques are, which is just about everywhere. So stop by your bank, AAA* or any American Express Travel Service Office and ask for Cheques *for Two*.

AMERICAN EXPRESS **Travelers Cheques**

Pack light.

Take the one number you need for any kind of call, anywhere you travel.

Checking in with your family back home? Calling for a tow truck? When you're on the road, the phone you use might not accept your calling card. Or you might get overcharged by an unknown telephone company. Here's the solution: dial 1 800 CALL ATT.[sm] You'll get flawless AT&T service, competitive calling card prices, and the lowest prices for collect calls from any phone, anywhere. Travel light. Just bring along this one simple number: 1 800 CALL ATT.

Bok Tower
Gardens, **26**

Cassadaga, **1**

Central Florida
Zoological Park, **2**

Charles Hosmer Morse
Museum of American
Art, **11**

Cornell Fine Arts
Museum, **10**

Florida Audubon
Society Madlyn
Baldwin Center for
Birds of Prey, **7**

Flying Tigers Warbird
Air Museum, **23**

Gatorland, **22**

Green Meadows
Farm, **24**

Lake Eola Park, **17**

Leu Botanical
Gardens, **15**

Loch Haven Park, **14**

Maitland Art Center, **6**

Mead Gardens, **12**

Mount Dora, **5**

Mystery Fun
House, **18**

Ocala National
Forest, **4**

Pirate's Cove
Adventure Golf, **21**

Ripley's Believe It or
Not!, **20**

Rollins College, **13**

Scenic Boat Tour, **9**

Terror on Church
Street, **16**

Water Mania, **25**

Wekiwa Springs State
Park, **3**

Wet 'n' Wild, **19**

Winter Park Farmer's
Market, **8**

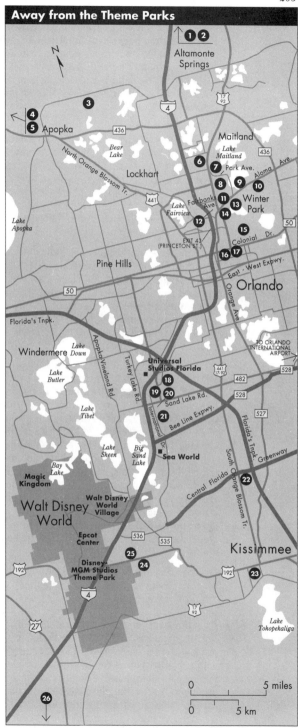

Away from the Theme Parks

If you're interested in more art, there is a concentration of galleries on Park Avenue. Half a block east is the elegant **Charles Hosmer Morse Museum of American Art**, which features an outstanding collection of stained-glass windows, blown glass, and lamps by Louis Tiffany. There's also a collection of paintings by 19th- and 20th-century American artists, as well as jewelry and pottery. *133 E. Welbourne Ave., Winter Park, tel. 407/645–5311. Admission: $2.50 adults, $1 students and children. Open Tues.–Sat. 9:30–4, Sun. 1–4.*

On Saturday, when the **Winter Park Farmer's Market** takes over a parking lot just west of Park Avenue, across the railroad tracks, you can see evidence of the real community that exists behind the upper-crust facade. The market is a long-standing tradition. Friends and neighbors gather to shop for fresh fruits and vegetables, breads and pastries, herbs, coffees, and plants. *W. Lyman and New York Aves., Winter Park, tel. 407/623–3275. Open Sat. 7–noon.*

Heading west out of town on Fairbanks Avenue, take the left fork onto Orange Avenue and, after ½ mile, turn left onto Denning Avenue for a visit to **Mead Gardens,** Winter Park's quite unusual park. Its 55 acres have intentionally been left to grow as a natural preserve. Walkers and runners are attracted to the trails that wind around the creek, and plans are under way to build a boardwalk to provide a better view of the delicate wetlands. *S. Denning Ave., Winter Park, tel. 407/623–3334. Admission free. Open daily 8–sundown.*

With entrances on both Rollins and Princeton streets (1 mile east off I–4's Exit 43), Orlando's **Loch Haven Park** is a grassy field with four of the city's cultural strongholds: Orlando Science Center, Orange County Historical Museum, Orlando Museum of Art, and Civic Theatre of Central Florida. All but the theater are open almost daily and have delightful gift shops chockablock with unusual items. The buildings, all air-conditioned, are delightfully cool on hot, humid days. The park itself doesn't offer much more than a pleasant walk from one building to another. However, off to the side are some old, shady oak trees—nice for a picnic—and a lovely lake is just across the street. The wide-open space hosts the Kite Festival in March and the Pet Fair in December, and it's frequently used by community groups for outdoor concerts and festivals.

Orlando Science Center is a place for action, and, best of all, touching is encouraged here. The Tunnel of Discovery has a variety of clever hands-on activities to teach the principles of physical science. Special traveling exhibits with themes ranging from dinosaurs to space travel all have interactive components. For preschoolers there's WaterWorks, where children, secured in plastic smocks, are turned loose to explore the properties of water. NatureWorks features an extensive collection of rocks and insects as well as live demonstrations with resident snakes, other reptiles, and amphibians. Films in the dome-shaped planetarium take viewers on a journey through the stars, and on weekend evenings Cosmic Concerts combines lasers and rock music in a psychedelic light show. There's a snack bar. *810 E. Rollins St., Orlando, tel. 407/896–7151. Admission: $6.50 adults, $5.50 children 3–11. Open Mon.–Thurs. and Sat. 9–5, Fri. 9–9, Sun. noon–5. Cosmic Concerts: admission $5; Fri. and Sat. 9 PM, 10:30 PM, and midnight.*

Adjacent to the Science Center is more sedate **Orange County Historical Museum,** a storehouse of Orlando memorabilia, photographs, and antiques. Exhibits explore Native American and native Floridian culture, and they show off a country store, Victorian parlor, and print shop; call for an update on the always-changing traveling exhibits. Fire Station No. 3, an actual 1926 brick firehouse behind the museum, houses antique fire trucks, fire-fighting memorabilia, and collectibles. Though most items are for looking only, there are some firefighters' bunks, hats, and jackets for youngsters to investigate. *812 E. Rollins St., Orlando, tel. 407/897–6350. Admission: $2 adults, $1.50 senior citizens, $1 children 6–11. Open Mon.–Sat. 9–5, Sun. noon–5.*

Across the park from the Science Center is the **Orlando Museum of Art.** The collection includes 19th- and 20th-century American art, displayed on a rotating basis year-round, and a permanent exhibit of pre-Columbian artifacts from a Mayan excavation. Young children will enjoy the first-class Art Encounter, created with the help of Walt Disney World. Hands-on activities, such as dressing up in colorful handwoven clothing from South America, stimulate imaginations and enhance children's understanding of the works in the galleries. The Museum Café opens off the rotunda, an atriumlike lobby done in glass and marble, and serves an upscale luncheon as jazz music plays (reservations accepted). Call for information on special exhibits. *2416 N. Mills Ave., Orlando, tel. 407/896–4231. Admission (suggested donation): $4 adults, $2 children 4–11. Open Tues.–Sat. 9–5, Sun. noon–5; tours Sept.–May, Wed. and Sun. 2 PM; Art Encounter Tues.–Fri. and Sun. noon–5, Sat. 10–5; café Tues.–Sun. 11:30–2:30.*

The **Civic Theatre of Central Florida** stages productions throughout the year. The MainStage Series offers traditional Broadway musicals and dramas; the SecondStage Series has off-Broadway-style, cutting-edge works; and family classics are performed in the Theatre for Young People. *1001 E. Princeton St., Orlando, tel. 407/896–7365.*

A short distance from Loch Haven Park is **Leu Botanical Gardens,** Orlando's 56-acre horticultural extravaganza. Formerly the estate of the late industrialist and citrus industry entrepreneur Harry P. Leu, it has a collection of historical blooms, many varieties of which were established before 1900. You'll see ancient oaks, a 50-foot floral clock, an orchid conservatory, and one of the largest camellia collections in eastern North America (in bloom October through March). Mary Jane's Rose Garden, named after Leu's wife, is filled with more than 1,000 bushes; it is the largest formal rose garden south of Atlanta. The simple 19th-century Leu House Museum, once the Leu family home, preserves the furnishings and appointments of a well-to-do, turn-of-the-century Florida family. From Loch Haven Park, continue east on Princeton Street to the end. Turn right on Mills Avenue and left on Virginia Avenue; bear left at the fork and look for the garden entrance on the left, just after the traffic light. *1730 N. Forest Ave., Orlando, tel. 407/246–2620. Admission: $3 adults, $1 children 6–16. Garden open daily 9–5; museum Tues.–Sat. 10–3:30, Sun. and Mon. 1–3:30.*

Tour 2: Lake County

As you drive northwest out of Orlando on U.S. 441, you head into aptly named Lake County, an area renowned for its pristine water and excellent fishing. Watch the flat countryside, thick with scrub pines, take on a gentle roll through citrus groves and pastures with live oaks. The lean orchards still show signs of the devastation caused by an unusually harsh freeze several years ago.

About 45 minutes northwest of Orlando is the quaint valley community of **Mount Dora,** west off U.S. 441 on either Old U.S. 441 or Route 44B. Built around the unspoiled Lake Harris chain of lakes, the town has a slow and easy pace, a rich history, New England–style charm, and excellent antiques shopping (*see* Off the Beaten Track in Chapter 6). Although the population of Mount Dora is only just over 7,000, there is plenty of excitement here, especially in fall and winter. There is an art festival, a sailing regatta, a bicycle festival, a crafts fair, and many other events. Palm Island Park offers nature trails and fishing, and Gilbert Park has a public dock and boat-launching ramp, picnicking facilities, and a playground. Take in one of the prettiest views in central Florida from the city dock at the end of Fourth Avenue, next to the Mount Dora Yacht Club; on a misty day, the lakes seem to go on forever. Or just amble through the Main Street district. The Mount Dora Chamber of Commerce provides a self-guided tour map that tells you everything you need to know—from historic landmarks to restaurants. *Chamber of Commerce, 341 Alexander St., Mount Dora, tel. 904/383–2165. Welcome center open weekdays 9–5, Sat. 10–4, Sun. noon–4; after hrs, maps set out on kiosk.*

A half-hour drive north of Mount Dora on Route 19 is **Ocala National Forest,** a 366,000-acre area between the Oklawaha and St. Johns rivers, known for its canoeing, hiking, swimming, camping, and invigorating springs. The visitor center, on Route 19, just north of Altoona, provides information on what to see and do. Alexander Springs, favored for its cold, fresh water, is just minutes away. From the center, continue north on Route 19 and turn right on Route 445; the entrance is on the left. After hiking down to the small beach, swim out, preferably with a snorkel and fins, to the steep drop-off at the head spring, where the water rushes out from rock formations below. It's not unusual to see friendly alligators sitting on the bank opposite the sandy beach, but you'll notice that natives leave the water before sundown—feeding time. Other choice springs in the national forest are Juniper and Salt springs. *Ocala National Forest visitor cen-*

ter, 45621 Rte. 19, Altoona, tel. 904/669–7495. Center open daily 9–5. Alexander Springs admission: $2; open daily 8–8.

Sightseeing Checklist

If you don't want to take a day trip, you might want to pick and choose individual attractions—peaceful, offbeat, enlightening, or just plain fun—to complement your time in the theme parks. You'll find there's more to culture here than Epcot Center, more to nature than Cypress Gardens, and more to animal life than Mickey and Shamu can offer.

The Natural World

Parks and Gardens If your appetite for natural beauty has been whetted, take a one-hour drive south of Orlando to **Bok Tower Gardens,** a quirky yet appealing sanctuary of plants, flowers, trees, and wildlife native to subtropical Florida. Shady paths meander through pine forests in this peaceful world of silvery moats, mockingbirds and swans, blooming thickets, and hidden sundials. You'll be able to boast that you stood on the highest measured point in the state, a colossal 324 feet above sea level. The majestic 200-foot Bok Tower is constructed of coquina (from seashells) and pink, white, and gray marble. The tower is carved with wildlife designs, and its bronze doors are decorated with reliefs that tell the complete story of Genesis. The tower houses a carillon with 57 bronze bells that ring every half-hour after 10 AM. Each day at 3 PM there is a 45-minute recital, which may include Early American folk songs, Appalachian tunes, Irish ballads, or Latin hymns. There are also moonlight recitals.

The landscape was designed in 1928 by Frederick Law Olmsted Jr., son of the planner of New York's Central Park. The tower was dedicated to the American people in 1929 by President Calvin Coolidge on behalf of Edward Bok, a Dutch immigrant who was editor of *Ladies' Home Journal* for 30 years. Also on the grounds is the 230-room, Mediterranean Revival–style Pinewood House, built in 1930. Take I–4 to U.S. 27 south. About 5 miles past the Cypress Gardens turnoff, turn right on Route 17A to Alternate U.S. 27. Past the orange groves, turn left on Burns Avenue and follow about 1½ miles to gardens. *Burns Ave. and Tower Blvd., Lake Wales, tel. 813/676–1408. Admission: $3 adults. Open daily 8–5. Pinewood House tours: admission (suggested donation): $5 adults, $4 children under 12; Sept. 15–May 15, Tues. and Thurs. 12:30 and 2, Sun. 2.*

In the heart of Orlando, on the eastern side of downtown, lies an inner-city victory, **Lake Eola Park.** Established in 1892, the family park experienced a series of ups and downs that left it run-down by the late '70s: The fountain in the lake was rusty, the bushes and trees havens for crime. With the support of determined citizens, the park gradually underwent a renovation, which restored the fountain and added a wide brick walkway around the lake. The circuit (.9 mi around) is well traveled by walkers and joggers; no bicycles, skateboards, or roller skates are allowed. The security is such that families with young children use the well-lighted playground in the evening and downtown residents walk their dogs late at night in safety. The Walt Disney Amphitheater, perched on the lake, is a dramatic site for the annual Shakespeare Festival (March and April), as well as for weekend community concerts and *FunnyEola*, a free, family comedy show performed the second Tuesday of every month. However, the most fun to be had at the park is a ride in a swan-shaped pedal boat; the view at dusk, as the fountain lights up and the sun sets behind Orlando's growing skyline, is spectacular. Take the I–4 Robinson St. exit, turn right at the bottom of the ramp, and go ¼ mile. *Bordered by Robinson St. and Rosalind Ave., Orlando, tel. 407/246–2827. Open daily 7 AM–midnight. Swan boats: rental: $5.30 for ½ hr; open daily noon–8 (to 10, June–Aug.); max. 3 people per boat. Eola Park Café open daily 10–9.*

Leu Botanical Gardens, formerly the Leu estate, has gardens teeming with all kinds of flowers, including orchids, camellias, and roses (*see* Tour 1, *above*).

Mead Gardens is a 55-acre nature preserve in Winter Park (*see* Tour 1, *above*).

Recreation Areas

North of Orlando, **Ocala National Forest,** known for its springs, is good for canoeing, hiking, and swimming (*see* Tour 2, *above*).

Where the tannin-stained Wekiva River meets the crystal-clear Wekiva headspring, there is a curious and visible exchange— like strong tea infusing in water. (Wekiva is a Creek Indian word meaning "flowing water.") The **Wekiwa Springs State Park** sprawls around this area on 6,400 acres. The parkland is well suited for camping, hiking, and picnicking; the spring for swimming; and the river for canoeing and fishing. Canoe trips can range from a simple hour-long paddle around the lagoon to observe a colony of water turtles, to a full-day excursion through less-congested parts of the river that haven't changed much since the area was inhabited by Timucuan Indians. Take I–4 Exit 49 (Longwood), and turn left on Route 434. Go 1¼ miles to Wekiwa Springs Road; turn right and go 4½ miles to entrance on right. *1800 Wekiwa Circle, Apopka, tel. 407/884–2009. Admission: $3.25 per vehicle. Open daily 8–sundown.*

Animals, Animals, Animals

A visit to 110-acre **Central Florida Zoological Park** will disappoint if you're expecting a grand metro zoo. However, this is a respectable display, of about 230 animals, tucked under pine trees, and, like the city of Orlando, it continues to grow. A new boardwalk has replaced most of the mulch-covered walkways and extends through wetlands. The elephant exhibit is popular, as are the playful otters and the exotic and native snakes housed in the herpetarium. The zoo is becoming specialized in small and medium-size exotic cats, including servals, caracals, and jaguarundis, and there is an aviary that houses American bald eagles that have been grounded due to injury. Children love the Animal Adventure, which has domestic and farm animals to pet and feed; elephant and pony rides are offered weekends from 11 to 4. Take I–4 Exit 52, and drive 1 mile east on U.S. 17–92 to entrance on right. *3755 N. U.S. 17–92, Sanford, tel. 407/323–4450. Admission: $5 adults, $3 senior citizens ($1.50 on Tues.), $2 children 3–12. Open daily 9–5.*

More than 20 different species of hawks, eagles, owls, falcons, and vultures make their home at the **Florida Audubon Society Madlyn Baldwin Center for Birds of Prey.** There is an earnestness to this humble, working facility on Lake Sybelia in Maitland, which takes in 500–600 injured wild birds of prey each year. About 43% are able to return to the wild; permanently injured birds continue to live at the center and can be seen in the aviaries along the pathways and sitting on outdoor perches. The center also tracks eagles and occasionally sets up a closed-circuit monitor to observe a nest, so visitors can watch a genuine nature show. Take I–4 Exit 47A then Maitland Boulevard East; turn right on Maitland Avenue, right on U.S. 17–92, right on Kennedy Boulevard, and right on Audubon Way. *921 S. Lake Sybelia Dr., Maitland, tel. 407/645–3826. Admission (suggested donation): $2 adults, $1 children 6–12. Open Tues.–Sat. 10–4.*

Long before Walt Disney World, there was **Gatorland.** This campy attraction south of Orlando on U.S. 441 has endured since 1949, without much change, despite competition from major attractions. Through the monstrous aqua gator-jaw doorway (a definite photo op) lie thrills and chills in the form of more than 5,000 alligators and crocodiles, swimming and basking in the Florida sun. In addition to the gators and crocs, there is a zoo that houses many other reptiles, mammals, and birds. A free train ride provides an overview of the park, and a three-story observation tower overlooks the breeding marsh, which is swamped with gator grunts, especially come sundown during mating season.

Don't miss the Gator Jumparoo show, in which gators leap out of the water for their food. The best Jumparoo is the first one in the morning, when the gators are hungriest. There's also a Gator Wrestling show, and though there's no doubt who's going to win the match, it's still fun to see the handlers take on those tough guys with the beady eyes. In the educational Snakes Alive show, high drama is provided by the 30–40 rattlesnakes that fill the pit around the speaker.

If your appetite builds, you may want to try out the smoked gator ribs or nuggets at Pearl's Smokehouse; there's more typical fare as well. The Gator Boutique is the epitome of a tacky tourist gift shop. Since Gatorland is a commercial alligator farm there are plenty of alligator-skin accessories, as well as gator sauce and gator chowder. Don't look for scrupulous Disney-style cleanliness here, and the personnel aren't polished with pixie dust either. This is a real Florida experience, and you'll walk out those aqua gator jaws knowing the difference between a gator and a croc. *14501 S. Orange Blossom Trail, between Orlando and Kissimmee, tel. 407/855–5496 or 800/393–JAWS. Admission: $10.95 adults, $7.95 children 3–11. Open daily 8–dusk.*

Friendly farmhands keep things moving on the two-hour guided tour of **Green Meadows Farm** in Kissimmee. There's little chance to get bored and no waiting in line because tours are always starting. Everyone who wants to gets to milk the fat momma cow, and chickens and geese are turned loose in their yard to run and squawk while city slickers try to catch them. Kids take a quick pony ride, and everyone gets jostled about on the old-fashioned hayride. Kids come away saying: "I milked a cow, caught a chicken, pet a pig, and fed a goat." Take I–4 Exit 25A (Kissimmee), go east on U.S. 192 for 3 miles to Poinciana Boulevard, turn right, and drive 5 miles. *1368 Poinciana Blvd., Kissimmee, tel. 407/846–0770. Admission: $9 adults, children under 3 free. Open daily 9:30–5 (last tour at 3).*

Museums

Art/Science Museums
Glass, both stained and blown, is the main attraction at the **Charles Hosmer Morse Museum of American Art** (*see* Tour 1, *above*).

Cornell Fine Arts Museum, at Rollins College, has a large collection of American and European art (*see* Tour 1, *above*).

Loch Haven Park contains Orlando's science, historical, and art museums and a community theater (*see* Tour 1, *above*).

It's local lore that the **Maitland Art Center,** a historic art museum near Lake Sybelia, is inhabited by the spirit of its artist-architect founder, Andre Smith. He began constructing his studio retreat in 1937, and the grounds and buildings themselves are works of art. The seemingly infinite reliefs and other details reflect Smith's fascination with Mayan and Aztec influences and further account for the mystical aura. An outdoor chapel is a favorite spot for weddings, and romantic gardens blend harmoniously with the natural surroundings. Inside, the galleries display an extensive collection of Smith's work as well as changing exhibits by local and national artists. Take I–4 Exit 47A and Maitland Boulevard East; turn right on Maitland Avenue and after ¾ mile, right again on Packwood Avenue. *231 W. Packwood Ave., Maitland, tel. 407/539–2181. Donations accepted. Open weekdays 10–4:30, weekends noon–4:30.*

Offbeat Museums
The **Orlando Museum of Art** (*see* Tour 1, *above*) has a new look and is attracting national touring exhibits of artists like Andy Warhol and William Wegman (he of humorous Weimaraner-posing fame).

Old warbirds never die—they just become attractions at the **Flying Tigers Warbird Air Museum** in Kissimmee. The working aircraft restoration facility is nicknamed "Bombertown USA," because most of the planes here are bombers. Once they are operational, they are usually flown away by private collectors, but the museum also houses a permanent collection of about 25 vintage planes in its hangar, with a few big ones out on the tarmac. Tour guides are full of facts and personality and have an infectious passion for the planes. There are also displays of memorabilia and artifacts. Go south on U.S. 441 to U.S. 192; turn right. After the Kissimmee Airport entrance, turn left on Hoag-land Boulevard (Airport Rd.). *231 Hoagland Blvd., Kissimmee, tel. 407/933–1942. Admission: $6 adults, $5 senior citizens and children 5–12. Open Mon.–Sat. 9–5:30, Sun. 9–5 (extended in peak seasons).*

A 10-foot-square section of the Berlin Wall. A pain and torture chamber. A Rolls-Royce constructed entirely of matchsticks. A 26-foot-by-20-foot portrait of Van Gogh made from 3,000 post-cards. These and almost 200 other oddities speak for themselves in the **Ripley's Believe It or Not!** museum in the heart of tourist territory on International Drive. It is said that the fruits of Robert Ripley's explorations are to reality what Walt Disney World is to fantasy. The building itself is designed to appear as if it's sliding into one of Florida's notorious sinkholes. Give your-self an hour or two to soak up the weirdness here, but remember this is a looking, not touching, experience, which may drive antsy youngsters—and their parents—crazy. Take I–4 to Exit 29 (Sand Lake Rd.); turn left. Turn right on International Drive (second traffic light); museum is ¼ mile on left. *8201 Interna-tional Dr., Orlando, tel. 407/363–4418. Admission: $8.95 adults, $5.95 children 3–11. Open daily 10 AM–11 PM (extended in peak seasons).*

Fun Houses and Miniature Golf

There are a variety of ways to attack the **Mystery Fun House.** You might just want to bring your quarters and visit the video arcade, for which there's no admission charge. Paying admission to the actual Fun House entitles you to a walk through the 18-chamber Mystery Maze, which comes with the warning that it is "90% dark" and full of gory and distorted images. Outside, there's an 18-hole Mystery Mini-Golf, a basic putt-putt course, laid out flat and simple, with some holes landing inside gator jaws, a gorilla, and so on. It isn't in the same league as Pirate's Cove, a golfer's wonder. The real highlight is the Starbase Omega laser-tag game. Equipped with laser guns and wearing reflector belts, players are transported on a simulated spaceship ride to the arena, where they try to zap each other (to score points) and avoid being zapped by the UFO spaceship hovering overhead. Underfoot, the playing surface feels like an air mat-tress, adding a simulated low-gravity element to the game. Take I–4 to Exit 34B (Universal Studios). Turn right on Kirkman Road and right again on Major Boulevard. *5767 Major Blvd., Orlando, tel. 407/351–3355. Admission: maze $7.95, minigolf $2.95, laser game $5.95, all 3 for $11.85. Open daily 10 AM–11 PM (to mid-night in peak seasons).*

You can play the crème de la crème of miniature golf at the two locations of **Pirate's Cove Adventure Golf.** Each site offers two 18-hole courses that wind around artificial mountains, through caves, over waterfalls, and into lush foliage. The beginner's course is called Captain Kidd's Adventure; a more difficult game can be played on Blackbeard's Challenge. The courses are op-posite Mercado Mediterranean Village and in the Crossroads of

Lake Buena Vista shopping plaza (*see* Shopping Villages in Chapter 6). *8601 International Dr., Orlando, tel. 407/352–7378; Crossroads Center (I–4 Exit 27), tel. 407/827–1242. Admission: Captain Kidd's Adventure $6, Blackbeard's Challenge $6.50, all day $12 (children 3–12 $5). Open daily 9 AM–11:30 PM.*

Visit a haunted house year-round at **Terror on Church Street.** This showcase of horror in the heart of downtown, a few blocks east of Church Street Station, is a 25-minute walking tour through a high-tech labyrinth featuring 23 scenes from horror films with live actors and state-of-the-art sound effects. Lines are long on weekends, but they move along quickly because groups of eight leave every five minutes. The gift shop is stocked with gargoyles, eyeballs, and blood, as well as masks and makeup for re-creating your favorite slasher scenes. Terror targets the 12–22 age group but won't disappoint horror-film fans of any age. Follow signs off I–4 to the Church Street Historic District. *Church St. and Orange Ave., Orlando, tel. 407/649–3327. Admission: $10 adults, $8 Florida residents and children under 18. Open Tues.–Thurs. and Sun. 7 PM–midnight, Fri. and Sat. 7 PM–1 AM.*

Water Parks

For aesthetics you can't beat River Country and Typhoon Lagoon, with their landscaping and design in spectacular Disney style. But they don't have the enclosed water slides that make the area's other water parks—Wet 'n' Wild and WaterMania—so popular. Both of these concrete and plastic attractions are packed in summer, and there are long lines at the popular rides. Both smell of chlorine and suntan lotion, and both are fashion shows of tacky swimwear. The basic difference is location. Wet 'n' Wild is on International Drive, the cruise strip for restless teenagers. It attracts locals as well as out-of-towners, who constitute the greatest part of visitors to WaterMania, which is in Kissimmee.

WaterMania has all the requisite rides and slides without Walt Disney World aesthetics. However, it's the only water park around to have Wipe Out, a surfing simulator, where you grab a body board and ride a continuous wave form. The giant Pirate Ship in the Rain Forest, one of two children's play areas, is equipped with water slides and water cannons. The Abyss, similar to Wet 'n' Wild's Black Hole (*see below*), is an enclosed tube slide through which you twist and turn on a one- or two-person raft for 300 feet of deep-blue darkness. The park also offers a sandy beach, a picnic area, snack bars, gift shops, and periodic concerts, which can be enjoyed while floating in an inner tube. Its 18-hole miniature golf course won't win any local prizes, considering the competition, but does give you another way to pass the time while you're out of the water. It's in Kissimmee (½ mile east of I–4 and 1½ miles from Walt Disney World). *6073 W. Irlo Bronson Memorial Hwy., Kissimmee, tel. 407/239–8448 in Orlando, 407/396–2626 in Kissimmee, or 800/527–3092. Admission:*

$19.95 adults, $17.95 children 3–12. Open 11–5 (to about 8 in summer) daily on Orlando's few very cold days.

Wet 'n' Wild, like WaterMania, is probably best known for its outrageous water slides, especially the Black Hole—a 30-second, 500-foot, twisting, turning ride on a two-person raft through total darkness propelled by a 1,000-gallon-a-minute blast of water. There's also an elaborate Kid's Park—for those 4 feet tall and under—full of miniature versions of the bigger rides. The latest addition is the Bubba Tub, a six-story, triple-dip slide with a tube big enough for the entire family. Take advantage of the half-price discount after 3 PM (5 in peak seasons), which not only saves money but also cuts down on exposure to the sun. Teens like the Top 40 concerts that take place frequently in summer. The park has snack stands, but visitors are allowed to bring their own food and picnic around the pool or on the lakeside beach. Take I-4 Exit 30A and make a left. *6200 International Dr., Orlando, tel, 407/351-3200. Admission: $19.95 adults, $16.95 children 3–9. Open daily 10–5 (to about 9 in summer) except for Orlando's few really cold days.*

Explorable Towns

About 35 miles northeast of Orlando is **Cassadaga,** headquarters of the Southern Cassadaga Spiritualist Camp Meeting Association. More than half of the 300 residents are psychics, mediums, and healers, which makes it the nation's largest such community. These mediums communicate with your spirit and the spirits of others primarily for purposes of healing a sickness of the soul. The camp welcomes visitors either to sit in on one of the church services (10:30–11:45 AM Sunday or 7:30–8:15 PM Wednesday at the Colby Memorial Temple at the end of Stevens Street). Spiritualist services are nonsensational meditative gatherings, with the most unconventional aspect being the "message" portion, during which certified mediums deliver specific messages to attendees from spirits in the beyond. Visitors are also encouraged to get a reading from a camp member; it is suggested that the best way to find a medium who is right for you is by walking or driving through this rustic, five-block-by-five-block neighborhood and stopping at a house that is giving off the right energy. A community rich in spirit, it doesn't offer much to the material world, except the modest Southern Cassadaga Bookstore (1112 Stevens St.; open Mon.–Sat. 9:30–5, Sun. noon–5). The people here are friendly and wholesome and accustomed to curiosity seekers, but they do request respect for their community. Take I-4 to Exit 54 (Cassadaga and Lake Helen). Turn right on Route 472 and right again on Route 4139 (first traffic light); continue 2 miles. *Cassadaga Spiritualist Camp, Box 319, Cassadaga, tel. 904/228-2880.*

Charming **Mount Dora** offers good antiques shopping and scenic lake views (*see* Tour 2, *above*).

6 Shopping

Updated by
Marianne
Camas

Shopping is part of the entertainment at Walt Disney World and throughout the Greater Orlando area. There's something in every price range in virtually every store, so even kids on allowances can get in on the act. You'll find everything from specialty stores, gift shops, and flea markets to factory outlets, department stores, and, of course, malls. Orlando is absolutely packed with malls. It is virtually impossible to step outside your hotel room without seeing a mall or a sign advertising one. Whatever your shopping interests, the area provides a great opportunity to do a lifetime of shopping in a few days. Most stores accept traveler's checks and major credit cards.

Walt Disney World

You'll be able to find Disney trinkets in every park, but there are a few shops throughout the property that carry unique items, like Magic Kingdom's Frontier Trading Post, where you can find western-style gifts. For top suggestions, *see* the shopping sections in Chapters 3 and 4. In addition, keep your eye out for wonderful finds tailored to special interests—tennis balls with Mickey Mouse logos, for instance, are available in the pro shops at the Contemporary and other hotels.

Disney-MGM Studios Theme Park

Check out Sid Cahuenga's **One-of-a-Kind** shop, to the left as you enter the park. Alongside old movie posters, autographed pictures, and assorted, one-of-a-kind knickknacks are original costumes once worn by stars in feature movies. The **Animation Gallery,** at the end of the Animation Tour, sells original Disney animation cels, books, collectibles, and exclusive limited-edition reproductions. If you've been searching for Christmas decorations with a Disney theme, try **It's a Wonderful Shop,** near New York Street.

Disney Village Marketplace

Nestled along the shores of Buena Vista Lagoon, this complex of 19 shops is packed with art, fashions, crafts, and more. If you are looking for one-stop Disney shopping, this is the place. **Mickey's Character Shop** is the largest Disney merchandise store in the world. Children can buy trinkets for a dollar or two or choose among hundreds of stuffed animals—from Bambi and Thumper to Pongo and Perdita. Serious Disney fans can spend thousands for original cel paintings of animated movies or for porcelain sculptures of Cinderella or Alice in Wonderland. **Team Mickey's Athletic Club** offers sports clothing and equipment with the Mickey logo or Disney University items. **Toys Fantastic** has a phenomenal selection of Barbie dolls and accessories, along with the latest character collectibles. Artisans demonstrate their skills throughout the day at **Eurospain** and **Cristal Arts.** The **Christmas Chalet** sells holiday merchandise year-round. Both Disney-themed and traditional yule items are available. The prices here are no better or worse than anywhere else

218

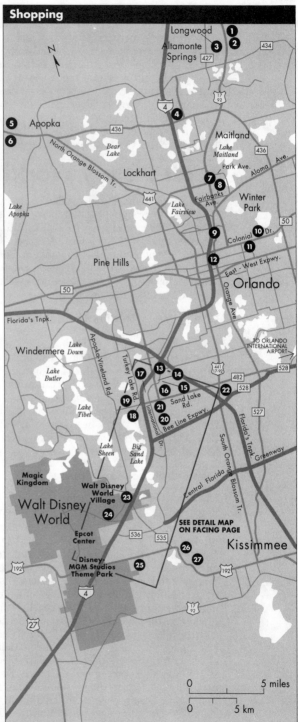

Shopping

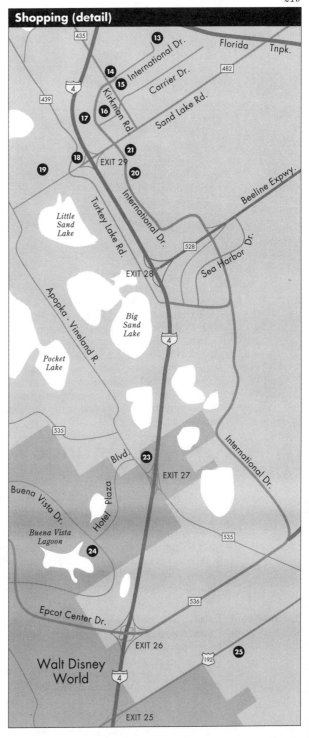

Shopping (detail)

in the country. While parents shop, kids 12 and up can rent watercraft at the marina. There are plenty of places to grab a snack or to relax with a heartier meal. Relatively quiet in the morning, the complex gets busier as the day goes on, especially since Pleasure Island, which has clubs, eateries, theaters, and more shops, is nearby. *Lake Buena Vista, tel. 407/824–4321. Open daily 9:30 AM–10 PM.*

Epcot Center

The real shopping here is done in the special interest shops at the pavilions in World Showcase (*see* Epcot Center in Chapter 3). The best place for souvenirs, however, is on the way out: **Centorium** in Future World's Innoventions has the largest selection of goodies with Epcot Center logos.

Magic Kingdom

Inside Cinderella Castle is the **King's Gallery,** where you can buy imported European clocks, chess sets, and tapestries while artisans perform intricate metalwork. Another nifty nook is **Harmony Barber Shop,** on the west side of Main Street, where old-time shaving items like mustache cups are sold. This will just whet your appetite for **Olde World Antiques** in Liberty Square, where you can find expensive antique jewelry, hutches, pewter, and brass. Serious collectors of Disney memorabilia will want to stop at **Disneyanea,** across the square from City Hall. Limited-edition sculptures, dolls, posters, and sometimes even park signs are available for purchase. To get monogrammed mouse ears, stop at the **Chapeau,** on the east side of Main Street (extremely crowded at the end of the day) or the **Mad Hatter,** in Fantasyland.

Greater Orlando Area and Kissimmee

Factory Outlet Malls

The International Drive area is filled with factory outlet stores, most on the northeast end. These outlets are clumped together in expansive malls or scattered along the drive, and much of the merchandise is discounted from 20% to 75%. You can find just about anything, some of it top quality, but be advised: These are not charming places to shop.

International Drive Area Belz Factory Outlet World is the area's largest collection of outlet stores—nearly 170, in two malls and four nearby annexes. A good place to find discount name-brand clothes for the whole family, the complex includes such stores as Carole Hockman Lingerie, Maidenform, Danskin, Anne Klein, Jonathan Logan, Calvin Klein, Harvé Benard, Van Heusen, Burlington Brands, Just Kids, Bugle Boy, Oshkosh, Young Generations, Bally Shoes, Bass Shoes, Etienne Aigner, and Capezio. Especially popular are the outlets for athletic shoes: Converse, Reebok, and Sneakee Feet (which sells Reebok, Nike, and Adidas). There are also good buys in housewares and linens in such outlets as Fieldcrest/Cannon, Pfaltzgraff, Corning/Revere, Mikasa, and Fitz & Floyd. Don't worry about carting home breakable or cumbersome items; these stores will ship your purchases anywhere in the United States by UPS. Although the mall isn't fancy, it is clean and pleasant. Mall 2 offers a carousel for children and an adequate food court. The information booth sells discount tickets to all the non-Disney theme parks and offers a foreign currency exchange service. *5401 W. Oakridge Rd. (at the northern tip of International Dr.), tel. 407/352–9600. Open Mon.–Sat. 10–9, Sun. 10–6.*

All the dinnerware, flatware, glassware, and cookware you can imagine is at **Dansk Factory Outlet**—and all of it is at discount prices. Many of these items are seconds, limited editions, and discontinued styles. *7024 International Dr., tel. 407/351–2425. Open daily 9–7.*

A great place for jeans, **Denim World** carries Levi's, Lee, Bugle Boy, Jordache, and Wrangler and often offers two-for-one deals on shirts. Although the selection in children's sizes is limited, most women's and men's sizes can be found. There are plenty of salesclerks to help you dig through the stacks of jeans, and a seamstress will make alterations while you wait (10 minutes if you're first, much longer if there's a line). Parking is limited. *7623 International Dr., tel. 407/351–5704. Open daily 8 AM–midnight.*

Edwin Watts Golf Shop is a no-handicap shop for golfing equipment. *7297 Turkey Lake Rd., tel. 407/345–8451. Open Mon.–Fri. 9:30–8, Sat. 9:30–6, Sun. 12–5.*

Quality Outlet Center and **Quality Center East** are two interconnected strip shopping centers containing more than 20 brandname factory outlet stores, including American Tourister, Great Western Boots, Corning/Revere, Royal Doulton, Villeroy & Boch, Florsheim Shoes, Laura Ashley, Magnavox, and Mikasa. *5409 and 5529 International Dr. (1 block north of Kirkman Rd.), tel. 407/423–5885. Open Mon.–Sat. 9:30–9, Sun. 11–6.*

Special Tee Golf carries all brands of golf and tennis equipment and sportswear at discounted prices. *5400 International Dr., tel. 407/352–3673. Open Mon.–Sat. 10–9, Sun. 11–5:30.*

U.S. 192 Area Although **Kissimmee Manufacturers' Outlet Mall** doesn't look too appealing from the road, this strip shopping center contains a nice selection of shops. The approximately 20 stores include Bass Shoes, American Tourister, Van Heusen, Bon Worth, London Fog, Levi's, Fieldcrest/Cannon, Manhattan, Totes, Acme Boots, and Brandname Shoes (Reebok and L.A. Gear). *2511–2557 Old Vineland Rd., just off U.S. 192 (Irlo Bronson Memorial Hwy., 1 mi east of Rte. 535), tel. 407/396–8900. Open Mon.–Sat. 10–9, Sun. 11–5.*

Flea Markets

When you see signs for flea markets, remember that most are collections of shops run by small-time retailers, not gigantic garage sales with vendors set up at card tables. Most of the stock is usually new, not used.

With 400 booths, **192 Flea Market Outlet** is about one quarter the size of Flea World (*see* Off the Beaten Track, *below*), but it's much more convenient to the major Orlando attractions and is open daily. The all-new merchandise includes toys, luggage, sunglasses, jewelry, clothes, beach towels, sneakers, and the obligatory T-shirts. *4301 W. Vine St. (also known as Irlo Bronson Memorial Hwy.), Kissimmee, tel. 407/396–4555. Open daily 9–6.*

Malls and Department Stores

While much of the rest of the country maintains a mall status quo, the Orlando area, with its burgeoning population and huge influx of tourists, continues to see mall construction. Several existing malls have been expanded, and a number of new ones are in the planning stages.

Central Orlando and Winter Park If you want to rub elbows with the locals, try shopping at **Colonial Plaza Mall,** Orlando's oldest mall. Anchor stores Byrons, Dillard's, and Belk Lindsey are connected by 70 specialty stores. Many vacant properties tell the tale of better days gone by. *2560 E. Colonial Dr. (2¹/2 mi east of I–4 Exit 41), Orlando, tel. 407/894–3603. Open Mon.–Sat. 10–9, Sun. noon–5:30.*

Gayfers, JC Penney, Burdines, and Sears are the anchors of **Orlando Fashion Square.** The 130 specialty shops include such chain stores as Camelot Music, the Gap, Lerner, and Lechters. Bebe's has special children's wear, including mother-daughter outfits, christening gowns, and dresses for big occasions. The White House sells women's lingerie, sportswear, and formal dresses, but only in shades of white and ivory. And, just in case you missed something at the home of the Mouse, there's a large Disney store. Souvenir prices are the same as in the park; however, the store stocks some clothing items and memorabilia not found anywhere else. There's a food court. *3201 E. Colonial Dr. (3 mi east of I–4 Exit 41), Orlando, tel. 407/896–1131. Open Mon.–Sat. 10–9, Sun. noon–5:30.*

At **Winter Park Mall,** anchor stores JC Penney and Dillard's are connected by 70 specialty shops. Don't miss the Basket Place, a wonderful little store featuring home accessories, wicker furniture, and gifts. Forget the food court here. *500 N. Orlando Ave. (U.S. 17–92), 1 block south of Lee Rd., Winter Park, tel. 407/647–2402. Open Mon.–Sat. 10–9, Sun. noon–5:30.*

International Drive Area The **Florida Mall,** the largest in central Florida, includes Sears, JC Penney, Belk Lindsey, Gayfers, Dillard's, 200 specialty shops, seven theaters, and one of the better food courts around. The specialty stores are mostly those you've seen before: County Seat, the Limited, Radio Shack, Waldenbooks, Athlete's Foot, and Gordon's Jewelers. At the Barefoot Mailman, however, you can purchase something special—authentic autographed pictures of Madonna, John Wayne, Michael Jackson, Elvis, and many others. Although the mall is supposedly divided into three distinct architectural areas (Victorian, Mediterranean, and Art Deco), you will probably not be aware of any striking differences. Because the mall attracts crowds of tourists, it offers many services, including car rental, airline reservations, check cashing, and currency exchange. Discount tickets to Universal Studios and other area attractions are also available here, as are brochures—many containing money-off coupons—describing local spots of interest. The **Florida Mall Terrace** is next door, with Byron, Phar-Mor, Service Merchandise, and more. *8001 S. Orange Blossom Trail (4½ mi east of I-4 and International Dr.), Orlando, tel. 407/851-6255. Open Mon.–Sat. 10-9:30; Sun. 11-6.*

Shopping Villages

These quaint shopping areas are filled with gift shops, antiques shops, clothing stores, and restaurants. Some are primarily for tourists, with tourist prices, but all are much more pleasant and relaxed than the malls.

Central Orlando and Winter Park   **Church Street Exchange** is a decorative, brassy, Victorian-theme "festival marketplace" filled with more than 50 specialty shops; still others are across the street. At the Exchange's Pearl Factory, you can choose a pearl from an oyster to create your own pearl ring, pendant, or earrings and get an informative explanation of how oysters make pearls. At Kandelstix, craftspeople show how the unique, refillable, hand-carved candles are designed. Perhaps the best demonstration is at Augusta Jansson, where free candy samples are distributed during a lighthearted look at the process of making fudge. Units sells women's clothing and accessories created to mix and match on a three-sizes-fit-all basis. Udderly Country is a New England–style country store with a cow theme. You can also find all the requisite upscale shops, such as Victoria's Secret and Benetton. Across the street from the complex is Bumby Emporium, a Church Street souvenir shop, and Buffalo Trading Company, where you can buy string ties, cowboy hats, and snakeskin boots; and across the railroad tracks is yet another collection of unusual shops and pushcarts, known as the Historic Railroad Depot. The Exchange has a small food court on the second floor (but remember there are some great restaurants on Church Street); children can spend some money on arcade and video games on the top floor at Commander Ragtime's Midway of Fun, Food and Games. *Church St. Station, 129 W. Church St., Orlando, tel. 407/422-2434. Open daily 11-11.*

The eight shops of **Ivanhoe Row,** in downtown Orlando, sell delightful but pricey antiques. The William Mosley Gallery carries a fine selection of 19th- and 20th-century paintings. Antiques to Cherish is known for its European and American silver, crystal, and porcelain, and Curator's Own has an unusual collection of African wood carvings and animal skins, American Indian and Eskimo crafts, and masks of all types. After antiquing, cross the street and take a stroll in the beautiful park surrounding Lake Ivanhoe. *1211–1231 N. Orange Ave., Orlando, tel. 407/896–9230 or 407/898–6050. (From I–4 Exit 43, follow Princeton Ave. east to N. Orange Ave. and turn right.) Open Mon.–Sat. 10–5.*

Longtime residents complain that **Park Avenue** is beginning to resemble a mall, as local one-of-a-kind stores are replaced by chains such as Banana Republic, Foot Locker, the Gap, Orvis, Laura Ashley, and Ann Taylor. Visitors, however, are usually charmed by this posh shopping district in Winter park, with its tiny courtyards ringed by restaurants, galleries, bookstores, and other little shops. Perfumery on Park specializes in hard-to-find fragrances. The Center Street Gallery features original artwork, Russian lacquer boxes, and wonderful gifts. Antiques and other items for the home can be found at Far East Treasures, Table Dressing, and Gallery of Collectibles. (*See* also Tour 1: Winter Park, in Chapter 5.) *Park Ave. between Fairbanks Ave. and Canton (east of I–4 Exit 45), Winter Park, tel. 407/644–8281. Most shops open Mon.–Sat. 10–5:30 (some also on Sun. noon–5).*

International Drive and WDW Area

The Crossroads of Lake Buena Vista, across the street from the entrance to the hotels at Lake Buena Vista, contains restaurants and nearly 20 shops that are convenient for tourists. Upscale and casual shops are geared toward sun and surf, electronics, and children, but the necessities, such as a 24-hour grocery and pharmacy, post office, bank, and cleaners, are also there. Though you'll find the usual franchised restaurants, there are also some local spots like the casual Pebbles (*see* The Orlando Area in Chapter 8). While you shop, your offspring can entertain themselves at Pirate's Cove Adventure Golf (*see* Fun Houses and Miniature Golf in Chapter 5). *12545–12551 Rte. 535 (off I–4 Exit 27), Orlando, tel. 407/827–7300. Hours vary.*

A neighborhood shopping center, **The Marketplace** provides all the basic necessities in one spot near International Drive. Stores include a pharmacy, post office, one-hour film processor, stationery and card store, bakery, dry cleaner, hair salon, optical shop, natural-food grocery, and 24-hour supermarket. Also in the Marketplace are three popular restaurants: Christini's, Enzo's, and the Phoenician (*see* The Orlando Area in Chapter 8). *7600 Dr. Phillips Blvd. (west of I–4 Sand Lake Exit), Orlando, tel. 407/345–8668. Hours vary.*

The Spanish-style **Mercado Mediterranean Village,** a relaxation stop for many bus tours, houses more than 60 specialty shops, such as Beach Club Orlando, which sells swimsuits and beach accessories; American Cola Company, which offers Coca-Cola and Anheuser-Busch memorabilia; and Once upon a Star, whose gifts and clothing have a movie motif. Earth Matters, a shop for environmentalists, sells items with a wildlife theme. A dinner theater and five restaurants (*see* Chapter 8) are found along the walkway that circles the festival courtyard, where live entertainment can be enjoyed at various times throughout the day. Near Mercado's front entrance is an office of the Orlando/Orange County Convention and Visitors Bureau. Here you'll find racks and racks of brochures on just about every conceivable area attraction. Discounted tickets to Universal Studios, dinner shows, and the water parks are sold here. The clean, quick, and large food court offers a selection of food from around the world. Although there is a variety show with animated birds for children every 20 minutes, this isn't a place you'll want to linger with your offspring. *8445 International Dr., Orlando, tel. 407/345–9337. Visitors bureau open daily 8–8, all others 10–10.*

Next door to Mercado is **Gooding's Plaza International,** a shopping plaza that caters to tourists. The 24-hour Gooding's Supermarket has a food court, one-hour photo developing, and an aisle devoted to Disney merchandise. Also here are an electronics store, Spec's music, and several restaurants, including a branch of the popular Jungle Jim's. *8255 International Dr., Orlando, tel. 407/352–4215. Hours vary.*

U.S. 192 The **Old Town** shopping-entertainment complex features a 1928 Ferris wheel, a 1909 carousel, and more than 70 specialty shops re-creating a turn-of-the-century Florida village. You can buy a nickel Coke at the General Store or gourmet popcorn at the Kissimmee Popcorn Company, watch the taffy maker at Coffelt's Taffy & Chocolates or the candlemaker at Candlelite, pan at Black Market Minerals, pan for gemstones and sharks' teeth or buy agate, onyx, quartz, or even dinosaur fossils. Every Saturday night there is a parade of classic automobiles. *5770 Irlo Bronson Memorial Hwy. (east of I–4), Kissimmee, tel. 800/843–4202; in FL, 800/331–5093. Open daily 10 AM–11 PM.*

Off the Beaten Track

Flea Markets and Antiques

Flea World claims to be America's largest flea market under one roof. More than 1,600 booths lend credence to the claim, but so much abundance sometimes means only that good bargains are hiding under unusually large piles of junk. Unlike flea markets in some areas, this one sells only new merchandise—everything from car tires, Ginsu knives, and pet tarantulas to gourmet coffee, leather lingerie, and beaded evening gowns. It's also a great place to buy cheap Florida and Mickey Mouse T-shirts. A free newspaper, distributed at the parking lot entrance, contains a map and directory. Kids love Fun World next door, which offers two unusual miniature golf courses, arcade games, go-carts, bumper cars, bumper boats, kiddie rides, and batting cages. *Located 3 mi east of I–4 Exit 50 on Lake Mary Blvd., then 1 mi south on U.S. 17–92, Sanford, tel. 407/321–1792. Open Fri.–Sun. 8–5.*

Advertised as Florida's biggest gathering of antiques and collectible dealers, **Renninger's Antique Center** is actually one large building with 150 "shops" arranged in rows of booths, similar to a flea market. Mother Daughter and the Victorian Rose sell fine 19th-century American and European furniture, Lyons Antiques specializes in American country furniture, and Lismore Antiques carries a large selection of steamer trunks. The aptly named Grandma's Attic, which is typical of many of the shops, offers china, quilts, toys, lamps, furniture, and collectibles from the 1890s through the 1950s. At bimonthly weekend Antique Fairs, as many as 500 antiques and collectibles dealers set up outdoor booths on the adjacent wooded, hilly acres; Renninger's triannual Extravaganzas draw 1,000 dealers. At the adjacent Renninger's Farmers' and Flea Market, 500 merchants sell fresh produce, meats, baked goods, crafts, and new and used household items. The best plan is to spend the morning at Renninger's and then move on to downtown Mount Dora in time for lunch. *U.S. 441, Mount Dora, tel. 904/383–8393 (Thurs.–Sun.). Admission charge ($10 Fri., $5 Sat., $2 Sun.) for Extravaganzas only. Open weekends 9–5, with Antique Fairs 7 weekends a year 8–5; Extravaganzas once each in Nov., Jan., and Feb.; Fri. 10–5, weekends 7–5; Farmers' and Flea Market weekends 8–5.*

Historic Shopping Towns

History buffs will especially enjoy shopping in the dozen or so quaint little shops in **Longwood,** a typical late-19th-century Florida town of towering live oak trees and brick-paved streets. The heart of the town, the Longwood Hotel, now an office building, went up in 1886 as a winter resort for sun-seeking northerners. The turreted Bradley-McIntyre House (1885), open for tours on the second and fourth Wednesdays of each month from 11 to 4, was a winter "cottage" in Victorian days. The shops, many of which are housed in historic homes, are scattered throughout this quiet neighborhood. The Apple Basket specializes in folk art, hand-thrown pottery, braided rugs, country furnishings, and hand-blown glass ornaments at holiday time. The Enchanted Cottage stocks country and Victorian furniture, plus Cat's Meow Villages, and Root and Yankee Candles. The Culinary Cottage sells wonderful gourmet foods, decorative accessories, and rubber stamps. In the Browser's Barn you can find antiques and collectibles. Candles, Etc. features not only its namesakes but also cards, incense, potpourri, oils, and sealing wax. Have breakfast, lunch, or afternoon tea in Elmira's Pantry, a charming, old-fashioned tearoom. *2¹/₂ mi east of I–4 Exit 49 on Rte. 434, then north on Rte. 427 to first traffic light (Church Ave.), then left. Most shops open Mon.–Sat. 10–5.*

If you love antiques or if you're just tired of amusement parks, treat yourself to a day in **Mount Dora** (*see* also Tour 2: Lake County in Chapter 5). Founded by homesteaders in 1874, this charming little town has 19th-century stores and houses tucked into rolling hills that overlook Lake Dora. There are dozens of crafts shops, boutiques, galleries, and antiques shops here. Schwab Antiques offers furniture, glass, china, silver, and clocks. Country Pine Newtiques has an extensive selection of Tom Clark gnomes, David Winter cottages, and other collectibles. The Art and Antique Union is a 16-dealer minimall. Arrive in time for lunch at Eduardo's Mexican & American Cantina or Windsor Rose Tea Room; stay for dinner at the Park Bench Restaurant, the Gables, or the Beauclaire Dining Room in historic Lakeside Inn, a famous turn-of-the-century resort that was later a favorite vacation spot of President and Mrs. Calvin Coolidge. *West off U.S. 441 on either Old U.S. 441 or Rte. 44B, Chamber of Commerce tel. 904/383–2165.*

Moviegoers may recognize **Sanford's** historic First Street, with buildings that date from the 1880s to the 1920s, as the place where Macaulay Culkin and Anna Chlumsky pedaled their bicycles in the movie *My Girl.* This sleepy town on the shores of Lake Monroe is sprinkled with crafts and antiques shops. I Remember That sells cut glass and Flow Blue china. The Country Courtyard offers quilting classes and supplies. Antiques and collectibles stock the Antique Station and Delightful Finds. The Cranberry House features handmade country and Victorian gifts. The First Street Gallery displays the work of some of Florida's best professional artists. The place to lunch is Soup to Nuts, a delightful little restaurant with a Vie de France bakery inside. Combine your shopping with a visit to the nearby Central Florida Zoological Park (*see* The Natural World in Chapter 5) or a St. Johns River cruise (*see* Action! in Chapter 7). *East on Rte. 46 off I–4 Exit 51. Most shops open Mon.–Sat., 10–5.*

Malls and Department Stores

With its renovation in 1989 and the addition of a food court in 1990, the **Altamonte Mall** has kept pace with and maybe even surpassed the others in the area. Sears, Gayfers, Burdines, and JC Penney department stores anchor the two-level property; its 165 specialty shops include branches of such chain stores as J. Riggings, Victoria's Secret, Foot Locker, Kay Bee Toys, B. Dalton, and Limited Express. To buy something unusual, try the San Francisco Music Box Company or, if you're really ready to splurge, the Wentworth Gallery, which has a fine selection of original art from around the world. Unlike the one-level malls in the area, this one has a light, airy, and spacious feeling. The many benches, central fountain, and towering palm trees invite you to relax. The neighboring **Renaissance Center** includes eight theaters, Byrons, Linens & Things, and Bookstop. *451 Altamonte Ave. (1/2 mi east of I–4 on Rte. 436), Altamonte Springs, tel. 407/830–4400. Open Mon.–Sat. 10–9, Sun. noon–5:30.*

7 Sports and the Outdoors

Action!

In the sports world, Orlando has more stature than many other cities its size. The Orlando Magic are big-time, and true baseball fans love the minor-league action. Local residents, who may visit the theme parks only when their great-aunt's in-laws are in town, fill the tennis courts and golf courses (there are some 60 in a 30-mile radius, staffed by nearly three dozen PGA pros). Anglers have their own place in the Orlando sun as well—on any of dozens of small lakes. And boating is big, both on these lakes and on backcountry rivers fed by clear, sweet springs.

Bicycling

At WDW
The most scenic bike riding in Orlando is on Walt Disney World property, along roads that take you past forests, lakes, golf courses, and Disney's wooded resort villas and campgrounds. Bikes are available for rent at **Caribbean Beach Resort** (tel. 407/934–2850) and **Fort Wilderness Bike Barn** (tel. 407/824–2742) for $3 an hour or $7 a day. At **Walt Disney World Village Resort,** Guest Services (tel. 407/827–6905) will rent you a bike for $3 an hour or $8 a day. Theoretically, bike rentals are only for those lodging on WDW property; in practice, rental outfits usually check IDs only in busy seasons. However, bikes must be used only in the area in which you rent them.

Elsewhere
Despite the presence of two large schools—the University of Central Florida and Rollins College—where you would expect to find large numbers of enthusiastic bicyclists, the Orlando area doesn't offer a lot in the way of biking opportunities. It's illegal to ride bikes on Orlando sidewalks (and the police discourage those who do), and bike trails are few and far between. Moreover, local motorists are often not particularly accommodating when it comes to sharing the road with two-wheeled traffic. There are some scenic routes, however.

The area near Rollins College, in Winter Park, offers views of lakes, tree-lined streets, and the homes of much of the area's old money. Most riders prefer to go west of town to the Clermont–Lake County area. Since it's out in the boonies, there isn't much traffic to worry about. There are lots of orange groves and some hills.

Florida Backroads, by Robert Howard ($14.95 in bookstores) contains detailed descriptions of biking areas, plus maps with mileage markers and routes for 40 excursions.

Fishing

Central Florida is covered with freshwater lakes and rivers teeming with all kinds of fish, especially largemouth black bass, but also perch, catfish, sunfish, and pike.

Licenses
To fish in most Florida waters (but not at Walt Disney World), anglers over 16 need a fishing license, available at bait-and-tackle shops, fishing camps, most sporting-goods stores, and

Walmarts and K-marts. Some of these locations may not sell saltwater licenses, or they may serve non-Florida residents only; call ahead to be on the safe side. The cost is $16.50 for seven days and $31.50 for one year (freshwater); $7 for three days, $17 for seven days, and $32 for one year (saltwater).

At WDW Two-hour fishing trips on Bay Lake depart from **Fort Wilderness Campground Resort** and include boat, equipment, and guide for up to five anglers. Reservations are required. *Fort Wilderness Campground, tel. 407/824–2621. Fee: $110, $50 for 3rd hr. Trips daily at 8, 11:30, and 3.*

There's fishing off the dock at the **Ol' Man Island Fishing Hole.** Catch and release is encouraged, but you can have your fish packed in ice to take home. You'll have to clean them yourself, though. *Dixie Landings, tel. 407/934–5409. Cane poles and bait: $3 per hr per person, $10 per hr for family of up to 6; no fee to use dock. Open daily 7–4.*

Elsewhere Top central Florida waters include **Lake Kissimmee, the Butler** and **Conway chains of lakes,** and **Lake Tohopekaliga** (don't bother to pronounce it—it's "Lake Toho" to locals). Your best chance for trophy fish is between November and April on Toho or Kissimmee; for good creels, the best producer is usually the Butler area, whose additional advantage is its scenery—lots of live oaks and cypresses, plus the occasional osprey or bald eagle. Toho and Kissimmee are also good for largemouth bass and crappie. The Butler chain yields largemouth, some pickerel, and the occasional huge catfish. A variety of services are available, from equipment and boat rental to full-day trips with guides and guarantees.

Fishing There are a number of excellent fishing camps in the area in the
Camps form of lakeside campgrounds that draw a more outdoorsy crowd than you find elsewhere in the area.

East Lake Fish Camp, on East Lake Tohopekaliga, has a restaurant and country store, sells live bait and propane, and rents boats and airboats. It also has 283 RV sites, 40 tent sites, and 24 cabins. Try to make reservations for the cabins at least two weeks in advance during the winter and spring. *3705 Big Bass Rd., Kissimmee, tel. 407/348–2040. RV sites $16 (2 people), tent sites $12, cabins $45 (2 people, $5 each additional).*

Red's Fish Camp, on West Lake Tohopekaliga, has RV sites. Most of the full hookups are booked year-round, but electrical and water hookups are usually available, as are rental boats, live bait, food, and drinks. *4715 Kissimmee Park Rd., St. Cloud, tel. 407/892–8795. RV sites $12. 14-foot motorboats $30 per day.*

Richardson's Fish Camp, also on West Lake Tohopekaliga, has cabins with kitchenettes, 16 RV sites, 12 tent sites, boat slips, and a bait shop. *1550 Scotty's Rd., Kissimmee, tel. 407/846–6540. RV sites $17.50, tent sites $13.50, cabins $33 for 1 bedroom, $49.50 for 2 bedrooms.*

Guides Guides fish out of each of the above fishing camps, and you can usually make arrangements to hire them through the camp office. Rates vary, but $125 for a half day and $175 for a full day are good rules of thumb. Many area guides are part-timers who fish on weekends or take a day off from their full-time job to guide; the following are full-timers, who hit a variety of local lakes, including those listed above and private lakes.

Bass Bustin' Guide (BBG) provides boat, tackle, transportation, and ice and soft drinks for bass fishing on local lakes—and guarantees fish! *5935 Swoffield Dr., Orlando, tel. 407/281–0845. 1/2 day from $125, full day from $175; extra person: $50 adult, $25 children under 17.*

Bass Challenger Guide (BCG) takes you out in boats equipped with tackle and drinks. Transportation can be arranged between fishing spots and local hotels. Bass is the only quarry, and they guarantee "No bass, no pay!" *Box 679155, Orlando, tel. 407/273–8045 or 800/241–5314. 1/2 day from $125, full day from $175.*

Cutting Loose Expeditions goes after bass, like the BBG and BCG (*see above*), but also arranges saltwater expeditions to the Indian River flats to light-tackle-cast for redfish, sea trout, tarpon, and snook. They'll arrange deep-sea charters out of Port Canaveral (*see* Chapter 11). All trips can include everything but food. They'll even pick you up at the hotel and take you to the fishing hole. *Box 447, Winter Park, tel. 407/629–4700 or 800/533–4746. 1/2 day from $175, full day $200–$300, $500–$600 offshore.*

Golf

With sunny weather practically year-round, Florida is a golfer's haven, offering more golf courses than any other state. Most of Florida is extremely flat, but many of the courses listed here have been sculpted by their designers to create rolling hills that make them more challenging. Many resort hotels let nonguests use their golf facilities. Some country clubs are affiliated with particular hotels, and their guests can play at preferred rates. If you're staying near a course you'd like to use, call and inquire.

Golfpac (Box 162366, Altamonte Springs 32701, tel. 407/260–2288) packages golf vacations and prearranges tee times at more than 40 courses around Orlando. Rates vary based on hotel and course, and 60–90 days' advance notice is required to set up a vacation.

What follows is a list of the best courses open to the public. All have dress codes, so call to find out the specifics at each, and be sure to reserve tee times in advance. The yardages listed are those from the blue tees. Since greens fees usually vary by season, the highest and lowest figures are provided, and all include mandatory cart rental.

At WDW Where else would you find a sand trap shaped like the head of a well-known mouse? Walt Disney World has five championship courses—all on the PGA Tour route. Eagle Pines and Osprey Ridge are the newcomers, flanking the Bonnet Creek Golf Club just north of Fort Wilderness. They join WDW's original courses, the Palm and the Magnolia, which flank the Shades of

Green Resort, to the west, and the Lake Buena Vista course, near Disney Village Marketplace.

Greens Fees   All five Disney courses have the same fees and discount policies: Guests at WDW resorts pay $85; all others pay $95 regardless of season. The twilight discount rate is $45 for everyone; this rate goes into effect at 2 PM during the winter and peak seasons and at 3 PM during the summer and off-seasons.

Tee Times   Tee times are available from 7:30 AM until dark on weekdays and
and   from 7 until dark on weekends. You can book them up to 30 days
Reservations   in advance if you're staying at a WDW-owned hotel, seven days ahead otherwise. For tee times at any course, call 407/824–2270; for private lessons, call Lake Buena Vista Club (tel. 407/824–1470).

Eagle Pines, one of two new courses, was designed by golf course architect Pete Dye. Greens are small and undulating, and fairways are lined with pines and punctuated by sand traps that broaden the challenge. *Golf View Dr., at Bonnet View Golf Club, north of Fort Wilderness. 6,722 yds. Par: 72. USGA: 72.3. 18 holes. Facilities: restaurant, private lessons, club and shoe rental, lockers, driving range, putting green.*

The **Lake Buena Vista** course winds among Disney Village Resort town houses and villas; greens are narrow—and hitting straight is important, since errant balls risk ending up in someone's bedroom. *Lake Buena Vista. 6,829 yds. Par: 72. USGA: 72.7. 18 holes. Facilities: restaurant, private lessons, club and shoe rental, lockers, driving range, putting green.*

The **Magnolia,** played by the pros in the Walt Disney World Golf Classic, is long but forgiving, with extra-wide fairways. *At Shades of Green. 6,642 yds. Par: 72. USGA: 72.5. 18 holes. Facilities: restaurant, private and small-group lessons, club and shoe rental, lockers, driving range, putting green.*

In designing **Osprey Ridge,** Tom Fazio leavened the challenge of the course with a relaxing tour into some of the still-forested, as yet undeveloped portions of the huge WDW acreage. Tees and greens as much as 20 feet above the fairways keep competitive players from getting too comfortable, however. Osprey Ridge opened in 1992 along with Eagle Pines. *Golf View Dr., Bonnet Creek Golf Club. 7,101 yds. Par: 72. USGA: 73.9. 18 holes. Greens fees: $85, $45 after 3 PM. Facilities: restaurant, private lessons, club and shoe rental, lockers, driving range, putting green.*

The **Palm,** one of WDW's original courses, has been confounding the pros as part of the annual Walt Disney World Golf Classic for years. It's not as long as the Magnolia, or as wide, and there are more trees. And don't go near the water! *At Shades of Green Resort. 6,957 yds. Par: 72. USGA: 73. 18 holes. Greens fees: $75, $35 after 3 PM. Facilities: restaurant, private and small-group lessons, club and shoe rental, lockers, driving range, putting green.*

Elsewhere   Greens fees at the following non-Disney courses fluctuate with the season. A twilight discount applies after 2 PM in busy seasons and after 3 PM during the rest of the year; the discount is usually half off the normal rate.

Cypress Creek Country Club is a demanding course with 16 water holes and lots of trees. *5353 Vineland Rd., Orlando, tel. 407/351–2187. 6,955 yds. Par: 72. USGA: 73.6. 18 holes. Greens fees: $25–$36. Special policies: tee times 7 days in advance. Facilities: restaurant, private lessons, club rental.*

Falcon's Fire Golf Club, designed by golf architect Rees Jones, has one of Orlando's newest courses. Its strategically placed fairway bunkers demand accuracy off the tee. *Seralago Blvd., Kissimmee, tel. 407/397–2777. 6,901 yds. Par: 72. USGA: 72.5. 18 holes. Greens fees: $45–$70. Special policies: tee times 7 days in advance. Facilities: restaurant, lounge, private and group lessons, club rental, lockers, driving range, putting green.*

Located about 45 minutes from Orlando, **Grenelefe Golf and Tennis Resort** has three 18-hole courses amid gentle hills. Length is the key here. The West Course, designed by Robert Trent Jones Sr., plays to 7,325 yards from the championship tees. An absence of water hazards (there are just two ponds) softens the course somewhat. The East Course is very tight, with small greens and lots of changes in elevation. Designed by Ed Seay, it requires accuracy. The South, designed by Ron Garl, has plenty of sand and water but wider fairways and larger greens. *3200 Rte. 546, Haines City, tel. 813/422–7511 or 800/237–9549. West Course 7,325 yds, par 72, USGA 75; East Course 6,802 yds, par 72, USGA 72.5; South Course 6,869 yds, par 71, USGA 72.6. 54 holes. Greens fees: $39–$94. Special policies: tee times 3 days in advance, but courses usually closed to public at busiest time of year (Jan.–Apr.). Facilities: 3 restaurants, 2 lounges, snack bar, private lessons, club and shoe rental.*

The Lloyd Clifton–designed **Hunter's Creek Golf Course** has large greens and 14 water holes. *14401 Sports Club Way, Orlando, tel. 407/240–4653. 7,438 yds. Par: 72. USGA: 72.8. 18 holes. Greens fees: $35–$50. Special policies: tee times 3 days in advance. Facilities: snack bar, private lessons, club rental.*

Marriott's Orlando World Center has a Joe Lee–designed course with 14 water holes and lots of sand. *1 World Center Dr., Orlando, tel. 407/239–4200 or 800/228–9290. 6,265 yds. Par: 71. USGA: 69.8. 18 holes. Greens fees: $60–$90. Special policies: tee times 7 days in advance for public, 90 days in advance for World Center guests. Facilities: 4 restaurants, sports bar, private and group lessons, club and shoe rental.*

MetroWest Country Club has a rolling, Robert Trent Jones Sr. course, with few trees but lots of sand. *2100 S. Hiawassee Rd., Orlando, tel. 407/299–1099. 6,500 yds. Par: 72. USGA: 70.3. 18 holes. Greens fees: $42–$62. Special policies: tee times 7 days in advance. Facilities: restaurant, private and group lessons, club rental.*

About five minutes from Walt Disney World's main entrance is **Orange Lake Country Club.** It has three 9-hole courses, all very similar. Distances aren't long, but fairways are very narrow, and there's a great deal of water, making the course very difficult. *8505 W. Irlo Bronson Memorial Hwy., Kissimmee, tel. 407/239–0000. Lake/Orange: 6,551 yds, par 72 USGA 72.2. Orange/Cypress: 6,654 yds, par 72, USGA 72.6. Cypress/Lake: 6,535 yds, par 72, USGA 72.3. Greens fees: $30–$61. Special policies: tee times 2 days in advance. Facilities: restaurant, cafeteria, pizzeria, club rental.*

About 18 miles southeast of Disney World is the **Poinciana Golf & Racquet Resort**—69 bunkers and 17 water holes nestled in a cypress forest. *500 Cypress Pkwy., Poinciana (near Kissimmee), tel. 407/933–5300. 6,400 yds. Par: 72. USGA: 70.8. 18 holes. Greens fees: $25–$40. Special policies: tee times 7 days in advance, discount coupons accepted. Facilities: restaurant, lounge, private and group lessons, club rental.*

Timacuan Golf and Country Club has a two-part course designed by Ron Garl. Part I, the front nine, is open, with lots of sand; part II, the back nine, is heavily wooded. *550 Timacuan Blvd., Lake Mary, tel. 407/321–0010. 6,582 yds. Par: 72. USGA: 71.5. 18 holes. Greens fees: $40–$55. Special policies: tee times 3 days in advance. Facilities: restaurant, snack bar, bar and grill, club/shoe rental, driving range.*

Health Clubs

At WDW Although most of the Walt Disney World health clubs accept only guests at Walt Disney World hotels (and some accept only guests of that particular hotel), some clubs have been known to stretch the rules—a fact worth noting if you're desperate for your workout.

Body by Jake, at the Dolphin, has step and regular aerobics classes, weights, and personal trainers. (The Walt Disney World Swan, nearby, has Universal weight machines, treadmills, and stationary bikes.) *The Dolphin, tel. 407/934–4264. Fee: $8 a day; $16 individual or $26 family for length of stay (hotel guests only). Open daily 6 AM–9 PM. Guests at other hotels admitted only by the day; must pay cash. Sauna.*

The **Olympiad Health Club** has Nautilus and hand weights, stairclimbers, cross-country ski machines, and treadmills, plus a tanning bed and booth. Massages are offered at the club or in your room. *Contemporary Resort, tel. 407/824–3410. Fee: $5 a day; massage: $35 a ½ hr; $50 an hr; $70 an hr in room. Open daily 6:30 AM–8 PM. Open to all Disney guests. Sauna.*

The glittering **St. John's Health Spa** has Nautilus, cardiovascular equipment, and a sauna. *Grand Floridian, tel. 407/824–3000, ext. 2433. Fee: $5.30 a day; $10.60 per individual or $15 per family for length of stay; massage $35 a ½ hr, $50 an hr. Open 6 AM–10 PM daily. Sauna.*

Exercise machines, a sauna, spa, and steam room are available at the **Ship Shape.** *Yacht and Beach Club, tel. 407/934–3256. Fee: $5 a day, $15 for length of stay; massage $35 a ½ hr. $50 an hr. Open daily 6:30 AM–10 PM. Open only to hotel guests.*

Elsewhere To find out what's hot when you visit, the best bet is to ask at your hotel because clubs outside WDW come and go. And don't forget about the local YMCAs, longtime local favorites. To find the one nearest where you're staying, phone the Metropolitan YMCA office (tel. 407/896–9220). Most accept guests on a single-visit basis, for $5–$10 a day, and you don't have to be a Y member.

The **Downtown YMCA** has Nautilus, free weights, racquetball, an Olympic-size pool, two gyms, and aerobics classes. It's an older property, but the weight room facilities were just revamped. *433 N. Mills Ave., Orlando, tel. 407/896–6901. Fee: $7 a day, free to YMCA members from outside Orlando. Open weekdays 5 AM–9:30 PM, Sat. 8–6:30, Sun. 1–5.*

The **International Drive YMCA** is definitely more posh. It has Nautilus, free weights, racquetball, two swimming pools (one Olympic-size), and a diving well. Call ahead to reserve racquetball courts. *8422 International Dr., Orlando, tel. 407/363–1911. Fee: $10 a day, $35 a week, free to YMCA members from outside Orlando. Open weekdays 6 AM–9 PM, plus Thurs. until 10, Sat. 8–4, Sun. 1–5.*

Horseback Riding

At WDW **Fort Wilderness Campground** offers tame trail rides through backwoods. Children must be over nine, and adults must be under 250 pounds. *Fort Wilderness Campground Resort, tel. 407/824–2803. Open to the public. Trail rides: $17 for 45 min. Rides daily at 9, 10:30, noon, and 2.*

Elsewhere Private lessons in hunter, jumper, and dressage are given at **Grand Cypress Equestrian Center.** Supervised novice and advanced group trail rides are also available. Call a week ahead for reservations in winter and spring. *Grand Cypress Resort, 1 Equestrian Dr., tel. 407/239–4608. Trail rides: $30 an hr for novice, $45 an hr for advanced; private lessons: $40 a 1/2 hr; $70 an hr. Open 8–5.*

Poinciana Riding Stables offers basic and longer, more advanced nature trail tours along old logging trails near Kissimmee. Private lessons and pony rides are also available, and the stable area has picnic tables, farm animals you can pet, and a pond to fish in. *3705 Poinciana Blvd., Kissimmee, tel. 407/847–4343. Trail rides: $24.95 for basic, $34.95 for advanced; private lessons: $25 an hr; pony rides: $4 for 10 min. Open 9–5.*

Ice Skating

Orlando sees frost only about once every other year, so ice-skating fever is not taking the city by storm. There are a couple of options, however, if you feel the urge to chill out.

Orlando Ice Skating Palace is either grungy or a look into pre-Disney Orlando, depending on your point of view. But if you are homesick for a winter chill, this should do the trick. *3123 W. Colonial Dr., Parkwood Shopping Plaza, Orlando, tel. 407/299–5440.*

Admission: weekdays and Sun. $5.95 adults, $4.95 children under 13; skate rental $1.50. Open in summer Mon.–Sat. 12:30–3:30, 4–7, 7:30–10:30, also Sat. 11 PM–1 AM, Sun. 2–5, 7:30–10:30; in winter closed Mon.–Tues., reduced hours Wed.–Sun.

Rock on Ice is definitely spiffier but seems touristy. *Dowdy Pavilion, 7500 Canada Ave., Orlando, tel. 407/363–7465. Skate rental $1.50. Admission prices and open-skating times vary; call for more information.*

Jogging

At WDW Walt Disney World has several scenic jogging trails. Pick up jogging maps at any Disney resort. **Fort Wilderness Campground** (tel. 407/824–2900) has a 2.3-mile jogging course with plenty of fresh air and woods as well as numerous exercise stations along the way. Early in the morning all the roads are fairly uncrowded, however, and make for good running. The roads that wiggle through **Disney's Village Resorts** are pleasant, as are the cart paths on the **golf courses.**

Elsewhere **Turkey Lake Park** (3401 S. Hiawassee Rd., Orlando, tel. 407/299–5581; park entry, $2 adults, $1 children under 13), not far from Disney, has a 3-mile biking trail that's also popular with joggers. Several wooded hiking trails also make for a good run.

In Winter Park, around **Rollins College,** you can jog along the shady streets and around the lakes, inhaling the aroma of old money. The **Orlando Runners Club** meets in the area every Sunday morning at 7 AM for 3-, 6-, and 12-mile jaunts; for details, call the Track Shack (1322 N. Mills Ave., Orlando, tel. 407/898–1313; open weekdays 10–7, Sat. 10–5).

Tennis

At WDW You can play tennis at any number of Disney hotels, and you'll find the courts a pleasant respite from the milling throngs in the parks. All have lights and are open from 7 AM to 10 PM, and most have lockers and rental racquets. All courts are open to all players, but court staff can opt to turn away nonguests when things get busy. (That doesn't often happen.)

The **Contemporary Resort** is the center of Disney's tennis program, with its sprawl of six DecoTurf courts. *Tel. 407/824–3578. Courts $10 per hr, $25 for length of stay, free 8 PM–10 PM. Court reservations available (up to 24 hr in advance). Clinics with video replay ($35), private lessons ($37–$45 per hr, $20–$25 per 1/2 hr), video reviews $10 extra.*

The **Dolphin** and **Swan** share eight asphalt courts. *Tel. 407/934–4396. Courts $12 per hr. Court reservations available to all (up to 24 hr in advance). Clinics with video replay ($35), private lessons ($45 per hr, $25 per 1/2 hr), video reviews $10. Arrange-a-game services, ball machines. Racquet rental, $5.*

Fort Wilderness Campground has two courts out in the middle of a field; they're popular with youngsters. If you hate players who are too free about letting their balls stray across their neighbors' court, this is not the place for you. *Tel. 407/824–2900. No charge for courts. No court reservations. No instruction.*

At the **Grand Floridian,** the two composition courts attract a somewhat more tennis-minded crowd. *Tel. 407/824–2438. Courts $12 per hr. Court reservations (up to 24 hr in advance). Private lessons $35 per hr.*

Village Clubhouse, with three secluded asphalt courts, draws a fairly sophisticated, generally adult group—WDW staff know they can always get a court here. *Tel. 407/828–3741. No charge. Court reservations (up to 24 hr in advance). No instruction.*

The **Yacht and Beach Club** has two blacktop courts. *Tel. 407/934–3256. No charge. Court reservations available (up to 24 hr in advance). No instruction.*

Elsewhere **Lake Cane Tennis Center** has 13 lighted asphalt courts. Four pros provide private and group lessons. *5108 Turkey Lake Rd., Orlando, tel. 407/352–4913. Courts $2 per hr weekdays, $4 per hr weekends. Lessons $30 per hr, $15 per 1/2 hr. Open 8 AM–10 PM.*

In addition to its golf courses, **Orange Lake Country Club** has 16 all-weather tennis courts, 10 of them lighted. It is five minutes from Walt Disney World's main entrance. *8505 W. Irlo Bronson Memorial Hwy., Kissimmee, tel. 407/239–0000. Courts free for guests, $4 per hr for nonguests. Court reservations unnecessary. Private lessons $30 per hr, $17.50 per 1/2 hr. Racquet rentals $2. Open dawn–11 PM.*

Orlando Tennis Center offers 16 lighted tennis courts (nine Har-Tru and seven asphalt), two racquetball courts, and four tennis pros. *649 W. Livingston St., Orlando, tel. 407/246–2162. Courts $5.80 for 1 1/2 hr on Har Tru, $3.68 for 1 1/2 hr on asphalt; Racquetball $2.12 per hr, no 1/2-hr rates. Court reservations unnecessary. Private lessons: $30 per hr, group lessons $5. Open weekdays 8 AM–10 PM, weekends and holidays 8–3.*

Red Bug Park has 16 lighted Plexipave courts and eight 4-wall racquetball courts. *3800 Red Bug Lake Rd., Casselberry, tel. 407/695–7113. Courts $2 per hr before 5, $4 per hr after; $4 per hr for racquetball. Court reservations available (up to 24 hr in advance). Private lessons $34 per hr. Open daily 8 AM–10 PM.*

Sanlando Park has 25 lighted Plexipave courts and eight covered, fan-cooled racquetball courts. *401 W. Highland St., Altamonte Springs, tel. 407/869–5966. Courts $2 per hr before 5, $4 per hr after; $4 per hr for racquetball. Court reservations available (up to 24 hr in advance). Private lessons $32 per hr, $16 per 1/2 hr. Open daily 8 AM–10 PM.*

Water Sports

At WDW Boating is big at Disney. There are marinas at the Caribbean Beach Resort, Contemporary Resort, Disney Village Marketplace, Fort Wilderness Campground, Grand Floridian, Polynesian Village, and Yacht and Beach Club, where you can rent

Sunfish, toobies, catamarans, motor-powered pontoon boats, pedal boats, and tiny two-passenger Water Sprites—a hit with kids—for use on **Bay Lake** and the adjoining **Seven Seas Lagoon, Club Lake, Lake Buena Vista,** or **Buena Vista Lagoon.** Most rent Water Sprites; otherwise, each hotel has its own rental roster, and you're sure to find something of interest. The Polynesian Village marina rents outrigger canoes. Fort Wilderness rents canoes for paddling along the placid canals in the area. And you can sail and water-ski on Bay Lake and the Seven Seas Lagoon; stop at the Fort Wilderness, Contemporary, Polynesian, or Grand Floridian marina.

Elsewhere   **Orange Lake,** a private lake at the Orange Lake Country Club next to Walt Disney World, has all types of boating—in rowboats, paddleboats, canoes, wave runners, Jet skis, and jet boats. You can even sign up for waterskiing school. *Rentals at Orange Lake Water Sports, 8505 W. Irlo Bronson Memorial Hwy., Kissimmee, tel. 407/239-4444. Fees: from $5 per ¹/₂ hr for canoes and Waverunners to $52 per ¹/₂ hr for a power boat; Jet skis $35 per ¹/₂ hr, $50 per hr, including instruction; waterskiing $45 for as long as it takes to teach you. Open 10–5.*

There's a ski ramp and slalom course on 140-acre **Sand Lake,** a fairly quiet scenic expanse of water rimmed mainly by villas. Jet skis keep swimmers away. *Rentals available at Splash 'n' Ski, 10000 Turkey Lake Rd. (west off I–4, Exit 29 on Sand Lake Rd.), Orlando, tel. 407/352–1494. Jet skis $40 per ¹/₂ hr; sailboards $25 per ¹/₂ day, waterskiing $45 per ¹/₂ hr. Open 10–5:30.*

A boat ride on **Shingle Creek** provides views of giant cypress trees dripping with Spanish moss. You can get around by airboat or rent a quiet electric swampboat or a canoe. *Airboat Rentals, 4266 Irlo Bronson Memorial Hwy., Kissimmee, tel. 407/847–3672. Airboats $22 per hr, swampboats and electric boats $16 per hr, canoes $5 per hr. Open daily 9:30–5.*

The **St. Johns River** winds through pine and cypress woods and past pastures where cows graze placidly, skirting the occasional housing development. There's good bird- and wildlife-watching; herons, ibis, storks, and sometimes bald eagles can be spotted, along with alligators and manatees. It's a favored local boating spot, for everything from a day of waterskiing to a weeklong trip in a houseboat. Rentals are available in De Land (west of I–4 Exit 56 via U.S. 44). *Holly Bluff, 2280 Hontoon Rd., De Land, tel. 904/822–9992 or 800/237–5105: Pontoon boats $60 for 4 hr, $100 a day, 44-ft houseboats $350 for 1 day, $560 for 2 days, $1,000 for a week; rates lower Dec.–Feb. Hontoon Landing Marina, 2317 River Ridge Rd., DeLand, tel. 904/734–2474 or 800/248–2474 in FL: Luxury houseboats $400–$1,395 for 1 day, $1,095–$2,495 for a week; Jet skis $30 per hr; $150 a day; ski boats $30 per hr, $100 a day; prices lower Dec.–Mar.*

Another great waterway for nature lovers is the **Wekiva River,** which runs through 6,397-acre Wekiva State Park into the St. Johns River. Bordered by cypress marshlands, its clear, spring-fed waters showcase a rich array of Florida wildlife, including otters, raccoons, alligators, bobcats, deer, turtles, and numerous birds. Canoes and battery-powered motorboats, whose quiet engines don't disturb the wildlife, are the best way to get around; they're available for rent. *Katie's Wekiva River Landing and Campground, 190 Katie's Cove, Sanford, tel. 407/628–1482. Canoes $5 per hr (2-hr minimum), $4 each additional hr, $18 per day; battery-powered motorboats $15 per hr (2-hr minimum), $60 per day. Group trips, restaurant, campsites, cabins, picnic tables.*

Alexander Creek and **Juniper Creek,** in Ocala National Forest just north of the greater Orlando area, also offer wonderful wilderness canoeing, with abundant wildlife and moss-draped oaks and bald cypresses canopying the clean, clear waters. Some of these runs are quite rough—lots of ducking under brush and maneuvering around trees. *Alexander Springs Canoe Rental, County Rte. 445, tel. 904/669–3522; canoes $10–$22 with $20 deposit and ID; open daily 8–dark. Juniper Springs Canoe Rental, State Rd. 40, tel. 904/625–2808; canoes $20–$25 with $20 deposit and ID.*

From the Sidelines

Not everything in Orlando is wholesome, Disney-style family fun. Wagering a wad of cash at the fronton or the dog track is guaranteed to wipe the refrain from "It's a Small World" right out of your head. And even if you bet and lose steadily, you won't necessarily spend more than you would at most of the attractions. In addition, there are team sports in various sports and leagues that play their regular seasons in and around Orlando, as well as major-league baseball clubs that make their spring-training home in the area.

Baseball

Watching a minor-league or spring-training game in a small ballpark can take you back to a time when going to a game didn't mean bringing binoculars or watching the big screen to see what was happening. Minor-league teams play from April to September and spring training lasts only a few weeks in March and early April, but it can be a thrill to watch stars up close while you, and they, enjoy a spring break before getting back to work. Tickets to the minors usually run $3–$6; spring training seats cost $8–$10.

Minor Leagues The **Orlando Cubs** are Chicago's Class AA Southern League affiliate. They play 69 home games at Tinker Field. *287 S. Tampa Ave. (west off I–4 Colonial Ave. Exit), Orlando, tel. 407/872–7593.*

The **Osceola Astros** are Houston's Class A team in the Florida State League and play at Osceola County Stadium. Arrive early because tickets are sold only at the stadium on a same-day, first-come basis. *1000 Bill Beck Blvd. (west of I–4, Exit 65), Kissimmee, tel. 407/933–5500 or 407/933–2520 for spring-training tickets.*

Spring Training Major-league baseball teams hold spring training all over Florida: in **Baseball City** (Kansas City Royals), **Bradenton** (Pittsburgh Pirates), **Clearwater** (Philadelphia Phillies), **Dunedin**

(Toronto Blue Jays), **Fort Lauderdale** (New York Yankees), **Fort Myers** (Boston Red Sox and Minnesota Twins), **Kissimmee** (Houston Astros), **Lakeland** (Detroit Tigers), **Melbourne** (Florida Marlins), **Plant City** (Cincinnati Reds), **Port Charlotte** (Texas Rangers), **Port St. Lucie** (New York Mets), **St. Petersburg** (Baltimore Orioles and St. Louis Cardinals), **Sarasota** (Chicago White Sox), **Vero Beach** (Los Angeles Dodgers), **West Palm Beach** (Atlanta Braves and Montréal Expos), and **Winter Haven** (Cleveland Indians). For dates and more information, get a copy of the free *Florida Spring Training Guide,* published each year in early February by the Florida Sports Foundation (107 W. Gaines St., Tallahassee 32399, tel. 904/488–8347).

Basketball

The **Orlando Magic** joined the National Basketball Association in the 1989–90 season and play in the 15,077-seat Orlando Arena. Seven-foot-one center Shaquille O'Neal and teammates have since driven the city to new heights of hoop fanaticism. Tickets to the '94 season sold out in one day, and the current waiting period for season tickets is 10 years. Your best bet for seeing a game is probably a sports bar (*see* Chapter 10, After Dark). *Box 76, 600 W. Amelia St. (2 blocks west of I–4 at Amelia St. Exit), Orlando; Ticketmaster tel. 407/839–3900, box office tel. 407/649–BALL, season tickets tel. 407/89–MAGIC. Admission: $17–$30.*

Dog Racing

Sanford Orlando Kennel Club has dog racing and betting as well as South Florida horse-racing simulcasts and betting. *301 Dog Track Rd., Longwood, tel. 407/831–1600. Admission: $1. Open Nov.–May, Mon.–Sat. at 7:30 PM; matinees Mon., Wed., Sat. at 1 PM.*

Seminole Greyhound Park, a newer, larger, and prettier track, is your other option for wagering on greyhounds and simulcast horse racing. *2000 Seminola Blvd., Casselberry, tel. 407/699–4510. Admission: $1 general, $2 clubhouse (children 1/2 price). Open May–Oct., Mon.–Sat. at 7:30 PM; matinees (most recently Mon., Wed., Sat. at 1 PM).*

Football

The **Orlando Predators** play in the Arena Football League, which differs from the National Football League in that teams have only eight players, each of whom holds both offensive and defensive positions. Games are held May to August at the Orlando Arena. *600 W. Amelia St., Orlando, tel. 407/648–4444 or 407/872–7362. Admission: $10–$21.*

Jai Alai

Orlando-Seminole Jai-Alai, about 20 minutes north of Orlando off I–4, offers south Florida horse-racing simulcasts and betting in addition to jai alai at the fronton. *6405 S. U.S. 17–92, Fern Park,* tel. 407/331–9191. *Admission: $1 general, $2 reserved seating. Open Wed.–Sat. at 7:30 PM; matinees Thurs. and Sat. at noon, Sun. 1 PM.*

8 Dining

*Updated by
Barbara
Freitag*

*Barbara
Freitag has
been eating out
around
Orlando three
or four nights
a week since
she moved here
20 years ago.*

Some of Orlando's finest restaurants are in the stylish hotels in areas close to Walt Disney World. These dining establishments like to flaunt their sophisticated menus and wine lists and to show off their big-city tastes. The thing is, many of them are overrated, nothing more or less than you'd expect of the best chain hotel restaurants anywhere in the United States. If you want convenience, decent food, and a cosmopolitan atmosphere, these hotel restaurants are a safe bet. On the other hand, if you're watching your pennies or like your restaurants with a certain regional flavor, it will be worth your while to drive a ways to eat in a local spot, where you'll find a taste of Orlando, as well as considerable savings. Many good restaurants are in rather mundane-looking shopping centers. It's a function of economics; people shop—and people need to eat.

Highly recommended restaurants are indicated by a star ★.

Local Specialties Try stone crabs, pompano (a mild white fish), small tasty Florida lobsters, and conch chowder. Fresh hearts of palm are a treat, too.

Dinner Shows Dinner shows, at which a themed show accompanies a rather ordinary meal, are big business throughout the area. Walt Disney World has several such wildly popular events, including the entertaining Hoop-Dee-Doo Musical Revue; there are also Arabian nights, cowboy, kings and queens, and medieval-themed entertainments, to name just a few. For our assessment and all the details, *see* Chapter 10, After Dark.

Dress Ties are always optional, though men on the far side of 30 commonly wear them. Casual dress prevails in all but the fanciest places; that means comfortably presentable.

Reservations They're always a good idea; otherwise a large group may arrive moments before you and keep you waiting. Orlando is not a big town, but getting to places is frequently complicated, so always call for directions.

Price

Category	Cost*
$$$$	over $40
$$$	$30–$40
$$	$20–$30
$	under $20

*per person, excluding drinks, service, and 6% sales tax

In and Around Walt Disney World

These are restaurants in Walt Disney World and close by it. In tourist heaven on the stretch of U.S. 192 between Walt Disney World and Kissimmee, most of the restaurants are either chains or large, overrated, and overpriced. On the other hand, Lake

Antonio's
La Fiamma, **3**

Ariel's, **47**

Authur's 27, **43**

Beeline Diner, **30**

Border Cantina, **6**

Capriccio's, **31**

Chalet Suzanne, **51**

Chatham's Place, **33**

Christini's, **34**

Ciao Italia, **32**

Del Frisco's, **8**

Dexter's, **9**

Donato's, **26**

Empress Lilly, **42**

Enzo's on the Lake, **1**

Enzo's at the
Marketplace, **37**

4-5-6, **16**

Florida Bay, **28**

Forbidden City, **11**

Gargi's Italian
Restaurant, **10**

Hard Rock Cafe, **25**

Harvey's Bistro, **17**

Hemingway's, **39**

Hollywood Brown
Derby, **49**

Jordan's Grove, **4**

La Coquina, **38**

La Scala, **2**

La Sila, **24**

Le Cordon Bleu, **7**

Le Coq au Vin, **20**

Le Provence Bistro
Français, **19**

Linda's La Cantina, **14**

Little Saigon, **18**

Lombardi's, **12**

Ming Court, **29**

New York
Chinatown, **48**

Pebbles, **41**

Phoenician, **35**

Planet Hollywood, **45**

Positano, **22**

Portobello Yacht
Club, **44**

Ran Getsu, **36**

Rolando's Cuban
Restaurant, **5**

Ronnie's, **13**

Rosario's, **50**

Sam Snead's
Tavern, **23**

Siam Orchid, **27**

Spicy Pot, **21**

Straub's Fine
Seafood, **15**

Victoria and
Albert's, **46**

White Horse
Saloon, **40**

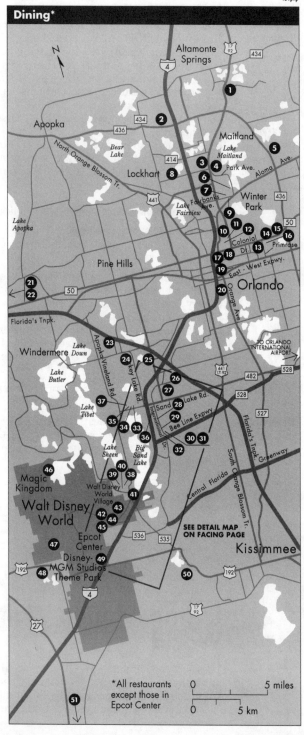

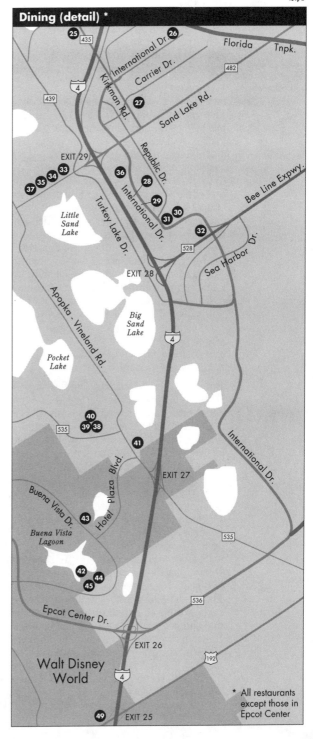

Buena Vista (also known as the Disney Maingate area) is full of great eating. (The **McDonald's** here is a destination in its own right; the playground out front is almost as big as the restaurant and is chockablock with bright-colored crawling and climbing apparatuses.) The same goes for International Drive.

American
$$$$
★

Victoria and Albert's. Don't let the Disney whimsy frighten you away from this fine restaurant. Yes, your two servers are called Victoria and Albert and they recite the day's specials in tandem, but the atmosphere is romantic and the food is divine. The intimate, circular dining room is enhanced by fabric-covered walls and marbleized columns; in the evening, a harpist adds another soothing touch. The six-course, prix-fixe menu changes substantially each day. Chef Vincent Panisset enjoys preparing exotic dishes but always offers something for less adventuresome palates as well. Appetizers might include velvety veal sweetbreads and rare New Zealand venison, artichokes in a lusty duxelles (mushroom-based) sauce, or jumbo sea scallops served over seaweed salad with warm beet vinaigrette. Entrées range from tender grilled pheasant or lean buffalo to perfectly prepared Angus sirloin or broiled Maine lobster. A deluxe version of the menu comes with four glasses of wine, each selected to complement a particular course. There are two seatings, the first beginning at six, the second at nine. A 14-seat private dining room is also available. *Grand Floridian Beach Resort, Walt Disney World Magic Kingdom resort area, tel. 407/824–2383. Reservations required. Jackets requested. AE, MC, V. Kosher and vegetarian meals by advance order.*

$$

Empress Lilly restaurants. The fire-engine-red paddle wheel of Disney's 220-foot, 19th-century Mississippi-style riverboat was never intended to move the boat even an inch from its mooring at the far end of Disney Village Marketplace. But much care was devoted to making the craft look like an old-fashioned Victorian showboat: it's complete with brass lamps, velvet love seats, and acres of gleaming mahogany paneling and moldings. Inside are four restaurants, each a little different. **Steerman's Quarters,** a cozy spot with its red walls, dark woodwork, and picture window framing a perfect up-close view of the paddle wheel, serves beef; **Fisherman's Deck,** replete with gingerbread woodwork painted in sunset pastels, offers seafood. In the **Baton Rouge Lounge,** John Charles performs musical comedy while you eat all you want from a Southern-style buffet, heavy on the carbohydrates. Overall, meals can be fun for families or groups that want congenial surroundings and don't mind the undistinguished food. For these restaurants, only 10% of the tables are open for reservations (up to a month in advance); without them, arrive early and add your name to the list. Then, depending on the length of the wait (it could be as much as an hour), you can sit on the Empress Lilly's promenade and have a drink, or you can dash through Disney Village Marketplace for some more shopping. The fourth restaurant, the **Empress Room,** is described later in this section. *Disney Village Marketplace, tel. 407/828–3900. Baton Rouge Lounge: no reservations; buffet 5 PM–8 PM. Steerman's*

Quarters and Fisherman's Deck: some reservations accepted up to a month in advance. Dress: casual. AE, MC, V.

Pebbles. This restaurant, full of hanging plants and with tiled floors, serves California cuisine with a Florida twist, using native produce and fish. A favorite of Orlando residents, the original restaurant in the suburbs now has several siblings in areas more accessible to tourists. With its cosmopolitan atmosphere and friendly, attentive service, it's casual enough that you'll feel at home in either shorts or a suit. The soups are tasty, particularly the black bean soup. Otherwise, best bets are the daily pasta and fresh fish specials, or possibly the Mediterranean salad, where sun-dried tomatoes put in their obligatory appearance. That rare Orlando dish, a good hamburger, is also served here. Desserts here are worth the calories, and the wine list is interesting and well priced. *In the Crossroads Shopping Center near the Lake Buena Vista entrance to Walt Disney World, Orlando, tel. 407/827–1111; 17 W. Church St., tel. 407/839–0892; 2516 Aloma Ave., Winter Park, tel. 407/678–7001; 2100 Rte. 434, Longwood, tel. 407/774–7111. No reservations. AE, D, DC, MC, V.*

Planet Hollywood. By late 1994, Demi Moore, Arnold Schwarzeneggar, Sylvester Stallone, and Bruce Willis will have collected enough movie memorabilia to open a new branch of their popular restaurant chain just outside the entrance to WDW's Pleasure Island. Besides film artifacts, guests will be able to take a gander at clips from soon-to-be-released movies and a waterfall, which spills down the center of the three-story, 20,000-square-foot structure. The menu is built around fresh, healthful dishes like turkey burgers, smoked and grilled meats, unusual pastas and salads, and a wide range of desserts. *Pleasure Island, Walt Disney World Village, tel. 407/363–7827. No reservations. Dress: casual. AE, DC, MC, V.*

White Horse Saloon. Put on your Texas duds and sashay on down to this western-themed saloon in the Hyatt Regency Grand Cypress for a night of serious eating. There are only four entrées to choose from in this casual restaurant: prime rib, roast free-range chicken, barbecued beef ribs, and vegetarian platters—and all come with salad, baked potato, and creamed spinach stuffed in a brioche. A Snickers candy bar that arrives at the end of the meal, on the house, should suffice as dessert; other sweets are extra. Keeping the atmosphere musically lively while you chow down is the Hand-Picked Trio, which has been here for years. *Hyatt Regency Grand Cypress, 1 Grand Cypress Blvd., Orlando, tel. 407/239–1234. Reservations advised. Dress: casual. AE, DC, MC, V.*

Chinese
$$
Ming Court. Although the names of some of the dishes may sound familiar, the creative flair of the kitchen of this fine restaurant makes each one stand out from the standard rendition. Try the jumbo shrimp in lobster sauce flavored with crushed black beans, or the Hunan *kung pao* chicken (with peanuts, cashews, and walnuts). Prices may seem high, but the elegant surroundings—glass walls allow you to look out onto a pond and floating gardens—make the expense worthwhile. Another plus is that Ming Court is within walking distance of the Orange

County Convention Center. *9188 International Dr., Orlando, tel. 407/351–9988. Reservations advised. AE, DC, MC, V.*

New York Chinatown. This spot on U.S. 192, a mile west of I–4, is a terrific place to take the family after a wearying day in the parks. The plain interior belies the quality of the food: Every entrée is made with the freshest ingredients and comes piping hot. The spareribs are lean and flavorful, and the egg rolls are light and delicate. In addition to those old favorites, try one of the vegetarian options. *7702 W. U.S. 192, Kissimmee, tel. 407/239–6972. Reservations accepted. Dress: casual. AE, DC, MC, V.*

Continental
$$$$

Arthur's 27. This fancy restaurant atop the Buena Vista Palace Hotel serves up not only one of the best views anywhere of the Magic Kingdom and Epcot Center but also elegant, well-prepared meals featuring specialties such as venison with papaya and dates, and sautéed breast of duck with honey-ginger sauce. You can choose a prix-fixe dinner with four courses for $45 (not including drinks) or pay $60 for one with six; if you order à la carte, expect the tab to go higher. Service is suitably attentive if bordering on the pretentious (watch the choreographed removal of the domed silver covers and add a percentage point or two to the tip if you're duly impressed); the wine list is formidable, featuring everything from reasonably priced Californias to some vintage Bordeaux of the sort that make news when sold at auction. Arthur's is popular on weekends and there is only one seating per night, so reserve your table when you reserve your room. And because dinners last several hours, go with someone you like. *Buena Vista Palace Hotel, Walt Disney World Village, Lake Buena Vista, tel. 407/827–3450. Reservations essential. Jacket required. AE, D, DC, MC, V.*

$$$

Empress Room. This small, gaudily luxurious Louis XV–style dining room on the *Empress Lilly* riverboat in Disney Village Marketplace is the kind of place that might bring out the Rhett Butler or Scarlett O'Hara in you, with its brass-and-crystal chandelier, damask-pattern wallpaper, and gilt moldings. Try the roast loin of veal with wild mushroom sausage in dry vermouth sauce or the John Dory topped with lobster and served with watercress sauce; there's always a soufflé of the day and a flourless chocolate cake. Thanks to recent improvements, you'll give the kitchen the kind of marks once reserved only for the team who designed the sumptuous room. *Empress Lilly, Disney Village Marketplace, tel. 407/828–3900. Reservations required (available up to a month in advance). Jacket required. AE, DC, MC, V.*

French
$$$

La Coquina. The menu of this restaurant in the Hyatt Regency Grand Cypress ranges from Normandy to Flanders and from the Basque country to the Côte d'Azur, and the food is always excellent. But for the most fun, try the Sunday brunch, which is lavishly laid out in the restaurant's kitchen. Be sure you're starving, because the huge spread of salads, smoked fishes, omelets, waffles, and pastries is so appealing you'll want to sample everything. Pace yourself, because it's not until near the end that you get to the entrées—the only French part of this all-American spread (seafood terrine, quartered duck, poached salmon). Try to sit by the windows so you can enjoy the tropical view as you listen to the harpist. The brunch price ranges from $33 to $115, depending on whether you order Chandon Napa Valley or Dom Perignon champagne to wash it all down. *Hyatt Regency Grand Cypress, 1 Grand Cypress Blvd., Orlando, tel. 407/239–1234. Reservations advised. Jacket and tie required for dinner only. AE, DC, MC, V.*

Italian **Capriccio's.** A relaxed atmosphere, more European than central
$$ Floridian, gives this restaurant appeal for locals as well as tourists. The marble-topped tables are arranged on the tile floors so that everyone can view the open kitchen and wood-burning pizza ovens, which turn out pies ranging from *pizza Margherita* (made with sun-dried tomatoes and smoked mozzarella, fontina, provolone, and Parmesan cheeses) to healthy *pizza bianco* (wholewheat crust with pecorino and Romano chese, broccoli, basil, olive oil, and black pepper). If you're not in the mood for pizza, try one of the mesquite-grilled fish, chicken, or beef entrées. *Peabody Hotel, 9801 International Dr., Orlando, tel. 407/352–4000. Reservations advised. AE, DC, MC, V. Brunch Sat. and Sun. Closed Mon.*

Ciao Italia. This charming little family-owned restaurant makes every item to order, so it isn't an in-and-out sort of place. Your patience will be rewarded, however: The Italian-speaking proprietors have managed to re-create a piece of Italy in central Florida. The proof is in the sweet New Zealand mussels, served with either white garlic or marinara sauce, and the light, flavorful, and colorful *pollo alla Tonino* (chicken breast with red and yellow peppers). For dessert, try the *tartufo* (chocolate-coated ice cream), but skip the cappuccino—it's watery. *Across from Sheraton World Hotel, 6149 Westwood Blvd., Orlando, tel. 407/354–0770. Reservations accepted. Dress: casual. AE, D, DC, MC, V. Beer and wine only. No lunch.*

Portobello Yacht Club. The Levys, longtime Chicago restaurateurs, have brought their highly touted hometown restaurant to Pleasure Island. However, it's pretty much in name only. (After all, this is Walt Disney World, and the standards of dining and service are more relaxed.) But the atmosphere is appealing, with the tile floors and charming waiters; the catch of the day is fresh; and the people-watching gets better the more sangria you drink. (Those who like their vino unadulterated will find the selection of Italian and domestic wines appealing.) Moreover, the kitchen keeps late hours—worth knowing about when you're partying the night away. *Pleasure Island, Walt Disney World, tel. 407/934–8888. Reservations accepted. Dress: casual. AE, DC, MC, V.*

$–$$ **Rosario's.** This little place, in a New England–style clapboard house that looks refreshingly out of place in the unsightly jumble of motels known as Kissimmee, is understated and cheerful, and serves Italian food that's way above average. The *spaghetti aglio olio* is sauced with fresh garlic, basil, and diced tomatoes sautéed in olive oil. The hearty *pasta e fagioli* soup is filled with Italian white beans, prosciutto, escarole, and pasta and flavored with both brandy and a touch of marinara sauce. All entrées come with a choice of soup or salad and plenty of crusty Italian bread. *4838 W. Irlo Bronson Hwy., Kissimmee, tel. 407/239–0118. AE, D, DC, MC, V. Beer and wine only. Closed for lunch.*

Fast Food **McDonald's.** The nation's largest McDonald's is no plain-Jane
$ burger joint. Although the menu is standard, the frills are pure Orlando: a 7,500-square-foot playground full of slides, tunnels, and seesaws; a theater where musicians and magicians perform; even a gift shop, called Mickey D's, full of T-shirts. You can chow down in the tiki bar–style Sunset Terrace area; the Maui Room, with a 600-gallon saltwater aquarium; or the Rock and Roll Room, featuring '50s memorabilia and a jukebox. *6875 Sand Lake Rd. and International Dr., Orlando, tel. 407/351–2185. No reservations. AE, MC, V.*

Japanese **Ran-Getsu.** The surroundings are definitely a Disney version of
$$ the Orient—but the food is fresh and carefully prepared. Sit at the curved, dragon's-tail-shaped sushi bar and order the *matsu* platter—an assortment of *nigiri-* and *maki*-style sushis. Or, unless you're alone, you can have your meal Japanese style at the low tables overlooking a carp-filled pond and decorative gardens. Specialties include sukiyaki and *shabu-shabu* (thinly sliced beef prepared tableside in a boiling seasoned broth and served with vegetables). If you feel more adventurous, try the deep-fried alligator tail. The servers are not great about educating unknowledgeable customers, so it helps to know a bit about Japanese cuisine when you come here. *8400 International Dr., Orlando, tel. 407/345–0044. Reservations advised. Dress: casual. AE, DC, MC, V.*

Seafood **Ariel's.** The centerpiece of this favorite of Disney executives,
$$$ named for the Little Mermaid, is a 2,500-gallon saltwater tank. The fare comes from Florida, the Northeast, and the Northwest, and it's most often simply grilled over a hardwood fire. Want something more exotic? Start with the Tuckernut shellfish gumbo with andouille sausage and then have Ariel's strudel— chicken and ricotta wrapped in a flaky basil-perfumed pastry. *Disney's Beach Club Resort, Lake Buena Vista, tel. 407/834–8000. Reservations accepted. Dress: casual. No smoking. AE, MC, V.*

$$–$$$ **Hemingway's.** Located by the pool at the Hyatt Regency Grand
★ Cypress, this restaurant serves up all sorts of sea creatures, from conch, scallops, and squid to grouper, pompano, and monkfish. Be sure to order Florida stone crabs during the season (October through March), and don't miss the beer-battered coconut shrimp. In addition to the regular menu, Hemingway's offers what is called Cuisine Naturelle—dishes that are low in fat, calories, sodium, and cholesterol and made with recipes that are approved by the **American Heart Association and Weight Watchers.** What more could you want? A piece of creamy Key lime pie for dessert. *Hyatt Regency Grand Cypress Resort, 1 Grand Cypress Blvd., Orlando, tel. 407/239–1234. Reservations advised. Dress: casual. AE, DC, MC, V.*

$–$$ **Florida Bay.** The food in this seafood restaurant, which is within walking distance of the Orange County Convention Center, is tasty, well prepared, and fairly priced. As a starter, try the Oriental stir-fry white cheese pizza (actually on a pita); for entrées, you can't go wrong with the seafood dishes or the grilled shrimp and mixed greens special. Florida Bay gives the feeling of a Key West yacht club, with its turquoise and gray color scheme and cement floors. It gets a well-dressed business crowd at lunch. *8560 International Dr., Orlando, tel. 407/352–6655. No reservations. Dress: casual. AE, D, DC, MC, V.*

Epcot Center

Epcot Center's World Showcase offers some of the finest dining to be found not only in Walt Disney World but in the entire Orlando area. The problems are that you have to pay Epcot Center admission to eat in these establishments; the top-of-the-line places, such as those in the French, Italian, and Japanese pavilions, can be expensive; and reservations can be hard to come by. On the other hand, most of them have a limited-selection children's menu with dramatically lower prices. Dress is informal—no one expects you to go all the way back to your hotel to clean up. And if you have unruly youngsters in tow, you probably won't be alone. Kosher and vegetarian meals are always available on request.

Reservations All restaurants, unless otherwise noted, are open for both lunch and dinner daily. For both meals, reservations are a must. However, unless you're staying on Walt Disney World property, you can't simply call up and make them by phone in advance but instead must present yourself at Epcot Center in person on the morning of the day you want to dine. Here's the drill: As soon as you get to Epcot Center, head for Earth Station, at the base of Spaceship Earth, and line up in front of the bank of interactive computer screens known as the WorldKey Information Center. You must arrive early, because the most popular seating times in the most popular restaurants are filled up within an hour of Epcot Center's official opening time (which, as you may remember, may be as much as 30 minutes ahead of the *published* opening time).

If the line is long when you get to Earth Station but you can move around quickly, it may pay to make a beeline for some of the other WorldKey kiosks, a bit farther away—there's one on the far side of of the Port of Entry shop, near the dock for the water taxi to Morocco, and another just before the bridge to World Showcase.

Alternatively, be flexible about your mealtimes. For the more popular establishments, it is much easier to get a reservation for lunch than for dinner, to get lunch reservations before noon, and to get dinner reservations for seatings before 6 PM and after 8 PM. And it's always worth stopping by the restaurant of your choice during the day in hopes of a cancellation.

Guests at most on-site hotels can avoid the battle of WorldKey by booking by phone (tel. 407/560–7277). When making reservations, you'll be asked your name, lodging place, and room number; in the restaurant, you must show your resort guest identification card.

No matter how you book, try to show up a bit early to be sure of getting your table. You can pay with cash; charge with American Express, MasterCard, or Visa; or if you're a guest at an on-site hotel on Disney property, charge the tab to your room.

The following are your best bets for both good food and atmosphere.

British
$$
Rose and Crown. At day's end, visitors mingle with Disney employees at this friendly British pub on World Showcase Lagoon while knocking off pints of Bass Ale and Guinness Stout with Stilton cheese. "Wenches" serve up simple pub fare, such as steak-and-kidney pie, and fish-and-chips. Dark wood floors, sturdy pub chairs, and brass lamps create a warm, homey atmosphere. At 4, a traditional tea is served. The food is relatively inexpensive, especially at lunch, and the terrace has a splendid view of IllumiNations, so all things considered, it's one of the best bets in Epcot Center.

French
$$$
Les Chefs de France. To create this sparkling French café-restaurant, three of France's most famous culinary artists came together: Paul Bocuse, who operates one restaurant north of Lyon and two in Tokyo; Gaston Lenôtre, noted for his pastries and ice creams; and Roger Vergé, proprietor of France's celebrated Mougins, near Cannes. The three don't actually prepare each meal, but they developed the menu, trained the chefs, and look in frequently to make sure the food and service stay up to snuff, which they do. Start with a chicken-and-duck pâté in a pastry crust, follow up with a classic coq au vin or broiled salmon with sorrel sauce, and end up with chocolate-doused ice cream–filled pastry shells. Some people say they feel transported back to fin-de-siècle France, if only for an hour or so.

$$–$$$
★
Bistro de Paris. The great secret at the France pavilion—and, indeed, in all of Epcot Center—is the Bistro de Paris, located around the back of the Chefs de Paris and upstairs. The sophisticated menu changes regularly and contains exciting offerings that reflect the cutting edge of French cooking. The dining salon is serene—and often filled with well-dressed French people, the mark of a successful transplant. Come late, ask for a window seat, and plan to linger to watch IllumiNations. The French wines are moderately priced and available by the glass. Open for lunch during busy seasons only.

German
$$
Biergarten. In this popular spot, Oktoberfest runs 365 days a year. The cheerful—some would say raucous—atmosphere is what you would expect in a place with an oompah band. Waitresses in typical Bavarian garb serve hot pretzels, hearty German fare such as sauerbraten and bratwurst, and stout pitchers of beer and wine, which patrons pound on their long communal tables—even when the yodelers, singers, and dancers aren't egging them on.

Italian **L'Originale Alfredo di Roma Ristorante.** If you love fettuccine
$$$ Alfredo, you owe it to yourself to try it in this restaurant, a cousin
of the one founded in 1914 by Alfredo de Lelio, who invented the
now-classic dish—pasta sauced with cream, butter, and loads of
freshly grated Parmesan cheese. Stick with pasta, for the other
menu items are undistinguished. Or try *lo chef consiglia* (the
chef's selection)—a spaghetti or fettuccine appetizer, a mixed
green salad, and a chicken or veal entrée such as *scaloppine alla
cacciatora*, a version of the familiar chicken dish. In addition,
during dinner the Italian waiters skip around singing Italian
songs and bellowing arias, a show in themselves.

Japanese **Mitsukoshi.** This complex of dining areas overlooking tranquil
$$–$$$ gardens is actually three restaurants: The **Yakitori,** a fast-food
★ stand in a small pavilion modeled on a teahouse in Kyoto's Kat-
sura Summer Palace, offers broiled skewers of chicken basted
with teriyaki sauce, and *guydon*, paper-thin beef simmered in a
spicy sauce and served with noodles. At the **Tempura Kiku,** two
dozen diners sit around a central counter and watch the chefs
prepare sushi, sashimi, tempura, batter-dipped deep-fried
shrimp, scallops, and vegetables. The food is first-class, and
though the menu doesn't list blowfish—the strange delicacy
whose charm is that ingesting it could be fatal—Japanese-food
lovers should be quite content. In the Mitsukoshi's third area—a
series of five **Teppanyaki Rooms**—chefs skillfully chop vegeta-
bles, meat, and fish at lightning speed and then stir-fry them at
grills set into communal dining tables. The **Matsunoma Lounge**
to the right of this area pours Japanese sake, plum wine, and
saketinis—martinis made with sake rather than vermouth.

Mexican **San Angel Inn.** The lush, tropical surroundings—cool, dark, and
$$ almost surreal—make this restaurant in the courtyard inside
★ the Mexican pavilion perhaps the most exotic in Walt Disney
World. It's popular among Disney execs as well as tourists. The
ambience is at once romantic and lively. Candlelit tables are com-
panionably close together, and the restaurant is open to the
"sky" in the inside of the pavilion and filled with the music of
folk singers, guitars, and marimbas. The best seats are along
the restaurant's outer edge, away from the entrance and directly alongside the Mexican's "river," where boatloads of sight-
seers stream by; above looms an Aztec pyramid, whose soft,
fiery light evokes a sense of the distant past. On the roster of
authentic dishes, one specialty is *mole poblano*—chicken sim-
mered until tender in a rich sauce of different kinds of chilies,
green tomatoes, ground tortillas, coriander seed, and 11 other
spices mixed with cocoa. Fresh tortillas are made every day and
served with beef, chicken, and cheese fillings as well as fresh
salsa verde (spicy green sauce).

Moroccan **Marrakesh.** Belly dancers and a three-piece Moroccan band set
$$–$$$ a North African mood in this restaurant that feels almost like a
set for a Disney *Casablanca*, if not quite like the African continent itself. The food is mildly spicy and relatively inexpensive.
Try the couscous, the national dish of Morocco, served with
vegetables; or *bastila*, an appetizer made of alternating layers

of sweet-and-spicy pork and a thin pastry, redolent of almonds, saffron, and cinnamon.

Norwegian
$

Restaurant Akershus. Norway's tradition of seafood and cold-meat dishes is highlighted at the *koldtbord*, or Norwegian buffet, in this restaurant, comprising four dining rooms that occupy a copy of Oslos's Akershus Castle. Hosts and hostesses explain the dishes and suggest which ones go together, then send you off to the buffet table. There is no need to shovel everything you see onto your plate at one time—it is traditional to make several trips. First, take your appetizers (usually herring, which comes several ways here), then go for cold seafood such as gravlax. Pick up cold salads and meats on your next trip, and then, on your last foray, fill up on hot lamb, veal, or venison. The selection of desserts, offered à la carte, includes cloudberries—delicate seasonal fruits that grow on the tundra.

Other Options

Future World's two full-service restaurants are Living Seas' tiered **Coral Reef Room**, which serves a finny menu and has a view of the pavilion's jumbo aquarium through 8-foot-high windows, and the **Garden Grill,** where you can eat American fare with a twist as the restaurant revolves, giving you an ever-changing view of each of the biomes of the Listen to the Land boat ride. In World Showcase, there's also China's **Nine Dragons,** which offers Chinese fare representing several regions—modified for American tastes—in a large, comfortable room decorated with Oriental motifs. If your hometown has a thriving Chinese community, you'll find the fare here uninspired.

Fast-food and cafeteria options are described in the section of Chapter 3 as Time Outs in the Exploring text; for an overview, *see also* that section's Dining text.

Meals with Disney Characters

At these breakfasts, brunches, and dinners staged in hotel and theme park restaurants all over Walt Disney World, kids can snuggle up to all the best-loved Disney characters. Sometimes the food is served buffet style, sometimes it's sit-down. Prices and times vary, so call ahead. Reservations are often required; places where they are not are crowded, so show up on the early side if you hate to wait. Smoking is not permitted at any of these.

Breakfasts

No reservations are required for many of these events. You can drop in from 8 to 10:30 at the **Buena Vista Palace** (tel. 407/827–2727; $8.95 adults, $4.95 children under 11); from 8 to 11 in a no-holds-barred buffet at the Contemporary Café in the **Contemporary Resort** (tel. 407/934–7639; $12.95 adults, $7.95 children 3–11); from 7:30 to 11 in the Cape May Café at **Disney's Beach Club** ($12.95 adults, $7.95 children under 12); from 7:30 to 10:15 Monday–Saturday at the **Polynesian Resort**'s Papeete Bay Verandah (tel. 407/824–1391; $12.95 adults, $7.95 children 3–11) and from 11 to 2 Sundays ($14.95 adult, $7.95 children 3 to 11); Saturdays from 8 to 11 in the Garden Grove at the **Walt Disney World Swan** (tel. 407/934–1281; about $11 for adults, $7 for children, depending on whether you go for the buffet or order from the menu); and at the counter-service Stargate Restaurant in Future World's CommuniCore East in **Epcot Center**. There, the characters are on hand from park opening until 10, with breakfast served for another hour; you don't have to buy food to enjoy the goings-on.

Reservations are required for other breakfasts, including **Breakfast à la Disney**, with seatings at 8:30 and 10 aboard the *Empress Lilly* (tel. 407/828–3900; $11.50 adults, $7.95 children 3–11), with Mickey & Co. in attendance, and from 7:30 to noon in the 1900 Park Fare Restaurant in the **Grand Floridian** (tel. 407/824–2383; $14.95 adults, $9.75 children 3–11), where Mary Poppins and her crew put in appearances.

Sunday Brunch The Disney characters show up for the lavish Sunday brunch from 8:30 to 12:30 at the Ristorante Carnivale at the **Walt Disney World Dolphin** (tel. 407/934–4025; $12.95 adults, $7.95 children 4–12). You can help yourself to everything from bacon and eggs and seafood crepes to pancakes and chocolate chip waffles in the distinctive circle-with-ears shape. Reservations are a good idea.

Dinner Mickey's Tropical Revue, a luau character show, is presented daily at 4:30 PM at the **Polynesian Resort** (tel. 407/W–DISNEY; $28 adults, $21.50 ages 12–20, $12.95 ages 3–11). Mickey and Minnie are at the buffet served from 5 to 9 daily at the 1900 Park Fare Restaurant in the **Grand Floridian** (tel. 407/824–2383; $17.95 adults, $9.95 children 3–11). The characters also appear during dinner, served 5:30–10 daily, at **Chef Mickey's Village Restaurant** (tel. 407/828–3723; entrées $10.25–$17.95, children's menu entrées from $8.75). You will need reservations for all of these. Every night at 8, near Fort Wilderness's Meadow Trading Post, there's also a **Character Campfire** and sing-along (free).

The Orlando Area

The following restaurants, in or near the city of Orlando, cater mostly to a local clientele.

American
$$ **Sam Snead's Tavern.** The prototype for a golf theme grill, this lively restaurant is a tribute to the venerable pro champion Sam Snead. The wood-paneled walls are chockablock with pictures and memorabilia of his illustrious career. The bar is busy seven nights a week, with a thirty-something crowd, and the dining rooms are usually filled with families and couples enjoying themselves. The kitchen does well with an eclectic variety of foods ranging from hamburgers and grilled chicken to veal chops and fish. The Caesar salad is excellent, as are the barbecued spareribs. The chocolate sack sounds weird but isn't: It's pound cake, ice cream, strawberries, and whipped cream packed into what looks like a paper bag made of chocolate, and it's much too much for one person. This is one of the few restaurants in town open as late as 1 AM. *2461 S. Hiawassee Rd., Orlando, tel. 407/295–9999. Reservations advised. Dress: casual. AE, DC, MC, V.*

$ **Dexter's.** Winter Park locals, from Rollins College students to the owners of the area's lakefront estates, hang out at this combination wine shop–wine bar. Sample the interesting vintages for sale by the glass, or have a meal at the counter or at bar-height wooden tables. The made-from-scratch soups are a hearty choice as is the ratatouille, served in a hollowed-out roll. Sandwiches and salads seem better than they are because of what's going on in the room. At dinner, there's often a jazz group and an interesting selection of tapas. *200 W. Fairbanks Ave., Winter Park, tel. 407/629–1150. Dress: informal. AE, MC, V. Closed Sun.*

Hard Rock Café Orlando. The popular Los Angeles Brat Pack hangout came to Orlando around the same time that Universal Studios Florida opened, and you can enter its guitar-shape building from the theme park or from the street. Besides ear-splitting rock music and rock memorabilia, Orlando's Hard Rock features hamburgers, barbecue, and sandwiches. *Universal Studios Florida, 5800 Kirkman Rd., Orlando, tel. 407/351–7625. No reservations accepted. Dress: casual. AE, MC, V.*

American-International
$$–$$$
★

Chatham's Place. The Chatham brothers, Culinary Institute of America graduates, prepare everything to order here, and the staff is genuinely concerned that every patron has a perfect experience. The professional office building that the restaurant calls home, across the street from the Marketplace shopping mall, lends nothing in the way of atmosphere; nor is the decor anything to get excited about—hanging plants, glass-topped paisley tablecloths, and a view of the kitchen. But the meticulously prepared food rises above the setting. Try the black grouper with pecan butter, the rosemary-infused rack of lamb, or the duck breast, grilled to crispy perfection. This is one of Orlando's best. *7575 Dr. Phillips Blvd., Orlando, tel. 407/345–2992. Reservations advised. Dress: casual. MC, V. Dinner only.*

Jordan's Grove. One of Orlando's most popular restaurants, Jordan's Grove occupies an old house built in 1912 next door to the only art theater in central Florida. The ambitious menu changes daily, and the prix fixe includes a choice of soup or salad, appetizer, entrée with vegetables, and dessert. That changing menu allows for some creative flexing of the kitchen's culinary muscles; depending on the day, the season, and the mood of the chef, the food ranges from weird to ordinary to quite extraordinary. Wine, the only alcoholic beverage served, is mostly American from smaller estates. *1300 S. Orlando Ave. (U.S. 17–92), Maitland, tel. 407/628–0020. Reservations advised. AE, DC, MC, V. Closed Mon. and lunch Sat.*

$$

Harvey's Bistro. In the Barnet Bank building downtown within walking distance of the Arena and the Centroplex, this clubby newcomer, with paneled walls and white tablecloths, has quickly collected an enthusiastic business crowd at lunch and concert-, theater-, and Arena-goers after dark. The menu offers a good selection of bistro and comfort foods. Soups are good (try the petite marmite au gratin), as are the oven-roasted saffron scallops, the duck cassoulet with white and black beans, and the thin-crusted pizza with caramelized onions, fresh spinach, and goat cheese. Late hours are a plus. *390 N. Orlando Ave., Orlando,* *tel. 407/246–6560. Reservations advised. Dress: casual. AE, D, DC, MC, V. No lunch Sat.; closed Sun.*

Chinese **The Forbidden City.** The Hunan-style food at this restaurant in
$–$$ a reconstructed gas station is terrific. Start with the diced
★ chicken with pine seeds in a package—icy lettuce cups wrapped around spicy chicken, which offer a delightful mix of cold and hot sensations. The sesame chicken—large chunks of sesame-coated poultry sautéed in a sweet sauce—goes perfectly with bright-green broccoli in a subtle garlic sauce. The traditional 10-ingredient lo mein is full of fresh shrimp, chicken, beef, and pork. You're in for a treat if you can get past the decor, or lack thereof; the former gas station's marquee is still there, and inside there are utilitarian tables and booths, with a few plastic plants to add that fresh, natural note. *948 N. Mills Ave., Orlando, tel. 407/894–5005. MC, V. Closed Sat. lunch and Sun.*

4-5-6. With its mirrored walls and emerald green carpet, this restaurant is sleek and clean-looking, setting the stage for the food, which is made without MSG or preservatives. There's an extensive choice of vegetarian and steamed entrées, and brown rice is provided as an alternative to the white. The best appetizer is steamed dumplings, served in the small aluminum dishes in which they're cooked; one person could easily consume an order. Dumplings sautéed in hot peanut butter sauce is the must for peanut butter fans. Specialties include chicken three ways (one platter that includes portions of General Tso's chicken, lemon chicken, and sliced chicken breast with snow peas), as well as Five Fresh Herbs Steamed Fresh Fish, made with sea bass. The friendly staff tries hard to accommodate, so be sure to speak up if you want your food spicy or served in a special casserole to keep it warm. *657 N. Primrose Dr., Orlando, tel. 407/898–1899. Reservations accepted. Dress: casual. Beer and wine only. AE, MC, V.*

Cuban **Rolando's Cuban Restaurant.** Cuban cuisine has become a Flor-
$ ida staple, and Rolando's is one of the best places in Orlando to
★ try it. Black bean soup, dirty rice, and chicken with yellow rice are just a few of the specialties. Brown Formica-topped tables with rickety metal legs and lush plastic greenery are the key features of the decor. It's a haul from WDW—35–40 minutes. *870 Semoran Blvd., Casselberry, tel. 407/767–9677. No reservations. Dress: casual. MC, V.*

Deli **Ronnie's.** Others have tried but failed to compete with Ronnie's,
$ which has been the only place in town to serve a decent corned-beef sandwich and Dr. Brown's soda for so long it has become an institution. At lunchtime, city bigwigs fill up the back tables, and hours after other Orlando restaurants have turned out their lights for the night, Ronnie's is still serving coffee and Danish. The tuna-fish salad is terrific. You can get takeout and baked goods next door. *Colonial Plaza, 2702 E. Colonial Dr. (bet. Bumby and Primrose Aves.), Orlando, tel. 407/894–4951. Cash or traveler's checks only. Open Sun.–Thurs. until 11, Fri. and Sat. until 1 AM.*

French **Le Cordon Bleu.** Over the past two decades, Georges and
$$$ Monique Vogelbacher have assembled a loyal clientele, who

come back night after night for French cuisine with a Swiss touch. With its print wallpaper, lace curtains, and white tablecloths, the room is comfortable, and so is the menu, which offers the kitchen's well-prepared version of Caesar salad, superb roast rack of lamb (for two) with an array of seasonal vegetables, and poached Norwegian salmon. In keeping with the trend toward lighter cuisine, Le Cordon Bleu has placed a number of low-fat dishes and fresh-fish specials on the menu as well. The dessert of choice is the Swiss roll, a crepe rolled around chocolate mousse with bittersweet chocolate on either end. The bread is really good. *537 West Fairbanks Ave., Winter Park, tel. 407/647–7575. Reservations advised. AE, D, DC, MC, V. Closed Sat. lunch and Sun.*

$$ **Le Coq au Vin.** The atmosphere here is country French, heavy ★ on the country. Charming owners Louis Perrotte and his wife, Magdalena, who acts as hostess, make the place feel warm and homey, and it is usually filled with friendly Orlando residents. The traditional French fare is first-class: homemade chicken liver pâté, fresh rainbow trout with champagne sauce, and Long Island duck with green peppercorns. For dessert, try the crème brûlée, and pat yourself on the back for discovering a place that few tourists know about. Ask to be seated in the main dining room—it's the center of the action. *4800 S. Orange Ave., Orlando, tel. 407/851–6980. Reservations advised. Dress: casual. AE, DC, MC, V.*

Le Provence Bistro Français. This charming two-story restaurant in the heart of downtown Orlando does a fine imitation of an out-of-the-way bistro on the Left Bank in Paris. Reasonable prices and first-rate service add to the delightful surroundings and excellent food. For lunch try the *salade niçoise*, made with fresh grilled tuna, French string beans, and hard-boiled eggs; or the *cassoulet toulousain*, a hearty mixture of white beans, lamb, pork, and sausage. At dinner you can choose between a six-course prix-fixe menu, a less pricey four-course version, or à la carte options. *50 East Pine St., Orlando, tel. 407/843–1320. Reservations advised. Dress: casual. AE, DC, MC, V. No lunch Sat.; closed Sun.*

Italian **Christini's.** Orlando is short on the kind of upscale Italian res- $$$ taurant you find so often in New York, so locals and tourists alike gladly pay the price at Christini's, one of Orlando's best for northern Italian cuisine. As a result, the place always feels as if there's a party going on, particularly in the center of the room. Owner Chris Christini is on hand nightly to make sure that everything is perfect. Try the pasta with lobster, shrimp, and clams or the huge veal chops, perfumed with fresh sage. And if you want to be removed from the hubbub, ask to be seated in the upper rooms on the right or left. *7600 Dr. Phillips Blvd., in the Marketplace, Orlando, tel. 407/345–8770. Reservations advised. AE, DC, MC, V.*

★ **Enzo's on the Lake.** Enzo's is Orlando's most popular restaurant. The Roman charmer who owns the place, Enzo Perlini, has turned a rather ordinary lakefront house in suburban Longwood, about 30 minutes' drive from I-Drive, into a delightful

Italian villa. It's worth the trip to sample the antipasto: a huge array of fresh grilled vegetables; the homemade frittatas and pâtés; bean salad; and marinated seafood salad, made up of tiny whole squid, tender calamari, and shrimp. The mussels, cooked in a heady broth of white wine and garlic, and the mild *bufalo mozzarella* cheese, flown in from Italy, make equally good starters. The *bucatini à la Enzo*, a combination of sautéed bacon, mushrooms, and peas served over long hollow noodles, is satisfying. Daily specials are consistently well done, particularly the fish. The electricity in the air is such that even people with reservations don't mind waiting at the bar (as is often necessary); they simply get into the party. Once you've adjusted to the clamor, your only problem will be deciding what to eat, because all the choices are irresistible. *1130 S. U.S. 17–92, Longwood, tel. 407/834–9872. Reservations necessary. Dress: casual. AE, DC, MC, V. Closed Sun.*

$$–$$$ **Antonio's La Fiamma.** Orlando residents count themselves lucky that this white two-story villa is on a busy local thoroughfare rather than on the hill in Tuscany, where it looks as if it belongs. The main section of the restaurant is upstairs, where an open wood-burning oven and grill anchor the rather stark but comfortable surroundings. Try the fennel and radicchio salad topped with orange zest, cracked pepper, shavings of Gruyère, and extra virgin olive oil. The *linguini alla cine di rapa*, linguini served with sautéed bitter greens, sausage, and slivered garlic, is a tantalizing marriage of tastes and textures. The *anitra con rosmarino all'agrodolce*, fully deboned and roasted duck with a sweet-sour sauce made of balsamic vinegar, rosemary, and honey, is heavenly. Grill favorites include the single- and double-broiled veal chops and the perfectly cooked Norwegian salmon. On weekends the restaurant can be noisy and the service slow, but the interesting choices that fill the wine list ease the wait. Downstairs is a gourmet grocery and wine shop that specializes in Italian food and produce, and alongside it, a deli purveying pizzas, salads, and cooked foods that you can take out or eat on the premises. The rosemary chicken is tender, juicy, and redolent of the oaky flavor of the fire. *611 S. Orlando Ave., Maitland, tel. 407/645–1035. Reservations advised. Dress: casual. AE, MC, V, Closed Sun.*

La Scala. Mirrored walls and gracious, sophisticated decor make this one of Orlando's most romantic restaurants. The fact that owner Joseph del Vento, a former opera singer, who once worked in New York's Tre Scalini, breaks into song every so often only adds to the charm. Go on Wednesday or Thursday for *osso bucco*, two-inch shanks of veal braised in a rich lemony broth. For pasta, order the dish called Chop, Chop, Chop—fresh seafood sautéed tableside, doused in marinara sauce, and served over fettuccine. Save room for homemade desserts such as the chocolate mousse cake with a hazelnut crust and raspberry sauce and the white chocolate mousse. La Scala was the first northern Italian restaurant in the city. *205 Loraine Dr., Altamonte Springs, tel. 407/862–3257. Reservations suggested. Dress: casual. AE, DC, MC, V. Closed Sat. lunch and Sun.*

La Sila. Although located in one of Orlando's ubiquitous shopping centers, La Sila offers consistently fresh, northern Italian cuisine in a gracious, sophisticated setting. A pianist plays in the cozy, wood-paneled bar, where friends meeting for a drink after work are as welcome as the couples who dance despite the lack of an official dance floor. The food is equally enjoyable: Pasta lovers will appreciate the large and original selection of dishes, including a penne with arugula and fresh tomato sauce that's an ideal mixture of bitter and sweet. The hefty, grilled veal chop or any of the fish specials are also sure to please. Because the restaurant's popularity continues to grow and because it's so convenient to WDW and Universal Studios, reservations are a must. *4898 Kirkman Rd., Orlando, tel. 407/295–8333. Reservations advised. Dress: casual. AE, DC, MC, V. Closed Sunday.*

$–$$ **Gargi's Italian Restaurant.** If you crave old-fashioned spaghetti and meatballs, lasagna, or manicotti made with sauces that you know have been simmering all day, this storefront hole-in-the-wall backed up against a railroad track in a commercial neighborhood just a little north of downtown is the place. Well-heeled Orlandoans eat here before Orlando Magic games; it's also a favorite of water-skiers from the lake across the street. Located well off the beaten tourist track, it's a welcome change from I-Drive. Get off I–4 at Ivanhoe and it's a minute away. *1421 N. Orange Ave., Orlando, tel. 407/894–7907. Reservations accepted. Dress: casual. Beer and wine only. MC, V. Closed Sun.*

Lombardi's. Orlando Magic fans and players as well as actors working at Disney-MGM and Universal Studios hang out at this downtown spot, 20 minutes from I-Drive. On weekends a jazz trio livens things up for the singles mingling around the bar. Specialties include crispy fried calamari served with a tomato-caper dipping sauce; *penne all'arrabiata*, short pasta tubes with a spicy tomato sauce flavored with pancetta, basil, olives, and Romano cheese; grilled marinated breast of chicken; and homemade pizzas. It's a big place but feels smaller, because the smoking and no-smoking sections are separate, on either side of the wood-burning oven that turns out the pizza. *800 N. Magnolia Ave., Orlando, tel. 407/839–0630. Weekend reservations advised. Dress: casual. AE, DC, MC, V. Closed Sat. lunch and Sun.*

Mexican **Border Cantina.** With its pink walls and neon lights, this third-floor restaurant at the southern end of Winter Park's Park Avenue is trendy Tex-Mex. But the kitchen does fajitas better than most, and the salsa is a fresh, chunky mix that will suit all tastes. Ask for something hotter if you prefer. *329 S. Park Ave., Winter Park, tel. 407/740–7227. Dress: casual. Reservations advised. AE, MC, V.*

$

Middle **Phoenician.** This is the latest addition to the rich culinary clique
Eastern at the Marketplace. Hummus flavored with tahini, *babaganoush*
$ (roasted eggplant purée), and *lebneh* (soft, seasoned, yogurt-based cheese) top the menu. The best bet is to order a tableful of mezes and then sample as many as possible. *7600 Dr. Phillips Blvd., in the Marketplace, Orlando, tel. 407/345–1001. No reservations. Dress: casual. AE, MC, V.*

Pizza
$–$$

Donato's. This family-owned restaurant, the only one on the north end of International Drive, is just steps away from the Belz Factory Outlet Mall. There's a takeout deli and grocery store as you walk in. But taking the time to eat in one of the two large dining rooms is worthwhile. Although the decor is delicatessen, the food is abundant and well prepared. There's real New York pizza, which you can order by the slice, or you can choose from a variety of southern Italian veal, chicken, or pasta dishes served with salad and either plain or garlic bread. Submarine sandwiches, deli sandwiches, and calzones round things out. *5159 International Dr., Orlando, tel. 407/363–5959. Reservations not necessary. Dress: casual. AE, DC, MC, V.*

Enzo's at the Marketplace. This pizzeria and deli combines the real Italian flavor of its Longwood sister with an atmosphere that's casual and a location that's more convenient for tourists. Owner Enzo Perlini, a food purist, imported the pizza ovens from Italy to ensure that his *pizza napoli* would have the proper thin, crispy crust. It does. The toppings are Italian style—fresh tomatoes and mozzarella, seafood, or grilled vegetables. If you don't feel like pizza, order the chicken cacciatore—a half bird served in a tangy marinara sauce—or one of the many pasta dishes (the chicken ravioli is a good bet). The deli has takeout. *7600 Dr. Phillips Blvd., in the Marketplace, Orlando, tel. 407/351–1187. Dress: casual. AE, D, DC, MC, V.*

★ **Positano.** One side of this cheerful restaurant is a bustling family-style pizza parlor; the other is a more formal dining room. Although you can't order pizza in the dining room, you can get anything on the entire menu in the pizzeria, which serves some of the best New York–style pies in central Florida. Try the unusual and piquant *ziti aum, aum*—ziti with mozzarella, Parmesan, eggplant, and basil in a tomato sauce. The delicious homemade soups—which are included in the full dinner—can also be a meal in themselves. Dessert offerings are all old reliables: spumoni, tortoni, and cannoli. If this place were on Disney property, it would be much more pricey—and you'd still be getting a good deal. *8995 West Colonial Dr., in Good Homes Plaza, Orlando, tel. 407/291–0602. Reservations in dining room only. Dress: casual. AE, D, DC, MC, V.*

Seafood
$$

Straub's Fine Seafood. Seafood restaurants in Orlando are surprisingly ordinary for a city that's so close to the coast. For adequate seafood at fair prices, try the Straub's establishments, which look like upscale coffee shops (with booths and Formica-topped tables with no tablecloths). The crab cakes, one of the better choices, are put together with plenty of fresh lump crabmeat and only a small amount of breadcrumbs. If you want fish, ask your server which is the freshest; you can order it blackened, grilled, or sautéed, with salad or coleslaw, and red potatoes or rice pilaf. The menu states the calorie count and fat content of every fish. *5101 E. Colonial Dr., Orlando, tel. 407/273–9330, and 512 E. Altamonte Dr., Altamonte Springs, tel. 407/831–2250. Reservations accepted. AE, D, DC, MC, V.*

Steak
$$$

Del Frisco's Prime Steak House. Orlando finally has a genuine New York–style steak house to call its own. The sound of Ol' Blue

Eyes belting the standards swirls about a clubby dining room, where big, juicy sirloins and porterhouses are the entrées of choice. Start with tomatoes and sliced onions with blue cheese vinaigrette or a crisp Caesar salad. Château potatoes and chopped spinach mixed with melted cheddar cheese and bacon bits come with the steaks and are sure to blow your low-fat diet. If you don't think you're up to devouring what seems like half a cow, try the lobster tails or some tender veal chops. This is decadent eating, but hey, you're on vacation. *729 Lee Rd., Orlando, tel. 407/645-4443. Reservations advised. Dress: casual but neat. AE, DC, MC, V. Closed Sun.*

$$ Linda's La Cantina. Twenty years ago, when this steak house was in a little frame house, customers would line up on its doorstep to eat the juicy, oversize New York strip and porterhouse steaks. A few years ago the owners replaced the original building with a big, unattractive, barnlike structure. But loyal customers still wait eagerly (though now in a bar around a fireside pit). Without exception this is Orlando's best and most popular steak house. Other than spaghetti with meat sauce, which is tasty, the Italian food seems offered only to fill up the menu. *4721 E. Colonial Dr., Orlando, tel. 407/894-4491. Reservations advised. Dress: casual. AE, DC, MC, V. Lunch only; closed Sun. and Mon.*

Thai **Siam Orchid.** One of Orlando's several elegant Asian restau-
$$ rants, Siam Orchid occupies a gorgeous structure a bit off I-Drive. Waitresses, who wear costumes from their homeland, serve authentic fare such as Siam wings—a chicken wing stuffed to look like a drumstick—and *pla lad prig,* a whole, deep-fried fish covered with a sauce flavored with red chili, bell peppers, and garlic. If you like your food spicy, say "Thai hot" and grab a fire extinguisher. Otherwise, a request to make a dish spicy will be answered with a smile, and your food will come merely mild. *7575 Republic Dr., Orlando, tel. 407/351-0821. Reservations advised. Dress: casual. AE, DC, MC, V.*

24-Hour **Beeline Diner.** This slick 1950s-style diner in the Peabody Hotel
$$ is not exactly cheap, but the salads, sandwiches, and griddle foods are tops. Though very busy at times, it can be fun for breakfast or a late-night snack. And for just a little silver, you get to play a lot of old tunes on the jukebox. *9801 International Dr., Orlando, tel. 407/352-4000. Dress: casual. AE, DC, MC, V.*

Vietnamese **Little Saigon.** As Orlando flourishes, so grow the ethnic restau-
$ rants, including a variety of Vietnamese eateries and shops, about 1½ miles east of I-4's U.S. 50 exit. The folks at Little Saigon are friendly and love to introduce novices to their healthy and delicious national cuisine. Sample the spring rolls or the summer rolls (spring roll filling in a soft wrapper), then move on to the grilled pork and egg, served atop rice and noodles, or the traditional soup, filled with noodles, rice, vegetables, and your choice of either chicken or seafood; ask to have extra meat in the soup if you're hungry, and be sure they bring you the mint and bean sprouts to sprinkle in. Ask for an English-speaking waiter if you're unfamiliar with the cuisine. *1106 E. Colonial Dr.,*

Orlando, tel. 407/423–8539. Reservations advised. Dress: casual. Beer and wine only. MC, V.

West Indian **The Spicy Pot.** One taste of the food in this luncheonette in a
$ rather dingy shopping center will take you straight to Trinidad. The roti sandwich is wrapped around a delicately spiced and curried filling of your choice—vegetable, potato, beef, or chicken. Be sure to drink sorrel or *mauby*, nonalcoholic beverages made from the bark of trees and the perfect accompaniment to the hot food. The traditional entrée is Jamaican jerk chicken, very spicy chunks of poultry served with vegetables and rice. On weekends there's music and dancing in a back room. The neighborhood is not appealing, but it's safe. *6203 Silver Star Rd., Orlando, tel. 407/297–8255. Dress: casual. No credit cards. Beer and wine only. Closed Sun. and Mon.*

Off the Beaten Track

Continental **Chalet Suzanne.** If you like to drive or are returning from a day
$$$$ at Cypress Gardens, consider making a dinner reservation at
★ this family-owned country inn and restaurant. Because of its charm and originality, Chalet Suzanne has earned praise from restaurant critics—and for good reason. It should provide one of the most memorable dining experiences of your Orlando stay. Expanded bit by quirky bit since it opened in the 1930s, this unlikely country inn looks like a small Swiss village—right in the middle of the orange groves. The furniture is a hodgepodge from all over the world. The place settings, china, glasses, chairs, and even the tables are of different sizes, shapes, and origins, which all work together strangly enough as the expression of a single sensibility. As an appetizer, try the broiled grapefruit, basted with a butter, cinnamon, and sugar mixture and served with a grilled chicken liver; then move on to shrimp curry, lobster Newburg, or filet mignon. Crepes Suzanne are a good bet for dessert. All meals are prix fixe, with seven courses; prices begin at $40 and are determined by the cost of your entrée. The wine list offers many excellent choices at reasonable prices. Guests may step into the cellar to taste some of the wines being featured that night. *3800 Chalet Suzanne Dr., U.S. 27 north of Lake Wales, about 10 mi past Cypress Gardens turnoff, tel. 813/676–6011. Reservations advised. Jacket required. AE, DC, MC, V. Closed Mon. in summer.*

9 Lodging

*Updated by
Edward
Schmidt Jr.*

Since Orlando's birth as a tourist mecca, the town's hotel business has boomed, and the number of hotels, motels, and resorts in the Orlando area is now simply astounding. There are more than 82,000 hotel rooms, and new ones of all sizes and varieties seem to open every day. Just about every U.S. hotel chain has at least one hotel in the vicinity. In the early days of Walt Disney World, the largest hotels tended to be on Disney property, but that has changed as convention business has taken off, and plenty of big properties now keep company on International Drive with the smaller ones that have been around for a long time.

Your basic options come down to properties that are (1) owned and operated by Disney on WDW grounds, (2) not owned or operated by Disney but located on Disney property, and (3) not located on WDW property. There are advantages to each.

How to Choose

When examining your options, give careful thought to the kind of vacation you want. Consider what you want to see during your Orlando visit and how long you want to stay. Within a given price category, compare the facilities of the available establishments to make sure that you get exactly what you want; our charts (*see below*) will help you do this. Don't overlook the savings to be gained from cooking your own breakfast and maybe a few other meals as well, which you can do if you choose an establishment with cooking facilities. If you're traveling with children, remember to ask about the cutoff age, the age at which the management considers your offspring to be adults (and makes you pay accordingly, even when they share your room).

**Staying in
WDW**

If you are coming to Orlando for only a few days and are interested solely in the Magic Kingdom, Epcot Center, and the other Disney attractions, the resorts on Disney property—whether or not they're owned by Disney—are the most convenient. You won't have to drive, because Walt Disney World buses and monorails—free to guests at on-site resorts—are efficient enough to make it possible to visit one park in the morning and another in the afternoon. You have the freedom to return to your hotel for R&R when the crowds are thickest, and if it turns out that half the family wants to spend the afternoon in one of the parks and the other half wants to float around Typhoon Lagoon, it's easy.

On-site hotels were built with families in mind. Older children can travel on their own on the transportation system without inviting trouble. Younger children get a thrill from knowing that they're actually living in Walt Disney World. Rooms are usually large enough to accommodate up to five; villas sleep six or seven. All accommodations offer cable TV with the Disney Channel and a daily events channel.

As an on-site guest, you receive a number of other perks as well: You can call in advance to make reservations at any of the restaurants in Epcot Center and at Disney-MGM Studios. (Outsiders can make reservations only in person in the park on the day they wish to dine, and their choice of seating times may be limited.) For Disney dinner-show reservations, on-site guests go to the head of the line as well. They can book as far in advance as they wish. (Outsiders, however, can reserve seats only 30–45 days in advance.) In addition, each day on-site guests can get in to one of three parks one hour before regular park opening. Even when the theme parks or water parks have reached capacity—as River Country, Typhoon Lagoon, and Disney-MGM Studios sometimes do—on-site guests are guaranteed entry. Then there are the small conveniences: Guests at Disney-owned properties are able to charge to their room most meals and purchases throughout WDW. To golfers, it's important that Disney guests also get first choice of tee times at the busy golf courses.

Staying Around Orlando If you're planning to visit attractions other than WDW or if the Disney resorts seem too rich for your blood, then staying off-site may hold a number of advantages. You'll enjoy more peace and quiet and may often have easier access to Sea World and Universal Studios—as well as to Orlando's shopping, dining, and entertainment facilities. Best of all, you're almost certain to save money.

The hotels closest to Walt Disney World are clustered in several principal areas: along International Drive within Orlando city limits; within the boundaries of Kissimmee, the town that is actually closest to Walt Disney World (where hotels tend to be small and cheap); and in the Disney Maingate area around WDW's northernmost entrance, just off I–4. Nearly every hotel in these areas provides frequent transportation to and from Walt Disney World. In addition, there are some noteworthy—if far-flung—options in the suburbs and the Greater Orlando area. Since the city isn't so big, even apparently distant properties are seldom much more than a half hour's drive from Disney toll plazas. If you're willing to make the commute, you're likely to save a bundle: Whereas accommodations at the Embassy Suites near Lake Buena Vista will cost you upwards of $120 a night, the sister property 30–40 minutes away in Altamonte Springs charges around $80 for equally luxurious quarters. Some of the simpler motels with Kissimmee addresses will put you up for $40 a night or even less.

Reservations

All on-site accommodations may be booked through the **Walt Disney World Central Reservations Office** (Box 10100, Suite 300, Lake Buena Vista 32830, tel. 407/W–DISNEY, or 934–7639); persons with disabilities can call **WDW Special Request Reservations** (tel. 407/354–1853; TTY 407/939–7670) to get information or book rooms. (*See* Hints for Travelers with Disabilities in Chapter 1 for more information.) Rooms at most non-Disney, chain hotels can be reserved by calling either the hotel itself or the toll-free number for the entire chain. Be sure to tell the reservationist exactly what you are looking for—Disney-owned property or not, price range, the number of people in your party, and the dates of your visit. If possible, stay flexible about dates;

many hotels and attractions offer seasonal discounts of up to 40%.

Deposits You must give a deposit for your first night's stay within three weeks of making your reservation. At many hotels you can get a refund if you cancel at least five days before your scheduled stay. However, individual hotel policies vary, and some properties may require up to 15 days' notice for a full refund. Check before booking.

When to Book Reservations should be made several months in advance—as much as a year in advance for the best rooms during high season.

Other Options If neither the WDW Central Reservations Office nor the off-site hotels have space on your preferred dates, try for an independent package such as those available through American Express and Delta; such operators have many rooms allotted to them for their travel packages. And because there are always cancellations, it's worth trying even at the last minute; for same-day bookings, call the property directly. *See* Chapter 1 for more on tours, packages, and seasons.

Packages, including cruises, car rentals, and hotels both on and off Disney property, can be arranged through your travel agent or **Walt Disney Travel Co.** (1675 Buena Vista Dr., Lake Buena Vista 32830, tel. 800/828–0228).

Ratings and Rates

Highly recommended properties are indicated by a star ★. Unless otherwise noted, rates are for two adults traveling during high season with up to two children under 18. Rates are lowest from early January to mid-February, from mid-April to mid-June, and from mid-August to December 20; low rates often remain in place longer at non-Disney properties. Always call several places—availability and special deals can often drive room rates at a "$$$$" hotel down into the "$$" range—and don't forget to ask if you're eligible for a discount. Many hotels offer special rates for members of, for example, the American Automobile Association or the American Association of Retired Persons.

Category	Cost*
$$$$	over $180
$$$	$120–$180
$$	$65–$120
$	under $65

All prices are for a double room, excluding 10% tax.

Walt Disney World Lodging

Name of Property	Number of Rooms/Suites	Number of Restaurants	Number of Lounges	Room Service	Complimentary Breakfast	
$$$$						
Buena Vista Palace and Palace Suite Resort	1,028	5	4	√		
Contemporary Resort	1,053	4	5	√		
Disney's Village Resort	592	4	4	√		
Fort Wilderness Resort Trailers	350	2	5			
Grand Cypress Resort	750	5	6	√		
Grand Floridian	901	5	4	√		
Hilton at WDW Village	813	7	2	√		
Marriott's Orlando World Center	1,504	7	3	√		
Peabody Orlando	891	3	2	√		
Polynesian Resort	855	3	4	√		
Stouffer Orlando Resort	778	5	2	√		
Vistana Resort	760	2	2			
WDW Beach and Yacht Club Resorts	1,215	5	5	√		
WDW Dolphin	1,510	8	3	√		
WDW Swan	758	3	3	√		
$$$						
Embassy Suites Hotel at Plaza International	246		1		√	
Embassy Suites International Drive South	245	1	1		√	
Embassy Suites Orlando—North	210	1	1	√	√	
Embassy Suites Resort Lake Buena Vista	280	1	2		√	
Grosvenor Resort	630	2	2	√		
Guest Quarters Suite Resort	229	1	1		√	
Howard Johnson at WDW Village	323	1	1			

	In-Room Kitchenettes	In-Room Microwaves	In-Room Coffeemaker	In-Room VCR	No. Swimming Pools	No. Tennis Courts (Lighted)	On-Site Golf	Arcade Game Room	Health Club	Boating	Supervised Children's Program	Baby-Sitting	Guest Laundry
	√	√	√	√	2	3(L)		√	√		√	√	√
					3	6(L)		√	√	√	√	√	√
	√	√	√		6	3(L)		√	√	√			
	√	√	√		2	2(L)		√		√	√	√	√
					2	12(L)	√	√	√	√	√	√	√
					1	2(L)		√	√	√	√	√	√
					2	2(L)		√	√		√	√	√
					4	12(L)	√	√	√		√	√	√
					1	4(L)		√	√		√	√	√
					2			√		√	√	√	√
					1	5(L)		√	√		√	√	√
					5	14(L)		√	√		√	√	√
					3	2(L)		√	√	√	√	√	√
					4	8(L)		√	√		√	√	√
					2	8(L)		√	√		√	√	√
	√	√	√		1			√	√			√	
					1							√	√
	√	√	√		1				√				
					1	1		√	√		√	√	
			√	√	2	2(L)		√	√			√	√
		√	√		1	2(L)		√	√			√	√
			√		3			√				√	√

Name of Property	Number of Rooms/Suites	Number of Restaurants	Number of Lounges	Room Service	Complimentary Breakfast	
Parc Corniche Resort	210	1	1			
Sol Orlando Resort	150	1	1		√	
Sonesta Villa Resort Orlando	369	2	1			
Summerfield Suites Hotel	146		1		√	
WDW Wilderness Lodge	729	2	3	√		
$$						
All-Star Sports and All-Star Music Resorts	1,920	2*	1			
Best Western Kissimmee	281	1	1			
Caribbean Beach Resort	2,112	1*	2			
Chalet Suzanne	30	1	1	√	√	
Clarion Plaza Hotel	810	2	2	√		
Crown Hotel	34	1	1			
Dixie Landings Resort	2,048	1/1*	1			
Doubletree Club Hotel	167	1	1	√		
Enclave Suites at Orlando	321	1	1			
Holiday Inn Maingate East	670	6	2	√		
Holiday Inn Sunspree Resort	507	1	1	√		
Hyatt Orlando Hotel	948	4	1			
Orlando Heritage Inn	150	1	1	√		
Orlando North Hilton and Towers	325	1	1	√		
Park Plaza Hotel	27	1	1	√	√	
Port Orleans Resort	1,008	1/1*	2			
Quality Suites Maingate East	225	1	2		√	
Radisson Inn Maingate	580	1	2	√		

*Food Court

In-Room Kitchenettes	In-Room Microwaves	In-Room Coffeemaker	In-Room VCR	No. Swimming Pools	No. Tennis Courts (Lighted)	On-Site Golf	Arcade Game Room	Health Club	Boating	Supervised Children's Program	Baby-Sitting	Guest Laundry
√	√	√	√	1		√	√				√	√
√	√	√		1	1		√	√			√	√
√	√	√		1	2(L)		√		√	√	√	√
√	√	√	√	1			√	√				√
				1			√		√	√	√	√
				2			√				√	√
√				2		√						
		√		6			√			√	√	√
				1					√			√
				1							√	√
				1								
				6		√	√			√		√
				1				√				
√	√	√		3	1(L)			√			√	√
√	√	√	√	2	2(L)		√				√	√
√	√	√	√	1						√		
				4	2(L)		√				√	√
				1							√	√
				1								
											√	√
				1			√				√	√
√	√	√		1			√					√
				1	2(L)						√	√

Name of Property	Number of Rooms/Suites	Number of Restaurants	Number of Lounges	Room Service	Complimentary Breakfast	
Ramada Resort Maingate at the Parkway	716	1	1			
Residence Inn by Marriott on Lake Cecile	160				√	
Royal Plaza	396	2	2			
Sheraton Lakeside Inn	651	2	1	√		
Travelodge Hotel	325	1	1			
Twin Towers Hotel and Convention Center	760	2	3	√		
$						
Casa Rosa Inn	54					
Comfort Inn Maingate	281	1	1			
Days Inn Orlando/Lakeside	695	1				
Fairfield Inn by Marriott	135					
Fort Wilderness Resort Campsites	825	2	5			
Knights Inn—Maingate	119					
Park Inn International	197	1				
Quality Inn Lake Cecile	222	1	1			
Record Motel	57					
Red Roof Inn	102					
Sevilla Inn	46					
Shades of Green on WDW Resort	288	2	1	√		
Wynfield Inn—Westwood	300		1			

In-Room Kitchenettes	In-Room Microwaves	In-Room Coffeemaker	In-Room VCR	No. Swimming Pools	No. Tennis Courts (Lighted)	On-Site Golf	Arcade Game Room	Health Club	Boating	Supervised Children's Program	Baby-Sitting	Guest Laundry
				1	2(L)							√
√	√	√	√	1	1				√			√
				1	4(L)		√				√	√
				3	4		√		√	√	√	√
		√		1			√				√	√
				1			√	√		√	√	√
				1								√
				1			√				√	√
√	√	√		3			√					√
				1			√					
				2	2(L)		√		√	√	√	√
√				1								
√				1			√				√	√
				1								√
				1								√
				1								√
				1								√
				2	2(L)	√	√	√			√	√
				2			√					√

Disney Hotels in WDW

Traditionally, guests have had to take a heavy hit in the wallet to stay in Disney-owned hotels. During the past several years, however, the number of moderately priced properties has boomed. With a wide selection of price ranges available, most lodging decisions come down to what area of WDW or what style hotel strikes your fancy. Resort hotels predominate but there are also campsites, trailers, and kitchen-equipped suites and villas. These accommodations are clustered together in four sections of Walt Disney World.

The **Magic Kingdom resort area** has ritzy hotels, all of which lie on the Magic Kingdom monorail route and are only minutes away from the park. Fort Wilderness Campground Resort, with trailers and RV and tent sites, is just southeast of this area. The **Epcot resort area,** south of the park, includes the luxurious Beach and Yacht Club resorts, as well as the popular Caribbean Beach Resort. Disney has plans to open another high-end property—with a Northeastern-boardwalk theme—in Epcot Center by summer '96. The **Disney Village resort area,** east of Epcot Center, is conveniently located near Pleasure Island and the Disney Village Marketplace. Accommodations include two mid-priced, Southern-themed resorts, as well as the Disney Village Resort, which has town houses and villas equipped with kitchens. The newest complex, **All-Star Village,** lies near the intersection of World Drive and U.S. 192, south of Epcot and the Magic Kingdom. The first two resorts, both moderately priced, are scheduled to open there between summer 1994 and early 1995.

Magic Kingdom Resort Area

Resort Hotels $$$$ ★ **Contemporary Resort.** Since the monorail runs right through the middle, this awkwardly modern 15-story A-frame feels like something straight out of Tomorrowland. But otherwise, what you've got is a place that always seems to be bustling in the best '90s fashion, from the crack of dawn until after midnight. Half the rooms are in the Tower, the main building, and these are the hotel's most expensive because of their spectacular views. (Those in the front look out toward the Magic Kingdom's Cinderella Castle, a great backdrop for the flaming Florida sunsets and a nightly fireworks show, while those on the back side have ringside seats for the Electrical Water Pageant and the sunrise through the mists of Bay Lake.) If you spring for 14th-floor all-suites, you'll enjoy the additional amenities of a new concierge package: free valet parking, afternoon tea, wine and cheese at night, fruit and juice in the morning, and nightly turndown. Tower rooms can be somewhat noisy at night—sounds rise through the busy atrium—so if you're a light sleeper, you may prefer a room in the hotel's North and South Gardens, where the other half of the rooms are located. Overlooking the hotel's pool and gardens, these cost less than Tower rooms; the best are on the shore of Bay Lake. (Try to avoid units described as having a view of the Magic Kingdom—they have an even better view of the parking lot.) Regardless of location, all rooms have a small terrace and most have two queen-size beds and a small additional bed, though you can request a room with a king-size bed and double sofa bed. Many recreational facilities are right on the property; one of the swimming pools is WDW's largest. The fast-paced Top of the World offers nightly Broadway revues and live jazz with dinner or drinks. Kids will enjoy meeting the Disney characters who show up for breakfast and dinner in the Contemporary Café. They'll also be happy to disappear into the Fiesta Fun Center, one of the biggest game rooms ever. It's also hard to beat the Contemporary's location. The monorail can take you to the Polynesian and Grand Floridian hotels as well as to the Magic Kingdom and Epcot Center; you can catch a motor launch to Discovery Island, Fort Wilderness, and River Country; and it's relatively easy to get everywhere else by bus. *WDW Central Reservations, Box 10100, Lake Buena Vista 32830, tel. 407/934–7639 or 407/824–1000 for same-day reservations. 1,053 rooms. Facilities: 4 restaurants, 2 snack bars, 5 lounges, room service, 3 heated outdoor pools, lakeside beach, beauty salon, health club, 6 lighted tennis courts, supervised children's program, baby-sitting, volleyball, shuffleboard, boat rentals, water skiing, game room, guest laundry, concierge services. AE, MC, V.*

★ **Grand Floridian.** At first you might think that Disney transported this gilded-age masterpiece from some turn-of-the-century coastal hot spot to the shores of the Seven Seas Lagoon. Not so. The gabled red roof, brick chimneys, and rambling verandas were all built from scratch on the site. Loving attention was paid to each detail, from the crystal chandeliers and stained-glass domes to the ornate balconies and aviary. Although equipped with every modern convenience, the softly colored rooms have real vintage charm, especially the attic nooks, up under the eaves. Even the resort's monorail station carries the elegant Victorian theme. There are many facilities, and the hotel is on the monorail and motor launch and bus lines. *WDW Central Reservations, Box 10100, Lake Buena Vista 32830, tel. 407/934–7639 or 407/824–3000. 901 rooms and suites. Facilities: 5 restaurants, 4 lounges, room service, large outdoor heated pool, beach, whirlpool, health club, 2 lighted tennis courts, marina, boat rentals, supervised children's program, baby-sitting, playground, guest laundry, concierge services. AE, MC, V.*

Polynesian Resort. The Great Ceremonial House, where visitors check in, sets the mood at this resort, the most popular of all owned by Disney. Right in the middle of the atrium, orchids bloom alongside coconut palms, and volcanic rock fountains create the constant sound of running water. If it weren't for the kids running around in Mickey Mouse caps, you might think you were in Fiji. Rooms are in 11 two- and three-story "longhouses" stretching from this main building. All offer two queen-size beds and a smaller sleeper sofa to accommodate up to five, and except for some second-floor rooms, all have a balcony or patio. If you want to be near the main building, request a room in the Bora Bora or Maui longhouses (named for exotic Pacific Islands, like all similar structures here). For the best view of the Magic Kingdom and the sandy, palm-trimmed Seven Seas Lagoon, stay in

Best Western
Kissimmee, **50**

Buena Vista
Palace, **24**

Casa Rosa Inn, **49**

Chalet Suzanne, **37**

Clarion Plaza
Hotel, **13**

Comfort Inn
Maingate, **35**

Crown Hotel, **1**

Days Inn-Orlando/
Lakeside, **6**

Doubletree Club
Hotel, **18**

Embassy Suites
International Drive
South, **10**

Embassy Suites at
Plaza International, **8**

Embassy Suites
Resort Lake Buena
Vista, **21**

Embassy Suites
Orlando North, **4**

The Enclave Suites at
Orlando, **7**

Fairfield Inn
by Marriott, **11**

Grand Cypress
Resort, **20**

Grosvenor
Resort, **30**

Guest Quarters Suite
Resort, **22**

Hilton at WDW
Village, **28**

Holiday Inn
Sunspree Resort
Lake Buena
Vista, **26**

Holiday Inn Main Gate
East, **41**

Howard Johnson
Resort at Walt Disney
World Village, **27**

Hyatt Orlando
Hotel, **39**

Knights Inn-
Maingate, **42**

Marriott's Orlando
World Center, **30**

Orlando Heritage
Inn, **14**

Orlando North Hilton
and Towers, **5**

Parc Corniche
Resort, **19**

Park Inn
International, **43**

Park Plaza Hotel, **3**

Peabody Orlando, **12**

Quality Inn Lake
Cecile, **37**

Quality Suites
Maingate East, **40**

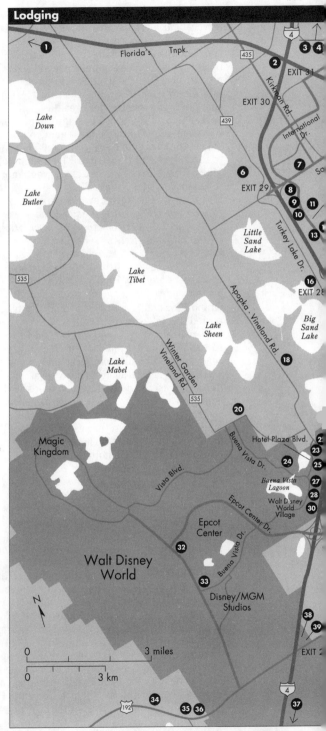

Lodging

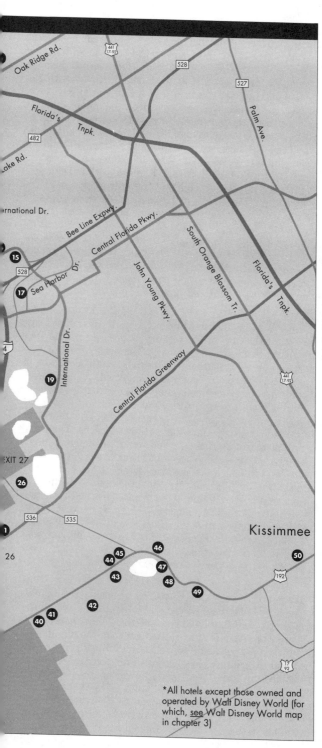

Radisson Inn Maingate, **36**

Ramada Resort Maingate at the Parkway, **38**

The Residence Inn by Marriott on Lake Cecile, **47**

Record Motel, **46**

Red Roof Inn, **45**

Royal Plaza, **23**

Sevilla Inn, **48**

Sheraton Lakeside Inn, **34**

Sol Orlando Resort, **44**

Sonesta Villa Resort Orlando, **16**

Stouffer Orlando Resort, **17**

Summerfield Suites Hotel, **9**

Travelodge Hotel, **25**

Twin Towers Hotel and Convention Center, **2**

Vistana Resort, **29**

Walt Disney World Dolphin, **32**

Walt Disney World Swan, **33**

Wynfield Inn-Westwood, **15**

*All hotels except those owned and operated by Walt Disney World (for which, see Walt Disney World map in chapter 3)

Samoa, Moorea, or Tonga. Lagoon-view rooms—the priciest—
are the most peaceful and include a host of upgraded amenities
and services that make them among the most sought after in
Walt Disney World. They also have a perfect view of the sparkling, once-nightly Electrical Water Pageant. Rooms with garden and pool view are slightly less quiet and slightly less
expensive; least expensive rooms overlook the other buildings,
the monorail, and the parking lot across the street. One of the
two pools is an extravagantly landscaped, free-form affair with
rocks and caverns; both are great for (and beloved of) children,
so if you want peace and quiet, head for the beach. Other recreational activities center on the hotel's marina, which rents sail-
boats, motorboats, and an eight-person outrigger canoe. The
Neverland Club, the hotel's child-care center, even offers its
guests a dinner show. No wonder more than half of the guests
have been here before. *WDW Central Reservations, Box 10100,
Lake Buena Vista 32830, tel. 407/934–7639 or 407/824–2000 for
same-day reservations. 855 rooms. Facilities: 3 restaurants, snack
bar, 4 lounges, room service, 2 outdoor heated pools, lakeside beach,
boating, beauty salon, barbershop, game room, playground, guest
laundry, supervised children's program, baby-sitting, concierge
services. AE, MC, V.*

$$$ **Walt Disney World Wilderness Lodge.** Guests at this rustic lodge
modeled after the turn-of-the-century structures in America's
national parks won't exactly rough it. The pricey, six-story es-
tablishment opened in summer 1994 on the southwest shore of
Bay Lake. Its centerpiece is a massive lobby with a huge, three-
sided stone fireplace, enormous chandeliers with iron bands in-
cised with silhouettes of Indians and buffalo, and two giant
totem poles that soar 55 feet. All over the property there are
porches, reading areas, and other intimate spaces. The large
swimming pool area begins as a hot spring in the main lobby,
flows under a window wall to become "Silver Creek" in an upper
courtyard, and widens into a rushing waterfall. You can satisfy
a hankerin' for buffalo, elk, or other unusual western-style
dishes at Artist Point, a dining room inspired by the Craftsman
era and featuring oversize landscapes of the Northwest. *WDW
Central Reservations, Box 10100, Lake Buena Vista 32830, tel.
407/934–7639. 729 rooms. Facilities: 3 restaurants, lounge, room
service, large heated swimming pool, children's pool, golf, game
room, guest laundry, supervised children's program, baby-sitting.
AE, MC, V.*

**Camp and
Trailer Sites**   The 780 acres of scrubby pine, tiny streams, and peaceful canals
known as **Fort Wilderness Resort and Campground** are on the
shore of subtropical Bay Lake opposite the Contemporary Re-
sort. There's always a feeling of excitement in the air, but the
mood is extremely relaxed (for Walt Disney World). There are
plenty of sports facilities and a marina where you can rent boats
to go out on Bay Lake. And though everyone has access to
WDW's River Country water playground, it's right at the door-
step of those who lodge in Fort Wilderness. To experience this
property, you can either bring your own trailer or tent and park
it at a site along the narrow blacktopped roads that meander

through the woods or rent one of the fully equipped RVs parked on the property (*see below*). *WDW Central Reservations, Box 10100, Lake Buena Vista 32830, tel. 407/W–DISNEY or 407/824–2900 for same-day reservations. Facilities: cafeteria, snack bar, grocery store, 2 outdoor heated pools, lakeside beach, bike paths, bike and canoe rental, jogging trail, petting farm, riding stable, guest laundry, game room, volleyball.*

$$$$ **Rental trailers.** For *House Beautiful* decor, stick to the resort hotels. Otherwise, these perfectly comfortable accommodations—more Motel 6 than Ritz-Carlton—are an excellent choice; they put the relaxed friendliness of Fort Wilderness within reach of families who haven't brought their own RV. The larger trailers can accommodate four grown-ups and two youngsters; the bedroom has a double bed and a bunk bed, and the living room has a double sleeper sofa or Murphy bed. The smaller trailers, without the bunk beds, sleep four. Both types come with full kitchen, a comfortable bathroom, air-conditioning, heat, daily housekeeping services, outdoor grill and picnic table, and even a color TV set with cable. *408 60- and 80-foot trailers.*

$ **RV and tent sites.** Bringing a tent or RV to Walt Disney World is
★ one of the cheapest ways to actually stay on WDW property, especially considering that sites accommodate up to 10. Tent sites with water and electricity are real bargains. RV sites cost more but come equipped with electrical, water, and sewage hookups as well as outdoor charcoal grills and picnic tables; you can even get maid service for your trailer. "Preferred sites," those closest to the lake (numbering from 100 to 500, in the 700s, and in the 1400s), have higher prices. *784 sites, 694 trailer hookups with water and electrical power and sewage hookups, 90 tent sites with water and electric hookups.*

Epcot Resort Area

Resort **Walt Disney World Beach and Yacht Club Resorts.** These two re-
Hotels latively new properties on a 25-acre lake, both accessible from
$$$$ Epcot Center via a boardwalk, are New England inns on a grand
★ scale. The five-story Yacht Club recalls the turn-of-the-century New England seacoast, with its hardwood floors, gleaming brass, gray clapboard facade, and evergreen landscaping; there's even a lighthouse on its pier. Rooms are similarly nautical. Equally impressive is the blue-and-white, three- to five-story Beach Club, where a croquet lawn, cabana-dotted white-sand beach, and staffers' 19th-century Jams and T-shirts set the scene. Guest rooms are summery, with wicker and pastel furnishings. Both establishments are refreshingly unstuffy, just right for families. Though each has its own restaurants and shops, the pair share certain facilities—the Sand Castle Club for children, a game room, a health club, and a huge water-recreation area with several sections of varying depths and a sandy bottom; there's even a shipwreck to clamber over (its mast is one long, exciting water slide). So far, Disney's attempts to introduce live freshwater fish here haven't worked. Maybe by the

time you check in, this great idea will have panned out. *WDW Central Reservations, Box 10100, Lake Buena Vista 32830, tel. 407/934–7639 or 407/934–8000 (Beach) and 407/934–7000 (Yacht). 1,215 rooms. Facilities: 5 restaurants, 5 lounges, room service, 2¹/₂-acre heated pool with water slides and 2 other pools, marina with boat rentals, health club, beauty salon, florist, guest laundry, golf, 2 lighted tennis courts, croquet court, volleyball court, concierge services, supervised program for children 3–12 (4:30–midnight), baby-sitting. AE, MC, V.*

$$ **Caribbean Beach Resort.** The first of Disney's moderately priced
★ accommodations, this immensely popular 200-acre property surrounding a 42-acre lake, just east of the Epcot Center and Disney-MGM Studios theme parks, is composed of five palm-studded island "villages," awash with the bright colors of the Caribbean. Each village is a complex of two-story buildings named for a different Caribbean island—Aruba, Barbados, Jamaica, Martinique, and Trinidad—and each has its own pool, guest laundry, and stretch of white-sand beach. Bridges over the lake connect the mainland with 1-acre, path-crossed Parrot Cay, where there's a play area for children. The hub of the resort is a building called Port Royale, which has a food court and a tropical lounge. The attractive, pastel-hued guest rooms, equipped with minibars and coffeemakers, are smaller than rooms in more expensive Disney resorts, but perfectly comfortable for smaller families. A promenade skirts the shores of the lake and makes for pleasant walking, jogging, and biking. You don't have the dining options that you do at other hotels in the same price range. Otherwise, the only thing missing is a supervised children's program. *WDW Central Reservations, Box 10100, Lake Buena Vista 32830, tel. 407/W–DISNEY. 2,112 rooms. Facilities: food court, 2 lounges, whirlpool, large heated outdoor pool with pirate fort and adjacent children's pool, 5 smaller pools, beach, playground, game room, bike rentals, marina with boat rentals, concierge services, minibar and coffeemaker in rooms, guest laundry, jogging track, baby-sitting. AE, MC, V.*

Disney Village Resort Area

Resort **Dixie Landings Resort.** While a mouse inspired the Magic King-
Hotels dom, Disney's Imagineers drew inspiration from the architec-
$$ ture of the Old South for this sprawling, moderately priced resort complex northwest of Disney Village Marketplace and Lake Buena Vista, not far from Fort Wilderness. Rooms, which accommodate four, are in three-story plantation-style mansions and two-story rustic bayou dwellings. The well-designed food court, Colonel's Cotton Mill and Market, offers burgers, sandwiches, breakfast items, and pizza (which can be delivered to your room upon request). The pool, a 3¹/₂-acre old-fashioned swimming-hole complex called Ol' Man Island, looks like something out of a Mark Twain novel; it has slides, rope swings, and an adjacent play area. A marina rents the usual Water Sprites and other craft. Alas, there's no children's program. Nonetheless, if you want to stay here, you'd better book early—rooms

go fast! *WDW Central Reservations, Box 10100, Lake Buena Vista 32830, tel. 407/W–DISNEY. 2,048 rooms. Facilities: food court, full-service restaurant, pizza delivery, whirlpool, large heated outdoor pools with adjacent children's pools, play area, golf, game room, boating, concierge services, guest laundry. AE, MC, V.*

Port Orleans Resort. Disney's version of New Orleans's French Quarter emulates the charm and romance of the original's old section but without the seediness. Ornate row-house buildings with wrought-iron balconies and hanging plants are clustered in small groups around squares that are anchored by stone fountains and lushly planted with magnolias and other typically Deep South trees. Throughout the complex, lamplit sidewalks edge the streets, which are named after authentic French Quarter thoroughfares. Crescent City specialties such as red beans and rice, jambalaya, Cajun chicken, beignets, and croissants are on the menu (along with the usual burgers, deli sandwiches, and pizza) at the Sassagoula Floatworks Factory, the hotel's food court. Bonfamille's Café, the hotel's full-service dining room, offers Creole and other Louisiana-style fare. Kids love the large, free-form pool ("Doubloon Lagoon"), which is one of the most exotic of all Disney hotel pools: The body of Neptune, a giant serpent, twists through the water and becomes a water slide; you zoom out through his mouth. The marina rents the usual assortment of boats. Note that most rooms here have two double beds and accommodate four; for quarters with one king-size bed, book early. The hotel doesn't have a child-care program. *WDW Central Reservations, Box 10100, Lake Buena Vista 32830, tel 407/W–DISNEY or 407/934–5502. 1,008 rooms. Facilities: food court, full-service restaurant, pizza delivery, whirlpool, large pool area, children's pool, game room, baby-sitting, concierge services, guest laundry, bike rentals. AE, MC, V.*

Villas with Kitchens If you're visiting WDW with your family or with a number of friends and want to stay together to avoid the expense of separate rooms, you may prefer to skip the resort hotels in favor of the five clusters of villas at **Disney's Village Resort,** in the Disney Village resort area; these share a single check-in point, the Village Resort Reception Center. Because none of these villa complexes are on the monorail, transportation to the parks can be slow. To get around within the village, a car or rented bike or golf cart is necessary. Free shuttle buses operate every 20 minutes to take you anywhere on the property. In addition, the accommodations are not quite as plush as those in the resort hotels. On the positive side, you get more space, not to mention proximity to great golf, WDW's most extensive shopping, and the lively after-dark action of Pleasure Island. *WDW Central Reservations, Box 10100, Lake Buena Vista 32830, tel. 407/934–7639 or 407/827–1100. Facilities: 4 restaurants, 4 lounges, room service, lounge, 6 outdoor pools (3 heated), in-room kitchenettes, game room, playground, health club, 3 lighted tennis courts, baby-sitting, guest laundry, boat rentals. AE, MC, V. Rates can vary depending on dates and party size.*

$$$$ **Grand Vista Suites.** These upscale, attractively furnished accommodations designed as prototypes for a housing development

are now available to rent. All the comforts of a luxury hotel are offered, including nightly turndown service and stocked refrigerators. *5 units.*

One-Bedroom Suites. The smallest and least expensive of the villas, these were designed to meet the needs of businesspeople attending meetings at the nearby WDW Conference Center. The accommodations are built of cedar and have one bedroom, a sofa bed in an adjacent sitting area, and a wet bar but no kitchen—they're the only villas without one. A few deluxe units with whirlpools sleep six, but most of the suites accommodate five. *324 units.*

One- and Two-Bedroom Villas. Originally built as the Vacation Villas and refurbished in 1986, these have complete living facilities with kitchens and either one or two bedrooms. The one-bedroom units have a king-size bed in one room and a queen-size sofa bed in the living room and sleep up to four. The two-bedroom units, which sleep six, have a sofa bed in the living room and either a king-size bed or two twins in each bedroom. *139 one-bedroom units, 87 two-bedroom units.*

★ **Treehouse Villas.** To really get away from it all, these out-of-the-way forest retreats on stilts, officially known as the Two-Bedroom Resort Villas with Study, are the best bet. Isolated within a peaceful, heavily wooded area ribboned with canals, these won't exactly make you feel like Tarzan or Jane, but the woods do occasionally reverberate with a howl or two late at night. All units accommodate six and have a kitchen and breakfast bar, two bathrooms, and two bedrooms with queen-size beds on the main level, plus a double-bedded study and a utility room with washer and dryer on a lower level. *60 units.*

Two-Bedroom Deluxe Villas. Built of cedar like the One-Bedroom Suites, these guest quarters are more tastefully decorated than those of some of the other villas and are very spacious. All have two bedrooms and a full loft and sleep up to six. They're right on the fairways of the Lake Buena Vista Golf Course. *64 units.*

All-Star Village

Resort Hotels
$$

All-Star Sports and All-Star Music Resorts. This large complex, in the northwest quadrant of the World Drive/U.S. 192 interchange, southwest of Disney-MGM Studios and Epcot Center, is the first phase of a project that is rumored to include a fourth major theme park. Though no one at Disney is confirming the speculation, gossip suggests that the new park will have an animal and jungle theme. Meanwhile, guests can enjoy the inventive design of the All-Star Sports Resort, which opened in summer 1994. Every aspect of the architecture, landscaping, and lighting display an over-the-top devotion to the theme: Five pairs of three-story buildings, each pair representing a different sport, include such eye-catching features as stairwells in the shape of soda cups, a courtyard that looks like a football field, and a pool shaped like a baseball infield. The rooms, each of which has two double beds, are intended to accommodate four. At press time, the opening date for the Music Resort had yet to be set. Music promises to have the same number of rooms, price scale, amenities, and layout as the Sports Resort—but look for Broadway, Country & Western, Calypso, Jazz, and Rock-and-Roll stylings to replace the sports paraphernalia. *WDW Central Reservations, Box 10100, Lake Buena Vista 32830, tel. 407/W– DISNEY. 1,920 rooms (at each). Facilities: food court, poolside bar, large pool area, guest laundry, game room, baby-sitting. AE, MC, V.*

Other Hotels in WDW

Although not operated by the Disney organization, the Swan and the Dolphin just outside Epcot Center, the military's Shades of Green Resort near the Magic Kingdom, and the seven hotels along Hotel Plaza Boulevard (by the Disney Village resort area) call themselves "official" Walt Disney World hotels. Having paid for the privilege, they are able to offer their guests many of the same courtesies available to guests at Disney-owned properties—for instance, telephone reservations for restaurants and dinner shows in Walt Disney World in advance of the general public. In addition, guests at any of the seven Hotel Plaza properties also receive a Preferred Guest Card; it provides discounts on meals and merchandise at each hotel, as well as unlimited transportation within Walt Disney World.

Hotel Plaza

$$$$ **Buena Vista Palace and Palace Suite Resort at Walt Disney World**
★ **Village.** This bold, modern hotel, the largest at Lake Buena Vista, seems small and quiet when you enter its lobby. Don't be fooled. Better indications of its enormity are its sprawl of parking lots, the height of its taller tower—27 stories—and its huge roster of facilities right down to a business center with translation and secretarial service. Restaurants and lounges include the Australian-theme Outback, which serves steaks and seafood; the Laughing Kookaburra Good Time Bar next door; and, at the top of the hotel, the Top of the Palace Lounge and the formal Arthur's 27 (*see* Chapter 8), which offer a ringside seat for the local sunsets and Epcot Center's nightly laser-and-fireworks show. Suites in the adjacent Palace Suite Resort, built in 1991, accommodate up to eight people and offer a nice alternative for larger families or people who just want extra space; these have private balconies, living rooms with sleeper sofas, and dining areas with appliances (sink, coffeemaker, microwave, and refrigerator). Both the new rooms and the originals have small balconies. Upper-floor rooms in the main hotel are more expensive; the best ones look out toward Epcot Center. Ask for a room in the main tower, where original rooms are, to avoid the late-night noise that reverberates through the atrium from the Kookaburra. All bedrooms come with one king- or two queen-size beds. *1900 Lake Buena Vista Dr, Lake Buena Vista 32830, tel. 407/827–2727 or 800/327–2990. 1,028 rooms. Facilities: 5 restaurants, 4 lounges, snack bar, room service, 1 indoor-outdoor heated*

pool, 1 heated outdoor lap pool, health club, whirlpool, playground, 3 lighted tennis courts, beauty salon, game room, business center, in-room kitchenettes, VCR in rooms, supervised children's program, baby-sitting, guest laundry. AE, DC, MC, V.

★ **Hilton at Walt Disney World Village.** One of the top establishments along Hotel Plaza Boulevard, the Hilton is also among the most expensive. Its facade is unimpressive, but after a recent $9-million renovation, public areas now sport a bright, tropical motif. A fountain, floral carpeting, shell-shaped cornices, and two large tanks of tropical fish enliven the lobby. The pool area has an attractive deck and gazebo. Guest rooms positively sparkle and, although not huge, are cozy and contemporary. Each has a king-size bed or two double beds, and amenities include cable TV plus in-room movies. The most expensive have views of Disney Village Marketplace and Lake Buena Vista, but poolview rooms are also good. Prices vary dramatically from one location, floor, and season to another. Keep in mind that if you must book a room at the lowest rate—on a lower floor with a mediocre view—the check-in clerk can assign you to a better room if one is available, at an extra charge of $30–$40. The luxurious rooms and suites on the 9th and 10th floors have a private lounge and their own check-in and checkout; rates include hors d'oeuvres in the late afternoon, complimentary Continental breakfast, and a newspaper each morning. Parents are particularly enthusiastic about the Hilton's Kids' Hotel, a supervised playroom with large-screen television and six-bed dormitory that operates every evening; meals are served on schedule, and the cost is $4 an hour. *1751 Hotel Plaza Blvd., Lake Buena Vista 32830, tel. 407/827–4000 or 800/782–4414 for reservations. 813 rooms. Facilities: 7 restaurants, 2 lounges, room service, Continental breakfast, 2 outdoor heated pools, outdoor whirlpool, 2 lighted tennis courts, supervised program for children 4–17 (4:30 PM–midnight daily), baby-sitting, health club, business center, lobby shops, guest laundry, valet parking. AE, DC, MC, V.*

$$$ **Grosvenor Resort.** Offering a wealth of facilities and comfortable rooms for a fair price, this attractive member of the Best Western chain is the best deal in the neighborhood. Rooms are average in size, but colorfully decorated, and have many amenities, including their own VCR; rent a movie in the lobby or, better yet, get a rental videocamera so you can record your day at the park and relive the experience that evening or months later. Public areas are spacious, with columns, high ceilings, cheerful colors, and plenty of natural light. Baskerville's, decorated with Sherlock Holmes memorabilia, serves Continental fare, and the homey Moriarty's pub has live entertainment. *1850 Hotel Plaza Blvd., Lake Buena Vista 32830, tel. 407/828–4444 or 800/624–4109. 630 rooms. Facilities: 2 restaurants, lounge, room service, 2 heated outdoor pools, children's pool, whirlpool, game room, 2 lighted tennis courts, playground, shuffleboard, basketball court, volleyball court, rental movies and videocameras, baby-sitting, guest laundry; in-room VCRs, safes, minibars, coffeemakers, and refrigerators. AE, DC, MC, V.*

★ **Guest Quarters Suite Resort.** Consisting exclusively of suites, this hotel is convenient for small families who want to avoid the hassle of cots and the expense of two separate rooms; it attracts a quiet family crowd and few of the noisy conventioneers often found at larger, splashier properties. Each unit has a bedroom with a king-size or two double beds, plus a separate living area equipped with a sofa bed; each can accommodate up to six (if not particularly comfortably). There's a television in each room plus another in the bathroom, as well as a refrigerator, wet bar, and coffeemaker; microwave ovens are available on request. The terrace restaurant and bar are fine for the complimentary buffet breakfasts, but you will probably want to drink and dine elsewhere. *2305 Hotel Plaza Blvd., Lake Buena Vista 32830, tel. 407/934–1000 or 800/424–2900. 229 units. Facilities: restaurant, lounge, ice cream parlor, pool bar, heated pool, children's pool, 2 lighted tennis courts, whirlpool, exercise room, jogging trail, refrigerator and coffeemaker in rooms, baby-sitting, guest laundry. AE, DC, MC, V.*

Howard Johnson Resort at WDW Village. Though somewhat charmless, with its lobbyful of white Formica and a nondescript 14-story atrium, this is undeniably one of the most reasonably priced places to stay on Walt Disney World property, and it's popular with young couples and senior citizens. The Howard Johnson's restaurant, open until midnight, is better than average. *1805 Hotel Plaza Blvd., Lake Buena Vista 32830, tel. 407/828–8888 or 800/223–9930. 323 rooms. Facilities: restaurant, lounge, 2 heated pools, children's pool, whirlpool, game room, coffeemaker in rooms, baby-sitting, guest laundry. AE, DC, MC, V.*

$$–$$$ **Royal Plaza.** Though dated in comparison to the slick hotels in the neighborhood, this casual, lively establishment is quite popular among families with young children and teenagers. Each of the generously proportioned rooms has a terrace or balcony, and the best ones overlook the pool. Be sure your quarters aren't too close to the ground floor if you have any interest in sleeping late or napping in the afternoon. The Giraffe, the hotel's Top-40 nightclub, hops until the wee, wee hours. *1905 Hotel Plaza Blvd., Lake Buena Vista 32830, tel. 407/828–2828 or 800/248–7890. 396 rooms. Facilities: 2 restaurants, 2 lounges, heated outdoor pool, whirlpool, sauna, tanning salon, 4 lighted tennis courts, putting green, guest laundry, baby-sitting. AE, DC, MC, V.*

Travelodge Hotel. This unexceptional property is a good choice for families especially now that its guest rooms have been refurbished with attractive furniture, touches of brass, and hues of baby blue, peach, and soft green. There's nightly entertainment in the 18th-floor Topper's Nightclub, which overlooks Epcot Center. *2000 Hotel Plaza Blvd., Lake Buena Vista 32830, tel. 407/828–2424, 800/423–1022 in FL, or 800/348–3765 outside FL. 325 rooms. Facilities: restaurant, lounge, 2 snack bars, heated pool, playground, game room, guest laundry, baby-sitting. AE, DC, MC, V.*

Epcot Resort Area

$$$$ **Walt Disney World Dolphin.** Not everyone takes to this ITT
★   Sheraton–operated bit of whimsy where the wild and imaginative run rampant. But no one questions that it's fast becoming
a Disney landmark. Two mythical 56-foot sea creatures—labeled dolphins by the hotel's noted architect, Michael Graves—
perch atop each end of the building; between them soars a
27-story pyramid, one of the highest structures in Walt Disney
World. A waterfall cascades down the facade from seashell to
seashell and then into a 54-foot-wide clamshell supported by
other giant dolphin sculptures; in true Florida spirit, the building's coral-and-turquoise facade displays a mural of giant banana leaves. Inside, chandeliers are shaped like monkeys, and
brightly painted wood benches sprout wood palm trees. Rooms
are equally colorfully furnished and are equipped with in-room
safes, minibars, and large vanity areas. The best overlook Epcot
Center and have a stunning view of its nightly fireworks-and-
laser show, IllumiNations. Special registration and concierge
services are available to those staying in the Tower, on the 12th–
20th floors. With its emphasis on the convention trade, this hotel
is more urban and adult than many other on-site properties. *1500
Epcot Resorts Blvd., Lake Buena Vista 32830, tel. 407/934–4000 or
800/227–1500. 1,510 rooms (140 suites and 185 Tower rooms). Facilities: 8 restaurants, 3 lounges, room service, 4 outdoor heated
pools, lakeside beach, 8 lighted tennis courts, beauty salon, game
room, safe and minibar in rooms, supervised children's program,
baby-sitting, multilingual concierge services. AE, DC, MC, V.*

Walt Disney World Swan. Two 45-foot swans grace the rooftop
of this coral-and-aquamarine hotel, which is connected to the
Dolphin by a covered causeway. Inside, architect Michael
Graves has canopied the ceiling with tall, gathered papyrus
reeds and lined up a regiment of columns with palm-frond capi-
tals. Guest rooms, located in the 12-story main building and two
7-story wings, are decorated in coral, peach, teal, and yellow
floral and geometric patterns; each has an in-room safe and
stocked refrigerator. As at the Dolphin, the atmosphere is more
grown-up and less family oriented than that at many other on-
site properties, though there are certainly plenty of facilities
that families will appreciate. *1200 Epcot Resorts Blvd., Lake
Buena Vista 32830, tel. 407/934–3000, 800/248–7926, or 800/228–
3000. 758 rooms (45 concierge rooms on 11th and 12th floors). Facilities: 3 restaurants, 3 lounges, room service, 2 outdoor heated
pools, lakeside beach, health club, 8 lighted tennis courts, beauty
salon, game room, safe and refrigerator in rooms, supervised program for children 3–11 (4–midnight), baby-sitting. AE, DC, MC,
V.*

Magic Kingdom Resort Area

$–$$ **Shades of Green on Walt Disney World Resort.** Formerly the
Disney Inn, this property is now operated by the U.S. Armed
Forces Recreation Center. Vacationing active-duty and retired
personnel from all branches of the armed forces as well as those

in the reserves, National Guard, and Department of Defense are eligible to stay at this quiet resort only two minutes by car from the Magic Kingdom. Even the rates are on a sliding scale based on rank. Situated between two world-class golf courses, the hotel offers spacious, country-style rooms that each accommodate up to five in two queen-size beds and a comfortable sleeper sofa. Choose among views of the fairways, lush gardens, or pools. *WDW Central Reservations, Box 10100, Lake Buena Vista 32830, tel. 407/824–3600. 287 rooms. Facilities: 2 restaurants, lounge, room service, 2 pools, children's pool, 2 lighted tennis courts, golf, game room, health club, guest laundry. AE, MC, V.*

International Drive

If you plan to visit other attractions besides Walt Disney World, the sprawl of newish hotels, restaurants, and shopping malls known as International Drive—"I-Drive" to locals and "Florida Center" in formal parlance—is a convenient point of departure. Parallel to I–4 (and accessible from Exits 28, 29, and 30), it's just a few minutes south of downtown Orlando. It's also near Sea World, Universal Studios, the vast Wet 'n' Wild water-slide park, and several popular dinner theaters.

Many veteran Orlando visitors consider the area the territory's most comfortable home base and its hotels some of the best around. But each part of the drive has its own personality. The southern end is classier; the concentration of cheaper restaurants, fast-food joints, and inexpensive malls increases as you go north.

$$$$ **Peabody Orlando.** Built by the owners of the landmark Memphis,
★ Tennessee, Peabody Hotel, this 27-story structure looks like a high-rise office building from afar. But don't be put off by its austere exterior. Inside, the place is very impressive and handsomely designed, from the lobby's rich marble floors and fountains to the sweeping views and the modern art throughout the hotel. As a grace note, there is also the famous Peabody tradition: Each day at 11, a flock of ducks waddles down a swath of red carpet through the lobby to a marble fountain, where they frolic until 5, then do the whole thing in reverse. The most panoramic rooms have views of Walt Disney World; those in the Peabody Club on the top three floors enjoy special concierge service. Even the restaurants are noteworthy: Capriccio's serves Italian fare; Dux is Continental; and the Beeline is a 24-hour 1950s-style diner (*see* Chapter 8). Located across the street from the Orange County Convention Center, the hotel attracts rock stars and other performers as well as conventioneers. *9801 International Dr., Orlando 32819, tel. 407/352–4000 or 800/732–2639. 891 rooms. Facilities: 3 restaurants, 2 lounges, room service, Olympic-size pool, children's pool, 4 lighted tennis courts, whirlpool, health club and spa, supervised children's program, baby-sitting, golf privileges, concierge services. AE, DC, MC, V.*

Stouffer Orlando Resort. From the folks who brought French bread pizza and Lean Cuisine to your grocery store comes an even more palatable product—the 10-story Stouffer Orlando Resort. This bulky building directly across the street from Sea World looks more like a Federal Reserve Bank than a comfortable hotel. Longer than a football field, its atrium lobby is billed as the world's largest. Occupying the entire core of the building, it is full of waterfalls, goldfish ponds, and palm trees; as guests shoot skyward in sleek glass elevators, exotic birds twitter in a large, hand-carved, gilded Venetian aviary. It's nice to be greeted with a glass of champagne when you register, but the spaciousness of the guest rooms is even more pleasant. The most expensive rooms face the atrium, but if you're a light sleeper, ask for an outside room to avoid the music and party sounds that come from gatherings there. *6677 Sea Harbor Dr., Orlando 32821, tel. 407/351–5555 or 800/468–3571. 780 rooms. Facilities: 5 restaurants, 2 lounges, room service, heated pool, children's pool, 5 lighted tennis courts, health club, game room, supervised children's program, baby-sitting, beauty salon, concierge services, guest laundry, golf privileges. AE, DC, MC, V.*

$$$–$$$$ **Sonesta Villa Resort Orlando.** This complex of multiunit town
★ houses not far from International Drive is like a huge luxury apartment complex on a lake. Each unit is a homey, comfortable apartment, small but fully equipped with a kitchenette, dining area, living room, small patio, bedroom, and private ground-floor entrance; some units are bilevel. The conveniently located outdoor facilities are equally attractive. Guests can sail and water-ski on the lake or sun themselves on the sandy beach. There are restaurants and a bar, but the only after-dark action consists of the outdoor barbecue buffet (even that's not always available). If you want to cook at "home" but are too busy to shop, the hotel will pick up groceries for you and deliver them while you're out. *10000 Turkey Lake Rd., Orlando 32819, tel. 407/352–8051 or 800/766–3782. 369 units. Facilities: 2 restaurants, lounge, pool bar and grill, ice cream parlor, heated outdoor pool, children's pool, 11 whirlpools, water sports (water ski, Jet ski, and paddleboat rental), 2 lighted tennis courts, supervised children's program, baby-sitting, volleyball, shuffleboard, jogging path, game room, grocery delivery service, guest laundry. AE, DC, MC, V.*

$$$ **Embassy Suites Hotel at Plaza International.** Another of the all-suite chain (*see above*), this member has a central atrium—wide, but somewhat smaller than at the Stouffer—that contains a lounge where a player piano sets the mood. The two-room suites can sleep up to six, and their kitchenettes, equipped with microwave, refrigerator, and coffeemaker, make it possible to eat in. *8250 Jamaican Ct., Orlando, 32819, tel. 407/345–8250 or 800/327–9797. 246 rooms. Facilities: lounge, indoor-outdoor pool, exercise room, whirlpool, sauna, coffeemaker in rooms, complimentary breakfast, baby-sitting, game room. AE, DC, MC, V.*

Embassy Suites International Drive South. The concept of an all-suites hotel that serves a free buffet breakfast with cooked-to-order items, pioneered by the Embassy Suites chain, has proved very popular in Orlando for a couple of reasons: The arrangement is comfortable; each unit has both a bedroom and a full living room equipped with wet bar, refrigerator, pullout sofa and two TVs. The even greater appeal is the modest cost—less than that of a single room in the topnotch hotels. This member of the chain seems part Deep South, part tropical. With its marble floors, pillars, hanging lamps, and ceiling fans, the lobby has an expansive, old-fashioned feel. Tropical gardens with mossy rock fountains give a distinctive Southern humidity to the atrium. Elsewhere, ceramic tile walkways and brick arches carry out the tropical mood. A fancy indoor pool is another distinctive touch. Breakfast and cocktails, served daily from 5 to 7, are included in the room rate. *8978 International Dr., Orlando 32819, tel. 407/352–1400 or 800/432–7272. 245 suites. Facilities: restaurant, lounge, complimentary breakfast and cocktails, indoor pool, whirlpool, steam room, sauna, supervised children's program, baby-sitting. AE, DC, MC, V.*

Parc Corniche Resort. Framed by an 18-hole Joe Lee–designed golf course called the International Golf Club, this all-suite resort is ideal for golf enthusiasts. Each of the one- and two-bedroom suites is decked out in pastels and tropical patterns and has a patio or balcony with a golf course view as well as a kitchen. The largest accommodations, a two-bedroom, two-bath unit, can sleep up to six. The resort serves a complimentary Continental breakfast daily, and Sea World is only a few blocks away. *6300 Parc Corniche Dr., Orlando 32821, tel. 407/239–7100 or 800/446–2721. 210 suites. Facilities: restaurant, lounge, in-suite kitchens, heated pool, children's pool, whirlpool, golf, playground, game room, baby-sitting, guest laundry. AE, D, MC, V.*

Summerfield Suites Hotel. A great option for big families, the all-suites Summerfield is small enough for guests to get plenty of personal attention, but accommodations are quite roomy. Two-bedroom units, the most popular, have fully equipped kitchens (complete with stove, coffeemaker, microwave, and jumbo refrigerator), plus a living room with TV and VCR. All the bedrooms have full baths and TVs. The courtyard shelters a small but pretty pool, with a poolside bar where you can get hot dogs and burgers; cocktails are served at the lobby bar every evening. If you don't want the hassle of whipping up eggs in the morning, you can sample the hotel's free Continental buffet—or stop in at one of the nearby International Drive restaurants. *8480 International Dr., Orlando 32819, tel. 407/352–2400 or 800/833–4353. 146 suites (42 with 1 bedroom, 104 with 2). Facilities: lounge, in-suite kitchen, heated outdoor pool, children's pool, convenience store, game room, exercise room, guest laundry, VCR in rooms, rental movies. AE, DC, MC, V.*

$$–$$$ **Enclave Suites at Orlando.** With three 10-story buildings surrounding an office, restaurant, and recreation area, this all-suite hotel is less a hotel than a condominium complex. Here, what you spend for a room in a fancy hotel gets you a complete apartment, with significantly more space than you'll find in other all-suite hotels. Accommodating up to six, the units have full kitchens, living rooms, two bedrooms, and small terraces. This is a great deal for families or small groups of friends who don't mind skipping the hotel hustle, and the studio suites are won-

derful for couples. The Enclave Beach Cafe is popular with local yuppies. *6165 Carrier Dr., Orlando 32819, tel. 407/351–1155 or 800/457–0077. 321 suites. Facilities: restaurant, lounge, in-suite kitchens, 2 heated outdoor pools, indoor pool, whirlpool, sauna, exercise room, lighted tennis court, playground, baby-sitting, guest laundry. AE, DC, MC, V.*

Twin Towers Hotel and Convention Center. Although this hotel has a big convention center and caters to meetings, it's a good choice for tourists, too. Who wouldn't appreciate the we-try-harder attitude or the great location just across from Universal Studios Florida? And don't worry about noisy conventioneers—the meeting and convention facilities are completely isolated from the guest towers. The comfortable if nondescript rooms have one king- or two queen-size beds, cable TV, and in-room movies. Among the dining-and-drinking options are a deli open around-the-clock, the Palm Court Restaurant (which serves three meals daily), and the Everglades Lounge (with live entertainment and a large-screen TV). The green neon that outlines the towers makes it easy to find your way home at night, and the swimming pool is surrounded by nicely landscaped grounds that include a playground. *5780 Major Blvd., Orlando 32819, tel. 407/351–1000 or 800/327–2110. 760 rooms, 30 suites. Facilities: 2 restaurants, 3 lounges, deli, room service, pool, children's pool, whirlpool, exercise room, sauna, game room, playground, supervised children's program, baby-sitting, guest laundry. AE, DC, MC, V.*

\$\$ Clarion Plaza Hotel. You'll see no shortage of wide-eyed conventioneers sporting name tags at this 12-story hotel alongside the Orange County Convention Center. Yet leisure travelers are gradually discovering both the hotel's prime location minutes from attractions and its long list of amenities generally found at more expensive properties. The dining line-up is exceptional for a hotel in this price range; there's the 24-hour Lite Bite; the upbeat Café Matisse, a coffee shop that serves elaborate buffets; and richly paneled Jack's Place, which serves steaks, seafood, and huge desserts on tables dressed in crisp white linens amid autographed caricatures of famous movie stars. *9700 International Dr., Orlando 32819, tel. 407/352–9700 or 800/627–8258. 810 rooms. Facilities: 2 restaurants, lounge, lobby bar, room service, heated outdoor pool, baby-sitting, guest laundry. AE, DC, MC, V.*

★ Orlando Heritage Inn. If you want a small, simple hotel with reasonable rates but plenty of charm, look into this establishment next door to the towering Peabody. Recalling Victorian-era Florida, it's full of reproduction turn-of-the-century furnishings, French windows, and brass lamps, interspersed with 19th-century antiques. In the guest rooms, folk art hangs on the walls, lace curtains adorn the double French doors, and quilted spreads cover the beds. The kitschy quaintness contrasts pleasantly with the anonymity of the area's other hotels, and the staff is strong on Southern hospitality. Dinner shows are presented in the rotunda several nights weekly. *9861 International Dr., Orlando 32819, tel. 407/352–0008 or 800/447–1890. 150 rooms. Facili-*

ties: *restaurant, lounge, dinner theater, room service, heated outdoor pool, baby-sitting, guest laundry. AE, DC, MC, V.*

$–$$ **Days Inn Orlando/Lakeside.** Among the budget motels in the International Drive area, this Days Inn is tops. That's not only because of its location on the shores of Spring Lake, across I–4 from International Drive, but also because of its good facilities. Rooms are basic but just fine, and suites with coffeemaker, microwave, and refrigerator are also available. Parents appreciate the chainwide policy that lets accompanying children age 12 and under eat free with a paying adult in its restaurants and cafeteria. The one drawback: There is no swimming or fishing in the hotel's lake. *7335 Sand Lake Rd., Orlando 32819, tel. 407/351–1900 or 800/777–3297. 695 rooms. Facilities: restaurant, cafeteria, snack bar; 3 outdoor pools (1 heated), lakeside beach, 2 playgrounds, insuites kitchenettes (coffeemaker, microwave, and refrigerator), game room, guest laundry, gas station. AE, DC, MC, V.*

Wynfield Inn–Westwood. If you don't want a room with just the bare essentials yet don't have the budget for luxury, this two-story motel is a find. Its cheerful, contemporary rooms are smartly appointed with colorful, floral-print bedspreads and understated wall hangings, there are in-room movies, and the lobby has been recently renovated; complimentary fruit, coffee, and tea are served there every day. The staff is friendly and helpful and acts more like the staff of a "do-anything-to-please" independent motel. Children 17 and under stay free in their parents' room (with a maximum of four guests per room). *6263 Westwood Blvd., Orlando 32821, tel. 407/345–8000 or 800/346–1551. 300 rooms. Facilities: 2 outdoor pools (1 heated), pool bar, game room, guest laundry. AE, D, MC, V.*

$ **Fairfield Inn by Marriott.** This understated, few-frills, three-story hotel—the Marriott Corporation's answer to the Motel 6 and Econolodge chain—is a natural for small families on a tight budget. You won't find the amenities of top-of-the-line Marriott properties, but nice perks such as complimentary coffee and tea, free local phone calls, remote-control TVs, and free cable TV give a sense of being at a much fancier property. *8342 Jamaican Court, Orlando 32819, tel. 407/363–1944 or 800/228–2800. 135 rooms. Facilities: heated outdoor pool, game room. AE, DC, MC, V.*

Maingate

Outside the northernmost entrance to WDW, just off I–4, the Maingate area is full of large hotels unaffiliated with Walt Disney World, mostly sprawling, high-quality resorts catering to Walt Disney World vacationers. Although they share a certain sameness with resorts the world over, they vary in size and price. As a rule, the bigger the resort and the more extensive the facilities, the more you can expect to pay. If you're looking for a clean, modern room, you cannot go wrong with any of them. All are equally convenient to Walt Disney World. One may emphasize one recreational activity more than another. So your ultimate decision may depend on how much time you plan to spend at your hotel and on which of your strokes—your drive or your backhand—requires most attention.

$$$$ **Grand Cypress Resort.** If you polled those familiar with Orlando
★ to name its most spectacular resort, few would hesitate to name the Grand Cypress. With more than 1,500 acres, it's huge and offers virtually every resort facility and then some. Golf facilities are first-class, with 45 Jack Nicklaus–designed holes, making up four courses, and a high-tech golf school. The huge, 800,000-gallon swimming pool has three levels and is fed by 12 cascading waterfalls, and there's a 45-acre Audubon nature reserve. Even the service is attentive. And as you'd expect of a first-class Hyatt resort, the hotel has a striking 18-story glass atrium filled with tropical plants and Oriental paintings and sculptures. Accommodations are divided between the 750-room Hyatt Regency Grand Cypress and the 146-unit Villas of Grand Cypress. Rooms are unmemorable but spacious; those with the best views overlook the pool and Lake Windsong. The restaurants are excellent (*see* Chapter 8). There's just one drawback: the king-size conventions that it commonly attracts. *1 Grand Cypress Blvd., Orlando 32836, tel. 407/239–1234 or 800/233–1234. 750 rooms. Facilities: 5 restaurants, 6 lounges, ice cream parlor, room service, 2 outdoor pools (1 heated), children's pool, 3 whirlpools, health club, 45-hole golf complex with clubhouse and golf school, 12 tennis courts (5 lighted), 2 jogging trails, fitness course, bicycle rental, equestrian center, croquet court, water sports on 21-acre lake (paddleboat, sailboat, and canoe rentals), game room, health club, supervised children's program, baby-sitting, guest laundry. AE, DC, MC, V.*

Marriott's Orlando World Center. To call this Marriott massive would be an understatement. The lineup of amenities seems endless; one of the four swimming pools is the largest in the state. The lobby is a huge, opulent atrium, and the rooms are clean and comfortable. Luxurious villas—the Royal Palms and Sabal Palms—are available for daily and weekly rentals. If you like your hostelries cozy, you'll consider the size of this place a definite negative; otherwise, its single unappealing aspect is the crowd of conventioneers it attracts. *8701 World Center Dr., Orlando 32821, tel. 407/239–4200 or 800/228–9290. 1,504 rooms. Facilities: 7 restaurants, 3 lounges, room service, 3 heated outdoor pools, 1 heated indoor pool, children's pool, 4 whirlpools, health club, 18-hole golf course, 12 lighted tennis courts, game room, beauty salon, supervised children's program, baby-sitting, guest laundry. AE, DC, MC, V.*

Vistana Resort. Consider this peaceful resort if you're interested in tennis: Its clay and all-weather tennis courts can be used without charge; private or semiprivate lessons are available for a fee. It's also a good bet if your family is large or you're traveling with a group of friends. The spacious, tastefully decorated villas and town houses spread over 95 landscaped acres and have two bedrooms each plus a living room and all the comforts of home, including a full kitchen and a washer and dryer. The price may seem high, but considering that each unit can sleep six or eight, the place is a positive bargain. *8800 Vistana Centre Dr., Orlando*

32821, tel. 407/239–3100 or 800/877–8787. 722 units. Facilities: 2 restaurants, 2 lounges, 5 heated outdoor pools, 5 children's pools, 7 whirlpools, health club, 3 basketball courts, shuffleboard, miniature golf course, game room, convenience store, concierge services, supervised children's program, baby-sitting, guest laundry. AE, DC, MC, V.

$$$-$$$$ **Embassy Suites Resort Lake Buena Vista.** This is a typical example of the popular all-suite chain (*see above*), although some local folks have been shocked by this hotel's wild turquoise, pink, and yellow facade. Clearly visible from I–4, it has become something of a local landmark. But it's an attractive option for other reasons. It's just 1 mile from Walt Disney World, 5 miles from Sea World, and 7 miles from Universal Studios Florida. The central atrium lobby, loaded with tropical vegetation and soothed by the sounds of a rushing fountain, is a great place to enjoy the complimentary breakfast. *8100 Lake Ave., Lake Buena Vista 32830, tel. 407/239–1144 or 800/362–2779. 280 suites. Facilities: restaurant, 2 lounges, snack bar, indoor-outdoor heated pool, children's pool, whirlpool, fitness room, lighted tennis court, shuffleboard, basketball, volleyball, fitness course, supervised children's program, baby-sitting, game room, playground. AE, DC, MC, V.*

$$-$$$ **Holiday Inn Sunspree Resort Lake Buena Vista.** From its sweeping, covered entrance to its striking, terra-cotta-colored facade, this big Holiday Inn is most impressive. It's also an excellent value. Furnished with two queen-size beds or one king and a sleeper, all rooms have a TV and VCR plus a kitchenette equipped with refrigerator, microwave, and coffeemaker. In the hotel courtyard is a wonderfully huge, free-form pool, plus a whirlpool and a vast wading pool. But what really earns the kudos here is Camp Holiday, a free children's program of magic shows, arts and crafts, movies, cartoons, and other supervised activities, day and night. Children even have their own restaurant, the Kid's Kottage. For a final nifty touch, the hotel rents beepers so that parents can have some time to themselves without worrying about the kids. *13351 Rte. 535, Lake Buena Vista 32821, tel. 407/239–4500, 800/366–6299, or 800/465–4329. 507 rooms. Facilities: restaurant, lounge, room service, kitchenettes, VCRs, heated outdoor pool, children's pool, whirlpool, free supervised program for children 2–12 (8 AM–midnight; must be potty trained). AE, DC, MC, V.*

★ **Ramada Resort Maingate at the Parkway.** With its attractive setting, good facilities, and competitive prices, this bright, spacious Ramada may offer the best deal in the neighborhood. Its delicatessen comes in handy when you want to assemble a picnic. Generously proportioned rooms are decked out in tropical patterns and pastel colors; those with the best view and light face the pool. *2900 Parkway Blvd., Kissimmee 34746, tel. 407/396–7000, 800/634–4774, or 800/225–3939 in FL. 716 rooms. Facilities: restaurant, lounge, deli, snack bar, heated outdoor pool, children's pool, 2 whirlpools, sauna, 2 lighted tennis courts, volleyball, guest laundry. AE, DC, MC, V.*

$$ ★ **Doubletree Club Hotel.** After traipsing through Orlando's theme parks and malls, what many visitors want most is to lounge around their living room just the way they do at home. This six-story hotel lets you do just that: It provides a 5,000-square-foot living room full of big couches, with a better-than-at-home big-screen TV. You don't expect such casual comforts when you see the building, which looks as if it belongs in a sterile office park anywhere in the United States. But homey touches abound, and the service and amenities more than make up for the less-than-inspiring facade. Each room has two phones and a TV with remote control. *8688 Palm Pkwy., Lake Buena Vista 32830, tel. 407/239–8500 or 800/228-2846. 167 rooms. Facilities: restaurant, lounge, room service, heated outdoor pool, whirlpool, health club. AE, DC, MC, V.*

Hyatt Orlando Hotel. Instead of a single tower, this very large hotel consists of nine 2-story buildings in four clusters. Each cluster is a community with its own heated pool, whirlpool, park, and playground at its center. The rooms are spacious, but otherwise unmemorable. The lobby is vast and mall-like, with numerous shops and restaurants; the Palm Terrace is kosher, and there is also a very good take-out deli. If you'll be spending most of your time attacking Orlando attractions, the convenience and reasonable rates will more than make up for the unremarkable nature of the place. *6375 W. Irlo Bronson Memorial Hwy., Kissimmee 34746, tel. 407/396–1234, 800/331-2003 in FL, or 800/544-7178 outside FL. 948 rooms. Facilities: 4 restaurants, deli, lounge, 4 heated outdoor pools, whirlpool, 2 lighted tennis courts, 4 play-grounds, jogging trail, game room, baby-sitting, guest laundry. AE, DC, MC, V.*

U.S. 192 Area

If you're looking for anything remotely quaint, charming, or sophisticated, move on. The U.S. 192 strip—a.k.a. the Irlo Bronson Memorial Highway, the Spacecoast Parkway, and Kissimmee—is crammed with mom-and-pop motels and bargain basement hotels, cheap restaurants, fast-food spots, nickel-and-dime attractions, gas stations, and minimarts in mind-numbing profusion. But if all you want is a decent room with perhaps a few extras for a manageable price, this is Wonderland. Room rates start at $20 a night—lower at the right time of year, if you can cut the right deal; otherwise, most cost $30–$70 a night, depending on facilities and proximity to Walt Disney World. Among the chain hotels—Best Western, Comfort Inn, Econolodge, Holiday Inn, Radisson, Sheraton, Travelodge, and so on—are a pride of family-owned properties, many of which are run by recent immigrants.

Whatever your choice, you will find basic rooms, grounds, and public spaces that vary little from one establishment to the next. As a rule, the newer the property, the more comfortable your surroundings, and the greater the distance from Walt Disney World, the lower the room rates. A few minutes' drive may save you a significant amount of money, so shop around. And if you wait until arrival to find a place, don't be bashful about asking to see rooms. It's a buyer's market.

$$$ **Sol Orlando Resort.** The brochure on this resort hotel complex stretches a point when it says it has the charm of a small village in the Spanish region of Andalusia. The red tile and stucco villas and palm-studded grounds are indeed attractive, but it's the spacious accommodations that are truly noteworthy. Each of the one-, two-, and three-bedroom units has a living and dining area, a kitchen, and two TVs; the three-bedroom villa has 1,200 square feet of living space and sleeps up to eight comfortably. Complimentary breakfast is also included. *4787 W. Irlo Bronson Memorial Hwy., Kissimmee 34746, tel. 407/397–0555. 150 villas. Facilities: restaurant, lounge, heated outdoor pool, children's pool, whirlpool, health club, tennis court, air-conditioned squash and racquetball court, game room, convenience store, guest laundry, minigolf complex next door. AE, MC, V.*

$$–$$$ **Residence Inn by Marriott on Lake Cecile.** Of the all-suite hotels on U.S. 192, this complex of four-unit town houses is probably the best. One side of the complex faces the highway; the other overlooks an attractive lake, where you can sail, water-ski, Jet-ski, and fish. Forty units are penthouses accommodating four, with complete kitchens, small living rooms, loft bedrooms, and fireplaces. All others accommodate two and are like studio apartments but still have full kitchens and fireplaces. Each suite has a private entrance. While the price may seem high considering the location, there is no charge for additional guests, so you can squeeze in the whole family at no extra charge, and both Continental breakfast and a grocery shopping service are complimentary. *4786 W. Irlo Bronson Memorial Hwy., Kissimmee 34746, tel. 407/396–2056, 800/648–7408 in FL, or 800/468–3027 outside FL. 159 units. Facilities: heated outdoor pool, whirlpool, tennis court, basketball court, playground, guest laundry. AE, DC, MC, V.*

Quality Suites Maingate East. This hotel, built in 1989, is an excellent option for a large family or groups of friends. The spacious rooms, designed to sleep six or 10, are decorated in green and gold and equipped with a microwave, refrigerator, and dishwasher. Suites have two bedrooms with two double beds each and a living room with a double pullout couch. A complimentary Continental breakfast is offered each morning. Kids will enjoy the motel's restaurant: A toy train chugs along overhead. No-smoking suites are available. *5876 W. Irlo Bronson Memorial Hwy., Kissimmee 34746, tel. 407/396–8040, 800/221–2222, or 800/848–4148 in FL. 225 units. Facilities: restaurant, lounge, poolside bar, heated outdoor pool, whirlpool, kitchenettes, playground, game room, convenience store, guest laundry. AE, D, DC, MC, V.*

$$ **Best Western Kissimmee.** Overlooking a nine-hole, par-three executive golf course, this independently owned and operated three-story hotel is a hit with golf-loving senior citizens as well as families. The two swimming pools in the garden courtyard are amply shaded to protect tender skins from the sizzling Southern sun. The spacious rooms are done in soft pastels, with

light wood furniture and attractive wall hangings. Units with king-size beds and kitchenettes are available. The hotel's restaurant, Casual Cuisine, serves dinners buffet style as well as from a varied menu. *2261 E. Irlo Bronson Memorial Hwy., Kissimmee 34744, tel. 407/846–2221. 281 rooms. Facilities: restaurant, lounge, 2 outdoor pools (1 heated), playground, picnic area, adjacent 9-hole golf course. AE, D, MC, V.*

Holiday Inn Maingate East. The service at this place is good, despite the fact that it's the world's biggest two-story Holiday Inn. But that's not the only reason to stay here. The rooms have TV, VCR, and kitchenettes with refrigerator, microwave, and coffeemaker; you can rent tapes and buy snacks and groceries in the lobby, and some of the restaurants serve buffet style—an added convenience. *5678 W. Irlo Bronson Memorial Hwy., Kissimmee 34746, tel. 407/396–4488, 800/366–5437, or 800/465–4329. 670 rooms. Facilities: 6 restaurants, 2 lounges, room service, 2 Olympic-size pools (1 heated), children's pool, 2 whirlpools, 2 lighted tennis courts, 2 game rooms, supervised program for children 3–12 (8 AM–midnight; must be potty trained), in-room kitchenettes, 2 playgrounds, small convenience store, VCRs and rental movies, guest laundry. AE, DC, MC, V.*

★ **Radisson Inn Maingate.** This sleek, modern hotel, just a few minutes from WDW's front door, has cheerful guest rooms, large bathrooms, and plenty of extras for the price. It's not fancy, but it is perfectly sufficient. The best rooms are those with a view of the pool. Two floors in each tower are reserved for non-smokers. *7501 W. Irlo Bronson Memorial Hwy., Kissimmee 34746, tel. 407/396–1400 or 800/333–3333. 580 rooms. Facilities: restaurant, lounge, deli, poolside bar, room service, heated outdoor pool, whirlpool, 2 lighted tennis courts, jogging trail, baby-sitting, guest laundry. AE, DC, MC, V.*

Sheraton Lakeside Inn. This comfortable if undistinguished resort, a complex of 15 two-story buildings spread over 27 acres, offers quite a few recreational facilities for the money. The nondescript beige rooms are available in the standard two double or one king-size bed configurations and each has a refrigerator and safe. The children's program has arts and crafts, movies, and miniature golf in a comfortable play area. *7769 W. Irlo Bronson Memorial Hwy., Kissimmee 34746, tel. 407/239–7919 or 800/848–0801. 651 rooms. Facilities: 2 restaurants, lounge, deli, room service, 3 outdoor pools (2 heated), children's pool, 4 tennis courts, supervised program for children 5–12 (Tues.–Fri. 2–9 PM, Sat. 11–5 PM), baby-sitting, miniature golf, 2 game rooms, paddleboat and fishing equipment rental, guest laundry. AE, DC, MC, V.*

$ ★ **Casa Rosa Inn.** For simple motel living—no screaming kids or loud music, please—this pink, Spanish style, family-run place is the one you want. It's simple and doesn't have much in the way of facilities aside from its pool and free in-room movies, but it's a good, serviceable option, and the price is right. *4600 W. Irlo Bronson Memorial Hwy., Kissimmee 34746, tel. 407/396–2020 or 800/432–0665. 54 rooms. Facilities: outdoor pool, guest laundry. AE, DC, MC, V.*

Comfort Inn Maingate. This hotel is close to Walt Disney World—just a mile away—so you can save a bundle without unduly inconveniencing yourself. Standard rooms are light and airy, with a mauve-and-soft-blue color scheme; deluxe rooms, overlooking a landscaped garden, have full-length mirrors, hair dryers, and refrigerators. Children 17 and under stay free. *7571 W. Irlo Bronson Memorial Hwy., Kissimmee 34746, tel. 407/396–7500 or 800/228–5150. 281 rooms. Facilities: restaurant, lounge, heated outdoor pool, game room, baby-sitting, guest laundry. AE, DC, MC, V.*

Knights Inn–Maingate. Part of a national chain, this one-story motel is not exactly an English charmer with its prefab Old World facade, but it does offer spacious, clean rooms at budget prices; some of them even have kitchenettes and sofas. Don't expect fine English antiques: Veneer is the predominant design statement. *7475 W. Irlo Bronson Memorial Hwy., Kissimmee 34746, tel. 407/396–4200 or 800/843–5644. 119 rooms. Facilities: outdoor pool, kitchenettes in some rooms. AE, D, MC, V.*

Park Inn International. The Mediterranean-style architecture is not likely to charm you off your feet, but the staff is friendly and the property is on a lake. Ask for a room as close to the water as possible. There is a restaurant, but for an extra $10 you can get a room with a kitchenette. *4960 W. Irlo Bronson Memorial Hwy., Kissimmee 34741, tel. 407/396–1376 or 800/327–0072. 197 rooms. Facilities: restaurant, outdoor pool, whirlpool, baby-sitting, game room, guest laundry. AE, C, DC, MC, V.*

Quality Inn Lake Cecile. Rooms at this plain Jane are adequate if not fancy. Try to get one as close to the lake as possible—it's prettier as well as quieter. *4944 W. Irlo Bronson Memorial Hwy., Kissimmee 34746, tel. 407/396–4455, 800/228–4427, or 800/432–1022 in FL. 222 rooms. Facilities: restaurant, lounge, outdoor pool, lakeside beach, fishing, guest laundry. AE, DC, MC, V.*

Record Motel. This simple property is the kind of few-frills, rock-bottom-rates, mom-and-pop operation that made U.S. 192 famous. Clean rooms with free HBO and a solar-heated pool are the major amenities. What the place lacks in luxuries and ambience it more than makes up for with the friendliness of its staff, who'll gladly direct you to equally inexpensive restaurants. *4651 W. Irlo Bronson Memorial Hwy., Kissimmee 34746, tel. 407/396–8400. 57 rooms. Facilities: heated outdoor pool, guest laundry. AE, MC, V.*

Red Roof Inn. If you want a clean, quiet room but don't want to gamble on an independent, this three-story chain motel delivers consistently. The small, comfortable rooms are decorated in blues and grays. A big plus are the many fast-food and budget-priced eateries within walking distance. The complimentary daily newspaper and coffee each morning are pleasant surprises. *4970 Kyng's Heath Rd., Kissimmee 34746, tel. 407/396–0065 or 800/843–7663. 102 rooms. Facilities: outdoor pool, heated whirlpool, guest laundry. AE, D, MC, V.*

Sevilla Inn. This classy, family-operated motel built in 1985 and expanded in 1990 is one of the best buys in the Orlando area. Stucco and wood on the outside, the three-story building has up-to-date rooms inside, with colorful bedspreads, tasteful wall hangings, a fresh paint job, and cable TV. If you need a place to just drop your bags and get some rest between theme parks, this is a good bet. The pool area, encircled by palm trees and tropical flowers, feels like something you'd find in a much fancier resort. *4640 W. Irlo Bronson Memorial Hwy., Kissimmee 34746, tel. 407/396–4135 or 800/367–1363. 46 rooms. Facilities: heated outdoor pool, guest laundry. AE, D, MC, V.*

Orlando Suburbs

Travel farther afield, and you can get more comforts and more facilities for your money, or some genuine Orlando charm—of the warm, cozy, one-of-a-kind, country inn variety.

Altamonte Springs

Staying among the suburban developments, office parks, and shopping malls of Altamonte Springs may not be as glamorous as dwelling with the Disney characters. But accommodations in this suburb 30–40 minutes' drive from the theme parks cost an average one-third less than comparable lodgings elsewhere in the Orlando area. And the suburban atmosphere offers relief from the frantic tourist scene farther south. In addition, the area is convenient to Enzo's on the Lake, one of Orlando's best restaurants, as well as to the jumbo Altamonte Mall (*see* Chapters 6 and 8).

$$$ **Embassy Suites Orlando-North.** All of the rooms in this member of the all-suite chain (*see above*) look out onto a lush tropical atrium. Although the sound of the waterfalls can be soothing, the same can't be said for that of the conventioneers at the tables around them. So for guaranteed peace and quiet, choose a suite on one of the upper floors. The accommodations are spacious and flawlessly kept, the staff friendly and helpful, and the complimentary cooked-to-order breakfast makes a great send-off for your day in the theme parks. *225 E. Altamonte Dr., Altamonte Springs 32701, tel. 407/834–2400 or 800/362–2779. 210 rooms. Facilities: restaurant, lounge, room service, in-suite kitchenettes, indoor heated pool, exercise room. AE, DC, MC, V.*

$$ **Orlando North Hilton and Towers.** Though the emphasis here is on the business traveler, tourists will also appreciate the hotel's quiet elegance. The comfortable rooms are decorated with peach and dark-green florals with brass accents. Facilities aren't extensive, although what there is is tasteful, and the staff is attentive. Renovated in fall 1992, this hotel also has two floors of more pricey, one- and two-bedroom Executive Suites and individual rooms with concierge service. The pool is sunny and surrounded by palm trees, and the bar is cozy for cocktails. *350 N. Lake Blvd., Altamonte Springs 32715, tel. 407/830–1985. 325 rooms. Facilities: restaurant, lounge, room service, heated outdoor pool, whirlpool, conference facilities. AE, D, DC, MC, V.*

Winter Park

Winter Park, Orlando's poshest and best-established neighborhood, is full of chichi shops and restaurants. Its heart is Central Park, a charming greensward dotted with huge trees hung with Spanish moss. It feels a million miles away from Orlando's tourist track, but it's still just a short drive from the major attractions.

$$–$$$ **Park Plaza Hotel.** Small and intimate, this 1922-vintage establishment feels almost like a private home, but there are nice touches: A newspaper is slid under your door each morning, and the complimentary breakfast is also brought to your room. Rooms—mostly on the small side—have either a double, queen-, or king-size bed; all open onto one long balcony abloom with ferns and flowers and punctuated by wicker chairs and tables, with views of Park Avenue or Central Park. This old-fashioned spot is definitely not for people who want recreational facilities or other special amenities. On the first floor is one of Orlando's most popular restaurants, the Park Plaza Gardens, where you can see and be seen by the fashionable folk of Winter Park over good Continental cuisine. This property is not suitable for young children. *307 Park Ave. S, Winter Park 32789, tel. 407/647–1072 or 800/228–7220. 27 rooms. Facilities: restaurant, lounge, room service, baby-sitting, guest laundry. AE, DC, MC, V.*

Off the Beaten Track

Mention should be made of a duo of unusual hotels off the beaten track—close enough to be part of the immediate Orlando area, but well away from the areas that draw most area visitors.

Lake Wales

$$–$$$ **Chalet Suzanne.** You'll find this conversation piece of a hotel in
★   orange-grove territory some 60 miles southwest of Orlando and about a half-hour drive from Walt Disney World in what seems the middle of nowhere. A homemade billboard directs you down a country road that turns into a palm-lined drive; then cobblestone paths lead to a balconied chalet-style house and cabins with thatched roofs. Fields and gardens extend to one side, a lake on the other. A friendly, homespun mom-and-pop operation, this assemblage has been in the Hinshaw family for generations. It became a country inn during the lean years of the Depression and has been added to bit by unlikely bit over the years; unusual features include an airstrip and a soup-canning plant. The happily quirky grounds are decorated with colorful tilework from Portugal, ironwork from Spain, pottery from Italy, and porcelain from England and Germany. In the rooms and public spaces, furnishings vary wildly from the rare and valuable to the garage-sale one-of-a-kind. As in the home of someone's rich, crotchety old uncle, each room has its own personality; all have eccentrically tiled bathrooms with old-fashioned tubs and washbasins. The most charming rooms face the lake. There is a good-

quality dining room, and guests receive a complimentary country breakfast. *Box AC, Lake Wales 33859, tel. 813/676–6011. 30 rooms. Facilities: restaurant, lounge, room service, swimming pool, boating, badminton court, guest laundry. AE, DC, MC, V.*

Inverness

$$ **Crown Hotel.** "Charming" is a word all too often applied to hotels that don't really deserve it. Not this one in Inverness, a small town north of Tampa (an easy hour-long drive from Orlando). Owners Jill and Nigel Sumner have bestowed on Florida's west coast a bit of Merrie Old England—their native land, via special touches like the portraits of English royalty that hang below the curving lobby staircase; there's even a display case filled with replicas of the crown jewels. Guest rooms, on the second and third floors, have pretty flowered wallpaper and huge old-fashioned washbasins with bright brass fixtures. Each room has a TV and either two twin beds or one double or queen-size bed. There's a small but beautiful pool out back, with a vine-covered wall for privacy. Churchill's in the hotel is well worth trying for its Continental food as well as its wine list; the cozy, dark-paneled Fox and Hounds is a good bet for snacks, sandwiches, and British beers—and oh, those chicken wings! *109 N. Seminole Ave., Inverness 32650, tel. 904/344–5555. 34 rooms. Facilities: restaurant, pub, outdoor pool. AE, MC, V.*

10 After Dark

Updated by
Mary
Meehan

If you know that adults traveling without children make up half of the more than 13 million travelers who visit Walt Disney World, it won't surprise you if the sidewalks don't roll up when the sun goes down. A recent surge in the number of night spots in the Orlando area shows no signs of letting up. Nightclubs in Orlando proper have significantly more character than those in the areas around Walt Disney World, and some are now producing all-night dance parties known as raves. However, for most very late night action, head for WDW. By virtue of Disney's independent legal status, clubs on Disney property are allowed to stay open later than bars elsewhere; you can get a drink there as late as 2:45 AM.

Walt Disney World

Inside Walt Disney World, every hotel has its quota of bars and lounges pushing specialty drinks in the colors of the rainbow. At the hotels and at Pleasure Island—Disney's dedicated after-dark destination—jazz trios and bluegrass bands, DJs and rockers tune up and turn on their amps after dinner's done. Plus, there are two long-run dinner shows that give you and your family an evening of song, dance, and dining, all for a single price. A pricey Broadway knockoff, *Broadway at the Top*, was canceled last year. Check with Guest Services to see if a replacement is being staged.

In the following text, "informal" means wear anything you want, while "casual" is a little dressier. Unless otherwise noted, men never need a jacket or jacket and tie.

Dinner Shows

The **Hoop-Dee-Doo Revue,** staged at Fort Wilderness's rustic Pioneer Hall, may be corny, but it is also the liveliest show in Walt Disney World. A troupe of jokers called the Pioneer Hall Players stomp their feet, wisecrack, and otherwise make merry while the audience chows down on barbecued ribs, fried chicken, corn on the cob, strawberry shortcake, and all the fixin's. There are three shows nightly, and the prime times sell out months in advance in busy seasons. But you're better off eating dinner too early or too late rather than missing the fun altogether—so take what you can get. And if you arrive in Orlando with no reservations, try for a cancellation. *Fort Wilderness Resort, tel. 407/934–7639 in advance (tel. 407/824–2748 on the day of the show). Dress: informal. Reservations required. Seatings at 5, 7:15, and 9:30 PM. Admission: $34 adults, $25 juniors 12–20, $17 children 3–11. No smoking.*

The **Polynesian Luau** is an outdoor barbecue with entertainment appropriate to its colorful, South Pacific setting at the Polynesian Resort. Its fire jugglers and hula-drum dancers are entertaining for the whole family, if never quite as endearing as the napkin-twirlers at the Hoop-Dee-Doo Revue. There are two shows nightly, plus an earlier wingding for children, called Mickey's Tropical Luau, wherein Disney characters do a few numbers, decked out in South Seas garb. *Polynesian Village Resort, tel. 407/934-7639. Dress: casual. Reservations normally necessary at least a month in advance. Polynesian Luau seatings at 6:45 and 9:30 PM. Admission: $32 adults, $24.50 juniors 12–20, $16.50 children 3–11. Mickey's Tropical Luau seating at 4:30 PM. Admission: $28 adults, $21.50 juniors, $12.50 children. AE, MC, V. No smoking.*

IllumiNations

You won't want to miss Epcot Center's grand finale, a laser show that takes place every night, just before the park closes, along the shores of the World Showcase lagoon. Orchestral music, including Tchaikovsky's *1812 Overture*, fills the air. The show starts with laser images moving on screens mounted on barges in the middle of the lagoon. Later, multicolored neon lasers streak across the sky in time to the music while fireworks explode high overhead and low to the water. More laser designs flicker on the clouds of smoke left behind. At the end, lasers trace the outline of the continents on Spaceship Earth, so that it looks like a slowly turning globe. It's a stellar performance.

Some places around the lagoon offer much better vantage points than others. The best locations are the Matsu No Ma Lounge in the Japan pavilion, the patios of the Rose and Crown in the United Kingdom pavilion, and Cantina de San Angel in Mexico. Another good spot is the World Showcase Plaza between the boat docks at the Showcase entrance, but this is often crowded with visitors who want to make a quick exit after the show. If you want to join them here, claim your seat at least an hour in advance. Because the fireworks create a good deal of smoke, use the old lick-the-finger test to see which way the wind is blowing, and position yourself accordingly.

Pleasure Island

Locals as well as tourists patronize this 6-acre after-dark entertainment complex which, like many Disney creations, has a fictitious history to go along with its craftily constructed facades. Ostensibly, the island's derelict factories and warehouses are left over from the sailmaking business of 19th-century entrepreneur Merriweather Adam Pleasure. The complex is connected to Disney Village Marketplace and the mainland by three footbridges; it's a short stroll from the *Empress Lilly*, a riverboat that houses several restaurants. In addition to seven clubs, the island has a few restaurants, shops, and a 10-screen AMC cinema that starts showing movies at 1:30 PM.

Things are always changing on Pleasure Island. New attractions include a '70s dance haven and a jazz club; the nightly New Year's Eve party—complete with fireworks—that started a couple of years ago is still going strong. One thing hasn't changed, and that's the pay-one-price admission that gets you into all the clubs and shows except the movie house. *Pleasure Island, tel. 407/934-7781. Dress: informal. Reservations not necessary. Clubs* *open 7 PM–2 AM year-round, shops 10 AM–1 AM, restaurants usually 11:30 AM–midnight. Cover: $13.95 (includes admittance to all clubs). No cover for shops and restaurants. Children accompanied by parent or guardian admitted to all clubs except Mannequins (same cover as adults).*

The **Adventurers Club** features the AudioAnimatronics showcased in many Disney rides and is supposed to re-create a private club of the 1930s. Apparently quiescent, mounted trophies may start talking, your bar stool may begin sinking, and it's sometimes questionable if the person at the next table is a guest or part of the live entertainment. *Guests under 18 must be accompanied by a parent.*

The **Comedy Warehouse** has evolved from a predictable troupe of comedians to an improvisational setup in which even Mickey and Walt are fair game. Nationally known acts perform in the club's Comics of the Month series, and Entertainment Television tapes its "Stand Up/Sit Down Comedy Show" here. There are five shows nightly. *Guests under 18 must be accompanied by a parent.*

In case the lava lamps and disco balls don't tip you off, the '70s are back at **8trax,** one of Pleasure Island's newest clubs. Slip on your love beads, strap on your platform shoes, and groove to the recorded tunes of Iron Butterfly, the Village People, or Donna Summers. *Guests under 18 must be accompanied by a parent.*

Most of the locals who come to Pleasure Island can be found dancing to Top-40 hits at **Mannequins Dance Palace,** a high-tech nightclub with a revolving dance floor, elaborate lighting, and such special effects as bubbles and snow. *Guests must be 21 or older.*

Live country-and-western music is the focus of the Southwestern-style **Neon Armadillo Music Saloon,** where you can also crack unshelled peanuts, drink a cold beer, or find a partner for the Texas two-step. *Guests under 18 must be accompanied by a parent.*

One of the better places for jazz in central Florida, the **Pleasure Island Jazz Company** presents nightly performances by accomplished soloists through six- or seven-piece bands. The decor recalls a '30s speakeasy, and the well-stocked tapas bar and assorted wines by the glass add a smooth '90s touch. *Guests under 18 must be accompanied by a parent.*

The three-tier **Rock & Roll Beach Club** is always crowded and throbbing with the rock music of the 1950s and 1960s. The live band and disc jockeys never let the action die down. *Guests under 18 must be accompanied by a parent.*

Other After-Dark Doings

Electrical Water Pageant This is one of Disney's small wonders, a 10-minute floating parade of sea creatures outlined in tiny lights, with a terrific blipping, bleeping, toe-tapping electronic score. You can see it from key beaches on Bay Lake and the Seven Seas Lagoon beaches at the Polynesian (at 9), the Grand Floridian (9:15), Fort Wilderness (9:45), the Contemporary (10:05), and, in busy seasons, the Magic Kingdom (10:20). Times occasionally vary so check with Guest Services.

Fireworks WDW is one of the earth's largest single consumers of fireworks. Traditionally there have been spectacular short shows at the Magic Kingdom and Disney-MGM Studios at 10. Times vary during the year, so check with Guest Services just to be certain. You can also find them at Pleasure Island as part of the every-night-is-New-Year's-Eve celebrations.

Movies With all the only-in-WDW activities, it seems a shame to do what you can always do at home. But there are nights when your feet won't walk even one more step. Try the tenplex theater at Pleasure Island (tel. 407/827–1309). It's state-of-the-art and plays all the latest.

Nightcaps Even the busiest hotels have quiet corners. At the Contemporary Resort, try the **Top of the World Lounge,** with its view of the Magic Kingdom, the tiny white lights lining the Main Street rooflines, and busy seasons' nightly fireworks. This is one of the few Disney locales that requires a jacket. At the Polynesian, Disney bartenders ring all the variations on rum punch and piña coladas at the **Tambu Lounge.** At the Grand Floridian, **Narcoossee's** serves jumbo beers. At the Caribbean Beach, **Captain's Hideaway** is the spot, with its tropical potables. At the Dolphin, try the **Copa Banana,** where the tabletops look like pieces of fruit. At the Beach Club, **Martha's Vineyard Lounge** pours a good selection of wines. At Disney Village Marketplace, drop in at **Cap'n Jack's** for huge, beautiful strawberry margaritas, which incorporate not only strawberries but also special strawberry tequila; and don't miss the homemade potato chips sold along with Old Man Rivers and other specialty drinks at the *Empress Lilly's* **Baton Rouge Lounge.** The **Empress Lounge** is the best part of the sumptuously gilt-and-crystal-bedecked Empress Room, also aboard the *Empress Lilly;* there's a harpist, but the place closes down early. The **Village Lounge,** at the Village Marketplace, is another unsung corner; here you can party till the wee hours.

Clubs and Bars The **Giraffe Lounge,** a flashy disco in the Hotel Royal Plaza at Lake Buena Vista, is full of spinning colored lights. It's small, and classy it ain't, but there's a lot going on, including live bands five nights a week, happy hour daily, and themed buffets (Mexican, Cajun, etc.); the place is usually densely packed on weekends. *Hotel Royal Plaza, Lake Buena Vista, tel. 407/828–2828. Dress: informal. Open 4 PM–2 AM; happy hour 4–9:30, buffets 4–8:30. No cover charge. AE, MC, V.*

A big hotel nightclub with live bands, the Australian-themed **Laughing Kookaburra Good Time Bar** draws a serious singles crowd of all ages. The music is loud and the dance floor can get very crowded. The bar serves up 99 brands of beer, plus cocktails. *Buena Vista Palace Hotel, Lake Buena Vista, tel. 407/827–*

3425. Dress: informal. Open Sun.–Thurs., 8 PM–2:30 AM; weekends until 3 AM (food until 1:30 AM). No cover charge. AE, DC, MC, V.

Spectro-Magic The Disney Imagineers have outdone themselves once again with this Magic Kingdom parade incorporating the latest gee-whiz technology in sound and lighting. If you thought the Main Street Electrical Parade couldn't be topped, you just have to see this one: It proceeds down Main Street and through the park nightly at 9—and again at 11 during peak seasons, when the park stays open until midnight. The early showing is for parents with children, while the later running gets night owls and others with the stamina and the know-how to hang around in order to enjoy the Magic Kingdom's most pleasant, least crowded time of day.

The Orlando Area

Disneyesque street signs with bright colors and engaging graphics are not the only new things in downtown Orlando. Night spots have sprung up and are thriving in areas that used to be deserted after the office workers went home. Orlando's club owners figured out that there's big money to be made by luring tourists into the city center. The result is a diverse collection of clubs and nighttime activities offering everything from cutting-edge dance palaces and quiet coffeehouses to jousting tournaments and murder/mystery buffets. Even locals who haven't ventured out in a few years are surprised.

The Arts

If the fantasy wears thin, check out the Orlando fine arts scene in *The Weekly*, a local entertainment magazine, or the "Calendar" in Friday's *Orlando Sentinel*. They are available at newsstands. The average ticket price for locally produced shows rarely exceeds $12 and is often half that.

Orlando has an active agenda of dance, classical music, opera, and theater, much of which takes place at the **Carr Performing Arts Centre** (401 W. Livingston St., Orlando, tel. 407/849–2020). The **Civic Theater of Central Florida** (1001 E. Princeton St., tel. 407/896–7365) presents a variety of shows, with evening performances Wednesday through Saturday and Sunday matinees.

During the school year, Winter Park's **Rollins College** (tel. 407/646–2233) has a choral concert series that is open to the public and is usually free. During the last week in February there is a Bach Music Festival (tel. 407/646–2182) that has been a Winter Park tradition for nearly 60 years. Also at the college is the Annie Russell Theater (tel. 407/646–2145).

The **Orange County Convention and Civic Center** (tel. 407/345–9800), at the south end of International Drive, and the **Orlando Arena** (tel. 407/849–2020), downtown on W. Amelia Street, play host to many big-name performing artists.

Church Street Station

Church Street Station is a complete entertainment complex, made up of old-fashioned saloons, dance halls, dining rooms, and shopping arcades (*see below*) that nearly match Disney in their attention to detail. It all started in the 1970s, when Church Street was distinguished by nothing more than a dilapidated hotel, a few run-down buildings, and a tired old train station. Developer Bob Snow started with just one bar, Rosie O'Grady's, then acquired neighboring properties as his business grew (and boomed). Now both sides of the block are restored. The newest addition to the complex is the **Church Street Exchange**, a razzle-dazzle marketplace with more than 50 specialty shops and restaurants on the first two floors and a jumbo games parlor on another (*see* Chapter 6).

Unlike much of what you see in Walt Disney World, this place doesn't just look authentic—it actually is. The train on the tracks is an actual 19th-century steam engine; the calliope was especially rebuilt to whistle its original tunes. Just about everything down to the cobblestones that clatter under the horse-drawn carriages is the real McCoy. Buildings have been completely redecorated with collectibles and memorabilia from around the world; don't be shy about asking where something came from. You may discover that a mahogany phone booth is actually a confessional salvaged from a French monastery.

You can either spend an entire evening in one part of the complex or wander from area to area, soaking up the peculiar atmosphere of each. Either way, you pay a single admission price. Food and drink cost extra and are not cheap. Parts of the complex are open during the day, but the area is usually quiet then; the pace picks up at night, especially on weekends, with crowds thickest from 10 to 11, when the streets can get insanely busy. The street scene alone is entertaining—saxophone players, singers, and balloon-bending clowns are among the street performers you're likely to spot. *129 W. Church St., Orlando, tel. 407/422–2434. Admission: $15.95 adults, $9.95 children 4–12 (includes admission to all of the following clubs; no admission required to enter Church Street Exchange, to wander through Church Street Station, or to eat in Lili Marlene's). Dress: casual. Reservations not necessary. AE, MC, V.*

Rosie O'Grady's Good Time Emporium, the original bar on Church Street, is a turn-of-the-century saloon with dark wood, brass trim, a full Dixieland band blaring out from a gazebo stage, banjo shows, tap dancers, and vaudeville singers. Is this a set for *The Music Man* or an evening at the Moulin Rouge? It's difficult to say. Multidecker sandwiches and hot dogs are available from 11 AM to 2 AM, along with sodas and such drinks as Flaming Hurricane Punch (served in a souvenir glass). *Open 11 AM–2 AM. Shows at 7:30, 9, 10:30, and midnight.*

Quiet **Apple Annie's Courtyard** offers recorded easy-listening music from Jimmy Buffett to James Taylor for your enjoyment either before or after dinner. It's also a good place to rest your feet after you've finished walking through the Church Street Exchange, to have a drink, and to do some people-watching. *Open 11 AM–2 AM.*

Lili Marlene's Aviator's Pub and Restaurant has the relaxed atmosphere of an English pub and the finest dining on Church Street. Food is hearty, upscale, and very American—mostly steaks, ribs, and seafood. Walls are wood paneled and decked with biplane-era memorabilia; from the ceiling hangs a large-scale model aircraft. There's no music. *Open for lunch 11–4, dinner 5:30–midnight.*

Phineas Phogg's Balloon Works, a Top-40 dance club, plays tunes on a sound system that will blow your argyle socks off. It draws a good-looking yuppie tourist crowd and a few locals, mostly young singles over 21 but with a sprinkling of old-timers showing off their moves on the dance floor. Much of the young crowd feels it is worth the price of admission into the Station just to come here. The place is jammed by midnight. *Open 7 PM–2 AM. Must be at least 21 to enter.*

In the **Orchid Garden Ballroom,** decorative lamps, iron latticework, arched ceilings, and stained-glass windows create a striking Victorian setting rather like an arcade where visitors sit, drink, and listen to a first-rate band pounding out popular tunes from the 1950s to the present. *Open 7:30 PM–2 AM. Shows at 8:30, 9:30, 10:45, midnight, and (Fri. and Sat. only) 1 AM.*

Cracker's Oyster Bar, behind the Orchid Garden, is a good place to get a meal of fresh Florida seafood and pasta or slam down a few oysters with a beer chaser. *Open 11 AM–midnight; lunch 11–4, dinner 4–midnight.*

The **Cheyenne Saloon and Opera House** is the biggest, fanciest, rootin'-tootin' saloon you may ever see. Occupying a trilevel former opera house, the place is full of moose racks, steer horns, buffalo heads, and Remington rifles; the seven-piece country-and-western band that plays there darn near brings the house down. With all the pickin', strummin', fiddlin', hollerin', and do-si-do-in', it's a fun place to people-watch. It's also one of the few places at Church Street to draw a big crowd every night. Make sure you wear your best stompin' shoes and cowboy hat, and practice up on your catcalls. The upstairs restaurant serves chicken-and-ribs fare. *Open 8:30 PM–2 AM; lunch 11–4, dinner 5–midnight. Shows at 8:30, 10, 11:30, and (Fri.–Sat. only) 1 AM.*

Clubs and Bars

If you were to judge only by the bars and nightclubs around Kissimmee, Lake Buena Vista, and International Drive, you would think that no one from Orlando ever went out. Not so. It's just that locals go elsewhere—and they have no shortage of options. Early in the week, many of the clubs are mostly deserted much of the night. Depending on your tastes, the absence of wall-to-wall crowds might make a visit worth the trip.

Downtown Orlando At **Dekko's,** an art deco–themed dance club, the pastel decor, massive light show, and a rainmaker of a sound system draw a 30ish crowd most nights. This is the dress-to-impress set—lots of minidresses and too-hip-to-touch ties. There are occasional progressive nights for the 20ish. *46 N. Orange Ave., tel. 407/648–8727. Cover: $6. Dress: informal (no sneakers). Open Mon. 8 PM–2 AM, Tues. and Wed. 9 PM–2 AM, Thurs. 9 PM–4 AM, Fri. and Sat. 5 PM–4 AM. AE, MC, V.*

The Edge, *the* current hot dance spot in downtown Orlando, is a multilevel converted warehouse with light shows and smoke machines; the pounding dance music is played just below the pain threshold. The musical offerings are schizophrenic: They vary from night to night and will probably change by the time you get here. Big-name acts also perform frequently in an adjoining concert field. *100 W. Livingston, tel. 407/426–9166. Cover: $4–$5. Dress: informal. Open Wed.–Sat. 9 PM–wee hours. AE, MC, V.*

Howl at the Moon has found the perfect solution to the rowdy bar patron who insists on crooning loudly with the band. Orlando's only sing-along bar encourages its patrons to warble the pop classics of yesteryear or campy favorites like the "Time Warp" and "Hokey Pokey" (turn yourself around). This isn't karaoke: Everybody sings at once, so the noise level is just below a sonic boom, but toss back a couple of long-neck beers or one of the house specialty drinks—served in souvenir glasses—and you won't care anymore. Piano players keep the music rolling in the evening, and The World's Most Dangerous Wait Staff adds to the entertainment. No food is served, but the management encourages you to bring your own or order out; several nearby restaurants deliver. *55 W. Church St., 2nd floor of Church St. Marketplace, tel. 407/841–4695. Cover: Wed.–Sat. $2–$4, Sun.–Tues. free. Dress: informal. Open daily noon–2 AM; piano players Sun.–Thurs. 8 PM–2 AM, Fri. and Sat. 6 PM–2 AM. AE, D, MC, V.*

Roomy, two-story **Mulvaney's Irish Pub,** as close to a real Irish pub as you can find in Orlando, has seven imports on tap, including Guinness, and traditional Irish music Wednesday through Saturday. It's packed to the fire-code limits and beyond on weekends and on Orlando Magic game nights. The kitchen serves mostly sandwiches but also has British staples such as shepherd's pie, fish-and-chips, and bangers and mash. *27 W. Church St., tel. 407/872–3296. No cover. Dress: informal. Open 11:30 AM–2 AM (food until 11). AE, MC, V.*

The **Rockin' Rooster** is a great place to see a (usually local) band. No ferns or pool tables to get in the way—just a stage, a few tables, and hordes of occasionally rowdy patrons. Appetizers are the only munchies available. *25 W. Church St., tel. 407/649–4806. Cover: occasional, and $5 or less. Dress: informal. Open Mon.–Sat. 5 PM–2 AM (food until 11). AE, DC, MC, V.*

Elsewhere **Bennigan's,** another young singles spot, is a favorite of people who work in the area. It draws crowds in the early evening and during happy hours from 2 to 7 PM and from 11 PM to midnight, with food served almost until closing. *6324 International Dr., Orlando, tel. 407/351–4436. Dress: informal. Open 11 AM–2 AM (food until 1:30 AM). AE, D, MC, V.*

As you can tell from the name of this tiny bar-and-restaurant, **Dad's Road Kill Café** strives to be different. The bar area is littered with things to keep you busy as you drink your beer and wine: games, puzzles, a computer, plus the obligatory pool table and dart boards. On Friday and Saturday nights, there's low-key live entertainment. The menu is eclectic, a little pricey, and better than most. To get there from I–4 take the Lee Road exit, head east to Orlando Avenue, turn left and go almost 1 mile, and look for the strip mall on the corner of Lake and Orlando. *106 Lake Ave., Maitland, tel. 407/647–5288. No cover. Dress: informal. Open Tues.–Sat. 11 AM–2 AM (food until 1 AM). AE, MC, V.*

J.J. Whispers, a trendy club-disco complex, draws young, fashion-conscious locals in their most tastefully outrageous attire and tries hard to maintain an image of cosmopolitan class. The place is multilevel, state-of-the-art disco. The over-30 set listens to music from the '40s, '50s, and '60s in the Showroom. J.J.'s is also home to Bonkerz, a comedy club featuring touring local and national comics from Thursday through Saturday nights; on Sundays it is transformed into 6 Feet Under, an industrial club that plays hard-core progressive music. Live entertainment regularly includes live bands, with a once-weekly all-male revue. There's always a cover (more on all-you-can-drink nights, often less for women on the assumption that guys will show up anyway); Bonkerz has a cover when a big-name comedian performs. J.J.'s is at the end of the Lee Road Shopping Center, 1½ miles west of I–4 (Lee Rd. exit) via Lee Road; watch for a sharp left-hand turn at Adanson Street. *5100 Adanson St., Orlando, tel. 407/629–4779 or 407/629–2665 (Bonkerz). Cover: $3–$10. Dress: tasteful but outrageous. Open 8 PM–2 AM (food until 2). AE, MC, V.*

Sullivan's Entertainment Complex is a newly renovated country-and-western dance hall with much right-friendly charm, where people of all ages and many families come to strut their stuff. Even Yankees are welcome. Big-name performers entertain on occasion; a house band plays from Tuesday through Saturday. Free country-dance lessons are offered on Sunday, Monday, Tuesday, and Thursday. *1108 S. Orange Blossom Trail (U.S. 441), tel. 407/843–2934. Cover: $2 and up depending on the show. Dress: informal. Open Mon.–Sat. 2 PM–2 AM, Sun. 6 PM–2 AM, with bands 8–2 (food until 2). AE, MC, V.*

Yab Yum is a bohemian refuge from the hustle and bustle of downtown Orlando. Local bands with names like Angel of the Odd or Gunga Din play on most Fridays and Saturdays. The crowd is heavy on aspiring-poet types, who hunch over espressos while giving form to their latest angst; luckily, you don't have to be tormented to enjoy a sandwich, the specialty coffees, or a tasty slab of fresh carrot cake or espresso flan. Beer, wine, and other drinks are also served. *25 Wall St. Plaza, Orlando, tel. 407/422–3322. Cover on band nights: $4. Open Mon.–Thurs. 8:30*

AM–1 AM, Fri. 8:30 AM–2:30 AM, Sat. 11:30 AM–2:30 AM. No credit cards.

Dinner Shows

Dinner shows are an immensely popular form of nighttime entertainment around Orlando. For a single price, these hybrid eatery-entertainment complexes deliver a theatrical production and a multiple-course dinner. Performances run the gamut from jousting to jamboree tunes and tend to be better than the usually forgettable meal; unlimited beer, wine, and soda are usually included, but mixed drinks will cost you extra. What the shows lack in substance and depth they make up for in color and the enthusiasm of the performers. The result is an evening of light entertainment, which youngsters in particular will enjoy. Most shows have seatings at 7 and 9:30, and at all but Mark Two, you sit with strangers at tables for 10 or more; that's part of the fun. Always call to make reservations in advance, especially for weekends. If you're in Orlando in an off-season, try to take in these dinner shows on a busy night—a show playing to a small audience can be pathetic and embarrassing. Also be on the lookout for discount coupons: You'll find them in brochure racks in malls, in hotels, and at the Orange County Convention and Visitor's Bureau in the Mercado Shopping Village on International Drive.

U.S. 192 Area   The **Arabian Nights** looks like an elaborate palace outside; inside it's more like an arena, with seating for more than 1,200 at long tables and a glass-enclosed sky box for private functions. The show features some 25 acts with more than 80 performing horses, music, special effects, and a chariot race; keep your eyes open for a unicorn. The three-course dinners are of prime rib or vegetarian lasagna. *6225 W. Irlo Bronson Memorial Hwy., Kissimmee, tel. 407/396–7400; in Orlando, 407/239–9223 or 800/553–6116; in Canada, 800/533–3615. Admission: $34.95 adults, $19.95 children 3–11. Dress: casual. Reservations advised. AE, D, DC, MC, V.*

Capone's Dinner and Show returns to the gangland Chicago of 1931, when mobsters and their dames represented the height of underworld society. The evening begins in an old-fashioned ice cream parlor, but say the secret password and you'll be ushered inside Al Capone's private Underworld Cabaret and Speakeasy. Dinner is an unlimited Italian buffet that's heavy on pasta. Beer and sangria are included. *4740 W. Irlo Bronson Memorial Hwy., Kissimmee, tel. 407/397–2378. Admission: $29.50 adults, $14.75 children under 13. Dress: casual. Reservations advised. AE, D, MC, V.*

Medieval Times, in a huge, ersatz-medieval manor house, portrays a tournament of sword fights, jousting matches, and other games on a good-versus-evil theme, featuring no fewer than 30 charging horses and a cast of 75 knights, nobles, and maidens. Sound silly? It is. Yet if you view it through the eyes of your children, this two-hour extravaganza is fabulous. That the show takes precedence over the hearty meat-and-potatoes fare is obvious from the dining setup: Everyone sits facing forward at long, narrow banquet tables stepped auditorium style above the tournament area. Additional diversions, in the $2 million Medieval Life area, include a dungeon and torture chamber to tour and demonstrations of antique blacksmithery, woodworking, and pottery making. *4510 W. Irlo Bronson Memorial Hwy., Kissimmee, tel. 407/239–0214 or 800/229–8300. Medieval Times admission: $31.95 adults, $21.95 children 3–12. Medieval Life open 4 PM–9 PM. Admission: $8 adults, $6 children. Dress: informal. Reservations necessary. AE, D, MC, V.*

Wild Bill's Wild West Dinner Show, in the 22-acre Fort Liberty complex, has the kind of slapstick theatrics and country-western shindigging that children really enjoy, including cancan girls, an authentic Texas lariat master, and Native American dancers. The chow, served by a rowdy chorus of cavalry recruits, is beef soup, fried chicken, corn on the cob, pork and beans, and pie and ice cream. Also part of the complex is an 1870s Main Street with shops, a stockade filled with western gifts and souvenirs, and a Brave Warrior Wax Museum. Between 11 AM and 2 PM, many of the acts in the dinner show perform in impromptu fashion in the courtyard. *5260 W. Irlo Bronson Memorial Hwy., Kissimmee, tel. 407/351–5151 or 800/883–8181. Admission: $31.95 adults, $19.95 children 3–11. Museum: $4 adults, $2 children 4–11. Dress: casual. Reservations advised. AE, DC, MC, V. No smoking in the show room.*

International Drive Area **Asian Adventure** is a two-hour Chinese variety show with acrobats, martial arts, magic, and aerial acts, all set in a generic Imperial Palace. A five-course Chinese dinner (with unlimited beer, wine, soft drinks, and coffee) is served during the show. American and children's meals are also available. *International Station, 5211 International Dr., Orlando, tel. 407/351–5655. Admission: $29.95 adults, $19.95 children 3–13. Dress: casual. Reservations advised. AE, D, DC, MC, V.*

King Henry's Feast. In a faux castle near the Orange County Convention Center, Orlando's own King Henry VIII holds court as a group of jesters, jugglers, dancers, magicians, and singers entertain; ostensibly, he is celebrating his birthday and commencing his quest for a seventh bride. Meanwhile, saucy wenches serve forth potato-leek soup, salad, chicken, and ribs. *8984 International Dr., Orlando, tel. 407/351–5151 or 800/883–8181. Admission: $31.95 adults, $19.95 children 3–11. Dress: casual. Reservations advised. AE, D, DC, MC, V.*

Jazzy, New Orleans–style **Mardi Gras** is the best of Orlando's dinner attractions (though youngsters tend to prefer the costumed period fantasies). Here a New Orleans jazz band plays during dinner, after which an hour-long cabaret showcases colorful song-and-dance routines to Dixieland jazz and Latin American and Caribbean beats. The fare is simple and undistinguished—vegetable soup, chicken nuggets, french fries, Key lime pie—just what you'd expect. *Mercado Mediterranean Village, 8445 International Dr., Orlando, tel. 407/351–5151 or 800/883–8181. Admission: $31.95 adults, $19.95 children 3–11. Dress: casual. Reservations advised. AE, D, DC, MC, V.*

Mark Two, Orlando's first true dinner theater, stages complete Broadway musicals such as *Oklahoma!, My Fair Lady, West Side Story,* and *South Pacific* throughout the year and musical revues chockablock with Broadway tunes during the Christmas holidays. For about two hours before curtain, you can order from the bar and help yourself at buffet tables laden with institutional seafood Newburg, baked whitefish, meats, and salad; dessert arrives during intermission. Sets, costumes, music, and choreography are all done in-house; direction is by the theater's owner; and actors are mostly local. Under the circumstances, you wouldn't expect the world's best *Oklahoma!* and you don't get it. But it can be a pleasure to revisit these old favorites while sitting comfortably with a drink in hand. Each show runs for six to eight weeks, with eight shows a week, including matinees. Note that unlike other dinner theaters, the Mark Two offers only tables for two and four. Young children usually find it impossible to sit through the shows, and the steep charge provides ample reason to leave them with a baby-sitter. *Edgewater Center, 3376 Edgewater Dr., Orlando (from I–4 take Exit 44 and go west), tel. 407/843–6275 or 800/726–6275. Admission: $29–$33 adults, $24–$27 children under 12. Dress: casual. Reservations advised. AE, D, MC, V. Performances Wed.–Sat. at 8; Wed., Thurs., Sat. at 1:15; Sun. at 6:30. Closed Mon. and Tues.*

If Sherlock Holmes has always intrigued you, head for **Sleuths Mystery Dinner Show,** where your four-course meal and unlimited soft drinks are served up with a healthy dose of conspiracy. The whodunit performance stops short of revealing the perpetrator; you get to question the characters and attempt to solve the mystery. Maybe it was the butler? Seven mysteries are rotated throughout the year. *7508 Republic Dr., Orlando, tel. 407/363–1985 or 800/393–1985. Admission: $31.95 adults, $21.95 children. Dress: casual. Reservations required. AE, D, MC, V. Performances Mon.–Sat. 6 and 9, Sun. 7:30.*

Sports Bars

So you're stuck in Orlando and the hotel bar isn't showing State U's biggest game of the year? No problem. Among about a dozen sports bars around town, the following pair offer dozens of games every week and are usually willing to tune their satellites in to pick up your requests.

Coaches Locker Room, a two-level sports palace, boasts seven satellite dishes, 20 satellite receivers, six big-screen TVs, and 12 smaller monitors. Coaches shows every pro football contest, plus every other kind of sport imaginable. The buffalo wings are worth trying. It's in the strip mall behind T.G.I.Friday's at the intersection of I–4 and Route 436. *249 W. Rte. 436, Altamonte Springs, tel. 407/869–4446. Dress: informal. Open 11 AM–2 AM (food until 2 AM). AE, D, DC, MC, V.*

The rambling, multiroom **Sports Dimension** has 12 satellite dishes and 12 big-screen TVs; more than 75 screens hang from the walls and ceiling and above the dance floor. There are even two sets in the men's room, lending new meaning to "standing room only." *3001 Curry Ford Rd., tel. 407/895–0807. Dress: informal. Open weekdays 4 PM–2 AM, weekends 11 AM–2 AM (food until 11 PM). AE, MC, V.*

11 The Cocoa Beach Area

Updated by
Dee Rivers

The most direct route from Greater Orlando to the coast, the Beeline Expressway, is arrow straight, cut through forests of long-needle pine and laid across the yawning savannas of the south-to-north St. Johns River, which begins life as a tiny stream in a place called Hell and Blazes, Florida. In this countryside of cedars, red maples, and palmettos, American egrets, blue herons, and shy limpkin wade and fish for dinner; ibis tend their chicks; and anhinga perch where they can, spreading their wings to dry. High above watery prairies yellow with wild mustard and butterflies, hawks hunt and osprey soar over their nests that crown stately sabal palms, Florida's official tree. It feels a million miles from the artificial worlds of the theme parks, and it's one good reason to make the trip from Orlando to Brevard County, on the east coast, only an hour away.

The laid-back beach communities are another. Although the winter season alone counts about 460,000 vacationers, the area's white sands are much less densely built up than Daytona area beaches. Sun worshipers don't have to worry about being run over as they frolic or stroll—no cars are allowed on the sands. Moreover, the area is home to Kennedy Space Center and Spaceport USA and offers water sports, fishing, golf, nature, nightlife, and some distinctive shopping.

Accommodations, restaurants, and shopping are relatively close to each other and to all of the region's points of interest. And if you're lucky enough to be in town during a space shot, you'll be treated to a spectacular sight.

If you have the time, the best plan is to set aside two or three days to enjoy the area.

Essential Information

Important Addresses and Numbers

Tourist Information
Contact the **Brevard County Tourist Development Council** (2725 St. Johns St., Melbourne 32940, tel. 407/633–2110 or 800/872–1969) and the **Cocoa Beach Area Chamber of Commerce** (400 Fortenberry Rd., Merritt Island 32952, tel. 407/459–2200). Both can provide general information as well as dates for rocket launches.

Medical Emergency
Cape Canaveral Hospital (701 W. Cocoa Beach Causeway, or Rte. 520, Cocoa Beach, tel. 407/799–7111).

Getting Around

The Beeline Expressway (Rte. 528) is accessible from either I–4 or the Florida Turnpike. Tolls for the trip, up to $2.45 for a car, are a bargain-basement fare for the scenery. The coast is about 90 minutes from WDW, 60 minutes from Orlando.

If you're heading to Cocoa Beach, don't get off the Beeline at any of the Cocoa exits. The expressway eventually turns into U.S. A1A, the beach area's main artery, which is also called At-

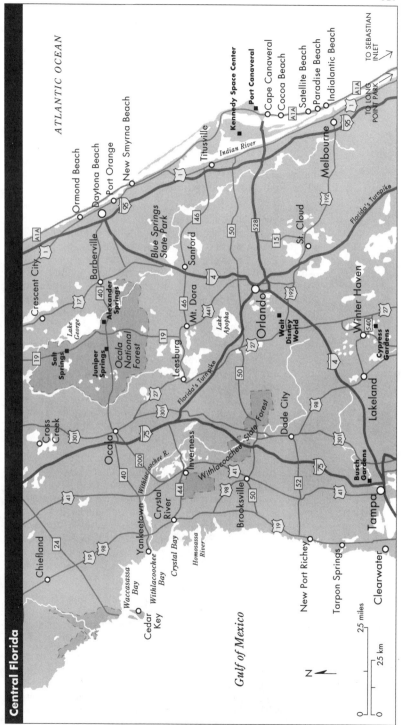

Central Florida

lantic Avenue. U.S. A1A's junction with Route 520, a few miles south of the Beeline changeover, marks the heart of Cocoa Beach.

Exploring the Cocoa Beach Area

To get a jump start on the day, rise and shine and watch the spectacular sunrise from the beach. Then head for Spaceport USA at the Kennedy Space Center, which is free—perhaps the best entertainment bargain in Florida. To get here from the Beeline, watch for signs for Kennedy Space Center, then take Route 407 to Route 405 and head east.

Kennedy Space Center To get an overview of the area and some historical background, take the two narrated **bus tours:** One passes by some of NASA's office and assembly buildings, including current launch facilities and the Space Shuttle launching and landing sites. The other goes to Cape Canaveral Air Force Station, where early launch pads and unmanned rockets illuminate the beginnings of the space program. Security concerns mandate that many sights be viewed through a tour bus window. However, live and recorded narrations are provided during both tours and there are historical exhibits at camera stops.

Even more dramatic is the IMAX film *The Dream Is Alive*, shown every 45 minutes in the IMAX I Theater. Projected onto a 5½-story screen, this overwhelming 40-minute film, shot mostly by the astronauts, takes you from astronaut training through a thundering shuttle launch and into the cabins where the astronauts live while in space, then back to Earth again. A second film, *The Blue Planet,* is shown about every 20 minutes in the IMAX II Theater.

In addition, you can stroll through the Spaceport's outdoor **rocket garden**, its lawns bristling with rockets, and tour a museum filled with spacecraft that have explored the last frontier. For a close-up of how space-related products have affected our daily lives, see *Satellites and You*, a free multimedia presentation at **Spaceport Central**. *Kennedy Space Center; tel. 407/452–2121. Bus tours: $7 adults, $4 children 3–11. IMAX film: $4 adults, $2 children 3–11; shown daily 10–6:35. Complex open daily 9 AM–dark; last tour 2 hr before dark. Closed on certain launch dates (call ahead).*

At the **United States Astronaut Hall of Fame** museum, one block east of U.S. 1, at the entrance to Spaceport USA, you can view videotapes of historic moments in the space program. *Tel. 407/269–6100. Admission: $6.95 adults, $4.95 children 3–11. Open daily 9–5, longer in summer.*

Port Canaveral After you leave the Space Center, going toward Cocoa Beach southbound on the Beeline and U.S. A1A, the first traffic light you reach marks the entrance to Port Canaveral, a once-bustling commercial fishing area where cruise ships and charter and party fishing boats now dock. It's not quaint and not densely populated with vessels, but it offers a glimpse into the Florida off the tourist path, particularly **Jetty Park,** where friendly conversations are hard to avoid; many locals like after-dark fishing from the jetties.

Cocoa Beach A few miles farther south on U.S. A1A is Cocoa Beach. From the center of town, go west for a couple of miles on Route 520; just before you reach the Cocoa Beach Causeway you'll come to the Banana River and the *Little River Queen,* an old-time riverboat that offers sightseeing and dinner cruises on which you'll see manatees, dolphins, many bird species, and some wonderful riverside homes. The *Little River Queen* sails only when at least 30 interested people make reservations. Book early and wait for a call back verifying that the cruise will sail. *500 W. Cocoa Beach Causeway, Cocoa Beach, tel. 407/783–2380. Sightseeing cruise Mon.–Fri. 2–4 PM; $10 adults, $6 children under 12. Lunch cruise Sat. and Sun. 11 AM–1:30 PM; $13 adults, $9 children. Buffet dinner cruise Sun.–Thurs. 6:30–9 PM; $19 adults, $11 children. Dixieland Jazz dinner cruise Fri. and Sat. 7–10 PM; $26 adults, $15 children.*

If you continue westbound on Route 520, you'll end up in **downtown Cocoa.** Cobblestone walkways wind through **Olde Cocoa Village,** a cluster of restored turn-of-the-century buildings now occupied by restaurants and specialty shops purveying pottery, macramé, leather and silvercraft, afghans, fine art, and clothing. Don't just stay on the main drag. If you'd like to explore the restored area from a horse-drawn buggy, call Mr. Olsson at Foxmeadow Farm (tel. 407/632–6754).

At 300 Delannoy Avenue, one street east of Brevard Avenue, is antique, high-ceilinged **Travis' Hardware,** a real vintage hardware store where, if you go there for thumbtacks or tape, you may not come out for four hours. **Ron Jon Surf Shop** (4151 N. Atlantic Ave., Cocoa Beach, tel. 407/799–8840) is marketing madness, a castle that's as purple, pink, and glittery as any amusement park monolith, except that it's plunked down in the middle of the beach community. It's a local attraction in its own right.

To see what the land was like in other eras, visit the **Brevard Museum of History and Natural Science.** Don't overlook the hands-on discovery rooms and the Collection of Victoriana. The museum's nature center has 22 acres of trails encompassing three distinct ecosystems—sand pine hills, lakelands, and marshlands. To get here from Cocoa Beach, take Route 520 to U.S. 1 and Michigan Avenue, then turn west and follow the signs. *2201 Michigan Ave., Cocoa Beach, tel. 407/632–1830. Admission: $3 adults, $1.50 students, children under 3 free. Open Tues.–Sat. 10–4, Sun. 1–4; closed Mon.*

Beaches

On Florida's mid-Atlantic coast from Ormond Beach south to Sebastian Inlet, there are about 100 miles of white-sand beaches. Generally, those below Satellite Beach—south of Cocoa Beach—tend to be rocky, with an uneven bottom.

The 57,000-acre **Canaveral National Seashore** (tel. 904/428–3384), just 8 miles south of New Smyrna Beach on U.S. A1A, is the home of more than 250 species of birds and animals. The area is undeveloped and hilly with dunes, and the strand itself is sprinkled with seashells. A hiking trail leads to the top of an Indian shell midden at Turtle Mound, where picnic tables are available. There's a visitor center on U.S. A1A. Parts of the park are closed before launches, sometimes as much as two weeks in advance, so call ahead.

Playalinda Beach (tel. 407/267–1110), part of the National Seashore, is the longest stretch of undeveloped coast on Florida's Atlantic Seaboard. It is remote, with pristine sands; hundreds of giant sea turtles come ashore here from May to August to lay their eggs, and the extreme northern area is favored by nude sun worshipers. Eight parking lots anchor the beach at mile intervals. There are no lifeguards, but park rangers patrol. Take Avon's Skin So Soft in case of horseflies. To get here, follow U.S. 1 north into Titusville to Route 406 (I–95, Exit 80), follow Route 406 east across the Indian River, then Route 402 east for 12 more miles. Do visit the **Merritt Island Wildlife Refuge** (tel. 407/861–0667; open weekdays 8–4:30, Saturday 9–5), which you'll pass on this stretch, to see up close, along nature trails, the same kind of scenery you whizzed past on the Beeline.

Cocoa Beach on U.S. A1A has dressing rooms, showers, playgrounds, picnic areas with grills, snack shops, and surfside parking lots. Beach vendors offer necessities, and guards are on duty in summer.

Satellite Beach is a sleepy little community just south of Patrick Air Force Base. Although no great shakes in the surfing world, it is the best place on the coast to surf right now. The only amenities are several picnic areas.

Small, scenic, 1,600-foot **Paradise Beach** (tel. 407/779–4008) is part of a 10-acre park north of Indianlantic on U.S. A1A. It has showers, rest rooms, a refreshment stand, and lifeguards in summer. Picnic tables must be reserved.

The 576-acre **Sebastian Inlet State Recreation Area** (tel. 407/984–4852), 12 miles south of Melbourne on U.S. A1A, offers 3 miles of interesting beach good for swimming, surfing, and snorkeling. The beach is rocky and the sand coarser than elsewhere along the coast, and the underwater drop-off is often sharp. It's fun for treasure hunters, because storms occasionally wash up pieces of eight from the area's ancient Spanish shipwrecks. Sebastian is also a favorite destination for Florida anglers. The park has a bathhouse, a concession, a fishing jetty, a boat ramp, campsites (tel. 407/589–9659), and the McLarty Treasure Museum (tel. 407/589–2147), built to commemorate the loss of the Spanish Treasure Fleet of 1715.

Sports

The **Recreation Complex of Cocoa Beach** (5000 Tom Warriner Blvd., tel. 407/868–3333) offers a variety of sports facilities. Its 27-hole championship golf course meanders for 4 miles along the Banana River. Touching the shores of 17 lakes, the course is also home to much wildlife. The complex offers 10 lighted tennis courts, a restaurant, and a riverside pavilion with picnic tables.

Biking

Although there are no bike trails as such in the area, biking is allowed on the beaches and the Cocoa Beach Causeway. Bikes can be rented hourly, daily, or weekly at Ron Jon Surf Shop (*see* Exploring the Cocoa Beach Area, *above*).

Fishing

Check *Florida Today*, the local newspaper, or bait-and-tackle shops to find out what's biting where. There's **surf casting** for bluefish, pompano, sea bass, and flounder; success is mixed and depends on the season. Anglers **fishing from piers** sometimes pull in mackerel, trout, sheepshead, and tarpon; the Titusville pier has good shrimping. All major beach towns have lighted piers (admission usually $1–$4). You can also fish from some bridges. And there are numerous **deep-sea charters** around Port Canaveral; contact Cape Marina (800 Scallop Dr., tel. 407/783–8410), Miss Cape Canaveral (630 Glen Cheek Dr., tel. 407/783–5274), or Pelican Princess (655 Glen Cheek Dr., tel. 407/784–3473).

Dining

Moderate prices and fresh seafood are the rule, but some restaurants have unusual themes. The Cocoa Beach Pier is the home of a lot of good eating: In addition to the Pier House Restaurant (*see below*), there's **Oh Shucks** (tel. 407/783–4050), where you can get oysters on the half-shell and burgers; **Marlin's** (tel. 407/783–7549), which serves light meals indoors; and the **Boardwalk** (tel. 407/868–0420), an open-air bar where finger food reigns and live music livens up weekends.

$$$ **Bernard's Surf.** Don't come to Bernard's for the view; there are no windows in its two main dining rooms. Come for steaks and local fish, particularly the crested red snapper, a house specialty crusted with seasoned red, yellow, and green bell peppers and topped with a mango-brandy sauce. Rusty's Raw Bar, the more casual part of the restaurant, offers 20 different seafood dishes as well as burgers and fries. *2 S. Atlantic Ave., Cocoa Beach, tel.*

407/783–2401. Dress: casual. Reservations advised. AE, D, DC, MC, V.

Mango Tree Restaurant. Candles, fresh flowers, white linen tablecloths, rattan basket chairs with fluffy cushions, and eggshell-color walls hung with tropical watercolors by local artists set a romantic mood here. The intimate dining room overlooks a garden aviary that is home to doves and pheasants. Try the broiled grouper topped with scallops, shrimp, and hollandaise sauce. *118 N. Atlantic Ave., Cocoa Beach, tel. 407/799–0513. Dress: casual. Reservations advised. AE, MC, V. Closed Mon.*

$$ **Ashley's.** The friendly servers in this snug wood-and-stucco restaurant will loan you the "U.S. Ghost Register" to read about the history of the place while you decide whether you want steak, seafood, or any of a wide range of other American favorites. Ladies may sense a presence in the powder room, purportedly the restless ghost of an ill-fated town girl; another spirit haunts the staircase, occasionally rudely pushing guests. Although Ashley's has a Rockledge address, it's only about 20 minutes from Cocoa Beach. *1609 S. U.S. 1, Rockledge, tel. 407/636–6430. Dress: casual. Reservations advised on weekends. MC, V.*

Black Tulip Restaurant. A tree is the room's centerpiece; fresh flowers and candlelight reflected in mirrored walls enhance the Continental cuisine, including roast duckling with apples and cashews, as well as mahimahi with scallops and herbs. The restaurant is in restored Cocoa. *207 Brevard Ave., Cocoa, tel. 407/631–1133. Dress: casual. Reservations recommended. AE, DC, MC, V.*

The Boathouse Restaurant. From the tables of this local favorite that opened in 1965, diners can watch the arrivals of both glittering cruise ships and working shrimp and scallop boats while enjoying the aerobatic antics of the gulls and pelicans that lobby for fishy snacks. The menu offers the freshest of the local catch, but you can also order chicken, lobster, prime rib, and beef. A nautical theme prevails, and a gallery displays autographed photographs of astronauts. *700 Scallop Dr., Port Canaveral, tel. 407/783–1580. Dress: casual. Reservations advised. AE, D, DC, MC, V.*

Dockside. Physically attached to Gatsby's Food and Spirits, Dockside is even more casual. You can eat outdoors on the deck and drink at the outside bar. Sundays at Dockside are a local tradition, for both the champagne brunch and the entertainment—usually a local band—that follows in the afternoon. *480 W. Cocoa Beach Causeway, Cocoa Beach, tel. 407/783–2380. Dress: casual. Reservations advised for brunch. AE, DC, MC, V.*

Gatsby's Food and Spirits. This friendly eatery on the banks of the Banana River offers prime rib, steaks, and seafood amid portraits of old-time movie stars, potted palms, brass railings, and other Roaring '20s touches. The bartender is famous for his penni wieni wo wos (sometimes known as shooters)—shots of peach schnapps, vodka, and cranberry juice. *480 Cocoa Beach Causeway, Cocoa Beach, tel. 407/783–2380. Dress: casual. Reservations advised. AE, DC, MC, V.*

Heidelberg. Roast duck and fillet Madagascar are the specialties at this elegant establishment, with its crisp linens, fresh flowers, and dark-red color scheme. All the soups and desserts are home-made; try the apple strudel and the rum-zapped almond-cream tortes. *7 N. Orlando Ave., opposite City Hall, Cocoa Beach, tel. 407/783–6806. Dress: casual. Reservations advised. AE, MC, V.*

Pier House Restaurant. In this elegant restaurant in a shopping, dining, and entertainment complex on Cocoa Beach Pier, you can enjoy fresh fish in a room with floor-to-ceiling windows that overlook the ocean. Try the mahimahi, or the grouper, which you can order broiled, blackened, grilled, or fried. *401 Meade Ave., Cocoa Beach, tel. 407/783–7549. Dress: casual. Reservations advised. AE, DC, MC, V.*

$ **Alma's Italian Restaurant.** Five crowded, noisy dining rooms keep the waitresses here busy. The specialty of the house is veal Marsala, and the cellar stocks more than 200 imported and do-mestic wines. The restaurant has a warm, casual atmosphere with red-checked tablecloths, stone floors, and a large stained-glass window. *306 N. Orlando Ave., Cocoa Beach, tel. 407/783–1981. Dress: casual. Reservations advised. AE, DC, MC, V.*

Herbie K's. This 1950s rock-and-roll diner has become a landmark since its 1987 opening. Servers dress, walk, and talk the '50s—you'll see saddle shoes and revisit such expressions as "Daddy-o" and "doll-face." Famous for its burgers, Herbie K's also serves home-style blue plate specials and old-fashioned ice-cream desserts. It's great for families. *2080 N. Atlantic Ave., Cocoa Beach, tel. 407/783–6740. Dress: informal. AE, D, DC, MC, V.*

Lone Cabbage Fish Camp. The natural habitat of wildlife and local characters, Lone Cabbage sits on the St. Johns River 9 miles north of Cocoa city limits on Route 520 and 4 miles west of I–95. The catfish, frogs' legs, turtle, country ham, and alliga-tor on the menu make the drive well worthwhile. A fun family outing, this one-of-a-kind spot also has a dock where you can fish, buy your bait, or rent a canoe for a trip on the St. Johns. On the first and third Sunday of every month, there's a fish fry and spirited country-and-western hoedown—not for the shy. *8199 Rte. 520, Cocoa Beach, tel. 407/632–4199. Dress: casual. No credit cards.*

Lodging

Most lodging in Cocoa Beach is on U.S. A1A around its intersec-tion with Route 520.

$$$ **Holiday Inn Cocoa Beach Resort.** When two adjacent beach ho-tels were redesigned and a promenade park landscaped between them, the Holiday Inn Cocoa Beach Resort was born. Public rooms are plush and modern, and there are many facilities. Op-tions include standard, king, or oceanfront suites (which include a living room with sleeper sofa), or you can opt for a villa or bilevel loft. All come with cable TV, including free Showtime. *1300 N. Atlantic Ave., Cocoa Beach 32931, tel. 407/783–2271. 500*

rooms. Facilities: Olympic-size outdoor heated pool, 2 lighted tennis courts, children's program, baby-sitting. AE, DC, MC, V.

Radisson Resort at the Port. This elegant new resort directly across the street from Port Canaveral is the closest beach-area resort to Walt Disney World, and though it's not on the ocean, the hotel provides complimentary transportation to the nearest strands as well as to restaurants and shopping on request. Tame peacocks roam the grounds. Rooms have a Caribbean motif, with wicker appointments, hand-painted wallpaper, and ceiling fans; they come with one king-size or two double beds and have TVs with cable and HBO. The pool is lavish, in the best central Florida fashion, tropically landscaped and complete with its 95-foot mountain waterfalls and its cascade. Facilities are equally abundant, as you'd expect of a resort of this caliber. *8701 Astronaut Blvd., Cape Canaveral 32920, tel. 407/784–0000 or 800/333–3333. 200 rooms. Facilities: restaurant, pool, children's pool, whirlpool, 2 lighted tennis courts, fitness center, convention center (with fax, photocopying, and secretarial support), playground, game room, guest laundry, complimentary local transportation, daily shuttle to Orlando International Airport. AE, D, DC, MC, V.*

$$ **Wakulla Motel.** This motel has the best occupancy rate on the beach. Its completely furnished five-room suites, designed to sleep six, are ideal for families; they include two bedrooms, a living room, dining room, and fully equipped kitchen and have cable TV with HBO. The grounds are landscaped with tropical vegetation. *3550 N. Atlantic Ave., Cocoa Beach 32931, tel. 407/783–2230. 116 suites. Facilities: 2 heated outdoor pools, shuffleboard court, outdoor grills, guest laundry.*

$ **Comfort Inn and Suite Resort.** This hostelry is across the street from the ocean and within walking distance of more than a dozen restaurants. You can choose from standard double rooms, minisuites, one-bedroom ocean-view suites, and fully equipped efficiencies. All are clean, comfortable, and decorated in light, tropical colors. The poolside bar has a waterfall, and there's a pond full of tropical fish, in addition to the many facilities. *3901 N. Atlantic Ave., Cocoa Beach 32931, tel. 407/783–2221. 40 rooms, 40 minisuites, 40 ocean-view suites, 40 efficiencies. Facilities: lounge, pool, whirlpool, lighted volleyball court, shuffleboard, table tennis, playground. D, MC, V.*

Pelican Landing Resort on the Ocean. This two-story beachfront motel is friendly and warm, so many guests call it a home away from home. Rooms have ocean views, microwaves, and TVs with cable and HBO; one even has a screened porch. Boardwalks to the beach, picnic tables, and a grill round out the amenities. *1201 S. Atlantic Ave., Cocoa Beach 32931, tel. 407/783–7197. 11 units. Facilities: beach, efficiencies with fully equipped kitchens. D, MC, V.*

Nightlife

In the Olde Cocoa area, the **Cocoa Village Playhouse** (300 Brevard Ave., Cocoa Beach, tel. 407/636–5050)—the area's community theater—mounts plays and musicals featuring local talent from September through March. The rest of the year the stage hosts touring professional productions, concerts, and, in summer, shows aimed at children on vacation.

At **Bumpers,** a cozy '50s-style lounge, they spin oldies for happy dancers amid memorabilia of the Eisenhower era; a 1957 Chevy serves as the DJ's booth, for example. Food is available from Herbie K's, the diner that shares the premises. *2080 N. Atlantic Ave., Cocoa Beach, tel. 407/783-9222. Open. Mon.–Thurs. 4 PM–midnight, Fri. and Sat. 4 PM– 2 AM. Dress: informal. AE, D, DC, MC, V.*

Coconuts, an oceanside night spot, draws under-40s with its Mr. Muscle and bikini contests and, in April, a Jet-ski rodeo. There's live music for dancing most evenings. *2 Minuteman Causeway, Cocoa Beach, tel. 407/784-1422. Open Mon.–Sat. 11 AM–2 AM, Sun. 10 AM–midnight. Dress: informal. AE, D, MC, V.*

Dino's, an intimate piano bar with mood lighting and great music, is a place to jam, sing, or just listen. A jazz combo plays on Wednesday, Friday, and Saturday. There's a small dance floor. *315 Cocoa Beach Causeway, Cocoa Beach, tel. 407/784-5470. Open noon–2 AM. Dress: casual. AE, D, DC, MC, V.*

Index

What's hot, where it's hot!

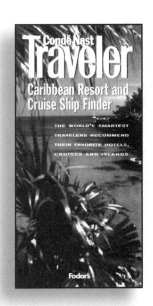

Condé Nast Traveler Caribbean Resort and Cruise Ship Finder
The World's Smartest Travelers Recommend Their Favorite Hotels, Cruises and Islands

Incorporating the results of the enormously influential *Condé Nast Traveler* survey with comprehensive Fodor's travel information — this brand new guide features 150 hotels and resorts, 30 cruise lines, 28 islands, and 60 pages of maps.

Cruises and Ports of Call 1995
Choosing the Perfect Ship and Enjoying Your Time Ashore

The most comprehensive cruise guide available offers all the essentials for planning a cruise: selecting the right ship, getting the best deals, and making the most of your time in port.

"A gold mine of information."
—New York Post

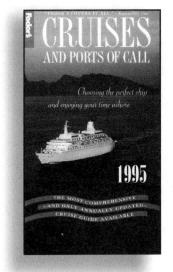

Fodor's Travel Guides

Available at bookstores everywhere, or call 1–800–533–6478, 24 hours a day.

U.S. Guides

Alaska	Las Vegas, Reno, Tahoe	Philadelphia & the Pennsylvania Dutch Country	USA
Arizona	Los Angeles	The Rockies	The Upper Great Lakes Region
Boston	Maine, Vermont, New Hampshire	San Diego	Virginia & Maryland
California	Maui	San Francisco	Waikiki
Cape Cod, Martha's Vineyard, Nantucket	Miami & the Keys	Santa Fe, Taos, Albuquerque	Walt Disney World and the Orlando Area
The Carolinas & the Georgia Coast	New England	Seattle & Vancouver	Washington, D.C.
Chicago	New Orleans	The South	
Colorado	New York City	The U.S. & British Virgin Islands	
Florida	Pacific North Coast		
Hawaii			

Foreign Guides

Acapulco, Ixtapa, Zihuatanejo	The Czech Republic & Slovakia	Japan	Provence & the Riviera
Australia & New Zealand	Eastern Europe	Kenya & Tanzania	Rome
Austria	Egypt	Korea	Russia & the Baltic Countries
The Bahamas	Euro Disney	London	Scandinavia
Baja & Mexico's Pacific Coast Resorts	Europe	Madrid & Barcelona	Scotland
Barbados	Florence, Tuscany & Umbria	Mexico	Singapore
Berlin	France	Montréal & Québec City	South America
Bermuda	Germany	Morocco	Southeast Asia
Brittany & Normandy	Great Britain	Moscow & St. Petersburg	Spain
Budapest	Greece	The Netherlands, Belgium & Luxembourg	Sweden
Canada	Hong Kong	New Zealand	Switzerland
Cancún, Cozumel, Yucatán Peninsula	India	Norway	Thailand
Caribbean	Ireland	Nova Scotia, Prince Edward Island & New Brunswick	Tokyo
China	Israel	Paris	Toronto
Costa Rica, Belize, Guatemala	Italy	Portugal	Turkey
			Vienna & the Danube Valley

Special Series

Fodor's Affordables

Caribbean

Europe

Florida

France

Germany

Great Britain

Italy

London

Paris

**Fodor's Bed &
Breakfast and
Country Inns Guides**

America's Best B&Bs

California

Canada's Great
Country Inns

Cottages, B&Bs and
Country Inns of
England and Wales

Mid-Atlantic Region

New England

The Pacific
Northwest

The South

The Southwest

The Upper Great
Lakes Region

The Berkeley Guides

California

Central America

Eastern Europe

Europe

France

Germany & Austria

Great Britain &
Ireland

Italy

London

Mexico

Pacific Northwest &
Alaska

Paris

San Francisco

**Fodor's Exploring
Guides**

Australia

Boston &
New England

Britain

California

The Caribbean

Florence & Tuscany

Florida

France

Germany

Ireland

Italy

London

Mexico

New York City

Paris

Prague

Rome

Scotland

Singapore & Malaysia

Spain

Thailand

Turkey

Fodor's Flashmaps

Boston

New York

Washington, D.C.

Fodor's Pocket Guides

Acapulco

Bahamas

Barbados

Jamaica

London

New York City

Paris

Puerto Rico

San Francisco

Washington, D.C.

Fodor's Sports

Cycling

Golf Digest's Best
Places to Play

Hiking

The Insider's Guide
to the Best Canadian
Skiing

Running

Sailing

Skiing in the USA &
Canada

USA Today's Complete
Four Sports Stadium
Guide

**Fodor's Three-In-Ones
(guidebook, language
cassette, and phrase
book)**

France

Germany

Italy

Mexico

Spain

**Fodor's
Special-Interest
Guides**

Complete Guide to
America's National
Parks

Condé Nast Traveler
Caribbean Resort and
Cruise Ship Finder

Cruises and Ports
of Call

Euro Disney

France by Train

Halliday's New
England Food
Explorer

Healthy Escapes

Italy by Train

London Companion

Shadow Traffic's New
York Shortcuts and
Traffic Tips

Sunday in New York

Sunday in San
Francisco

Touring Europe

Touring USA:
Eastern Edition

Walt Disney World and
the Orlando Area

Walt Disney World
for Adults

**Fodor's Vacation
Planners**

Great American
Learning Vacations

Great American
Sports & Adventure
Vacations

Great American
Vacations

Great American
Vacations for Travelers
with Disabilities

National Parks and
Seashores of the East

National Parks
of the West

**The Wall Street
Journal Guides to
Business Travel**

*The only guide to explore a
Disney World you've never seen before:*

The one for grown-ups.

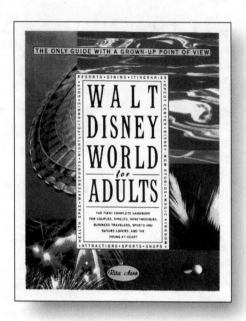

This is the only guide written specifically for the millions of adults who visit Walt Disney World each year <u>without</u> kids. Upscale, sophisticated, packed full of facts and maps, *Walt Disney World for Adults* provides up-to-date information on hotels, restaurants, sports facilities, and health clubs, as well as unique itineraries for adults. With *Walt Disney World for Adults* in hand, you'll get the most out of one of the world's most fascinating, most complex playgrounds.

At bookstores everywhere, or call **1-800-533-6478.**

Wet 'n Wild

$3 OFF

Present this coupon and save $3.00 off the regular all–day adult or child admission price. Coupon good for up to six people. Not to be used in conjunction with any other discounted offer or afternoon pricing.

Expires 12/31/95.

Wet 'n Wild®

$3 OFF

Present this coupon and save $3.00 off the regular all-day adult or child admission price. Coupon good for up to six people. Not to be used in conjunction with any other discounted offer or afternoon pricing.

Expires 12/31/95.

BUSCH GARDENS.

〜〜〜〜 TAMPA BAY, FLORIDA 〜〜〜〜

NEW FOR 1993

KUMBA

THE SOUTHEAST'S LARGEST & FASTEST ROLLER COASTER!

$3.00 OFF

ADMISSION

Present this coupon at the Main Entrance prior to entering the park and receive $3.00 off the regular daily general adult or child's admission price. Coupon good only on the dates specified. Coupon has no cash value and cannot be used in combination with any other discount offer. Limit six guests per coupon. Coupon cannot be duplicated. Operating hours and general admission prices subject to change without notice.

COUPON VALID THRU DEC. 31, 1995
PLU# 2791c/2792a

Anheuser-Busch Theme Parks

BUSCH GARDENS.
TAMPA BAY, FLORIDA

SEE A RARE BREED AND SAVE

$2.50 OFF

ADMISSION!

See the rare manatee up close, both above and below the water at Sea World's newest attraction, *Manatees: The Last Generation?*[SM]!

Manatees: The Last Generation?

Plus, learn how to help this gentle, endangered animal. You'll also have the chance to enjoy *Pacific Point Preserve*[SM] sea lion habitat and the hilarious new sea lion and otter show, *Hotel Clyde and Seamore!*

Limit six guests per coupon. Not valid with other discounts or on purchase of multi-park/multi-visit passes or tickets. Present coupon before bill is totaled. Redeemable only at time of ticket purchase. Photocopies not accepted. Prices subject to change without notice. **Valid through 12/31/95 only.**

© 1993 Sea World of Florida, Inc. All rights reserved.

4147/4148

Sea World®
Orlando, Florida
Make Contact With Another World®
An Anheuser-Busch Theme Park

$3⁰⁰ OFF
All-Day Studio Pass
Regular admission price $35⁰⁰ (plus tax)

RIDE THE MOVIES®!

At Universal Studios Florida® you'll find yourself "in the movies" at every turn! So get ready to ride the blockbusters like E.T.® Back to the Future®...The Ride,℠ Earthquake® and more as you see how movie magic is recreated at THE #1 MOVIE STUDIO AND THEME PARK IN THE WORLD!

10% OFF
General merchandise at the Universal Studios Store

Coupon excludes candy, tobacco, film and sundry items.
Not valid with other discounts. Valid through 12/31/95.

20% OFF
Food and beverages purchased for your party (up to six) at Studio Stars Restaurant or Finnegan's Pub.

Present coupon to your server when ordering. Tax and gratuity not included. This coupon has no cash value and is not valid with other specials or discounts. Valid through 12/31/95.

$3.00 OFF All-Day Studio Pass

$3.00 discount valid through 12/31/95. Coupon valid for up to 6 people and must be presented at the time of purchase. This offer has no cash value and is not valid with any other special discounts. Subject to change without notice. Parking fee not included.

6183920001990

ENJOY PREMIER SHOPPING!

You'll find everything from Nickelodeon® novelties to electronic toys at the Universal Studios Store. Select the perfect gift or souvenir to remind you of your trip to Universal Studios Florida,® and save 10% with this coupon.

DINE HOLLYWOOD-STYLE

Be a part of the scene at the Studio Stars Restaurant (across from Ghostbusters®) or drop into Finnegan's Pub for Irish spirits, ales and entertainment. Your 20% discount is good for a party of six! Remember to present this coupon when ordering.